es Titles

Grammar and Composition: Third Course
Grammar and Composition: Fourth Course
Grammar and Composition: Fifth Course
Grammar and Composition: Complete Course

ementary Materials (for each course)

ated Teacher's Edition
er's Resource Book
ook

uting Writers

e Harris
Tomlinson

Editorial	Sue Martin (Managing Editor), Barbara Brien (Project Editor), Carol Clay, Lynn Duffy, Peg McNary, Mary Ellen Walters; *Freelance Assistance:* Karen Gabler, Anne Jones, Judy Keith, William Ray, Ellen Whalen
Services	Marianna Frew Palmer (Manager), K. Kirschbaum Harvie
Design	Sally Thompson Steele
r Design	Dawn Ostrer Emerson
oduction	Maureen LaRiccia

edgments: page 653

he United States of America

imultaneously in Canada

al Standard Book Number: 0-669-15968-9

3 4 5 6 7 8 9 0

Heath Grammar and Com

with
Process
t

Authors
Carol Ann Bergman
J. A. Senn

Contributing Author
Margaret M. Withey

D.C. Heath and Com
Lexington, Massachusetts / Tor
HEATH

Heath
Grammar and Composition

with a Process Approach to Writing

Series Consultants

Henry I. Christ
Former Chairman of the English Department
Andrew Jackson High School
St. Albans, New York

Richard Marius, Ph.D.
Director of the Expository Writing Program
Harvard University
Cambridge, Massachusetts

Reviewers

Alabama

Fran West
Red Bay High School
Red Bay, Alabama

California

Dorothy Gillmann
Portola Junior High School
Tarzana, California

Florida

Sonya M. Crown
Ely High School
Pompano Beach, Florida

Elynore Schott
South Broward High School
Hollywood, Florida

Illinois

Margaret J. Blaufuss
Glenbard East High School
Lombard, Illinois

Marion P. Johnson
Andrew High School
Tinley Park, Illinois

Virginia Riedel
Willowbrook High School
Villa Park, Illinois

Sister Julia Ann Rogers
Driscoll Catholic High School
Addison, Illinois

Maine

Michael S. Weatherwax
Camden-Rockport High School
Camden, Maine

Massachusetts

Lorraine A. Plasse, Ph.D.
Springfield Public Schools
Springfield, Massachusetts

David C. Reid
Minuteman Vocational Technical High School
Lexington, Massachusetts

Shirley M. Westrate
Hamilton-Wenham Regional High School
South Hamilton, Massachusetts

Michigan

Marilyn Bright
Andover High School
Bloomfield Hills, Michigan

New York

Joseph F. Cammarano
Patchogue-Medford High School
Medford, New York

Joseph R. Teta
Baldwin High School
Baldwin, New York

Oregon

Deborah L. Sommer
Cedar Park School
Portland, Oregon

Paul Williamson
Cedar Park School
Portland, Oregon

Pennsylvania

Sandra M. Couch
Solanco High School
Quarryville, Pennsylvania

Bernadette Fenning
Cardinal O'Hara High School
Springfield, Pennsylvania

South Carolina

Francie C. Brown
Dreher High School
Columbia, South Carolina

Idris B. McElveen, Ph.D.
Spring Valley High School
Columbia, South Carolina

Zelder N. Pressley
Keenan High School
Columbia, South Carolina

Texas

Karen Hibbs
Richland Senior High School
Fort Worth, Texas

Frankye Taylor
Euless Junior High School
Euless, Texas

Virginia

Cindy K. Driskill
Clover Hill High School
Midlothian, Virginia

Washington

Cindy Mar
Liberty High School
Issaquah, Washington

Contents

Contents

Contents

UNIT 2   USAGE

Contents

UNIT 3 MECHANICS

UNIT 4   VOCABULARY AND SPELLING

Contents

Contents

UNIT 7   TEST TAKING

APPENDIX

To the Student

This book is about communication—the act of expressing your thoughts and ideas effectively to someone else. Think of how much of your day is spent speaking with members of your family, friends, and many others in your school and community. Speaking, however, is only one means of communication. Writing is another, and writing clearly and concisely is an essential skill. In this electronics age, more and more businesses are using computers to communicate information. The written word—whether displayed on a computer screen or printed in books—is the backbone of communication.

Although this book is divided into different units, it has one unified goal: to help you speak and write clearly and effectively. The first unit, on grammar, shows you how the structure of the English language gives you choices to improve your speaking and writing. The next unit, on usage, explains ways to speak and write with clarity and exactness of meaning. Mechanics, the third unit, emphasizes the importance of capitalization and punctuation in precisely transmitting your written message. The fourth unit, on vocabulary and spelling, points out the power of individual words within your total message. The fifth and sixth units show you how to find, organize, and communicate information, including your own ideas and insights. The last unit, on test taking, will help you communicate what you know in a test situation.

The composition unit in this book is unique. Each chapter includes all the help and information you need to understand and write a different type of composition—from a single paragraph to an essay or a report. Within chapters, you are taken step by step through the four stages in the writing process. In the *prewriting* stage, you learn how to choose and limit a subject and how to find and organize your thoughts or information. In the *writing* stage, you learn how to write a topic sentence or a thesis statement; how to write the body of a paragraph, an essay, or a report; and how to write a conclusion. In the *revising* stage, you learn how to pull your writing together—how to give it unity and coherence. Finally, in the *editing* stage, you learn how to polish your work by applying the information in the first three units.

Going through these writing stages is like having someone sit beside you as you learn to drive a car for the first time. If you are unsure of yourself, there is an abundance of help in the form of practice, models, and checklists to show you exactly what to do, how to do it, and when to do it. Following these stages in the writing process will ensure success and build your confidence in your ability to write well.

To The Student

As you go through each unit in this book, remember its underlying purpose: to help you speak and write clearly and effectively. Each chapter has been written with this goal in mind, because speaking and writing are essential skills for success in today's world.

Special Helps

Your teacher will probably go through some of the chapters in this book with you. All of the chapters, however, have been written and organized so that you can refer to them and use them on your own throughout the year. You may find some of the following features of the book particularly helpful.

Keyed Rules All the rules are clearly marked with keyed blue arrows. An index at the back of the book tells you where to find each rule.

Tinted Boxes Throughout the text, important lists, summaries, and writing steps are highlighted in tinted boxes for easy reference.

Application to Writing These sections in the first three units of the book clearly show you how you can use the various grammatical concepts you have learned to improve your writing.

Diagnostic and Mastery Tests You can use the diagnostic and mastery tests to measure your progress. The diagnostic test at the beginning of a chapter will show you what you need to learn; the mastery test at the end will show you how well you learned it.

High-Interest Exercises Many of the exercises throughout the book are based on interesting topics. You will not only practice learning a particular skill, but you will also find the material in these exercises informative and interesting.

Composition Models Clearly marked models in the composition chapters provide interesting examples by professional writers.

Composition Checklists Almost all the composition chapters end with a checklist that you can follow—step by step—when you are writing a paragraph, an essay, or a report.

Standardized Tests Standardized tests, which follow five of the units, give you practice and build your confidence in taking tests.

Appendix In a clear, concise format, the appendix at the end of the book provides assistance with various study skills, communication skills, and career skills. For example, you will find helpful information about taking notes, using proofreading symbols, speaking to an audience, and completing a job application.

Unit 1

Grammar

1
The Sentence

Number your paper 1 to 10. Then write the subjects and the verbs in the following sentences.

EXAMPLE   Pat and I are going to Boston today.
ANSWER   Pat, I — are going

1. Our class watched a movie yesterday.
2. The guests seemed tired after the neighborhood block party.
3. Carmen waited for ten minutes and then left.
4. Haven't you done your homework yet?
5. Into the bowl of punch splashed the ball.
6. Here are the pens.
7. The cherries and the grapes should be washed and put into the fruit salad.
8. Trucks and cars roared through the tunnel at the end of the highway.
9. Did you read the newspaper this morning?
10. Melissa should never have loaned Anthony her record albums.

In casual conversation people sometimes express their ideas incompletely.

> Kim: "Do you want to go skiing?"
> Allen: "In this weather? No way!"

Kim easily understood Allen's reply even though he used only parts of a sentence to answer her. Although Allen's remarks might be effective in conversation, written words should express complete thoughts.

RECOGNIZING SENTENCES

Before you can write sentences, you first must be able to recognize them.

1a A **sentence** is a group of words that expresses a complete thought.

The following groups of words are incomplete thoughts.

> The man in the black suit.   Running in the corridor.
> Ate all the roast beef.   When the race was over.

Groups of words that express incomplete thoughts are called *sentence fragments*. To change these fragments into sentences, you must add the missing information.

> The man in the black suit **is my teacher.**
> **My brother** ate all the roast beef.
> Running in the corridor **is forbidden.**
> When the race was over, **we held a party for the winner.**

EXERCISE 1   Recognizing Sentences
Label each group of words *S* if it is a sentence or *F* if it is a fragment.

1. The fans at the hockey game cheered wildly.
2. Because the weather turned cold.
3. Sent the package to her yesterday.

4. A history teacher at the middle school.
5. Roberto works on Saturday afternoons.
6. Skiing down a mountain for the first time.
7. Since we are going out for dinner.
8. George does 20 push-ups each morning.
9. Laughed at Antonia's jokes.
10. After the corn is planted in the far field.

EXERCISE 2   Completing Sentences
Add the information needed to make each fragment in
Exercise 1 a sentence. When you write each sentence,
remember to use a capital letter and punctuation.

SUBJECTS AND PREDICATES

To write a complete sentence, you must have a subject
and a predicate. A *subject* names the person, place, or thing
the sentence is about. The *predicate* tells something about
the subject.

1b ▶ A sentence has two main parts: a **subject** and a **predicate.**

	SUBJECT	PREDICATE
PERSON	Our science teacher	organized the fair.
PLACE	Florida's beaches	attract many tourists.
THING	Jamie's car	is ten years old.

Complete and Simple Subjects

The *complete subject* of a sentence usually contains more
than one word.

1c ▶ A **complete subject** includes all the words used to identify the
person, place, thing, or idea that the sentence is about.

To find a complete subject, ask yourself *Whom?* or *What?* the sentence is about.

> **The salesperson in the store** explained the computer. [Whom is this sentence talking about? Who explained the computer? *The salesperson in the store* is the complete subject.]
>
> **The bananas on the table** aren't ripe yet. [What is this sentence talking about? What isn't ripe yet? *The bananas on the table* is the complete subject.]

EXERCISE 3   Finding Complete Subjects
Write the complete subject in each sentence.

Animal
Oddities

1. A huge grizzly bear has the speed of an average horse.
2. The largest elephant in Africa may weigh over seven tons.
3. The ancient Egyptians trained baboons as waiters.
4. The opossum dates back 45 million years.
5. A panda weighs about four ounces at birth.
6. The greyhound can run over 40 miles per hour.
7. The one-ton African rhinoceros is easily tamed.
8. Cattle branding was practiced 4,000 years ago.
9. Herds of camels roamed Alaska 12,000 years ago.
10. The ancestors of the modern horse were only a foot tall.

Simple Subjects.   Within each complete subject, one word directly answers the question *Who?* or *What?*

1d ▸ A **simple subject** is the main word in the complete subject.

In the following examples, the simple subjects are in heavy type.

┌────── complete subject ──────┐
The **athletes** on the field stood at attention.

┌────── complete subject ──────┐
The lone gray **horse** galloped across the field.

Sometimes a complete subject and a simple subject are the same.

> **Luis Sanchez** will sing a solo at the concert.
> [*Luis Sanchez* is the simple subject. Both words are considered one name.]
>
> **He** will return my science book.
>
> **Everyone** completed the assignment.

NOTE: Throughout the rest of this book, the simple subject will be called the *subject.*

EXERCISE 4   Finding Complete and Simple Subjects
Write the complete subject in each sentence. Then underline each simple subject.

EXAMPLE   The huge oak door opened with a groan.
ANSWER   The huge oak <u>door</u>

1. My friends from school met me at the football game.
2. Nearsighted penguins mistake stones for their eggs.
3. Pigs always sleep on their right side.
4. The back wheel on my bicycle is loose.
5. Seven different colors are found in the human eye.
6. Twenty new students enrolled in our school this year.
7. Ferdinand Magellan made the first voyage around the world.
8. Everyone voted for Tom for class president.
9. The leaves from the tree in the backyard must be raked.
10. The tusks of an elephant grow throughout its lifetime.

EXERCISE 5   Finding Simple Subjects
Write the simple subject in each sentence.

1. Early settlers used acorns for food.
2. My homework in math will take one hour.
3. Loud music bothers my father.
4. Most snakes in the United States are harmless.

5. My brother's friend will eat dinner with us.
6. The large red apple was hard and juicy.
7. Identical twins always have the same eye color.
8. That picture of my family was taken last year.
9. The center of the United States is located in Castle Rock, South Dakota.
10. The tiger's huge eyes surveyed the scene.

EXERCISE 6 Writing Sentences
Write five sentences that tell about things you might see during a walk down the main street of your city or town. Then underline each subject in your sentences.

Complete and Simple Predicates

Besides a subject, every sentence needs a predicate.

1e ▶   A **complete predicate** includes all the words that tell what the subject is doing, or that tell something about the subject.

To find a complete predicate, first find the subject. Then ask, *What is the subject doing?* or *What is being said about the subject?*

The wild horses **roamed across the prairie.** [The subject is *horses.* What did the horses do? They roamed across the prairie. *Roamed across the prairie* is the complete predicate.]

Our car **has front-wheel drive.** [The subject is *car.* What is being said about the car? It has front-wheel drive. *Has front-wheel drive* is the complete predicate.]

EXERCISE 7 Finding Complete Predicates
Write the complete predicate in each sentence.

The Statue of Liberty

1. The Statue of Liberty stands in New York Harbor.
2. The tablet in her left hand reads, "July 4, 1776."
3. Seven rays surround her head.
4. Broken chains lie at her feet.

5. She weighs 225 tons.
6. Her index finger extends eight feet.
7. The French people gave the statue to the United States as a birthday present.
8. The formal presentation took place in 1886.
9. One million sightseers visit the statue each year.
10. She remains the best-known statue in the world today.

Simple Predicates. A predicate has one main word or phrase that tells what the subject is doing or tells something about the subject. This key word or phrase is always the verb.

1f ▸ A **simple predicate,** or **verb,** is the main word or phrase in the complete predicate.

In the following examples, the verb is in heavy type.

┌─ complete predicate ─┐
Everyone in the audience **enjoyed** the play.

┌──── complete predicate ────┐
The airplane **landed** safely in the field.

┌──── complete predicate ────┐
My brother **is** a fine soccer player.

Verbs that tell something about a subject are sometimes hard to find because they do not show action. Following is a list of common verb forms that are used to make a statement about a subject.

Verbs That Make Statements
am   is   are   was   were   be   being   been

EXERCISE 8   Finding Complete Predicates and Verbs
Write the complete predicate in each sentence. Then underline each verb.

EXAMPLE   His coat hangs on that hook.
ANSWER   <u>hangs</u> on that hook

1. Hank Aaron hit 755 home runs during his career.
2. My cat chases the neighbor's dog every morning.
3. That camera is the least expensive model.
4. The United States paid Russia only two cents an acre for Alaska.
5. A cow gives less milk in hot weather.
6. The school board met for five hours last night.
7. Both George Washington and Thomas Jefferson were six-footers.
8. The principal conducted the first assembly.
9. The temperature fell ten degrees last night.
10. Luther Crowell invented the paper bag in 1867.

EXERCISE 9 Finding Verbs
Write the verb in each sentence.

1. The United States issued the first patent in 1790.
2. I started a savings account last month.
3. Evenings in the fall are quite cool.
4. Otters always entertain the visitors at Sea World.
5. The color on the television needs some adjustment.
6. The lifeguard shouted a warning to the swimmers.
7. My parents insulated our house this year.
8. Edgar Rice Burroughs was the creator of Tarzan.
9. The dog eagerly ate its dinner.
10. The elephant's tusks weighed over 200 pounds.

EXERCISE 10 Time-out for Review
Number your paper 1 to 20. Then write the subject and the verb in each sentence.

A Joint Venture

1. This true story tells about a cat and a famous man, Eli Whitney.
2. Together they changed the course of history.
3. The man with the cat's help invented the cotton gin.
4. As a result, the South gained great wealth.
5. In colonial days people removed the seeds from cotton.
6. They pulled the cotton apart by hand.
7. One person cleaned only a few pounds each day.

8. This manual labor was very expensive.
9. Cotton planters wanted a cheaper method.
10. Eli knew their problems.
11. On a sleepless night, he hunted for a solution.
12. He went to the window for some fresh air.
13. He saw a stray cat in the alley.
14. It clawed at a dead chicken through the slots of a crate.
15. Its sharp claws raked only feathers through the slots.
16. The space between the slots was very narrow.
17. The chicken remained inside the crate.
18. Suddenly Eli thought of an idea for his invention!
19. In his machine, sharp teeth pull cotton fibers through narrow openings.
20. That nameless cat helped Eli with the invention of the cotton gin.

Verb Phrases

The main verb in the following example is *mow*. However, to show that Tom's action will take place in the future, the word *will* must be added to the verb.

Tom **will mow** the lawn tomorrow.

Words such as *will* are called auxiliary verbs, or *helping verbs*. The main verb plus any helping verbs make up a *verb phrase*. The helping verbs in the following examples are in heavy type.

┌ verb phrase ┐
Eva **is** watching the football game now.

┌── verb phrase ──┐
Those seeds **can be** planted next month.

┌──── verb phrase ────┐
You **should have been** warned about the penalty.

NOTE: As you can see from the examples above, a verb phrase can include as many as three helping verbs plus the main verb.

Common Helping Verbs

be	am, is, are, was, were, be, being, been
have	has, have, had
do	do, does, did
others	may, might, must, can, could, shall, should, will, would

EXERCISE 11 **Finding Verb Phrases**

Write the verb phrase in each sentence.

EXAMPLE   Greg will be working on weekends now.
ANSWER   will be working

1. The first photograph was taken in 1826.
2. The election results will be announced on Monday.
3. Dandelion leaves can be eaten raw like lettuce.
4. Their sneakers are drying in the sun.
5. The invitation must have given the time.
6. You should have spoken to me first.
7. The Girl Scouts was founded on March 12, 1912.
8. American Indians could make beads from shells.
9. The award should have gone to her.
10. With help, babies can swim at an early age.

Interrupted Verb Phrases.   Verb phrases are often interrupted by other words.

A bloodhound **can** easily **follow** a day-old scent.
Betsy **has** never **seen** the ocean.

In a question the subject sometimes comes in the middle of a verb phrase.

Is Tony **running** in the marathon on Saturday?

Although *not* and its contraction *n't* are never part of a verb phrase, they often interrupt a verb phrase.

Dan **is** not **going** with us to the movies.
Beth **doesn't like** ice cream.

11

NOTE: Throughout the rest of this book, the term *verb* will refer to the whole verb phrase.

EXERCISE 12 Finding Verbs
Write the verb in each sentence. Remember that words can interrupt a verb phrase.

1. Did you join the track team this year?
2. Some parts of Brazil have never been explored.
3. The roses in our garden haven't bloomed yet.
4. Would you like corn instead of peas?
5. Isn't she wanted in the office?
6. Valuable antiques can sometimes be found at flea markets.
7. Have you eaten your lunch yet?
8. I must have lost the keys to the house.
9. Platinum was first discovered in Colombia.
10. Cats were not tamed until about 5,000 years ago.
11. The oldest hat in the world may well be the familiar chef's hat.
12. A person can now travel over 9,000 miles in 8 hours.
13. A regular lead pencil can write about 50,000 words.
14. The English didn't invent the umbrella.
15. How often does Halley's comet make an appearance?

EXERCISE 13 Writing Sentences
Write five sentences that describe a child who is learning to ride a bicycle. Then underline the verb in each of your sentences. Be sure to include helping verbs.

EXERCISE 14 Time-out for Review
Number your paper 1 to 10. Then write the subject and the verb in each sentence.

An Accidental Discovery

1. Long ago Egyptians would mix hippo fat with moldy bread crumbs.
2. This mixture was then used as a medicine.
3. The moldy bread contained a medicine—penicillin.

12

4. In 1928, Alexander Fleming was growing bacteria for an experiment.
5. His helper didn't cover the dish of bacteria.
6. Some mold blew in the window.
7. It fell on the bacteria.
8. Fleming noticed the dead bacteria.
9. He eventually named the mold penicillin.
10. Since then, penicillin has saved millions of lives.

Compound Subjects

Many sentences have a single subject. Others have two or more subjects joined by a conjunction such as *and* or *or*.

1g A **compound subject** is two or more subjects in one sentence that have the same verb and are joined by a conjunction.

In the following examples, each subject is underlined once, and each verb is underlined twice.

> ONE SUBJECT   <u>Janice</u> <u>spent</u> the day at the beach.
> COMPOUND SUBJECT   <u>Janice</u> and <u>Kate</u> <u>spent</u> the day at the beach.
> COMPOUND SUBJECT   <u>Janice</u>, <u>Kate</u>, and <u>Sue</u> <u>spent</u> the day at the beach.

The conjunctions *and, or,* and *nor* are used to connect compound subjects. Pairs of conjunctions, such as *either/or, neither/nor, not only/but also,* and *both/and* may also be used.

> Either <u>chicken</u> or <u>veal</u> <u>will be served</u> at the banquet.

EXERCISE 15   Finding Compound Subjects
Number your paper 1 to 10. Then write the subjects in each sentence.

EXAMPLE   Both Otis and Pearl went to the game.
ANSWER   Otis, Pearl

1. Hikers and cyclists often camp by the brook.
2. Neither Gladys nor Rosalie can baby-sit for us.
3. The best baseballs and footballs are made of leather.
4. Shells, starfish, and driftwood are among her souvenirs.
5. Insects and disease are the major enemies of trees.
6. My family and I will fly to Arizona next week.
7. *Jane, Jean,* and *Joan* are forms of the same ancient name.
8. Both basketball and volleyball were first played in Massachusetts.
9. Carnations and zinnias last a long time.
10. Breakfast, lunch, and dinner were included in the price of a room.

Compound Verbs

Just as some sentences have compound subjects, some sentences may also have compound verbs. Conjunctions such as *and, or, nor,* and *but* are used to connect the verbs.

1h   A **compound verb** is two or more verbs in one sentence that have the same subject and are joined by a conjunction.

In the following examples, each subject is underlined once, and each verb is underlined twice.

ONE VERB   Jeff milks the cows.
COMPOUND VERB   Jeff milks the cows and gathers the eggs.
COMPOUND VERB   Jeff milks the cows, gathers the eggs, and feeds the chickens.

A sentence can include both a compound subject and a compound verb.

Nancy and Peg went to Orlando and visited Disney World.

EXERCISE 16   Finding Compound Subjects and Compound Verbs

Number your paper 1 to 15. Then write the subjects and the verbs in the following sentences.

1. The gymnast jumped from the bar and bowed.
2. Linda wrote her report but left it at home.
3. The train departed on time but arrived ten minutes late.
4. Pure gold is soft and can be molded with the hands.
5. Kate arranged the flowers and set the table.
6. Ted and I hired mules and rode through the Grand Canyon.
7. Hank and Ida grabbed the rope and pulled the boat to shore.
8. The scouts and their leader pitched the tents and cooked dinner.
9. The male moose sheds its antlers every winter and grows a new set the following spring.
10. Hal fell and limped off the field.
11. Miguel will go to the movies or play football.
12. Both honeybees and bumblebees gather pollen and live in colonies.
13. Both the deer and her fawn looked cautiously and then darted across the open field.
14. A new jet makes vertical takeoffs and flies horizontally.
15. At birth a rattlesnake has poison fangs and is very dangerous.

EXERCISE 17 **Writing Sentences**

Write ten sentences that use the following compound subjects and compound verbs. Remember to use capital letters and punctuation marks correctly.

EXAMPLE   eat and run
POSSIBLE ANSWER   Every morning I eat breakfast and run to the bus stop.

1. books and magazines
2. hockey and football
3. Beth and George
4. a cat, a dog, and three rabbits
5. eggs and cheese
6. will read and decide
7. worked but will study
8. swim or jog
9. whistled, shouted, and clapped
10. waited and worried

EXERCISE 18 Time-out for Review

Number your paper 1 to 10. Then write the subjects and the verbs in the following sentences.

Twins:
A Case
Study

1. Jim Lewis and Jim Springer are twins but were adopted by different parents.
2. They had neither met nor talked to each other for 30 years.
3. Some unusual facts were then discovered.
4. Their wives were both named Betty.
5. James Allen and James Alan were the names of their first sons.
6. Math and woodworking were hobbies of both of them.
7. The twins drove the same make of car and had vacationed at the same beach in Florida.
8. These similarities sound like coincidences.
9. Some researchers don't think so.
10. They have now found identical brain-wave patterns in twins.

Position of Subjects

In most sentences, the subject comes before the verb. Sometimes, however, the normal subject-verb order is changed to create sentence variety.

When the verb or part of a verb phrase comes before the subject, the sentence is in *inverted order*. To find the subject and the verb, put the sentence in its natural order. In the following examples, each subject is underlined once, and each verb is underlined twice.

INVERTED ORDER   Onto the football field marched the band.
NATURAL ORDER   The band marched onto the football field.

INVERTED ORDER   Directly overhead flew the helicopter.
NATURAL ORDER   The helicopter flew directly overhead.

Finding the subject in an inverted sentence is sometimes easier if you first find the verb. After finding the verb, then ask who or what is doing the action, or about whom or what a statement is being made.

Around the corner raced a blue car. [The verb is *raced*. What raced? *Car* is the subject.]

Questions. One type of inverted order occurs in a question. Quite often part of a verb phrase will come before the subject. To find the subject in a question, turn the question around so that it makes a statement.

QUESTION   <u>Did</u> José <u>bring</u> his camera?
STATEMENT   José <u>did bring</u> his camera.

QUESTION   <u>Should</u> Peg <u>go</u> to the meeting?
STATEMENT   Peg <u>should go</u> to the meeting.

Sentences Beginning with *There* and *Here*. Inverted order can also occur in a sentence that begins with the word *there* or *here*. When a sentence begins with one of these words, the verb will come before the subject.

To find the subject of this kind of sentence, drop the word *there* or *here*. Then put the rest of the words in their natural order. Just remember that *there* or *here* can never be the subject of a sentence.

INVERTED ORDER   Here <u>comes</u> the <u>plane</u> down the runway.
NATURAL ORDER   The <u>plane</u> <u>comes</u> down the runway.

INVERTED ORDER   There <u>are</u> two <u>cardinals</u> at the feeder.
NATURAL ORDER   Two <u>cardinals</u> <u>are</u> at the feeder.

EXERCISE 19   Finding Subjects in Inverted Order
Write the subject and the verb in each sentence.

1. There are a thousand millimeters in a meter.
2. Over the waves roared the speedboat.
3. High on the mountain stood the hikers.
4. Can you see her in the crowd?
5. There goes the last hamburger.
6. Why can't Cara or Lee bring the records?
7. Here are the muffins and bagels.
8. Did your teacher give you a choice of subjects?
9. Around the track raced the motorcycles.

17

10. Between Las Vegas and Barstow lies a great desert.
11. There are my brother and sister.
12. Are your parents going to the open house at the school?
13. What did Lou tell you about the camp?
14. There are four basic taste sensations: sweet, bitter, sour, and salty.
15. Amid the large crowd wandered a puppy.

Understood Subjects

Once in a while, the subject of a sentence is not stated. It is understood. This happens when a command is given or a request is made.

Look at the beautiful sunset.

If you ask who should look at the sunset, the answer is *you*—the person (or persons) receiving the command. Notice that *you* is the understood subject of each of the following sentences.

(you) Turn down the radio!
(you) Put the cat outside.
Virginia, (you) please come here.

NOTE: In the last example, the person receiving the request is called directly by name. Nevertheless, *you* is still the understood subject.

EXERCISE 20   Finding Subjects

Write the subject and the verb in each sentence. If the subject is an understood *you,* write it in parentheses.

EXAMPLE   Lower your voice.
ANSWER   (you) Lower

1. Take the dog for a walk.
2. Lend me your notes from math class.
3. Michael, carry these packages for me.
4. Here comes dinner right now.
5. Get some milk at the store.

6. Leave the keys on the table.
7. Has Roger spoken to you about the meeting?
8. Stephanie, meet me at three o'clock.
9. Answer the questions very carefully.
10. Into the gym raced the eager players.

EXERCISE 21 Time-out for Review

Number your paper 1 to 10. Then write the subjects and the verbs in the following sentences.

1. Has the countdown for the space shuttle begun?
2. Near the water hole were many animal tracks.
3. There will be food, games, and prizes at the picnic.
4. What do you remember about the accident?
5. Mail the package at the post office.
6. Here is the Sunday newspaper.
7. The horse galloped fast and jumped the fence easily.
8. Which job should we give to Susan?
9. On the walls hung colorful paintings of birds.
10. Tulips and crocuses bloom in spring and last for weeks.

DIAGRAMING SUBJECTS AND VERBS

A *sentence diagram* is a picture made up of lines and words. It can help you clearly see the different parts of a sentence.

Subjects and Verbs. All sentence diagrams begin with a base line. A straight, vertical line then separates the subject (or subjects) on the left from the verb (or verbs) on the right. Notice in the following diagram that the capital letter in the sentence is included, but not the punctuation. Also notice that the whole verb phrase is included on the base line.

She has remembered.

Inverted Order. A sentence in inverted order, such as a question, is diagramed like a sentence in natural order.

Were you talking?

Understood Subjects. When the subject of a sentence is an understood *you,* put parentheses around it in the subject position.

Stop!

When a name is included with the understood subject, place it on a horizontal line above the understood subject.

Ted, listen.

Compound Subjects and Verbs. Place compound subjects and verbs on parallel lines. Put the conjunction connecting them on a broken line between them. Notice in the first example that two conjunctions are placed on either side of the broken line.

Both cameras and computers were displayed.

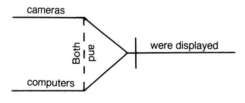

Jan has gone but will return.

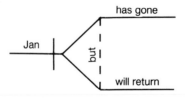

Balloons, streamers, and horns were bought but have been lost.

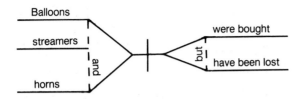

EXERCISE 22 Diagraming Subjects and Verbs

Diagram the following sentences or copy them. If you copy them, draw one line under each subject and two lines under each verb. If the subject is an understood *you,* write it in parentheses.

1. Crickets were chirping.
2. Hurry!
3. Both seeds and bulbs have sprouted.
4. Were you sleeping?
5. Pepe swung but missed.
6. Lilacs are blooming.
7. Sue and Cathy have arrived and are rehearsing.
8. Roy, wait.
9. Have tornadoes been spotted?
10. Reports were given and have been discussed.

Application to Writing

One way to avoid a choppy style in your writing is to combine short sentences. By doing that, you also will be able to drop some unnecessary words. You can combine two sentences that have either the same verb but different subjects or the same subject but different verbs.

TWO SENTENCES   Inés plays soccer. Rachel plays too.

COMPOUND SUBJECT   Inés and Rachel play soccer.

TWO SENTENCES   The dog sat up. It barked twice.

COMPOUND VERB   The dog sat up and barked twice.

EXERCISE 23 **Combining Sentences**

Combine each pair of sentences into one sentence with a compound subject or a compound verb. Use the conjunctions *and* or *but.*

1. Edgar Allan Poe wrote mystery stories. O. Henry wrote them also.
2. Many tomatoes were planted in the field. They were destroyed by the drought.
3. The eagle circled the ridge. It landed in its nest.
4. Sherlock Holmes appeared in many movies. Charlie Chan did also.
5. Rain fell last night. Sleet also fell.
6. Curtains were bought for the new house. Rugs were bought too.
7. Dogs make good pets. Cats make good pets.
8. Beth left at seven. She still missed her bus.
9. I read Isaac Asimov's latest book. I enjoyed it.
10. Pete plays basketball. He also swims.

CHAPTER REVIEW

A. Number your paper 1 to 10. Then write the subjects and the verbs in the following sentences. If the subject is an understood *you,* write it in parentheses.

1. Bob has stacked the shelves in the den with books.
2. The children raked the leaves and put them into bags.
3. How many cassettes do you own?
4. Angie and Martin can operate a computer.
5. Here are your glasses.
6. Alberto shouldn't have worked all day.
7. Will Shirley go to Texas with you?
8. Dave, fix the faucet for me.
9. On Saturday my brother bowled in the afternoon and went to a concert in the evening.
10. At the top of the hill stood a statue.

B. Number your paper 1 to 10. Then write the subjects and the verbs in the following sentences. If the subject is an understood *you*, write it in parentheses.

1. The tibia is located in the lower leg.
2. Peru was once ruled by the Incas.
3. The Nile and the Amazon are the two longest rivers in the world.
4. There are no fish in the Dead Sea.
5. Do arteries carry blood from the heart or to the heart?
6. The only perfect game in the World Series was pitched by Don Larsen.
7. Mississippi floods can usually be predicted six months in advance.
8. Look at that spectacular red sunset!
9. The water supply on the earth neither increases nor diminishes.
10. Traffic lights didn't appear until 1914.

MASTERY TEST

Number your paper 1 to 10. Then write the subjects and the verbs in the following sentences.

1. The warm bread melted in my mouth.
2. Candy and soda can cause cavities.
3. Vicky's watch has never lost a minute.
4. They might not have known our address.
5. Under the cupboard ran the tiny mouse.
6. Jim thought for a while and then made a decision.
7. The men remained friends for 30 years.
8. There goes my last dollar.
9. Why can't you go to the dance next Saturday?
10. The Gregsons and the Smiths own that boat and use it each summer.

2

Nouns and Pronouns

Number your paper 1 to 10. Make two columns on your paper. Label the first column *nouns* and the second column *pronouns*. Then under the proper column, write each noun and pronoun.

EXAMPLE   I asked Fred for his slide rule.

ANSWER   nouns   pronouns
         Fred, slide rule   I, his

1. Our vacation to Florida ended on Labor Day.
2. On their anniversary the Hendersons celebrated with friends and relatives.
3. Everyone at the dance had a wonderful time.
4. What happened during halftime at the game?
5. Some of my friends play chess the first Wednesday of each month.
6. I like both of these very much.
7. Who led the parade down Main Street?
8. We enjoyed seeing the monkeys and the elephants at the zoo.
9. Jill built herself shelves for her books.
10. At the police station, I could learn nothing about the accident.

A classroom dictionary lists thousands of words. An unabridged dictionary includes even more. All of these words, however, can be divided into eight groups called the *parts of speech*. A word's part of speech is determined by the job it does in a sentence.

The Eight Parts of Speech

noun [names]   **preposition** [relates]
pronoun [replaces]   **conjunction** [connects]
verb [states action or being] **interjection** [expresses
adjective [describes, limits]   strong feeling]
adverb [describes, limits]

NOUNS

In English, there are more nouns than any other part of speech.

2a ▶ A **noun** is the name of a person, place, thing, or idea.

Nouns that name people, places, and things are usually easy to spot. Nouns that name ideas and qualities are harder to recognize.

PEOPLE   sailor, brother, Dr. Adams, senators, Ed
PLACES   forest, North Carolina, rooms, England
THINGS   rug, explosion, piano, bird, rain, trucks,
         minutes, wind, flu, chipmunk
IDEAS   freedom, happiness, fun, love, inflation,
         bravery, anger, honesty, sickness, faith

EXERCISE 1   Finding Nouns
Number your paper 1 to 30. Then write the nouns in the following paragraph.

25

What a
Car!   A car totally run by a computer now exists. A key has been replaced by a card made of plastic. The driver inserts it into a slot in the dashboard. The seat and the mirrors are automatically adjusted first. Then a device uses radar to sense vehicles and objects ahead and puts on the brakes if necessary. If rain begins, the wipers turn on by themselves. A map gives instructions on the best route to follow. The carburetor checks itself to ensure the best mileage from a tank of gas. The car can even follow commands given by voice. To own such an amazing car is the dream of many people.

Compound and Collective Nouns

Some nouns include more than one word. *Office* is one noun, but *post office* is also one noun. A noun that includes more than one word is called a *compound noun*. Compound nouns can take one of three forms.

SEPARATE WORDS   living room, home run, record player
HYPHENATED   break-in, attorney-at-law, twenty-one
COMBINED   birdhouse, headband, flashlight

NOTE: It is not always easy to know how a particular compound noun should be written. The best way to find out is to check in the dictionary.

Collective Nouns.   A noun can also name a group of people or things. This kind of noun is called a *collective noun*.

COLLECTIVE NOUNS   team, family, herd, choir, jury

EXERCISE 2   Finding Nouns
Number your paper 1 to 10. Then write the nouns in each sentence.

1. The pilot pulled the plane out of the nose dive.
2. Last summer Mark went to a dude ranch for two weeks.
3. Our class will meet with the mayor at city hall.
4. The new high school will open next week.
5. My sister went to school at night to study speed-reading.

6. The private detective compared the fingerprints.
7. Ken and I spent the day doing a jigsaw puzzle.
8. My brother-in-law lost his credit cards recently.
9. Will you give me a rain check on that invitation?
10. The prizewinner was surrounded by a group of fans.

Common and Proper Nouns

All nouns are either common nouns or proper nouns. A *common noun* names any person, place, or thing. A *proper noun* names a particular person, place, or thing. All proper nouns begin with a capital letter.

COMMON NOUNS	PROPER NOUNS
man	Mr. Henry Collins
city	Chicago
building	World Trade Center
team	Los Angeles Rams

NOTE: A proper noun sometimes includes more than one word. For example, even though *World Trade Center* is three words, it is considered one noun. It is the name of *one* place.

EXERCISE 3   Finding Common and Proper Nouns

Number your paper 1 to 10. Make two columns on your paper. Label the first column *common nouns* and the second column *proper nouns*. Then under the proper column, write each noun.

EXAMPLE   Ronald Taylor from California thinks that most bugs make tasty treats.

ANSWER   <u>common nouns</u>   <u>proper nouns</u>
bugs, treats   Ronald Taylor, California

Foods
of the
Future

1. In Colombia, ants are sold as snacks from carts along the street.
2. Fried worms are eaten in Mexico.
3. People in Uganda crush flies and shape them into pancakes for lunch.

4. In other parts of Africa, termites are munched like pretzels.
5. Certain spiders are roasted in New Guinea.
6. These insects taste like peanut butter, but they don't stick to the roof of your mouth.
7. Restaurants in New York City serve ants and grasshoppers dipped in chocolate.
8. In recent years the North American Bait Farms have held a bake-off using worms.
9. In some cookbooks you can find a recipe for green peppers stuffed with earthworms.
10. Some people think that moths taste better than potato chips.

EXERCISE 4 Writing Sentences
Write five sentences that describe what you might find in an old trunk in your home. Then underline each noun.

EXERCISE 5 Time-out for Review
Number your paper 1 to 10. Then write the nouns in each sentence.

How Did
Houdini
Do It?

1. How did Houdini escape from jails, straitjackets, and strange containers?
2. Sometimes he kept keys in his throat.
3. He used the same method sword-swallowers use.
4. Once when escaping from a jail in New York, he hid a piece of metal in a callus in his heel.
5. He attached it to a wire that he had hidden in his hair to make a key.
6. He also designed trick cabinets with locks and hinges in secret places.
7. This magician also had great strength and agility.
8. Like a professional athlete, he kept his body fit.
9. Moreover, he had a great gift; he could dislocate his joints.
10. His skill enabled him to mystify audiences throughout the world.

✐ *Application to Writing* —————

Words create certain pictures in the minds of readers. The nouns you choose can make these pictures dull and fuzzy or clear and exact. Vague, general nouns should always be replaced with specific nouns.

GENERAL On a **holiday** we went to a **lake** for a ride in a **boat.**

SPECIFIC On **Labor Day** we went to **Ryan Lake** for a ride in a **rowboat.**

EXERCISE 6 Using Specific Nouns

Number your paper 1 to 10. For each underlined word or words, substitute a specific noun.

EXAMPLE For lunch <u>the man</u> ate <u>food</u>.
ANSWER For lunch Mr. O'Connor ate a turkey sandwich.

1. <u>The boy</u> made <u>a dessert</u> for dinner.
2. <u>Appliances</u> were on sale at <u>the store</u>.
3. I play <u>a musical instrument</u> in the band at <u>school</u>.
4. <u>The woman</u> bought <u>an art object</u> at the auction.
5. <u>The girl</u> ordered <u>flowers</u> from the florist.
6. The <u>family</u> just moved here from <u>another city</u>.
7. We saw <u>the movie</u> at <u>the theater</u>.
8. The <u>tree</u> was covered with <u>insects</u>.
9. The new <u>car</u> was parked on <u>a street</u>.
10. The <u>athlete</u> spoke to the students in <u>a building</u>.

PRONOUNS

Holly took Holly's books with Holly.

Speaking and writing would be very repetitious if there were no words to take the place of nouns. *Pronouns* do this job. With the substitution of pronouns for nouns, the example above reads more smoothly and is easier to understand.

Holly took **her** books with **her.**

2b ▶ A **pronoun** is a word that takes the place of one or more nouns.

Pronoun Antecedents

The noun that a pronoun refers to or replaces is called its *antecedent*. In the following examples, an arrow has been drawn from the pronoun to its antecedent. Notice that the antecedent usually comes before the pronoun.

Dion said that **he** couldn't go.

Alan caught the **ball** and threw **it** to first base.

Lynn asked **Sandy**, "Did **we** miss a turn?"

EXERCISE 7 Finding Antecedents
Write the antecedent for each underlined pronoun.

EXAMPLE   The Pedersens just left on their vacation.
ANSWER   Pedersens

1. Ellen carried her umbrella to school.
2. Walter said, "I like mashed potatoes best."
3. Steve asked Anita to go to the dance with him.
4. Randy and Margo said they were going to the movies.
5. Sandy told Robert that she was having a party.
6. The sky has a rosy tint to it.
7. Did Clara and Ann wear their uniforms?
8. Jeff asked Leda, "Are you leaving now?"
9. Albert said that he was going to play hockey.
10. The coach asked the team, "Are you ready to win?"

Personal Pronouns

All the pronouns in Exercise 7 are *personal pronouns*. These are the most commonly used pronouns. Personal pronouns are divided into the following three groups.

Personal Pronouns

FIRST PERSON	(The person speaking)
SINGULAR	I, me, my, mine
PLURAL	we, us, our, ours
SECOND PERSON	(The person spoken to)
SINGULAR	you, your, yours
PLURAL	you, your, yours
THIRD PERSON	(The person or thing spoken about)
SINGULAR	he, him, his, she, her, hers, it, its
PLURAL	they, them, their, theirs

The following sentences show how personal pronouns are used.

FIRST PERSON PRONOUNS	**I** want to take **my** dog with **me.**
	We think **our** way is best for **us.**
	That boat is **ours.**
SECOND PERSON PRONOUNS	Did **you** clean **your** room?
	Are these sneakers **yours?**
THIRD PERSON PRONOUNS	The reporter took **his** camera with **him.**
	They like **their** soup very hot.

EXERCISE 8   Finding Personal Pronouns

Number your paper 1 to 10. Then write the personal pronouns in each sentence.

1. She slung the camera over her shoulder.
2. My friends and I went to a football game.
3. Are the tickets yours or ours?
4. Your mother called you an hour ago.
5. We decided to bring our dog with us.
6. Do they plan to invite him or me?
7. The record albums are mine, but the stereo is hers.
8. He gave the car its first oil change.
9. Should we meet at his house or theirs?
10. They carried their raincoats with them.

EXERCISE 9   Finding Personal Pronouns

Number your paper 1 to 10. Write each personal pronoun and its antecedent.

EXAMPLE   Jim thought he should talk with his father.
ANSWER   he, his — Jim

1. Because Mr. Ogawa had left his briefcase at home, he went back to get it.
2. The children asked their father if they should take their sleeping bags with them.
3. Betty told Karen, "You go now, and I will come later."
4. The Keiths will take their dog with them to Denver.
5. As Nina watched the parade, she saw Juan in it.
6. Carlos asked Bob, "Will you help me repair my car?"
7. Jim asked Mike if he would try out for the play with him.
8. Frank told Margie, "Chad can ride with you and me."
9. Mary said to Joyce, "I think this book is yours."
10. The Lees borrowed the rake, but they will return it.

Other Kinds of Pronouns

Besides personal pronouns, there are a few other kinds of pronouns. Four of these kinds will be discussed in this section. A fifth kind, *relative pronouns*, will be covered in Chapter 10.

Reflexive Pronouns.   These pronouns are formed by adding *-self* or *-selves* to certain personal pronouns.

Reflexive Pronouns

SINGULAR   myself, yourself, himself, herself, itself
PLURAL   ourselves, yourselves, themselves

Miguel bought **himself** a new notebook.

The guests served **themselves** at the buffet.

NOTE: Do not write or say *hisself* or *theirselves*.

EXERCISE 10 Finding Personal and Reflexive Pronouns
Number your paper 1 to 10. Then write each personal or reflexive pronoun. Beside each pronoun, write its antecedent.

1. The Harrisons bought themselves a video recorder.
2. "Tell me what you heard," Mark told Michele.
3. Doris gives herself a manicure every week.
4. The cat tossed its toy mouse into the air and caught it.
5. The students wrote their reports and turned them in.
6. "Did you teach yourself to ski?" Anne asked David.
7. "I will help myself by exercising more," Barbara said.
8. Dick took his turn after Paula took hers.
9. "Can you tell me if Pedro is here?" Bruce asked Mary.
10. "The Morrisons spoke highly of you when they were here," Audrey told Chris.

Indefinite Pronouns. These pronouns very often refer to unnamed people or things. They usually do not have definite antecedents as personal pronouns do.

Several have qualified for the contest.
Many attended the school concert.
I've heard **everything** now!

Common Indefinite Pronouns			
all	both	few	nothing
another	each	many	one
any	either	most	several
anybody	everybody	neither	some
anyone	everyone	none	someone
anything	everything	no one	something

EXERCISE 11 Finding Indefinite Pronouns
Number your paper 1 to 10. Then write each indefinite pronoun.

1. The invitation was extended to everyone.
2. Both of you know everything that happened.

3. No one saw anyone from the other school at the dance.
4. Each of the witnesses knew something about the accident.
5. Some arrived early, but many came late.
6. All except Mary attended the class meeting.
7. One of my friends will go with me.
8. None of the dinner had been eaten.
9. Did you tell anybody about either of our ideas?
10. Most of my friends sent me a card on my birthday.

Demonstrative Pronouns. These pronouns are used to point out people, places, and objects.

This is Mary's coat on the hanger.
Are **these** John's glasses?

Demonstrative Pronouns
this   that   these   those

Interrogative Pronouns. These pronouns are used to ask questions.

What is known about the case?
Who is coming to the party?

Interrogative Pronouns
what   which   who   whom   whose

EXERCISE 12 Finding Demonstrative Pronouns and Interrogative Pronouns

Number your paper 1 to 10. Then write each demonstrative and interrogative pronoun in the following sentences.

1. What is the starting time of the game?
2. If that is true, who will help us?

3. Bob can't decide between these or those.
4. Whom did Alex meet at the dance?
5. That is my sweater.
6. These are Mike's gloves and those are Anne's.
7. If Mom has the keys, then whose are these?
8. This is Amy's first trip to the East.
9. Which of those does Lucy want?
10. What does Ruth think this could be?

EXERCISE 13 Time-out for Review
Number your paper 1 to 10. Then write all the pronouns in each sentence.

1. After the party, most of the guests said they enjoyed it very much.
2. What is Tom doing in our garage?
3. Meg thinks she found the candles and their holders.
4. Teresa cooked herself an egg for breakfast.
5. Everyone donated something to the fund.
6. The judge asked the jury, "Is this your verdict?"
7. Both of the girls took their skates with them to the rink.
8. What does that mean to you?
9. One of the parakeets got out of its cage.
10. When George finished his homework, he put it into his notebook.

Application to Writing

As you have learned in this chapter, pronouns provide shortcuts in writing. These shortcuts create a smoother flow to your writing.

EXERCISE 14 Substituting Pronouns for Nouns
The following paragraph repeats some nouns too often. Rewrite the paragraph by replacing nouns with pronouns where they are needed. Then underline your changes.

Gorillas
Are
Smart

Investigations into the intelligence of gorillas show that gorillas are much smarter than people once thought gorillas were. Gorillas will stack boxes to help gorillas reach bananas that are too high to pick. Gorillas will use sticks as tools to pull food into gorillas' cages. One scientist, Dr. James White, trained a female gorilla named Congo to perform various actions. When the scientist returned some years later, Congo remembered the scientist. Congo also repeated some of the actions the scientist had taught Congo.

CHAPTER REVIEW

Number your paper 1 to 20. Make two columns on your paper. Label the first column *nouns* and the second column *pronouns*. Under the correct column, write each noun and pronoun. Then underline each proper noun.

EXAMPLE Pat and I skied in Aspen last winter.

ANSWER nouns   pronouns

Pat, Aspen, winter   I

1. Tim just bought himself something at the mall.
2. The newspaper praised Rhoda for her calmness and courage after the accident.
3. The long snout and tongue of the anteater enable it to burrow in the ground for its dinner.
4. After Alaska, the state with the smallest population is Wyoming.
5. Lee had his hair cut and his suit pressed for the wedding on Sunday.
6. Some of your books from the library are due next week.
7. A ring around the moon is a sign of rain or snow.
8. Lynn bought herself a painting of a flock of geese in a meadow.
9. Harvey Kennedy became a multimillionaire because he invented the shoelace.
10. The first person in history to swim the English Channel was Matthew Webb.
11. Everyone goes to the new shopping center in Newton.

12. I heard Mary say that last night at the game.
13. At any given moment, there are about 2,000 thunderstorms brewing in the atmosphere.
14. If this doesn't fit me, do you want it?
15. After most of the guests had arrived, Sheila opened her gifts.
16. Steve bought his mother a music box for her birthday.
17. My family and many of our relatives held a reunion in June.
18. These are the ones you should buy.
19. Which of the girls was chosen to be the leader of the group?
20. He explained to me everything about the concert in Melbourne Auditorium.

MASTERY TEST

Number your paper 1 to 10. Make two columns on your paper. Label the first column *nouns* and the second column *pronouns*. Then under the proper column, write each noun and pronoun.

1. Will you play tennis with me on Saturday?
2. I have lived in the state of Washington for five years now.
3. Animals usually show loyalty and obedience to their owners.
4. What is that on the edge of the table?
5. Pat wants to buy the small radio in the window.
6. Who will help Ralph with a hard problem in math?
7. We thought the special effects in the movie were amazing.
8. Do you think this is a good price for both of them?
9. Something is wrong with the brakes on your bicycle.
10. Crowds gathered on Lake Street to watch the parade as it passed.

3
Verbs

Number your paper 1 to 10. Write the verb or the verb phrase in each sentence. Then label each one *action* or *linking*.

EXAMPLE   Has her temperature remained high?
ANSWER   has remained — linking

1. The rabbit scampered into the bushes.
2. Your radio is loud!
3. You should have known the answer.
4. Mr. Jenkins will become the new police chief next November.
5. The snow has been falling very heavily for three hours now.
6. The group did postpone the trip.
7. Ken carefully tasted the hot soup.
8. Mrs. Davidson has lived in that yellow house for seven years.
9. Do you feel warm?
10. The study hall was quiet all period.

Verbs breathe life into sentences. One kind of verb gives a subject action and movement. Another kind of verb tells something about a subject. It can state the condition of the subject or state the fact that the subject exists. This chapter will explain these kinds of verbs. You will also learn how to choose the best verbs when you write.

ACTION VERBS

The most frequently used verb is the *action verb*.

3a An **action verb** tells what action a subject is performing.

Most action verbs show physical action.

Dad **plants** tulip bulbs every fall.
Karen **skated** across the frozen pond.

Some action verbs show mental action. Others show owner-ship or possession.

José **remembered** the formula.
Toby **has** a new friend.

In Chapter 1 you learned that *helping verbs* are often used with an action verb to form a *verb phrase*.

3b A **verb phrase** is a main verb plus one or more helping verbs.

Notice in the following examples that a verb phrase may contain more than one helping verb. It may also be inter-rupted by other words. *(See page 11.)*

John **should have announced** the contest.
Barbara **can** surely **help** you with your math.
Shouldn't Robin **go** with us?

Verbs

Following is a list of the common helping verbs.

Common Helping Verbs	
be	am, is, are, was, were, be, being, been
have	has, have, had
do	do, does, did
others	may, might, must, can, could, shall, should, will, would

EXERCISE 1   Finding Action Verbs
Write the verb or the verb phrase in each sentence.

The
Amazing
Dolphins

 1. Dr. Lilly, a scientist from California, has been experimenting with dolphins for 20 years.
 2. He has made some curious claims about them.
 3. Dolphins have larger brains than humans.
 4. Their language contains at least 50,000 words.
 5. Their brains can handle four conversations at one time.
 6. They can also judge between right and wrong.
 7. Dolphins can remember sounds and series of sounds.
 8. They can even communicate among themselves.
 9. They use a series of clicks, buzzes, and whistles.
10. Dolphins have discharged some of these sounds at the rate of 700 times a second.

EXERCISE 2   Finding Verb Phrases
Write the verb phrase in each sentence.

 1. The party should have started an hour ago.
 2. A diamond will not dissolve in acid.
 3. An average person's liver can weigh three and a half pounds.
 4. Mark has had a coin collection for ten years.
 5. Chewing gum had first appeared in 1848.
 6. Some tortoises can live about 100 years.
 7. Steve couldn't stay for lunch.
 8. Larry must have just finished his chores.
 9. Didn't you sleep well last night?

10. Pigs actually do exhibit great intelligence.
11. Romans had originally named the Colosseum the Flavian Amphitheater.
12. Didn't you see the red light?
13. In Houston you can visit the first domed stadium.
14. A storm had never caused such severe damage before.
15. A mother bird may feed its fledglings over 1,200 times a day.
16. The current horse population in the United States has reached 72 million.
17. Haven't you taken algebra yet?
18. Lack of air in the lungs can frequently cause yawns.
19. I didn't recognize him with a beard.
20. After a long, hard climb, some of the group did finally reach the summit.

EXERCISE 3   Writing Sentences

Write three sentences that tell how to cook an egg. Then underline each action verb.

Transitive and Intransitive Verbs

All action verbs can be either transitive or intransitive. To decide whether a verb is transitive or intransitive, say the subject and the verb. Then ask the question *What?* or *Whom?* A word that answers either question is called an *object*. An action verb that has an object is *transitive*. An action verb that does not have an object is *intransitive*.

TRANSITIVE   Josh always **eats** dinner late. [Josh eats what? *Dinner* is the object. Therefore, *eats* is a transitive verb.]

INTRANSITIVE   The car **skidded** on the icy road. [The car skidded what? The car skidded whom? Since there is no object, *skidded* is an intransitive verb.]

41

EXERCISE 4   Identifying Transitive Verbs and Intransitive Verbs

Write the action verb in each sentence. Then label each one *transitive* or *intransitive*.

1. Eagles keep the same nests throughout their lives.
2. Hummingbirds sometimes fly backward.
3. The dog buried its bone in the backyard.
4. My family eats fresh vegetables every day.
5. The papers scattered all over the lawn.
6. A human eye winks in one fortieth of a second.
7. Suddenly lightning struck the massive tree.
8. In 1932, Babe Didrikson broke three Olympic records.
9. The trees blew gently in the breeze.
10. The Empire State Building has 6,400 windows.

Transitive or Intransitive?   The same verb can be transitive in one sentence and intransitive in another sentence.

TRANSITIVE   Carrie **sang** a song for us. [Carrie sang what? *Song* is the object.]

INTRANSITIVE   Carrie **sang** at the Civic Center. [Carrie sang what? There is no object. *At the Civic Center* is a prepositional phrase.]

EXERCISE 5   Distinguishing between Transitive and Intransitive Verbs

Write the action verb in each sentence. Then label each one *transitive* or *intransitive*.

1. Jeff quickly turned the pages.
2. My mother often speaks at school meetings.
3. On Fridays Ann plays at Symphony Hall.
4. My brother always drives carefully.
5. Kim speaks English, French, and Spanish.
6. The birdhouse hung from a rope on the oak tree.
7. They turned down the dark alley.
8. Anne drives her car to school.
9. We hung new curtains in my bedroom.
10. Rob usually plays tennis on the weekends.

LINKING VERBS

Verbs that link or join the subject with another word in the sentence are called *linking verbs*.

3c ▶ A **linking verb** links the subject with another word in the sentence. The other word either renames or describes the subject.

Tim **is** my brother. [*Is* links *brother* and the subject *Tim*. *Brother* renames the subject.]

The weather **has been** very cold. [*Has been* links *cold* and the subject *weather*. *Cold* describes the subject.]

Following is a list of common linking verbs. They are all forms of the verb *be*. Any verb phrase ending in *be* or *been* is a form of *be* and can be used as a linking verb.

Common Forms of *Be*		
be	shall be	have been
is	will be	has been
am	can be	had been
are	could be	could have been
was	should be	should have been
were	would be	may have been
	may be	might have been
	might be	must have been

The forms of the verb *be* are not always linking verbs. To be a linking verb, a verb must link the subject with another word in the sentence that renames or describes it. In the following examples, the verbs simply make statements.

I **was** there.
They **will be** in the library.

EXERCISE 6 Finding Linking Verbs

Write the linking verb in each sentence. Then write the two words that the verb links.

EXAMPLE   The roses were a gift.
ANSWER   were, roses — gift

1. The comforter was very warm.
2. The Minakos will be our new neighbors.
3. Alex should have been the captain.
4. The elephant is the only animal with four knees.
5. The light here should be brighter.
6. In China the dragon is a symbol of good luck.
7. You might be the winner.
8. Is the butter too hard?
9. Some fish are smaller than ants.
10. Lenny may be correct about the score.
11. The winner of the first Super Bowl was the Green Bay Packers.
12. No two fingerprints are exactly alike.
13. That road may have been the turnoff to Route 6.
14. This holiday should be happy for everyone.
15. The inventor of the thermometer was Galileo.
16. The Taylors have been our neighbors for 15 years.
17. Would you be my lab partner?
18. The largest desert in the world is the Sahara.
19. Baseball will always be my favorite sport.
20. Lincoln was the 16th president of the United States.

Additional Linking Verbs

Besides the verb *be*, a few other verbs can be linking verbs.

Additional Linking Verbs			
appear	grow	seem	stay
become	look	smell	taste
feel	remain	sound	turn

Just like forms of *be*, these verbs link the subject with a word that either renames or describes the subject.

Burt **remained** captain of the team for two years.
[*Captain* renames the subject.]

Lucy **looks** very healthy since her vacation.
[*Healthy* describes the subject.]

Like action verbs, linking verbs may be used with helping verbs.

The weather **will turn** colder tomorrow.

EXERCISE 7 Finding Linking Verbs

Write the verb or the verb phrase in each sentence. Then write the two words that the verb links.

1. That hat looks ridiculous on you!
2. Hector has grown braver.
3. Judy became the new treasurer of the club.
4. The rabbit's fur felt extremely soft.
5. My mother appears quite content.
6. Her hands remained steady throughout her speech.
7. His voice sounded very stern.
8. The grapefruit tasted unusually sour.
9. Does Betsy seem sad to you?
10. The roasting turkey smelled delicious.

EXERCISE 8 Finding Linking Verbs

Write the verb or the verb phrase in each sentence. Then write the two words that the verb links.

1. For some people a bee sting may be fatal.
2. Andrew Jackson was the seventh president.
3. That rumor sounds untrue to me.
4. The stew tastes salty.
5. Tommy is growing more restless by the minute.
6. Alaska is the only state without a state motto.
7. I have been sick for two weeks.

8. The towels from the dryer felt warm.
9. "The Star-Spangled Banner" did not become our national anthem until 1931.
10. René should have been the candidate.

Linking Verb or Action Verb?

Most of the linking verbs listed on page 44 can also be action verbs.

LINKING VERB   The medicine **tasted** very bitter. [*Bitter* describes the subject.]

ACTION VERB   Marvin nervously **tasted** the lobster. [*Tasted* shows action. It tells what Marvin did.]

To decide whether a verb is a linking verb or an action verb, ask two questions. *Does the verb link the subject with a word that renames or describes the subject? Does the verb show action?*

LINKING VERB   Your costume **looks** perfect.
ACTION VERB   She **looks** in the mailbox each day.

EXERCISE 9   **Distinguishing between Linking Verbs and Action Verbs**

Write the verb or the verb phrase in each sentence. Then label each one *linking* or *action*.

1. Did you turn the record over?
2. The evening breeze felt cool.
3. My neighbor grows tomatoes in her backyard.
4. Peggy looked everywhere for Penny.
5. Have you felt the material on the sofa?
6. Her voice sounds so pleasant over the phone.
7. Our cat always grows hungry at night.
8. Those shoes look very comfortable.
9. The bugle sounded the start of the race.
10. The photographs turned dull with age.

EXERCISE 10 Writing Sentences
Write two sentences for each of the following verbs. First use the verb as a linking verb. Then use it as an action verb. Label each one *linking* or *action*.

1. taste   2. look   3. smell   4. appear   5. grow

EXERCISE 11 Time-out for Review
Write the verb or the verb phrase in each sentence. Then label each one *linking* or *action*.

The Study of Cold

1. Cryogenics is the study of cold.
2. At very cold temperatures, your breath will turn to a liquid.
3. At colder temperatures, it actually freezes into a solid.
4. Cold steel becomes very soft.
5. A frozen banana can serve as a hammer.
6. Shivers can raise the body temperature by seven degrees.
7. People with a low body temperature feel lazy.
8. People should wear layers of clothing for the best protection from the cold.
9. Chipmunks have found a good solution to the cold.
10. They hibernate all winter long.

Application to Writing

At the beginning of this chapter, you read that verbs can breathe life into a sentence. This is true; however, some verbs can breathe more life into a sentence than other verbs. The dictionary and the thesaurus usually provide colorful alternatives to dull, lifeless verbs such as *say* and *walk*.

LIFELESS VERB   The roller coaster **went** down the steep slope.

COLORFUL VERB   The roller coaster **roared** (thundered, crashed, hurtled) down the steep slope.

EXERCISE 12 Listing Colorful Verbs
Number your paper 1 to 10. Then write at least two colorful verbs that have about the same meaning as each of the following overused verbs.

1. tell   3. sit   5. throw   7. go   9. speak
2. walk   4. eat   6. look   8. move   10. hurry

EXERCISE 13 Using Colorful Verbs
Choose ten of the following colorful verbs. Then write a sentence for each one of them.

1. shattered   6. scurried   11. whirled   16. rumbled
2. slithered   7. dribbled   12. mumbled   17. blazed
3. whimpered   8. toppled   13. twirled   18. gasped
4. scattered   9. scowled   14. rippled   19. hissed
5. volleyed   10. kindled   15. sprang   20. crept

EXERCISE 14 Writing Sentences
Write three sentences that describe the action of a football, baseball, or other game. Use colorful verbs.

CHAPTER REVIEW

A. Write the verb or the verb phrase in each sentence. Then label each one *action* or *linking*.

1. Hollywood has made 19 films about Dracula.
2. Ms. Edwards will become the school's new track coach.
3. The flowers still look very fresh.
4. Have you gone to the new science museum?
5. A female condor lays a single egg every two years.
6. For two weeks they have been looking for a job.
7. A human can detect the smell of a skunk a mile away.
8. Daisies have always been my favorite flower.
9. They should have telephoned the restaurant first.
10. Rice is the chief food for half the people of the world.
11. Lettuce is the world's most popular green vegetable.
12. It can be colder in winter in New York than in Iceland.

13. Didn't you sing in the chorus last year?
14. I have always attended the meetings.
15. Rico remains my best friend.
16. Turn right at the next intersection.
17. Guinea pigs are not members of the pig family.
18. At first, the exercise appeared very difficult.
19. Some turtles do not breathe at all during the winter.
20. Have you tasted Mildred's potato salad?

B. Write the verb or the verb phrase in each sentence. Then label each one *transitive* or *intransitive*.

1. Most of the apples fell from the tree during the storm.
2. Spiders have transparent blood.
3. Antonio scored two runs in the second inning.
4. Most American horns beep in the key of F.
5. I have seen that movie five times now.
6. Will you take a picture of me and my dog?
7. Cut the grass tomorrow.
8. From outside no one can hear the phone.
9. Thomas Jefferson invented the calendar clock.
10. Have you taken the radio outside?

MASTERY TEST

Number your paper 1 to 10. Write the verb or the verb phrase in each sentence. Then label each one *action* or *linking*.

1. You should buy two quarts of milk at the store.
2. Anita will be happy with your decision.
3. Are you going to the game on Saturday?
4. The sky turned dark in the afternoon.
5. You should have told me that sooner.
6. Is Sue your best friend?
7. The movie is starting in ten minutes.
8. The storm has delayed my flight.
9. The portrait of Martha was very flattering.
10. Have you tasted her homemade chili?

4

Adjectives and Adverbs

DIAGNOSTIC TEST

Number your paper 1 to 10. Make two columns on your paper. Label the first column *adjectives* and the second column *adverbs*. Then under the proper column, write each adjective and adverb. Do not include articles.

EXAMPLE   The three yellow-breasted birds flew away.

ANSWER   <u>adjectives</u>   <u>adverbs</u>
         three, yellow-breasted   away

1. Jeff carefully read the long instructions.
2. Alan spoke briefly but convincingly before the entire faculty.
3. The unusually smart horse could do many tricks.
4. Unsteadily the very nervous actor appeared on stage.
5. A Sunday brunch of waffles is always delicious.
6. During a two-week vacation, we visited the islands.
7. Amanda received three scarves for a present.
8. The Mexican dancers whirled swiftly around the large hats.
9. One rose remained in the rather large glass vase.
10. Haven't these books been returned to the library?

A sentence with only nouns or pronouns and verbs would be very short and dull.

Dogs bark.

Adjectives and *adverbs*, however, can be added to give color and sharper meaning to nouns, pronouns, and verbs.

Those three huge dogs bark constantly.

Adjectives and adverbs are called *modifiers* because they change or make more precise the meaning of other parts of speech.

ADJECTIVES

What was your day like yesterday? Was it *pleasant, boring, happy, sad, successful,* or *nerve-racking?* All of these possible answers are *adjectives.*

4a ▶ An **adjective** is a word that modifies a noun or a pronoun.

To find an adjective, first find each noun and pronoun in a sentence. Then ask yourself, *What kind? Which one(s)? How many?* or *How much?* about each one. The answers to these questions will be adjectives.

WHAT KIND?   The **old** car needs to be painted.

Do you like **fresh** broccoli?

WHICH ONE(S)?   **These** boots belong to Stacy.

I like the **white** one.

HOW MANY?   **Thirty** people attended the meeting.

He owns **many** tapes.

HOW MUCH?   **Little** room was left in the suitcase.

She deserves **much** praise for her work.

51

NOTE: The words *a*, *an*, and *the* form a special group of adjectives called *articles*. Keep in mind that *a* comes before words that begin with a consonant sound, and *an* comes before words that begin with a vowel sound. You will not be asked to list articles in the exercises in this book.

EXERCISE 1 Finding Adjectives

Number your paper 1 to 10. Then write the adjectives in the following sentences.

1. Nancy laughed at the silly joke.
2. The hike up the mountain took three hours.
3. Would you like to ride a powerful motorcycle?
4. We had little time to shop for a pair of comfortable shoes.
5. The spicy aroma of the chili welcomed the hungry guests.
6. The hectic pace of a dynamic city is enjoyable.
7. On a clear night you can see countless stars.
8. The beautiful painting brightened the dark hallway.
9. Michael pulled the wooden oars of the squeaky rowboat.
10. We walked on the long, narrow path through the green forest.

EXERCISE 2 Supplying Adjectives

Write an adjective that completes each sentence.

1. The _____ building will be torn down soon.
2. I counted _____ birds in that tree yesterday.
3. Do you want a _____ sweater for your birthday?
4. I enjoyed eating the _____ dessert.
5. _____ time was given for the assembly.
6. There weren't _____ people left when I arrived.
7. Ellen's _____ choice for a vacation was California.
8. She could easily be seen in her bright _____ coat.
9. Kent thought the book was very _____.
10. The _____ flowers decorated the table.

Position of Adjectives

Adjectives can modify different nouns or pronouns, or they can modify the same noun or pronoun.

DIFFERENT NOUNS   Buy **six** pears and a **big** watermelon.

THE SAME NOUN   I just bought **six big** tomatoes.

Usually an adjective comes in front of the noun or the pronoun it modifies. However, an adjective can also follow a noun or a pronoun, or it can follow a linking verb.

BEFORE A NOUN   Her **soft** voice couldn't be heard.

AFTER A NOUN   The dog, **sad** and **wet,** whined.

AFTER A LINKING VERB   Ron looks quite **cheerful** today.

EXERCISE 3 Finding Adjectives

Number your paper 1 to 10. Write the adjectives in each sentence. Then beside each adjective, write the word it modifies. There are 30 adjectives.

Fancy Dressers

1. For many years men dressed with more color and greater style than women.
2. During the 1600s, men wore lacy collars and fancy jackets with shiny buttons.
3. Long, curly hair reached the shoulder.
4. Men even carried small purses on huge belts.
5. After all, there were no pockets in the warm, colorful tights they wore.
6. By 1850, clothing had become drab and conservative.
7. Gone were elegant white silk shirts, purple vests, lacy cuffs, and stylish black boots.
8. Clothing stayed colorless and dreary until the popular Beatles came along in the 1960s.
9. The way they dressed, bright and informal, created a new style for men.
10. Today people don't follow one style; everyone dresses to suit personal tastes.

Proper and Compound Adjectives

You have learned that a proper noun is the name of a particular person, place, or thing—*Mexico* and *Northeast*. A *proper adjective* is an adjective that is formed from a proper noun—*Mexican* food and *Northeastern* states. Notice that a proper adjective begins with a capital letter—just as a proper noun does.

PROPER NOUNS	PROPER ADJECTIVES
England	**English** countryside
Shakespeare	**Shakespearean** dramas
Greece	**Greek** food

Some proper adjectives keep the same form as the proper noun.

New York	**New York** skyline
Roosevelt	**Roosevelt** era
Monday	**Monday** traffic

Compound Adjectives. You have also learned that compound nouns are nouns that are made up of two or more words. *Compound adjectives* are adjectives that are made up of two or more words.

COMPOUND ADJECTIVES   **rooftop** apartment
                            birdseye view
                            homesick student
                            far-off horizon

EXERCISE 4   Finding Proper and Compound Adjectives
Number your paper 1 to 10. Write the proper adjective and the compound adjective in each sentence. Then beside each adjective, write the word it modifies.

EXAMPLE   The farsighted investor purchased Mexican art.
ANSWER   farsighted—investor, Mexican—art

1. Francisco lives in a seafront cottage on a Hawaiian island.
2. The topic of the after-school discussion will be the American economy.
3. Japanese people enjoy fast-food restaurants.
4. The blue-eyed girl was from a Scandinavian country.
5. The Republican congressman spoke of widespread poverty.
6. The pint-size car is a French import.
7. The all-star team will play the Australian team in the tournament.
8. The reporter's straightforward questions surprised the Russian diplomat.
9. Canadian friends of ours met us this morning at the waterfront hotel.
10. Third-class mail is sent by boat to European countries.

EXERCISE 5   Writing Sentences

Write five sentences that describe your favorite dessert. Then underline each adjective in your sentences.

Adjective or Noun?

The same word can be an adjective in one sentence and a noun in another sentence.

ADJECTIVE   Her editorial appeared in the **school** paper. [*School* tells what kind of paper.]

NOUN   I've gone to this **school** for three years. [*School* is the name of a place.]

ADJECTIVE   Did you buy **plant** food?

NOUN   The **plant** is doing very well here.

NOTE: *Plant* can also be used as a verb.

Plant the evergreen here.

**EXERCISE 6 Distinguishing between Adjectives
and Nouns**

Write the underlined word in each sentence. Then label each word *adjective* or *noun*.

1. Have you seen the <u>garden</u> tools?
2. The <u>television</u> series was canceled after two shows.
3. We need two panes of <u>glass</u> to repair this window.
4. Don't touch the hot <u>oven</u>!
5. I need to buy a <u>picture</u> frame for this snapshot.
6. Margo planted irises in her <u>garden</u>.
7. When was that <u>picture</u> of you taken?
8. Jane received a tiny <u>glass</u> owl as a present.
9. Do they own an <u>oven</u> thermometer?
10. Did you see the special on <u>television</u>?

EXERCISE 7 Writing Sentences

Write two sentences for each of the following words. In the first sentence, use the word as an adjective. In the second sentence, use the word as a noun. Label the use of each one.

1. birthday   2. rose   3. bicycle   4. top   5. paper

Adjective or Pronoun?

These words can be used as adjectives or pronouns.

Words Used as Adjectives or Pronouns			
Demonstrative	Interrogative	Indefinite	
that	what	all	many
these	which	another	more
this		any	most
those		both	neither
		each	other
		either	several
		few	some

All these words are adjectives if they come before a noun and if they modify a noun. They are pronouns when they stand alone.

ADJECTIVE I bought **this** bread yesterday.
PRONOUN Do you like **this?**
ADJECTIVE **What** time is it?
PRONOUN **What** did the choir sing?
ADJECTIVE We phoned you **several** times.
PRONOUN **Several** of the students received awards.

NOTE: The possessive pronouns *my, your, his, her, its, our,* and *their* are sometimes called *pronominal adjectives* because they answer the question *Which one?* Throughout this book, however, they will be considered pronouns.

EXERCISE 8 Distinguishing between Adjectives and Pronouns

Write the underlined word in each sentence. Then label each word *adjective* or *pronoun*.

1. This is my coat on the chair.
2. Which of the bridesmaids should come first?
3. Both of you will make magazine racks.
4. May I have some peace and quiet?
5. These are the perfect curtains for my room.
6. I like this course the most.
7. John will take both suitcases with him.
8. Which record do you want to play first?
9. Can you tell me the price of these scarves?
10. Mr. Kent spoke with some of Peg's teachers.

EXERCISE 9 Writing Sentences

Write two sentences for each of the following words. In the first sentence, use the word as an adjective. In the second sentence, use the word as a pronoun. Label the use of each one.

1. many   2. each   3. what   4. several   5. that

EXERCISE 10   Time-out for Review
Number your paper 1 to 20. Write all the adjectives in the following paragraph. Then beside each adjective, write the word it modifies.

A
Helping
Hand

A Russian athlete named Nikolai helped the American team win the Olympic ice-hockey championship in 1960. The Americans had beaten the Canadian team and the Russian team. Now all they had to do was defeat the Czechs in the final game. After two periods the Americans were losing. The thin air in the California mountains was slowing them down. During the intermission between the second period and the third period, Nikolai visited the weary Americans. Unfortunately he didn't speak any English. Through many gestures, however, he told them to inhale some oxygen. The team immediately felt lively and energetic. The Americans went on to beat the Czechs 9–4. This was the first time an American team had won the title.

Application to Writing ————————————

Adjectives should make your writing more colorful and interesting. Some adjectives, however, are used so often that they no longer mean anything. Look at the difference between the following sentences.

OVERUSED ADJECTIVE   The movie at the Plaza was **great.**
FRESH ADJECTIVE   The movie at the Plaza was **hilarious** (matchless, extraordinary).

When you write, refer to the dictionary and the thesaurus for fresh adjectives.

EXERCISE 11   Using Fresh Adjectives
Write at least two fresh adjectives for each of the underlined adjectives.

1. The picnic lunch tasted <u>good</u>.
2. The music at the concert was <u>loud</u>.
3. We enjoyed the <u>nice</u> mountain view.

4. Your puppy is <u>playful</u>.
5. Their house is always <u>clean</u>.
6. The <u>dull</u> speech made me sleepy.
7. The dance at the school was <u>bad</u>.
8. That's a <u>pretty</u> sunset.
9. Our trip to the Grand Canyon was <u>enjoyable</u>.
10. My sister looked <u>beautiful</u> in her wedding dress.

EXERCISE 12   Expanding Sentences
Choose five of the following sentences. Expand each one by adding words. Each expanded sentence should include at least two adjectives. Then underline each adjective.

EXAMPLE   The boy wrote.
POSSIBLE ANSWER   The <u>four-year-old</u> boy wrote his name in <u>huge</u> letters.

1. A sailboat glided.
2. The athlete jumped.
3. The horse pranced.
4. An ambulance raced.
5. An airplane soared.
6. A storm struck.
7. The woman investigated.
8. The waves crashed.
9. The dog growled.
10. The candle flickered.

EXERCISE 13   Writing Sentences
Write a five-sentence advertisement for the best bicycle in the world. Use colorful, fresh adjectives.

ADVERBS

Adjectives add more information to nouns and pronouns. *Adverbs* make verbs, adjectives, and other adverbs more precise.

4b An **adverb** is a word that modifies a verb, an adjective, or another adverb.

Many adverbs end in *-ly*.

> **Recently** Congress voted **unanimously** for the bill.
> **Absentmindedly** Carl strolled **casually** into the wrong classroom.

Following is a list of common adverbs that do not end in *-ly*.

Common Adverbs			
again	ever	often	somewhere
almost	here	perhaps	soon
alone	just	quite	then
already	later	rather	there
also	never	seldom	today
always	not	so	too
away	now	sometimes	very
even	nowhere	somewhat	yet

NOTE: *Not* and its contraction *n't* are always adverbs.

> I could**n't** find the broom.

Adverbs That Modify Verbs

Most adverbs modify verbs. To find these adverbs, first find the verb. Then ask yourself, *Where? When? How?* or *To what extent?* about the verb. The answers to these questions will be adverbs. The adverbs in the following examples are in heavy type. An arrow points to the verb each adverb modifies.

WHERE? Look **everywhere** for the watch.

Put the newspapers **there.**

WHEN? I **frequently** visit my grandparents.

Sometimes I wax the car.

HOW? He **quickly** and **accurately** threw the ball to third base.

Roy has **carefully** read the contract.

TO WHAT EXTENT? Stan **completely** enjoyed the dinner.

I have **almost** finished my report.

An adverb can come before or after a verb. It can also come in the middle of a verb phrase.

EXERCISE 14 Finding Adverbs That Modify Verbs
Number your paper 1 to 10. Write the adverbs in each sentence. Then next to each one, write the verb it modifies.

EXAMPLE Pearl suddenly laughed heartily.
ANSWER suddenly—laughed, heartily—laughed

1. The old train slowly chugged forward.
2. The huge watchdog growled fiercely and angrily.
3. I haven't seen that movie yet.
4. He often makes decisions quickly.
5. Julio will soon call his relatives in Mexico.
6. Our cat seldom goes outside.
7. The small plane landed smoothly and safely.
8. Old houses are rapidly being remodeled.
9. We already hung decorations everywhere.
10. Was the moon shining then?

Adverbs That Modify Adjectives and Other Adverbs

A few adverbs modify adjectives and other adverbs.

MODIFYING AN ADJECTIVE The coat was **too** long.

MODIFYING AN ADVERB Dennis talks **very** fast.

To find adverbs that modify adjectives or other adverbs, first find the adjectives and the adverbs. Then ask yourself, *To what extent?* about each one. Notice in the preceding examples that the adverbs that modify adjectives or other adverbs usually come before the word they modify.

EXERCISE 15   Finding Adverbs That Modify Adjectives and Other Adverbs

Number your paper 1 to 10. Write each adverb that modifies an adjective or another adverb. Then beside each adverb, write the word it modifies.

EXAMPLE   The actor spoke quite clearly.
ANSWER   quite — clearly

1. The exceptionally long walk exhausted me.
2. The extremely nervous center fumbled the ball.
3. That was a rather funny speech.
4. The old bike works surprisingly well.
5. Read the directions very carefully.
6. The river near our house seems unusually high.
7. My brother is never ready on time.
8. The job at the supermarket is just right for me.
9. They were sitting somewhat close to the front.
10. David arrived much later than Scott.

Adverb or Adjective?

As you have seen in the previous section, many adverbs end in -ly. You should, however, be aware that some adjectives also end in -ly. Always check to see how a word is used in a sentence before you decide what part of speech it is.

ADVERB   Ralph receives the magazine **monthly.**

ADJECTIVE   He pays on a **monthly** basis.

ADVERB   Tom whacked the ball quite **hard.**

ADJECTIVE   The test was very **hard.** [an adjective that follows a linking verb]

**EXERCISE 16   Distinguishing between Adverbs
and Adjectives**

Write the underlined word in each sentence. Then label
each one *adverb* or *adjective.*

1. My <u>early</u> appointment was canceled.
2. The music was too <u>lively</u> for me.
3. Their large historic house is located <u>high</u> on the grassy knoll.
4. We <u>carelessly</u> locked the keys in the car.
5. Our new microwave oven works <u>well</u>.
6. Bears are definitely not <u>friendly</u>.
7. Car prices are very <u>high</u> right now.
8. Don't speak so <u>loudly</u> in the library.
9. The snowstorm arrived <u>early</u>.
10. You should feel <u>well</u> again in a day or two.

EXERCISE 17   Time-out for Review

Number your paper 1 to 20. Write the adverbs in the following paragraphs. Then beside each adverb, write the word or
words it modifies.

The
First
Roller
Skates

The first pair of roller skates appeared in 1760. They were unsuccessfully worn by Joseph Merlin. Merlin had unexpectedly received an invitation to a very large party. Quite excitedly he planned a grand entrance. The night finally arrived. Merlin rolled unsteadily into the ballroom on skates as he played a violin. Unfortunately he couldn't stop. He crashed into an extremely large mirror. The mirror broke into a million pieces. Merlin also smashed his violin and hurt himself severely.

Roller skates were never used again until 1823. Robert Tyers eventually made another attempt. His skates had a single row of five very small wheels. In 1863, James Plimpton finally patented the first pair of four-wheel skates. With these skates, people could keep their balance easily. They could even make very sharp turns.

DIAGRAMING ADJECTIVES AND ADVERBS

Adjectives and adverbs are diagramed on a slanted line below the words they modify.

The huge crowd cheered wildly.

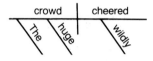

Two Adjectives or Adverbs Joined by a Conjunction. The conjunction is placed on a broken line between the two adjectives and/or adverbs.

My small but strong brother swam fast and skillfully.

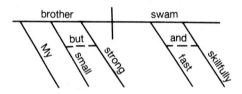

NOTE: Possessive pronouns, such as *my* in the sentence above, are diagramed like adjectives.

An Adverb That Modifies an Adjective or Another Adverb. This adverb also is connected to the word it modifies. It is written on a line parallel to the word it modifies.

The extremely smart child won.

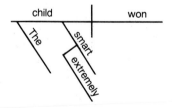

She ate too quickly.

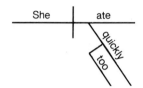

EXERCISE 18   Diagraming Adjectives and Adverbs
Diagram the following sentences or copy them. If you copy
them, draw one line under each subject and two lines under
each verb. Then label each modifier *adjective* or *adverb*.

1. The brick wall collapsed.
2. A large silver trophy has disappeared.
3. The happy cat purred softly.
4. The weary but happy winner grinned.
5. You should never swim alone.
6. A rather large yacht sailed past.
7. The colorful new uniforms have arrived.
8. The children were playing very noisily.
9. A cheetah can run rapidly and gracefully.
10. Those little red ants bite.

✒ *Application to Writing*

To give your writing added variety, begin some sentences
with an adverb.

REGULAR ORDER   The hikers **wearily** trudged into camp.
VARIETY   **Wearily** the hikers trudged into camp.

EXERCISE 19   Creating Sentence Variety with Adverbs
Choose ten of the following adverbs and use each one in a
sentence. Then change five of the sentences around so that
they begin with the adverb. Remember to use capital letters
and end punctuation.

EXAMPLE   cleverly
POSSIBLE   The missing foxes escaped cleverly.
ANSWERS   Cleverly the young foxes escaped.

1. hesitantly	6. clumsily	11. soon
2. bashfully	7. closer	12. today
3. suddenly	8. loudly	13. happily
4. overhead	9. twice	14. quickly
5. silently	10. away	15. noisily

CHAPTER REVIEW

A. Make two columns on your paper. Label the first column *adjectives* and the second column *adverbs*. Under the proper column, write each adjective and adverb.

EXAMPLE   Afterward everyone watched an adventure film.
ANSWER   adjectives   adverbs
           adventure   afterward

1. The Siamese cat was chosen first.
2. Have you read that book yet?
3. The car stopped abruptly at the red light.
4. Canadian bacon tastes delicious.
5. The first face-to-face meeting between the two opponents was extremely awkward.
6. Cautiously the young man climbed the ladder.
7. Lee complained of too much homework.
8. We completely filled the large basket with beets.
9. The sneakers were worn-out and dirty.
10. Didn't you answer the question correctly?

B. Number your paper 1 to 10. Write the underlined words in each sentence. Then label each one *noun, pronoun, adjective,* or *adverb.*

1. Your <u>apple</u> pie tastes much better than <u>this</u>.
2. <u>Both</u> of my brothers went to the <u>play</u> rehearsal.
3. <u>Most</u> drivers couldn't see the <u>street</u> sign.

4. <u>Some</u> of the fawns stood <u>close</u> to their mothers.
5. I have waited a long time to see <u>this</u> <u>play</u>.
6. The <u>car</u> roared down the <u>street</u>.
7. The <u>kindly</u> gentleman offered <u>some</u> good advice.
8. <u>Most</u> of the <u>car</u> dealers are holding sales.
9. <u>Apples</u> were given to <u>both</u> children.
10. She spoke <u>kindly</u> of her <u>close</u> friend.

MASTERY TEST

Number your paper 1 to 10. Make two columns on your paper. Label the first column *adjectives* and the second column *adverbs*. Then under the proper column, write each adjective and adverb. Do not include articles.

1. The large American flag waved gently in the breeze.
2. She spoke softly and tenderly to the baby.
3. Noreen and Pat wrapped the expensive presents beautifully.
4. Which test schedule did you just see?
5. The gentleman from the German embassy in the light-blue suit seemed very friendly.
6. The market will soon receive the Idaho potatoes.
7. These tomatoes were grown here in the backyard.
8. The black-and-white dog doesn't have a home.
9. The math test was extremely long and hard.
10. Sally dreamed of visiting a far-off land.

5

Other Parts of Speech

DIAGNOSTIC TEST

Number your paper 1 to 10. Make three columns on your paper. Label the first column *prepositions*, the second column *conjunctions*, and the third column *interjections*. Then under the proper column, write these parts of speech.

EXAMPLE   Okay! I'll go to the doctor either today or tomorrow.

ANSWER
prepositions	conjunctions	interjections
to	either, or	okay

1. Despite the storm, I'm going with her.
2. Wow! Did you see him run and slide into third base?
3. Behind the house grew a small but healthy oak tree.
4. Are you leaving now or staying through Sunday?
5. Yikes! I almost hit the ball through the window.
6. The awards assembly was scheduled for today, but the team captain is not in school.
7. Because of his broken arm, Jeff can neither write nor eat easily.
8. Gee! I can't wash and dry the dishes by myself.
9. Either Michael or Jon will take you to school.
10. Sean saw both Celeste and Roberta last night.

This chapter will cover three parts of speech. A *preposition* shows relationships between words. A *conjunction* connects words. An *interjection* shows strong feelings.

PREPOSITIONS

The letter $\left\{\begin{array}{l} \textbf{to} \\ \textbf{from} \\ \textbf{about} \end{array}\right.$ Meg was lost.

Changing just one word in the sentence above alters the meaning of the whole sentence. Each of the three words in heavy type shows a different relationship between Meg and the letter. These words are called *prepositions*.

5a ► A **preposition** is a word that shows the relationship between a noun or a pronoun and another word in the sentence.

Following is a list of the most common prepositions.

Common Prepositions				
aboard	before	down	off	till
about	behind	during	on	to
above	below	except	onto	toward
across	beneath	for	opposite	under
after	beside	from	out	underneath
against	besides	in	outside	until
along	between	inside	over	up
among	beyond	into	past	upon
around	but (except)	like	since	with
as	by	near	through	within
at	despite	of	throughout	without

A preposition that is made up of two or more words is called a *compound preposition*.

Common Compound Prepositions		
according to	by means of	instead of
ahead of	in addition to	in view of
apart from	in back of	next to
as of	in front of	on account of
aside from	in place of	out of
because of	in spite of	prior to

EXERCISE 1 Supplying Prepositions

Number your paper 1 to 10. Then write two prepositions that could fill each blank in the following sentences.

EXAMPLE   Roger will go _____ you.

POSSIBLE ANSWERS   in place of, with

1. The bushes _____ the house need trimming.
2. Frank should go _____ the store.
3. The package _____ the chair is mine.
4. We cannot go _____ the storm.
5. Ken hid _____ the boat.
6. Gloria will attend the meeting _____ Howard.
7. The ball rolled _____ the street.
8. Janet walked _____ the water.
9. Carl sat _____ Marcy at the game.
10. The plane flew _____ the storm clouds.

Prepositional Phrases

A preposition is always part of a group of words called a *prepositional phrase.* A prepositional phrase begins with a preposition. It ends with a noun or pronoun called the *object of the preposition.* Any number of modifiers can come between a preposition and its object.

Margaret missed the train **by two minutes.**
The birds flew **between the old wooden beams.**

A sentence can have several prepositional phrases, and the phrases can come anywhere in the sentence.

Without a moment's hesitation, the cat leaped **through the open window.**

In view of the memo *from* the office *of* the principal, afternoon classes will be canceled tomorrow.

EXERCISE 2   Finding Prepositional Phrases

Number your paper 1 to 10. Then write each prepositional phrase. There are 20 phrases.

Agatha
Christie
Saves
a Life

1. A nurse at a London hospital had a young girl in her ward.
2. None of the doctors could find a cure for her.
3. Before work, the nurse began reading another chapter in a mystery by Agatha Christie.
4. After several pages she put the book into her bag and hurried to the hospital.
5. According to the book, someone had taken a rare poison called thallium.
6. The description of the victim's symptoms exactly matched the symptoms of the young girl.
7. The nurse placed the book in front of the doctors.
8. She told them about her suspicions.
9. Within minutes the doctors prescribed a new series of treatments for the girl.
10. Because of a mystery by Agatha Christie, a young girl's life was saved.

Preposition or Adverb?

The same word can be a preposition in one sentence and an adverb in another sentence. Just remember that a preposition is always part of a prepositional phrase. An adverb stands alone.

PREPOSITION	*Below the stairs* is extra storage space.
ADVERB	The sailor climbed **below.**
PREPOSITION	The children slid *down the hill.*
ADVERB	Don't put your books **down** on the floor.

EXERCISE 3 Distinguishing between Prepositions and Adverbs

Write the underlined word in each sentence. Then label it *preposition* or *adverb*.

1. Walk the pony <u>around</u> the rink.
2. "Be careful that you don't fall <u>off</u>," he shouted.
3. Everyone sang as the flag went <u>up</u>.
4. George did his exercises <u>before</u> breakfast.
5. If you go <u>outside</u>, take your key.
6. <u>Up</u> the hill raced the boys on their bikes!
7. All the marbles rolled <u>off</u> the table.
8. We looked <u>around</u> but couldn't find them.
9. Haven't I met you <u>before</u>?
10. A blizzard was raging <u>outside</u> our warm house.

EXERCISE 4 Time-out for Review

Number your paper 1 to 15. Then write the prepositional phrases in the following paragraph.

A
Tasty
Meal

In the Beartooth Mountains of Montana, there is a most unusual glacier. Within the ice of the glacier are frozen millions of grasshoppers. According to scientists, an immense swarm of grasshoppers made a forced landing on the glacier two centuries ago! They were then quickly frozen by a snowstorm. Today the grasshoppers are still excellently preserved. During the warm weather, many birds and animals throughout the region flock to the glacier in addition to their normal sources of food. When the ice melts, the grasshoppers provide them with a most unusual meal.

Application to Writing

Sentence variety can be created by starting some sentences with a prepositional phrase.

REGULAR ORDER   The child coughed **throughout the night.**

VARIETY   **Throughout the night** the child coughed.

EXERCISE 5   **Creating Sentence Variety with**
                 Prepositional Phrases

Choose ten of the following prepositions. Then write a sentence using each one. Begin at least five of your sentences with the prepositional phrase.

1. in place of	6. through	11. inside	16. along
2. because of	7. next to	12. beyond	17. as of
3. in back of	8. during	13. across	18. from
4. opposite	9. behind	14. aboard	19. into
5. ahead of	10. out of	15. until	20. near

CONJUNCTIONS

A word that connects is called a *conjunction*.

5b ► A **conjunction** connects words or groups of words.

There are three kinds of conjunctions. A *coordinating conjunction* is a single connecting word.

Coordinating Conjunctions
and   but   for   nor   or   so   yet

WORDS   Her *ring* **and** *bracelet* were lost. [nouns]

She **or** *he* will be elected. [pronouns]

Greg *came* to the party **but** *left* early. [verbs]

Wear the *white* **or** *red* gloves. [adjectives]

He joins us *now* **and** *then*. [adverbs]

GROUPS   The dog ran *through the door* **and** *into the*
OF WORDS   *kitchen*. [prepositional phrases]

The spring water tasted especially good, **for** we were very thirsty. [sentences]

73

Correlative conjunctions are pairs of connecting words.

Correlative Conjunctions

both/and   either/or   neither/nor
not only/but also   whether/or

Both dogs **and** cats can get fleas.
You should take **either** Route 2 **or** Fowler Highway.

NOTE: A *subordinating conjunction* is the third kind of conjunction. It will be covered in Chapter 10.

EXERCISE 6 Finding Conjunctions
Write the coordinating or correlative conjunctions in each sentence.

1. Neither Mercury nor Venus has a natural satellite.
2. We looked for her keys in the house and on the lawn.
3. Linda raised her hand and answered the question.
4. The alarm didn't go off, so I was late for school.
5. I will go with either Nancy or her sister.
6. Sam not only played the piano but also sang.
7. The story was both interesting and informative.
8. Pierre spoke only French, yet we became good friends.
9. Swiftly but carefully he ran the course.
10. The Bucks or the Hornets will win the tournament.

EXERCISE 7 Writing Sentences
Write ten sentences that follow the directions below.

1. Use *both/and* with two nouns.
2. Use *but* with two adjectives.
3. Use *either/or* with a noun and a pronoun.
4. Use *and* with two sentences. (Use a comma before *and*.)
5. Use *and* with two prepositional phrases.
6. Use *neither/nor* with two proper nouns.
7. Use *not only/but also* with two verbs.

8. Use *and* with two adverbs.
9. Use *for* with two sentences. (Use a comma before *for*.)
10. Use *but* with two verbs.

INTERJECTIONS

Some words show strong feelings or emotions, such as joy or anger. These words are called *interjections*.

5c ▶ An **interjection** is a word that expresses strong feeling or emotion.

Interjections usually come at the beginning of a sentence. Since they are not related to the rest of the sentence, they are separated from it by an exclamation point or a comma.

What! Are you sure?
Wow! That sounds great.
Oh, I just locked myself out!

Sometimes another part of speech can be used as an interjection as well.

Surprise! It's a party.
Great! We finished on time.
Well! Who ate my dessert?

NOTE: Do not use too many interjections when you write. If you use them sparingly, they will have the impact they are meant to have.

EXERCISE 8 Writing Sentences
Number your paper 1 to 10. Then write a sentence for each of the following interjections.

1. Oops!   3. Aha!   5. Great!   7. Ugh!   9. Whew!
2. Hurrah! 4. Ouch! 6. Alas!   8. Wow! 10. Gee!

CHAPTER REVIEW

Number your paper 1 to 20, skipping a line between each number. After you write each sentence, label each preposition *(prep.)*, conjunction *(conj.)*, and interjection *(interj.)*. Then underline each prepositional phrase.

EXAMPLE   Both Ellie and Cheryl went to Maine.

ANSWER   Both Ellie and Cheryl went <u>to Maine</u>.
conj.   conj.   prep.

1. Without a pause Paul threw the ball quickly and accurately.
2. Because of the heat, Mae and Allison went swimming.
3. Neither our dog nor our cat likes cold food from the refrigerator.
4. For her lunch Glenda ordered soup and a salad.
5. Between you and me, she is the right person for the job.
6. The test in science was hard, yet I did very well.
7. Our trip throughout Alaska was long but exciting.
8. Seriously! Either some of your books or some of your records must go.
9. Wayne can't come until noon, so the game will be delayed.
10. She not only has won meets but also has set records in the broad jump.
11. Are we going to an Italian or Chinese restaurant?
12. Incredible! After a poor season, the team won 20–0.
13. Both Juanita and Maureen applied for the job.
14. Either Steve or Mary Ellen will meet you at the airport.
15. Instead of driving, Chris and he walked across town.
16. Congratulations! You are the winner of the contest.
17. Beneath the murky water, the divers swam toward the sunken ship.
18. Marianna not only plays the piano but also studies the harpsichord.
19. Please park the car within the white lines.
20. In spite of the efforts of many people, the candidate lost the election by a few votes.

MASTERY TEST

Number your paper 1 to 10. Make three columns on your paper. Label the first column *prepositions,* the second column *conjunctions,* and the third column *interjections.* Then under the proper column, write these parts of speech.

1. Today the judges will choose both the finalists and the semifinalists.
2. Heat has been restored throughout the school, so classes will be held tomorrow.
3. Ahem! This is neither the time nor the place for the discussion.
4. The scouts will take their tents in addition to a camper.
5. Not only Lesley but also Brenda must go with us.
6. Great! I will meet you within the hour.
7. The stars glittered in the dark but clear sky.
8. Around March, tryouts for both the tennis team and the baseball team will be held.
9. Ugh! I don't like the taste of clams or oysters.
10. During the night the snow piled against the door.

6

Parts of Speech Review

In the first five chapters of this book, you learned the eight parts of speech. You also learned that one word can be used in more than one way. How a word is used in a sentence determines its part of speech. For example, the word *near* can be used as four different parts of speech.

VERB	She will **near** the halfway point soon.
ADJECTIVE	I will join the club in the **near** future.
ADVERB	The date of her interview drew **near.**
PREPOSITION	Plant the bushes **near** the house.

To find out what part of speech a word is, read the sentence carefully. Then ask yourself, *What is each word doing in this sentence?* Following is a summary of questions you can ask to determine a word's part of speech.

NOUN   Is the word naming a person, place, thing, or idea?
Tom bought **milk** at the **store.**

PRONOUN   Is the word taking the place of a noun?
This is **my** favorite brand of soup.

VERB   Is the word showing action?
Greg **jogged** four miles.

Does the word link two words in a sentence?
Ellen **is** the captain of the team.

ADJECTIVE   Is the word modifying a noun or pronoun? Does it answer the question *What kind? Which one(s)? How many?* or *How much?*

Three yellow tulips bloomed today.
You can have **these** few.

ADVERB   Is the word modifying a verb, an adjective, or another adverb? Does it answer the question *How? When? Where?* or *To what extent?*

He drove **too fast** on a **very** dark road.

PREPOSITION   Is the word showing a relationship between a noun or pronoun and another word in the sentence? Is it a part of a phrase?

Because of *their length,* I finished both **of** *the chapters.*

CONJUNCTION   Is the word connecting words or groups of words?

Jim **and** I like **neither** lima beans **nor** broccoli.
Mom turned the key, **but** the car wouldn't start.

INTERJECTION   Is the word expressing strong feelings?

Hurray! We won the championship.

EXERCISE 1   Determining Parts of Speech

Number your paper 1 to 25. Write the underlined words. Then beside each word, write its part of speech: *noun, pronoun, verb, adjective, adverb, preposition, conjunction,* or *interjection.*

The Magic of Music

(1) <u>Caution</u>! Music may wilt (2) <u>your</u> leaves. In 1969, (3) <u>Dorothy Retallack</u> (4) <u>ran</u> some experiments with plants (5) <u>and</u> music. (6) <u>She</u> proved music affects the growth of plants. (7) <u>In</u> one test (8) <u>loud</u> rock music (9) <u>greatly</u> stunted the growth of (10) <u>corn</u>, squash, and (11) <u>several</u> flowers. In another test (12) <u>several</u> of the plants (13) <u>grew</u> tall, (14) <u>but</u> their leaves (15) <u>were</u> extremely (16) <u>small</u>. Also they (17) <u>needed</u> water, and (18) <u>their</u> roots were (19) <u>very</u> short. (20) <u>Within</u> several weeks (21) <u>all</u> of the marigolds in (22) <u>one</u> experiment died. Identical healthy flowers, however, bloomed (23) <u>nearby</u>. These (24) <u>flowers</u> had been listening (25) <u>to</u> classical music!

EXERCISE 2   Determining Parts of Speech

Number your paper 1 to 10. Write the underlined words in each sentence. Then beside each word, write its part of speech: *noun, pronoun, verb, adjective, adverb, preposition, conjunction,* or *interjection.*

1. Do you shut off the <u>lights</u> <u>in</u> a room when you leave?
2. When you are <u>not</u> watching <u>television</u>, is it turned off?
3. Do <u>you</u> close the refrigerator door <u>tightly</u>?
4. If your <u>answer</u> is yes, you are saving <u>electricity</u>.
5. <u>Use</u> electricity wisely <u>and</u> you conserve energy.
6. <u>Water</u> is a <u>natural</u> resource that can also be conserved.
7. A dripping faucet <u>or</u> a leaking pipe can waste gallons <u>of</u> water.
8. When you cook with water, save <u>it</u> for your <u>house</u> and garden plants.
9. Weather strips on doors and windows keep heat <u>inside</u> <u>during</u> cold weather.
10. <u>Fantastic</u>! Some communities even <u>recycle</u> paper, bottles, tin cans, and metal.

EXERCISE 3 Determining Parts of Speech

Number your paper 1 to 10. Write the underlined words in each sentence. Then beside each word, write its part of speech: *noun, pronoun, verb, adjective, adverb, preposition, conjunction,* or *interjection.*

1. <u>Gee</u>! In 1937, real <u>life</u> almost imitated the movies.
2. The earth came <u>close</u> to massive destruction from <u>outer</u> space.
3. An asteroid called Hermes <u>came</u> within 500,000 miles of <u>us</u>.
4. Had <u>Hermes</u> hit our planet, <u>it</u> could have created a crater 100 miles wide.
5. It also could have caused a <u>massively</u> <u>destructive</u> tidal wave.
6. <u>According to</u> probability, three large asteroids will strike the earth within the next <u>million</u> years.
7. You should not, however, be afraid of <u>this</u> <u>or</u> any other attack from outer space.
8. <u>For</u> one thing, a million years <u>is</u> a long time.
9. For another thing, <u>asteroids</u> can <u>now</u> be stopped.
10. Nuclear devices can destroy <u>them</u> in <u>space</u> before they strike.

EXERCISE 4   Determining Parts of Speech
Write the underlined word in each sentence. Then beside each word, write its part of speech: *noun, pronoun, verb, adjective, adverb, preposition, conjunction,* or *interjection.*

1. Half of those wooden <u>blocks</u> are missing.
2. <u>Call</u> your sister to dinner.
3. <u>Those</u> jeans are made very well.
4. Let's go and sit <u>outside</u>.
5. May I have a snack before <u>dinner</u>?
6. Have another <u>try</u> at the game.
7. Where did you put the <u>snow</u> shovel?
8. <u>Well</u>! That certainly is a surprise.
9. Construction always <u>blocks</u> the traffic here.
10. The private stiffly saluted the <u>major</u>.
11. How many of <u>those</u> do you want?
12. The long-distance <u>call</u> is for you.
13. The television doesn't work very <u>well</u>.
14. Can you see anything <u>outside</u> the window?
15. The <u>snow</u> fell gently to the ground.
16. In college Tim will <u>major</u> in French.
17. Will you <u>try</u> again next year?
18. The old <u>well</u> produces crystal-clear water.
19. It was my <u>major</u> reason for volunteering.
20. We'll need 15 <u>dinner</u> plates.

EXERCISE 5   Determining Parts of Speech
Number your paper 1 to 20. Write the underlined words in each sentence. Then beside each word, write its part of speech: *noun, pronoun, verb, adjective, adverb, preposition, conjunction,* or *interjection.*

1. I'm reading a <u>very</u> exciting historical <u>novel</u>.
2. A <u>prune</u> is <u>nothing</u> more than a dried plum.
3. <u>Jamie</u> and Charles are <u>fast</u> friends.
4. <u>Either</u> coat will be <u>warm</u> enough.
5. <u>We</u> will have to climb <u>through</u> the open window.
6. Was <u>that</u> an interesting <u>book</u>?
7. Can you <u>picture</u> me <u>on</u> the stage?

8. The <u>garage</u> door is frozen <u>fast</u> to the concrete.
9. <u>Everyone</u> voted for his <u>novel</u> idea.
10. I need a <u>book</u> bag <u>for</u> school.
11. <u>You</u> may have <u>either</u>.
12. Was <u>that</u> <u>picture</u> taken at your home?
13. <u>He</u> bought a shirt <u>besides</u>.
14. <u>Put</u> the bicycle in the <u>garage</u>.
15. The bucket should be <u>either</u> <u>here</u> or in the basement.
16. Be careful! <u>This</u> might fall <u>in</u>.
17. We will <u>book</u> our reservations <u>to</u> Florida next week.
18. Does <u>this</u> <u>picture</u> frame fit the photograph?
19. When will you <u>prune</u> the <u>bushes</u>?
20. <u>Besides</u> my job at the supermarket, <u>I</u> also have a paper route.

EXERCISE 6   Labeling Parts of Speech

Copy the following sentences, skipping a line between each one. Then above each word, label its part of speech, using the following abbreviations. Remember that articles are adjectives.

noun = *n.*   adjective = *adj.*   conjunction = *conj.*
pronoun = *pron.*   adverb = *adv.*   interjection = *interj.*
verb = *v.*   preposition = *prep.*

EXAMPLE   For breakfast I especially like eggs and bacon.

ANSWER
prep. n. pron. adv. v. n. conj. n.
For breakfast I especially like eggs and bacon.

1. My grandmother will visit us during this week or next week.
2. Oops! I almost dropped this very expensive plate.
3. Which of the cartoons in the Sunday paper do you enjoy?
4. During history class we watched a film about the American Revolution.
5. Do you ever help your brother with his homework?
6. The small airplane delivers food but does not transport heavy items.

7. Terry lent me a pencil so I could copy the address from the Boston directory.
8. Leslie brought us good news about the construction of a new gymnasium.
9. Grain crops like wheat and barley are grown widely in the Midwest.
10. From the questions, everyone can usually judge the difficulty of a test.

EXERCISE 7 Writing Sentences

Number your paper 1 to 5, skipping a line between each number. Then write two sentences for each direction.

1. Use *light* as a verb and a noun.
2. Use *that* as a pronoun and an adjective.
3. Use *below* as a preposition and an adverb.
4. Use *these* as a pronoun and an adjective.
5. Use *secret* as an adjective and a noun.

EXERCISE 8 Completing Sentence Skeletons

Following are ten sentence skeletons. Make up a sentence that matches each skeleton. You can use an article (*a, an,* or *the*) for an adjective. If necessary, refer to the list of abbreviations in Exercise 6.

EXAMPLE adj. n. prep. adj. n. v. adj.
POSSIBLE ANSWER The winner of the match was happy.

1. n. v. adj. adj. n.
2. pron. v. adv.
3. adj. adj. n. v. adv.
4. n. v. adj.
5. pron. v. adj.
6. adj. adj. n. v. adj. adj. n.
7. adj. adj. n. prep. adj. n. v. adj.
8. adj. adj. n. v. adv. prep. adj. n.
9. n. conj. n. v. adv. adj.
10. n. v. adj. prep. adj. n.

CHAPTER REVIEW

Write the underlined words. Then beside each word, write its part of speech: *noun, pronoun, verb, adjective, adverb, preposition, conjunction,* or *interjection.*

Great
Finds

In 1928, a farmer was planting (1) <u>horseradishes</u> in a field (2) <u>in</u> Petersburg, (3) <u>West Virginia</u>. He noticed a greasy, (4) <u>shiny</u> stone. He picked it (5) <u>up</u> and brought (6) <u>it</u> home as a curiosity (7) <u>piece</u>. (8) <u>Ten</u> years later (9) <u>he</u> made a startling (10) <u>discovery</u>. The stone (11) <u>was</u> a (12) <u>32-carat</u> diamond. (13) <u>Wow!</u> (14) <u>Imagine</u> how (15) <u>he</u> felt.

Diamonds, however, are (16) <u>not</u> necessarily (17) <u>rare</u> in the United States. The Eagle diamond (18) <u>weighs</u> 16 carats and was found in Wisconsin a (19) <u>few</u> years ago. (20) <u>Other</u> large stones have (21) <u>also</u> been discovered in Ohio, Illinois, (22) <u>and</u> Indiana. The (23) <u>largest</u> diamond found in the United States weighs 40 (24) <u>carats</u>. It was mined (25) <u>near</u> Murfreesboro, Arkansas.

MASTERY TEST

Number your paper 1 to 10. Write the underlined words in each sentence. Then beside each word, write its part of speech: *noun, pronoun, verb, adjective, adverb, preposition, conjunction,* or *interjection.*

1. Have you <u>ever</u> seen a British <u>stamp</u>?
2. <u>Everyone</u> at the <u>concert</u> had a wonderful time.
3. Did <u>you</u> see the <u>stop</u> sign at the corner?
4. Jerry has <u>just</u> started a <u>stamp</u> collection.
5. Her birthday <u>is</u> on Saturday <u>or</u> Sunday.
6. <u>No!</u> You cannot go <u>into</u> that office now.
7. <u>Because of</u> the <u>storm</u>, school was closed.
8. The <u>concert</u> tickets were very <u>expensive</u>.
9. <u>Stamp</u> your feet <u>and</u> clap your hands for warmth.
10. <u>Recently</u> all the lights in our house <u>went</u> out.

85

7

Complements

DIAGNOSTIC TEST

Number your paper 1 to 10. Write the underlined complement in each sentence. Then label each one *direct object, indirect object, predicate nominative,* or *predicate adjective.*

EXAMPLE   Janice received a <u>trophy</u> at the banquet.
ANSWER   trophy — direct object

1. Lois entered her <u>dog</u> in the pet show.
2. Send <u>me</u> a copy of your editorial.
3. Mr. Reynolds was a <u>sergeant</u> in the army during World War II.
4. The milk in the refrigerator has turned <u>sour</u>.
5. The squeak in the bicycle was very <u>loud</u>.
6. Mr. Dolan offered <u>Keith</u> an after-school job at the dry cleaners.
7. Will you drive <u>me</u> to school this morning?
8. The stones in her ring were <u>sapphires</u>.
9. Do you want a big or little <u>piece</u> of watermelon for dessert?
10. Is your toast <u>cold</u> too?

Sometimes a complete thought can be expressed with just a subject and a verb. At other times, a subject and a verb need another word to complete the meaning of the sentence.

Greg likes.   Ruth seems.

To complete the meaning of these subjects and verbs, a completer, or *complement,* must be added.

Greg likes **pears.**   Ruth seems **unhappy.**

COMPLEMENTS

There are four common kinds of complements. *Direct objects* and *indirect objects* complete the meaning of action verbs. *Predicate nominatives* and *predicate adjectives,* called *subject complements,* complete the meaning of linking verbs. Together a subject, a verb, and a complement are called the *sentence base.*

Direct Objects

Direct objects complete the meaning of action verbs.

| 7a | A **direct object** is a noun or pronoun that receives the action of the verb. |

To find a direct object, first find the subject and the action verb in a sentence. Then ask yourself *What?* or *Whom?* after the verb. The answer to either question will be a direct object. In the following sentences, subjects are underlined once, and verbs are underlined twice.

d.o.
Jean borrowed my English **book** yesterday. [Jean borrowed what? *Book* is the direct object.]

d.o.
Kenneth invited **Penny** to the dance. [Kenneth invited whom? *Penny* is the direct object.]

Verbs that show ownership are action verbs and take direct objects.

d.o.

Mom owns a 1980 **Ford.**

Sometimes two or more direct objects, called a *compound direct object,* will follow a single verb. On the other hand, each part of a compound verb may have its own direct object.

d.o.   d.o.

Have you done your **math** and **science** yet? [one verb]

d.o.   d.o.

I took the **pictures** and developed the **film.** [two verbs]

A direct object can *never* be part of a prepositional phrase.

d.o.

Nancy took only **one** of the puppies. [*One* is the direct object. *Puppies* is part of the prepositional phrase *of the puppies.*]

Marjorie walked through the park. [*Park* is part of the prepositional phrase *through the park.* Even though this sentence has an action verb, it has no direct object.]

EXERCISE 1 · **Finding Direct Objects**

Number your paper 1 to 20. Then write each direct object. If a sentence does not have a direct object, write *none* after the number.

1. Rattlesnakes periodically shed their fangs.
2. Philip thanked his father for all his help with the woodworking project.
3. The energetic students raced into the school yard before the bell.
4. The meadowlark can sing 50 different songs.
5. I ripped the wrapping paper off the box and slowly opened the lid.
6. Gorillas eat fruits and vegetables.
7. John emptied the contents of the box onto the floor.

8. Did you see her at the dance last night?
9. A grapefruit tree can bear 1,500 pounds of fruit each year.
10. Nathan went to the shopping mall.
11. Susan placed the clean sheets and pillowcases on the bed in the guest room.
12. Ecuador gets its name from the equator.
13. Have you ever had a parrot for a pet?
14. Joel cut the apple into quarters and then ate it.
15. Heat may damage the film in a camera.
16. We jogged on the path by the pond.
17. He bought two posters for his room and hung them up.
18. The flounder has both of its eyes on the right side of its body.
19. Robin drove slowly down the dark road.
20. Make your bed and clean your room.

EXERCISE 2   Writing Sentences
Number your paper 1 to 5. Write a sentence that answers each of the following questions. Then underline each direct object.

1. What do you see to your left?
2. What did you eat for breakfast today?
3. What do you want most for your next birthday?
4. What is your favorite subject in school?
5. What did you buy when you last went shopping?

Indirect Objects

If a sentence has a direct object, it also can have another complement called an *indirect object*.

7b An **indirect object** answers the questions *To* or *for whom?* or *To* or *for what?* after an action verb.

To find an indirect object, first find the direct object. Then ask yourself, *To whom? For whom? To what?* or *For what?*

about each direct object. The answer to any of these questions will be an indirect object. An indirect object always comes before a direct object in a sentence.

i.o.   d.o.
Gordon <u>sent</u> his **mother** flowers on her birthday. [*Flowers* is the direct object. Gordon sent flowers to whom? *Mother* is the indirect object.]

i.o.   d.o.
Jennifer <u>gave</u> her **story** a title. [*Title* is the direct object. Jennifer gave a title to what? *Story* is the indirect object.]

A verb in a sentence can have two or more indirect objects, called a *compound indirect object.*

i.o.   i.o.   d.o.
The <u>teacher</u> <u>read</u> her **boys** and **girls** a story. [To whom?]

i.o.   i.o.   d.o.
<u>Mrs.</u> <u>Samuels</u> <u>gives</u> **dogs** and **cats** obedience training. [To what?]

Keep in mind that an indirect object is *never* part of a prepositional phrase.

i.o.   d.o.
The guide showed **us** a map of the trail. [*Us* is the indirect object. It comes between the verb and the direct object, and it is not a part of a prepositional phrase.]

d.o.
The guide showed a map of the trail to us. [*Us* is *not* an indirect object. It does not come between the verb and the direct object. It follows the direct object and is part of the prepositional phrase *to us.*]

NOTE: You cannot have an indirect object without a direct object in a sentence.

EXERCISE 3 Finding Indirect Objects

Number your paper 1 to 10. Then write each indirect object. If a sentence does not have an indirect object, write *none* after the number.

1. Will you lend me your umbrella?
2. Tad gave the fence a fresh coat of paint.
3. We will visit them during our school vacation.
4. Please read that article to us.
5. Mrs. Jenkins showed our class a film.
6. We loaned Tony and Maria our skis.
7. Show Sam the pictures of your trip to Alabama.
8. My sister sent him a card on his birthday.
9. Show me your new watch.
10. I gave the essay to my teacher.

EXERCISE 4   Finding Direct Objects and Indirect Objects

Number your paper 1 to 10. Write each direct object and each indirect object. Then label each one *direct object* or *indirect object*.

A Star
Is Born

1. Pal, the first Lassie, worried his owners.
2. He barked fiercely, chased cars, and chewed things.
3. In desperation his owners gave him obedience lessons.
4. The Weatherwax brothers owned the local obedience school.
5. After a few lessons, they gave Pal a screen test.
6. Pal got the role of Lassie in the movie *Lassie Come Home*.
7. People throughout the world loved the dog.
8. Millions sent him fan mail.
9. After several other movies, a producer made Pal's owners an offer of a television series.
10. Since then audiences have seen seven other Lassies.

Predicate Nominatives

Direct objects and indirect objects follow action verbs. Two other kinds of complements follow linking verbs. They are called *subject complements* because they either rename or describe the subject. One kind of subject complement is called a *predicate nominative*.

Complements

7c ▶ A **predicate nominative** is a noun or a pronoun that follows a linking verb and identifies, renames, or explains the subject.

To find a predicate nominative, first find the subject and the verb. Check to see if the verb is a linking verb. Then find the noun or the pronoun that identifies, renames, or explains the subject. This word will be a predicate nominative. Notice in the second example that a predicate nominative can be compound.

Melba <u>has</u> <u>become</u> my best **friend.** [friend = Melba]

George <u>will be</u> a **reporter** or an **announcer.**
[reporter = George, announcer = George]

Following is a list of common linking verbs.

Common Linking Verbs	
BE VERBS	is, am, are, was, were, be, being, been, shall be, will be, can be, should be, would be, may be, might be, has been, etc.
OTHERS	appear, become, feel, grow, look, remain, seem, smell, sound, stay, taste, turn

Like a direct object and an indirect object, a predicate nominative cannot be part of a prepositional phrase.

Peggy <u>is</u> **one** of the leaders. [*One* is the predicate nominative. *Leaders* is part of the prepositional phrase *of the leaders.*]

EXERCISE 5 Finding Predicate Nominatives
Number your paper 1 to 20. Then write each predicate nominative.

1. Amethyst is another name for purple quartz.
2. Last night the rain became sleet.
3. The best hitters on the team are she and Sally.

4. The two countries have remained allies for centuries.
5. A white potato is a swollen stem.
6. Pure water is an odorless and tasteless liquid.
7. The bus was his only means of transportation.
8. Many stamps today are also beautiful pictures.
9. His present should be a book or a record.
10. The Siberian tiger is the largest member of the cat family.
11. The chief authors of *The Federalist* were Alexander Hamilton, James Madison, and John Jay.
12. Igor Sikorsky was the inventor of the helicopter.
13. Illinois became a state in 1818.
14. Chippendale is a unique style of furniture.
15. For many years the most popular dog in America was the poodle.
16. New York City has always been the headquarters of the United Nations.
17. Harvard was the first American college.
18. Willie and Roy became friends last year.
19. These tablecloths might be the ones on sale.
20. Is New Orleans the home of the Sugar Bowl?

Predicate Adjectives

The second kind of subject complement is a *predicate adjective.*

7d ▶ A **predicate adjective** is an adjective that follows a linking verb and modifies the subject.

Notice the difference between a predicate nominative and a predicate adjective in the following examples.

Some <u>dinosaurs</u> <u>were</u> small **animals.** [A predicate nominative renames the subject.]

Some <u>dinosaurs</u> <u>were</u> **small.** [A predicate adjective modifies the subject.]

93

To find a predicate adjective, first find the subject and the verb. Check to see if the verb is a linking verb. Then find an adjective that follows the verb and describes the subject. This word will be a predicate adjective. Notice in the second example that predicate adjectives can be compound.

Does the lemonade taste **sour** to you? [*Sour* describes the lemonade.]

The weather tomorrow will be **warm** and **humid.** [*Warm* and *humid* describe the weather.]

Do not confuse a regular adjective with a predicate adjective. Remember that a predicate adjective must follow a linking verb and describe the subject of a sentence.

REGULAR ADJECTIVE   Henry was an **excellent** speaker.

PREDICATE ADJECTIVE   Henry was **excellent** as a speaker.

EXERCISE 6   Finding Predicate Adjectives

Number your paper 1 to 20. Write each predicate adjective. If a sentence does not have a predicate adjective, write *none.*

1. Human beings are taller every century.
2. Was Lian nervous before her piano recital?
3. A piece of watermelon is a refreshing snack.
4. Pure seawater is colorless.
5. The cereal tasted too sweet.
6. Diamonds can be totally black.
7. The winter day grew dark and dreary.
8. Today was the best day of my life!
9. Everyone's nails and hair are dead.
10. The trail up the mountain was steep and rocky.
11. Dinosaurs became extinct for many reasons.
12. These apples are hard but juicy.
13. Doesn't the weather seem cool for this time of year?
14. I feel quite warm and uncomfortable.
15. Before 1863, postal service in this country was free.

16. The spaghetti sauce tasted unusually spicy.
17. Since his graduation, Tim has been extremely busy.
18. Everyone in the theater became noisy during the long intermission.
19. Playing cards in India are round.
20. The whole incident sounds very mysterious to me.

EXERCISE 7 Finding Subject Complements

Write each subject complement. Then label each one *predicate nominative* or *predicate adjective.*

1. The photographer was an expert in her field.
2. The elm remains an endangered tree.
3. The actor seemed nervous and scared.
4. Isn't Russ allergic to seafood?
5. Sirius is the brightest star.
6. Our blackberries will be ripe very soon.
7. Opals are beautiful but soft stones.
8. The movie was very long and tiresome.
9. The female cheetah is a tender parent but an effective hunter.
10. The storm became more and more intense.

EXERCISE 8 Time-out for Review

Number your paper 1 to 20. Write each complement. Then label each one *direct object, indirect object, predicate nominative,* or *predicate adjective.*

The Sixties

1. In 1960, Chubby Checker started a new dance craze.
2. Dancers loved the twist.
3. The most popular rock group was the Beatles.
4. At that time the Beatles' hair was fairly short.
5. The Beach Boys were also popular.
6. In 1961, parents bought their children Garloo.
7. He was a green robot-monster doll.
8. Young people used expressions like *tough toenails, out of sight,* and *flake out.*
9. The miniskirt became the leading fashion.

10. Elephant jokes were the rage in the early 1960s.
11. For example, why do elephants wear green sneakers?
12. Their blue ones are dirty.
13. Fifteen-year-old Oliver Knussen conducted the London Symphony Orchestra.
14. Eleven-year-old Mike Grost became a freshman at Michigan State.
15. Everyone watched more and more television.
16. *Sesame Street* started on television and taught young boys and girls letters and numbers.
17. Howdy Doody and Soupy Sales were popular with young people.
18. Sometime during every show, someone would throw a pie in Soupy Sales's face.
19. Other popular television programs were *Captain Video* and *Captain Midnight*.
20. In 1969, *Mister Rogers' Neighborhood* became an instant sensation.

DIAGRAMING COMPLEMENTS

Together a subject, a verb, and a complement are called the *sentence base*. Since complements are part of the sentence base, they are diagramed on or below the baseline.

Direct Objects. A direct object is placed on the baseline after the verb. It is separated from the verb by a vertical line that stops at the baseline. Notice in the second example that the parts of a compound direct object are placed on parallel lines. The conjunction is placed on a broken line between them.

Some sharks have no natural enemies.

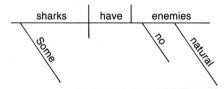

We studied Jupiter and Saturn.

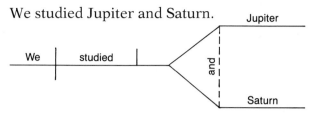

Indirect Objects. An indirect object is diagramed on a horizontal line that is connected to the verb. Notice in the second example that the parts of the compound indirect object are diagramed on parallel horizontal lines. The conjunction is placed on a broken line between them.

Phil prepared his friends a big dinner.

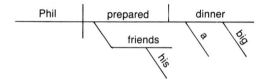

Give Bart and Ken this message.

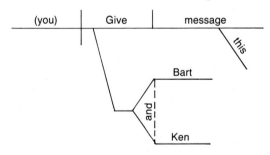

Subject Complements. Both subject complements are diagramed in the same way. They are placed on the baseline after the verb. They are separated from the verb by a slanted line that points back toward the subject. Notice in the third example that a compound subject complement is diagramed just like a compound direct object, except for the slanted line.

This tree is an oak.

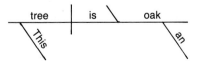

97

The painting is very old.

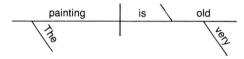

The winners are two freshmen and one senior.

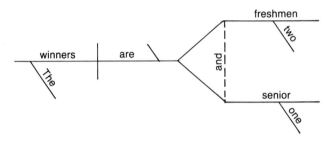

EXERCISE 9 Diagraming Complements

Diagram the following sentences or copy them. If you copy them, draw one line under each subject and two lines under each verb. Then label each complement *d.o.*, *i.o.*, *p.n.*, or *p.a.*

1. My soft sculpture won first prize.
2. Don gave me a new notebook.
3. The director is a wonderful man.
4. I have visited Cypress Gardens and Disney World.
5. That flower looks so delicate.
6. Will you show Jan and me your coin collection?
7. Haven't you given him your answer yet?
8. The books were very old and dusty.
9. Sing us another song.
10. My favorite sports are basketball and baseball.

✐ *Application to Writing*

The boy ran.

The four-year-old boy ran frantically down the street after his puppy.

Both of these sentences are exactly alike in one respect. They both follow the same subject-verb sentence pattern.

Even though there are an endless number of sentences that can be written, there are only a few basic sentence patterns. Following are the most common ones.

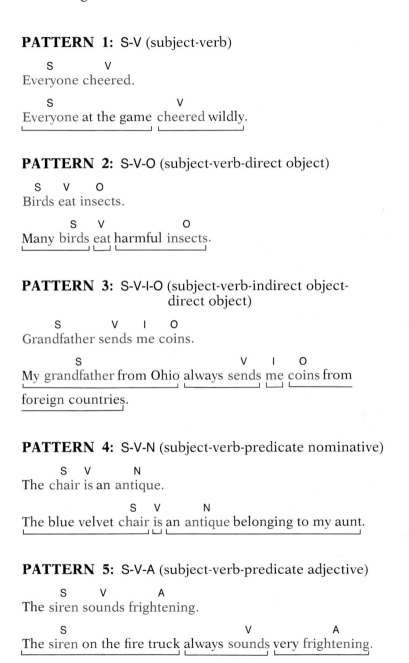

PATTERN 1: S-V (subject-verb)

    S   V
Everyone cheered.

    S   V
Everyone at the game cheered wildly.

PATTERN 2: S-V-O (subject-verb-direct object)

  S   V   O
Birds eat insects.

      S V   O
Many birds eat harmful insects.

PATTERN 3: S-V-I-O (subject-verb-indirect object-
                    direct object)

      S   V I O
Grandfather sends me coins.

        S   V   I   O
My grandfather from Ohio always sends me coins from
foreign countries.

PATTERN 4: S-V-N (subject-verb-predicate nominative)

    S V   N
The chair is an antique.

             S V   N
The blue velvet chair is an antique belonging to my aunt.

PATTERN 5: S-V-A (subject-verb-predicate adjective)

    S   V   A
The siren sounds frightening.

    S   V   A
The siren on the fire truck always sounds very frightening.

EXERCISE 10   Determining Sentence Patterns

Write the sentence pattern that each sentence follows.

EXAMPLE   The jacket with the hood is the one for me.
ANSWER   S-V-N

1. The scholarship award was a check for five hundred dollars.
2. The Japanese have developed a half-inch camera.
3. The action in a hockey game is fast and furious.
4. My radio alarm doesn't work anymore.
5. A guppy is a small tropical fish.
6. The holiday catalogue was large and colorful.
7. The principal gave the athlete a trophy.
8. My grandparents from Iowa travel extensively.
9. Pure radium resembles ordinary table salt.
10. The computer gave us the answer to the question.

EXERCISE 11   Using Patterns to Write Sentences

Write two sentences that follow each sentence pattern. Add as many modifiers and prepositional phrases as you want.

CHAPTER REVIEW

Number your paper 1 to 20. Write each complement. Then label each one *direct object, indirect object, predicate nominative,* or *predicate adjective.*

1. Matt promised me some help with my homework.
2. The moon looked hazy behind the thick clouds.
3. Before his retirement, Mr. Berger had been a teacher.
4. The loud crash of thunder frightened our dog and cat.
5. Ricardo is the captain of the soccer team and the president of the National Honor Society.
6. Have you seen Claire in the school play?
7. Eric is only one of the contestants in the show.
8. The receptionist greeted Mary and me at the door.
9. The crowd at city hall sounded loud and angry.

10. Send your grandmother and grandfather a card for their anniversary.
11. I offered Lalia a slice of freshly baked bread.
12. The first prize is a silver cup.
13. Hand me the scissors.
14. Dad scattered some seed on the lawn.
15. Babysitting is a pleasure to Sarah.
16. The coach shouted encouraging words to the team.
17. Jody mailed his parents his marks from college.
18. The librarian is ill today.
19. The fall asters in the vase were brilliant purple.
20. The concert was a great success.

MASTERY TEST

Number your paper 1 to 10. Write the underlined complement in each sentence. Then label each one *direct object, indirect object, predicate nominative,* or *predicate adjective.*

1. Angie used a <u>computer</u> for the first time yesterday.
2. Can you tell <u>me</u> the assignment?
3. The first dance of the year was a huge <u>success</u>.
4. The coats on the rack are not very <u>expensive</u>.
5. The recent documentary on television was very <u>educational</u>.
6. The new play on Broadway will be a big <u>hit</u>.
7. I couldn't carry the large <u>box</u> of books.
8. Did you give <u>Luis</u> your address?
9. On Saturday Meg raked the <u>leaves</u> around her house.
10. The first song on the record sounds <u>familiar</u>.

8
Phrases

Number your paper 1 to 10. Write the prepositional phrases and the appositive phrases in the following sentences. Then label each one *adjective, adverb,* or *appositive.*

EXAMPLE   Pat, my young cousin, is moving to Texas.
ANSWER   my young cousin — appositive
           to Texas — adverb

1. Throughout the house we searched for the cat.
2. Throw the newspapers by the door into the trash.
3. Our dog, a golden retriever, barks at strangers.
4. Do you know the contents of the box on the table?
5. Several of my friends work on weekends.
6. The mud from your boots stained the carpet in the living room.
7. After the game everyone gathered at Pam's house.
8. The editor of our school newspaper interviewed Mr. Cruz, the town poet.
9. The spare set of keys to the house is missing.
10. Eva seems content with her job at the radio station.

In Chapter 5, you were introduced to phrases.

A **phrase** is a group of related words that function as a single part of speech. A phrase does not have a subject and a verb.

In that chapter you learned to recognize one kind of phrase, a *prepositional phrase*. In this chapter you will learn that a prepositional phrase can be used as an adjective or an adverb. You also will learn about another kind of phrase, an *appositive phrase*. This kind of phrase identifies or renames a certain noun or a pronoun in a sentence.

PREPOSITIONAL PHRASES

When you studied prepositional phrases in Chapter 5, you learned two things. You learned that a prepositional phrase begins with a preposition. You also learned that a prepositional phrase ends with a noun or a pronoun called the *object of the preposition*. The prepositional phrases in the following sentences are in heavy type.

The sweater **in the box** is a present **from Sue and Carol.**
Because of rain the game was delayed **until Monday.**

Following is a list of common prepositions. *(See pages 69 and 70 for additional prepositions.)*

Common Prepositions			
above	beside	inside	over
across	between	instead of	past
after	by	into	to
ahead of	down	next to	toward
among	during	of	under
around	for	on	until
at	from	on account of	up
before	in	out	with
behind	in addition to	out of	within
below	in back of	outside	without

EXERCISE 1 Finding Prepositional Phrases

Number your paper 1 to 10. Then write the prepositional phrases in the following sentences.

1. Smiling is good exercise for your face.
2. At birth the average newborn weighs about seven pounds.
3. Driving within the speed limit saves lives.
4. On account of George Washington, we celebrate a national holiday.
5. Fresh fruit provides a delicious snack without excess calories.
6. In addition to liver, carrots, pumpkins, and eggs contain vitamin A.
7. Colonial women made colorful quilts out of old scraps of fabric.
8. Today many women work toward careers.
9. Why do people choose one vocation over another?
10. During adolescence, many important decisions are made.

EXERCISE 2 Finding Prepositional Phrases

Number your paper 1 to 10. Then write the prepositional phrases in the following paragraph.

Tight Going

In 1859, Charles Blondin walked across Niagara Falls on a tightrope. He was high above the water. Later he crossed with a blindfold over his eyes. Then he crossed on stilts. Finally he really amazed everyone. Halfway across the falls, he stopped for breakfast. He cooked some eggs, ate them, and continued to the other side.

Adjective Phrases

A prepositional phrase can be used as an adjective to modify a noun or a pronoun. When it does, it is called an *adjective phrase.*

SINGLE ADJECTIVE   The **library** book is due.
ADJECTIVE PHRASE   The book **from the library** is due.

> **8b**   An **adjective phrase** is a prepositional phrase that is used to modify a noun or a pronoun.

Like a single adjective, an adjective phrase answers the question *Which one(s)?* or *What kind?* about a noun or a pronoun.

WHICH ONE(s)?   The dog **with short legs** is a dachshund.

WHAT KIND?   Please empty this bag **of groceries.**

An adjective phrase usually modifies the noun or the pronoun directly in front of it. Occasionally an adjective phrase will modify a noun or a pronoun in another phrase.

The movie *about* **creatures** *from* **another planet** was scary.

Two adjective phrases can also modify the same noun or pronoun.

The glass *of* **milk** *on* **the table** is yours.

EXERCISE 3 · Finding Adjective Phrases

Number your paper 1 to 20. Write each adjective phrase. Then beside each phrase, write the word it modifies. Some sentences have more than one adjective phrase.

EXAMPLE   The preserves in that jar are homemade.
ANSWER   in that jar — preserves

1. The radio in the kitchen doesn't work.
2. The last 20 minutes of the movie at Cinema I were very funny.
3. None of the Pilgrims on the *Mayflower* had a middle name.
4. The captain of the debating team met the principal.

5. A tablespoon of butter contains 100 calories.
6. The article about animals without a home was sad.
7. Edgar Allan Poe is the father of the detective story.
8. The little boat with the two masts is a yawl.
9. The pot of soup on the stove should be removed.
10. The car in front of the school is illegally parked.
11. One of my brothers joined the tennis team at school.
12. He accidentally dropped the last carton of milk.
13. I took a picture of my grandparents from Utah.
14. Twenty-six species of insects have become extinct.
15. Parrots usually have a vocabulary of only 20 words.
16. I need the box of nails in the top drawer.
17. The wettest city in the United States is Miami, Florida.
18. The tallest species of tree in the world is a kind of eucalyptus.
19. Some of these trees reach a height of almost 400 feet.
20. Each human being has a total of 46 chromosomes.

EXERCISE 4 Writing Sentences
Write a sentence that uses each of the following prepositional phrases as an adjective phrase. Then underline the
word each phrase modifies. Remember that an adjective
phrase must modify a noun or a pronoun.

1. on that shelf
2. with the black stripes
3. on the desk
4. inside the barn
5. near the river
6. at the party
7. under the bed
8. on the front door
9. next to the garage
10. around the package

Adverb Phrases

A prepositional phrase can also be used as an adverb. It
can modify a verb, an adjective, or an adverb. When it does,
it is called an *adverb phrase.*

8c An **adverb phrase** is a prepositional phrase that is used to
modify a verb, an adjective, or an adverb.

106

The following examples show how adverb phrases may be used to modify verbs.

SINGLE ADVERB The baseball whizzed **by.**

ADVERB PHRASE The baseball whizzed **by the batter.**

SINGLE ADVERB Everyone came **here.**

ADVERB PHRASE Everyone came **to my house.**

Like a single adverb, an adverb phrase answers the question *Where? When? How? To what extent?* or *To what degree?* Most adverb phrases modify the verb. Notice that an adverb phrase modifies the whole verb phrase, just like a single adverb does.

WHERE? Next summer the Rogers will drive **to California.**

WHEN? We should meet **during intermission.**

HOW? John answered the questions **with confidence.**

Adverb phrases also modify adjectives and adverbs.

MODIFYING Sam was happy **with his report card.**
AN ADJECTIVE
The material was rough **against her skin.**

MODIFYING The meeting ran late **into the night.**
AN ADVERB
The kite soared high **into the sky.**

An adverb phrase does not necessarily come next to the word it modifies. Several adverb phrases can also modify the same word.

On **Saturday** meet me *at* **ten o'clock** *at* **Harvey's.**

EXERCISE 5 Finding Adverb Phrases
Number your paper 1 to 20. Write each adverb phrase. Then beside each phrase, write the word or words it modifies. Some sentences have more than one adverb phrase.

1. Hockey pucks are kept in a refrigerator before a game.
2. A blue whale may weigh 5,000 pounds at birth.
3. Since Wednesday we have been rehearsing the play.
4. The band performed on the field during halftime.
5. On the river bank a small boy fished for trout.
6. During the winter a person cannot catch a cold at the North Pole.
7. I am very happy about your promotion.
8. A bird sees everything at once in total focus.
9. During the marathon we sat on the curbstone.
10. Napoleon was defeated at Waterloo by British, Dutch, and German soldiers.
11. Some lizards can run on their hind legs.
12. Within the week your report must be given to Mr. Robertson.
13. The Mexican hedgehog cactus can live five years without any water.
14. On Thursday Pedro's photograph will appear in the local paper.
15. At certain times snow falls in the Sahara Desert.
16. The tailless Manx cat is common in the Far East.
17. Throughout the state, apple trees bloom in spring.
18. After English class I went to the cafeteria.
19. On Sunday we should meet for breakfast.
20. In spite of the cold weather, the picnic was held at the fairgrounds.

Punctuation with Adverb Phrases

If a short adverb phrase comes at the beginning of a sentence, usually no comma is needed. You should, however, place a comma after an introductory adverb phrase of four or more words or after several introductory adverb phrases.

NO COMMA **After dinner** we went to a movie.

COMMA **Because of the heavy traffic on Route 2,** we were late for dinner.

EXERCISE 6   Writing Sentences

Write a sentence that uses each of the following prepositional phrases as an adverb phrase. Then underline the
word or words each phrase modifies.

1. across the bridge
2. during dinner
3. around the house
4. in the morning
5. over the top

6. from the library
7. after six o'clock
8. about the dance
9. into the pool
10. since breakfast

EXERCISE 7   Time-out for Review

Number your paper 1 to 15. Write each prepositional
phrase. Then label each one *adjective* or *adverb*.

Louis
Braille

1. The Braille family lived in a village near Paris, France, in the early 1800s.
2. On account of an accident, three-year-old Louis Braille became blind.
3. Louis went to the school in his neighborhood.
4. He could listen to his teacher's words, but he couldn't learn from books.
5. At ten, he entered a school for the blind in Paris.
6. Children at that school were reading from special books.
7. Letters of the alphabet were pressed into thick, heavy paper.
8. This created raised outlines on the other side of the paper.
9. The students would feel the outlines with their fingers, and they could read.
10. All the books were extremely large and heavy because of the huge letters.
11. One day a retired army captain came to the school with a secret code.
12. His system of dots and dashes ultimately proved too difficult for everyone.

13. By the age of 15, Braille developed a new system of only dots.
14. Now on the door of Braille's home appears a tribute to his accomplishments.
15. It reads, "He opened the doors of knowledge to so many."

Misplaced Modifiers

Because a prepositional phrase is used as a modifier, it should be placed as close as possible to the word it describes. If a phrase gets too far away from the word it modifies, it may result in a *misplaced modifier*. Misplaced modifiers create confusion and misunderstanding for readers.

MISPLACED   The puppy belongs to the man with long ears.

CORRECT   The puppy **with long ears** belongs to the man.

EXERCISE 8   Correcting Misplaced Modifiers
Rewrite the following sentences, placing each misplaced modifier closer to the word it modifies.

1. With a screech Mr. Reynolds stopped the car.
2. Inside the cereal box I looked for the coupons.
3. Charles told us about his vacation in the kitchen.
4. On the ocean floor the professor described sea life to the class.
5. We looked for a cat in the want ads.
6. Behind the bars of the cage John waved to the lion.
7. We heard that the President was ill on television.
8. On top of the cake Elizabeth counted 14 candles.
9. The bird flew to the girl with red feathers.
10. The passengers sighted whales on the deck of the cruise ship.
11. Tonight on the shelf in the closet we will use the new tablecloth.
12. At the age of two my mother taught my brother to count.

13. On the stage the audience applauded the performers.
14. The realtor is looking for a ranch house for the Rogers with a split level.
15. The acrobats bowed to the crowd in sequined tights.

APPOSITIVES AND APPOSITIVE PHRASES

A noun or a pronoun is sometimes immediately followed by another noun or pronoun that identifies or explains it.

My sister **Pat** is coming home in June.

In the restaurant he ordered his favorite drink, **milk.**

This identifying noun or pronoun is called an *appositive.*

8d ▶ An **appositive** is a noun or a pronoun that identifies or explains another noun or pronoun in the sentence.

Most of the time an appositive is used with modifiers to form an *appositive phrase.*

Our car, **a small compact,** gets great gas mileage.

The award went to Mrs. Kenny, **Sue's mother.**

NOTE: A prepositional phrase can be part of an appositive phrase.

Jack made dinner, **chicken with rice.**

EXERCISE 9   Finding Appositives and Appositive Phrases
Write the appositive or the appositive phrase in each sentence. Then beside each one, write the word or words it identifies or explains.

1. American artist Norman Rockwell selected scenes from everyday life.
2. Have you ever read the poem "The Road Not Taken" by Robert Frost?

3. We discussed *Moby Dick,* the classic tale of a man's quest for the white whale.
4. July was named after Julius Caesar, a Roman ruler.
5. August was named after Augustus, Caesar's nephew.
6. At the Mardi Gras, a famous carnival in New Orleans, people wear costumes.
7. The church organist Franz Gruber wrote the music for "Silent Night."
8. My sister has mastered calligraphy, the art of beautiful handwriting.
9. Eating a meal with chopsticks, two narrow wooden sticks, is an oriental custom.
10. The herbs parsley, mint, and rosemary grow well indoors at a sunny window.

EXERCISE 10 **Finding Appositives and Appositive Phrases**

Write the appositive or the appositive phrase in each sentence. Then beside each one, write the word or words it identifies or explains.

1. My sister plays the cornet, a wind instrument.
2. I just finished reading a story by the famous science-fiction writer Isaac Asimov.
3. *Voyager I* photographed Jupiter, our largest planet, in 1979.
4. My dog Fred is never late for a meal.
5. Nora's brother, an explorer scout, will attend an Outward Bound program this summer.
6. Have you seen the play *The Diary of Anne Frank?*
7. Juanita would like to take up the popular sport wind surfing.
8. The first man to drive a vehicle on the moon was David Scott, an American.
9. Juneau, the capital of Alaska, has a deep harbor.
10. The dingo, an Australian dog, has to be taught how to bark.

Punctuation with Appositives and Appositive Phrases

If the information in an appositive is essential to the meaning of a sentence, no commas are needed. The information is essential if it identifies a person, place, or thing. However, a comma is needed before and after an appositive or an appositive phrase if the information is not essential to the meaning. The information is not essential if it could be removed without changing the basic meaning of the sentence.

ESSENTIAL On Tuesday we watched the play ***Romeo and Juliet*** on television. [Commas are not used because the appositive is needed to identify the play.]

NOT ESSENTIAL *Romeo and Juliet*, **a play by William Shakespeare,** can be seen on television on Tuesday. [Commas are used because the appositive is additional information. It could be dropped from the sentence.]

EXERCISE 11 Writing Sentences

Write five sentences that include appositives or appositive phrases. Use commas if needed. Then underline each appositive or appositive phrase.

EXERCISE 12 Time-out for Review

Number your paper 1 to 10. Write the prepositional phrases and the appositive phrases in the following sentences. Then label each one *adjective, adverb,* or *appositive.*

Food Facts

1. The average American annually consumes a total of two and a half tons of food.
2. In parts of China, roast dog is considered a gourmet's delight.
3. Truffles, a subterranean fungus, is the most expensive food in the world.
4. In the eastern part of Texas, a rich spinach-growing area, farmers have erected a statue of Popeye.

5. A 220-pound wheel of cheese can require a ton of milk.
6. The apple had spread throughout Europe before the dawn of recorded history.
7. In addition to caffeine, chocolate contains *theobromine*, a mild stimulant.
8. Many Americans caught their first glimpse of the banana at the 1876 Exposition in Philadelphia.
9. Rennet, a common substance in cheese, is taken from the inner lining of a calf's stomach.
10. Throughout the United States, consumption of green and yellow vegetables has decreased since the 1940s.

DIAGRAMING PHRASES

In a diagram a prepositional phrase is connected to the word it modifies. The preposition is placed on a connecting slanted line. The object of a preposition is placed on a horizontal line that is attached to the slanted line.

Adjective Phrases. An adjective phrase is connected to the noun or pronoun it modifies.

The squirrel with the fluffy tail gathered nuts from the ground.

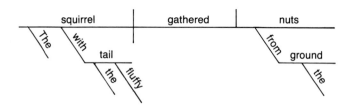

Sometimes a phrase modifies the object of a preposition of another phrase.

I chose a brand of cereal without sugar.

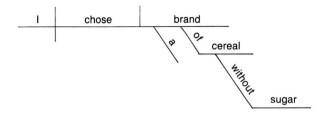

Adverb Phrases. An adverb phrase is connected to the verb, adjective, or adverb it modifies.

We drove to the park on Saturday.

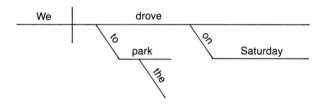

The score was tied early in the inning.

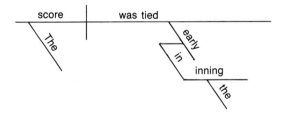

Notice in the last example that an adverb phrase that modifies an adjective or an adverb needs an additional line.

115

Appositives and Appositive Phrases. An appositive is diagramed in parentheses next to the word it identifies or explains.

My cousin George will visit us.

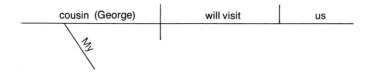

I bought a new calendar, one with pictures of horses.

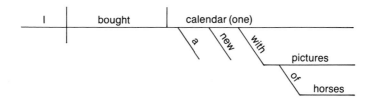

EXERCISE 13   Diagraming Phrases

Diagram the following sentences or copy them. If you copy them, draw one line under each subject and two lines under each verb. Then put parentheses around each phrase and label it *adj., adv.,* or *appos.*

1. Many children can swim at an early age.
2. I just bought a new radio, a small portable one.
3. The posters for the dance are beautiful.
4. I went to Mexico with my sister.
5. My friend Bert collects stamps from foreign countries.
6. The tips of the daffodils showed through the snow.
7. Meg left the store with the groceries.
8. Wendy, my best friend, went to the horse show.
9. At the signal every swimmer dived into the water.
10. The summit of Mount McKinley is always covered with snow.

Application to Writing

To avoid a choppy writing style, you can combine sentences by using phrases.

TWO SENTENCES	Mary Lee had her picture taken. She wore a nineteenth-century costume.
ONE SENTENCE	Mary Lee had her picture taken in a nineteenth-century costume. [prepositional phrase]
TWO SENTENCES	Baby's breath is used in many bouquets. It is a fine spray of tiny white flowers.
ONE SENTENCE	Baby's breath, a fine spray of tiny white flowers, is used in many bouquets. [appositive phrase]

EXERCISE 14 Combining Sentences

Combine each pair of sentences into one sentence, putting some of the information into a prepositional phrase or an appositive phrase. Use commas if needed.

1. I called you last night. It was at seven o'clock.
2. Poppy Seed is a big gray mare. She is the fastest horse at Mr. Miller's stables.
3. Have you read this book about Mark Twain? It was written by Albert Paine.
4. My brother is reading *Great Expectations*. It is a story about wealth and vanity.
5. After our breakfast we hiked to Emerald Pond. We ate pancakes and bacon.
6. Dad bought some Indian jewelry. He bought it in New Mexico.
7. The bicycle has a flat tire. It is in the garage.
8. I visited my grandmother. I visited her during spring vacation.
9. I walked to the library. It is on Main Street.
10. Mount Vernon was the home of George Washington. It is 15 miles south of Washington, D.C.

CHAPTER REVIEW

A. Number your paper 1 to 10. Write the prepositional phrases and the appositive phrases in the following sentences. Then label each one *adjective, adverb,* or *appositive*.

1. Diamonds sometimes fall from the sky in meteorites.
2. Mr. Leonard, our principal, sings in the church choir.
3. A grasshopper's sense of hearing is centered in its front knees.
4. The Chinese New Year always begins during the period between January 20 and February 20.
5. Silk material from India is very soft to the touch.
6. The lead guitarist in that band is Rufo Ortiz, my next-door neighbor.
7. I now work after school at the supermarket.
8. Some members of the dinosaur family were the size of rabbits.
9. My father, the man in the blue suit, will be the speaker at the assembly.
10. Musicians tune instruments to the pitch of middle A.

B. Number your paper 1 to 10. Write the prepositional phrases and the appositive phrases in the following sentences. Then label each one *adjective, adverb,* or *appositive*.

1. The center of the earth, a ball of solid iron and nickel, has a temperature of 9,000° F.
2. Don't use the switch in the kitchen by the door.
3. Oysters on trees are a common sight on many islands in the Caribbean Sea.
4. The Abyssinian, a beautiful short-haired feline, developed entirely from the African wildcat.
5. The geographic center of North America is located in North Dakota.
6. The jigsaw puzzle of the mountains in Japan is very difficult.
7. John Tyler, the tenth president of the United States, served from 1841 to 1845.

8. By the end of the weekend, we should know the results of the tests.
9. The largest member of the python family grows to a length of 25 feet.
10. The whale, the mightiest creature of the seas, has fins.

MASTERY TEST

Number your paper 1 to 10. Write the prepositional phrases and the appositive phrases in the following sentences. Then label each one *adjective, adverb,* or *appositive.*

1. We have enjoyed the box of oranges from Florida.
2. The trees in our backyard should be pruned in the spring.
3. Cirrus clouds, the thin feathery type, are always made of ice crystals.
4. Most of the streets in our town have been repaved.
5. Pam arrived with her present, a music box.
6. Everything outside is buried under two feet of snow.
7. The cars on the parkway crawled for miles.
8. The assembly on Friday lasted for an hour.
9. The stamps in her collection are valued at two thousand dollars.
10. On Tuesday I had a long talk with Julie.

9

Verbals and Verbal Phrases

Number your paper 1 to 10. Write the verbal phrase in each sentence. Then label it *participial, gerund,* or *infinitive.*

EXAMPLE Running swiftly, he caught the football.

ANSWER   running swiftly — participial

1. Slipping quietly into the kitchen, Kaya surprised everyone.
2. Remember to call Sam after dinner.
3. They had hoped to find John's wallet.
4. It is easy to swim in salt water.
5. Do you enjoy flying in an airplane?
6. We heard Tommy hammering in the basement.
7. Hitting high notes was easy for Ellen.
8. Finding her house was difficult.
9. They planned the party before sending out the invitations.
10. Her jacket, covered with mud, was finally found.

You are already familiar with some of the information in this chapter. For example, you already know that the words *exhausted* and *cheering* in the following sentence are used as adjectives.

The **exhausted** singer bowed before the **cheering** fans.

What you might not know is that they belong to a special group of words called *verbals.*

VERBALS AND VERBAL PHRASES

Verbals are unique words. A verbal has the form of a verb but it is not used as a verb. Instead, a verbal is used as some other part of speech. In the example above, for instance, *exhausted* and *cheering* look like verbs but are used as adjectives. Verbals can add variety and conciseness to your writing. There are three kinds of verbals: *participles, gerunds,* and *infinitives.*

Participles

The words *exhausted* and *cheering* in the example above are participles.

9a A **participle** is a verb form that is used as an adjective.

To find a participle, ask the adjective question *Which one?* or *What kind?* about each noun or pronoun. If a verb form answers one of these questions, it is a participle. The participles in the following examples are in heavy type. An arrow points to the noun or the pronoun each participle modifies.

The **starving** hikers gobbled up Mom's **baked** ham.

The teddy bear, **worn** and **frayed,** lay beside the

sleeping child.

There are two kinds of participles. *Present participles* end in *-ing. Past participles* usually end in *-ed,* but some have irregular endings, such as *-n, -t,* or *-en.*

PRESENT PARTICIPLES   starving, sleeping, missing
PAST PARTICIPLES   baked, frayed, worn, bent, fallen

Everyone enjoyed the smell of the **burning** leaves.

The **defrosted** hamburgers are ready to cook.

EXERCISE 1   Finding Participles

Number your paper 1 to 10. Write each participle that is used as an adjective. Then beside each one, write the word it modifies.

1. No one answered the ringing doorbell.
2. The flag of Denmark is the oldest unchanged national flag in existence.
3. The meeting, noisy and disorganized, was a waste of time.
4. The redwoods are the tallest living things on our planet.
5. The speeding car almost crashed.
6. Please empty the overflowing trash.
7. The hikers, hungry and exhausted, returned to camp.
8. The barking dog kept me awake all night.
9. Don't step on the broken glass on the floor.
10. Those nails, rusted and bent, are a hazard.

Participle or Verb?

Because a participle is a verb form, you must be careful not to confuse it with the main verb in a verb phrase. To be the verb of a sentence, a participle must have a helping verb.

PARTICIPLE   The **injured** bird lay still.
VERB   Sandra **was** not **injured** in the accident.
PARTICIPLE   The **winning** team held a victory party.
VERB   Barbara **is winning** the race right now.

EXERCISE 2   Distinguishing between Participles and Verbs

Write the underlined word in each sentence. Then label it *participle* or *verb*.

1. A <u>talking</u> doll was one of Thomas Edison's many clever inventions.
2. The strawberries were <u>frozen</u> last summer.
3. Maria <u>discarded</u> her old sneakers.
4. The dog <u>buried</u> its bone in the backyard.
5. Our <u>reserved</u> seats at the restaurant were located beside a window.
6. Why are you <u>talking</u> so softly?
7. Have you ever hunted for <u>buried</u> treasure?
8. They warmed their <u>frozen</u> feet by the fire.
9. Have you <u>reserved</u> the book from the library?
10. The <u>discarded</u> lamp was soon missed.

Participial Phrases

Because a participle is a verb form, it can have modifiers or a complement. A participle plus any modifiers or complements form a *participial phrase*.

9b ▶ A **participial phrase** is a participle with its modifiers and complements—all working together as an adjective.

The following examples show three variations of the participial phrase. Notice that a participial phrase can come at the beginning, the middle, or the end of the sentence.

PARTICIPLE WITH AN ADVERB	**Flying low,** the plane circled the airport.
PARTICIPLE WITH A PREPOSITIONAL PHRASE	The elm **growing in our yard** is 20 years old.
PARTICIPLE WITH A COMPLEMENT	The grand prize will go to the person **giving the right answer.**

Verbals and Verbal Phrases

NOTE: Once in a while an adverb will precede a participial phrase. That adverb is still considered part of the phrase.

Quickly raising his hand, Joe was called on first.

EXERCISE 3   Finding Participial Phrases

Write the participial phrase in each sentence. Then underline the participle.

Facts
and
Figures

1. James Zaharee, using a fine pen and a microscope, printed the Gettysburg Address on a human hair.
2. The largest jigsaw puzzle, made in 1954, contained over 10,000 pieces.
3. One of the oldest games, played since prehistoric times, is marbles.
4. Living off the coast of Japan, the largest crabs in the world stand 3 feet high and weigh 30 pounds.
5. Bloodhounds, often used in detective work, can detect a ten-day-old scent.
6. Swimming rapidly, John Sigmund traveled 292 miles down the Mississippi River in 90 hours.
7. The smallest bird is the bee hummingbird, measuring only two and a half inches.
8. In Ohio someone found an eagle's nest weighing two tons.
9. The highest wind velocity recorded in the United States was 231 miles per hour.
10. Oranges, cantaloupes, and strawberries are fruits containing vitamin C.

EXERCISE 4   Finding Participial Phrases

Write the participial phrase in each sentence. Then beside each one, write the word it modifies.

1. We watched the chickadees fluttering around the bird feeder.
2. Quacking loudly, the ducks paddled toward the shore.
3. The soybean, first grown in the United States as fodder for livestock, is rich in vitamins.

4. Rearing on its hind legs, the deer cropped off the lower branches of the juniper tree.
5. The swordfish has a powerful snout shaped like a sword.
6. The nest of the weaver bird looks like a bottle hanging down from a tree branch.
7. The storm heading toward us could have winds over 50 miles per hour.
8. Costing only a few dollars, the old bookcase was a real bargain.
9. In his lifetime John D. Rockefeller gave away sums totaling $550 million.
10. A piece of pie eaten once each week can add three pounds of body weight in a year.

Punctuation with Participial Phrases

A participial phrase that comes at the beginning of a sentence is always followed by a comma.

Speaking softly, the mother encouraged the child.

Participial phrases, however, that come in the middle or at the end of a sentence may or may not need commas. If the information in the phrase is essential, no commas are needed. Information is essential if it identifies a person, place, or thing in the sentence. If the information is nonessential, commas are needed to separate it from the rest of the sentence. A participial phrase is nonessential if it can be removed without changing the meaning of the sentence.

ESSENTIAL The painting **hanging near the door** is Lee's. [Commas are not used because the participial phrase is needed to identify which painting is Lee's.]

NONESSENTIAL My down vest, **given to me as a present,** keeps me toasty warm. [Commas are used because the participial phrase could be removed from the sentence without changing its meaning: *My down vest keeps me toasty warm.*]

EXERCISE 5 Writing Sentences

Write a sentence for each of the following participial phrases. Use commas where needed.

1. lost in the woods
2. walking down the street
3. enjoying the picnic
4. laughing hysterically
5. found in the backyard
6. using a dictionary
7. recently discarded
8. stored in the attic
9. broken into pieces
10. cooking dinner

Gerunds

Another kind of verbal is called a *gerund*. Both the gerund and the present participle end in *-ing*. A gerund, however, is used as a noun, not as an adjective.

9c ▶ A **gerund** is a verb form that is used as a noun.

A gerund can be used in all the ways a noun can be used.

SUBJECT	**Singing** is my best talent.
DIRECT OBJECT	Do you like **skiing?**
INDIRECT OBJECT	His trimmer waistline gave his **dieting** a big boost.
OBJECT OF A PREPOSITION	I can't stop her from **speaking.**
PREDICATE NOMINATIVE	My favorite pastime is **reading.**
APPOSITIVE	I have found a new exercise, **jogging.**

EXERCISE 6 Finding Gerunds

Write the gerund in each sentence. Then use one of the following abbreviations to label its use.

subject = *subj.*	object of a preposition = *o.p.*
direct object = *d.o.*	predicate nominative = *p.n.*
indirect object = *i.o.*	appositive = *appos.*

1. Swimming is one of the best forms of exercise.
2. She has just finished a course in typing.
3. Please stop that yelling!

4. An early method of food preservation was pickling.
5. The hungry boys gave eating their full attention.
6. Their whispering bothered everyone in the movie.
7. Lee has a new hobby, painting.
8. A common experience for everyone is dreaming.
9. The hardest part of skating is balance.
10. Kim has always enjoyed cooking.

Gerund or Participle?

It is easy to confuse a gerund and a present participle because they both end in *-ing*. Just remember that a gerund is used as a noun. A participle is used as an adjective.

GERUND   My neighbor earns extra money by **sewing.** [*Sewing* is the object of the preposition.]

PARTICIPLE   I think I'll take a **sewing** class. [*Sewing* modifies *class.*]

EXERCISE 7   **Distinguishing between Gerunds and Participles**
Write the underlined word in each sentence. Then label it *gerund* or *participle.*

1. Are you a member of the <u>rowing</u> team?
2. <u>Reading</u> does not weaken the eyes.
3. I'm joining the <u>swimming</u> team this year.
4. Connie's <u>singing</u> has greatly improved.
5. Do you have a copy of the ninth grade <u>reading</u> list?
6. The movie showed the hazards of <u>smoking</u>.
7. <u>Swimming</u> is the best exercise for asthmatics.
8. The local <u>singing</u> group is becoming famous.
9. By noon my muscles were sore from <u>rowing</u>.
10. The <u>smoking</u> oven meant the roast had burned.

Gerund Phrases

Like a participle, a gerund can be combined with modifiers or a complement to form a *gerund phrase.*

9d ▶ A **gerund phrase** is a gerund with its modifiers and complements—all working together as a noun.

The following sentences show four variations of the gerund phrase.

GERUND WITH AN ADJECTIVE	**The loud talking** bothered the people in the library.
GERUND WITH AN ADVERB	**Exercising daily** is important for everyone.
GERUND WITH A PREPOSITIONAL PHRASE	**Jogging in a park** is a pleasant form of exercise.
GERUND WITH A COMPLEMENT	**Watching a football game** is one of my favorite pasttimes.

NOTE: Use the possessive form of a noun or a pronoun before a gerund. A possessive form before a gerund is considered part of the phrase.

We were surprised at **Tom's** winning the award.
Mom encouraged **our** climbing Mount Snow.

EXERCISE 8   Finding Gerund Phrases

Write the gerund phrase in each sentence. Then underline the gerund.

1. Galileo made his first telescope by placing a lens at each end of an organ pipe.
2. Sinking 499 free throws in a row is Harold's claim to fame.
3. A snail can cross the edge of the sharpest razor without cutting itself.
4. The ancient Egyptians avoided killing any sacred animal.
5. Josh's plan, rushing the passer, seemed sound to us.
6. Kingfishers build nests by tunneling into the sides of riverbanks.
7. I appreciate your helping me with my homework.

8. There are many different ways of growing vegetables and flowers in small containers.
9. Decreasing the Amazon rain forests threatens one of the earth's most important natural resources.
10. Bagdad, California, once went 767 days without receiving a single drop of rain.

EXERCISE 9 Finding Gerund Phrases

Write the gerund phrase in each sentence. Then use one of the following abbreviations to label its use.

subject = *subj.*	object of a preposition = *o.p.*
direct object = *d.o.*	predicate nominative = *p.n.*
indirect object = *i.o.*	appositive = *appos.*

1. Next week Missy will try diving from the high board.
2. You can call almost anywhere by dialing directly.
3. My plan for the future is going to college.
4. David enjoys reading science fiction.
5. Part of Una's morning routine is getting up at seven.
6. Rubbing paraffin on the shoe part of your ice skates will prevent cracks.
7. Arriving on time for a job interview creates a good impression.
8. My part-time job, baby-sitting for the Murphys, pays well.
9. Walking the dog is one of my afternoon chores.
10. Gabriel Fahrenheit made the thermometer more accurate by substituting mercury for alcohol.

EXERCISE 10 Writing Sentences

Write a sentence for each of the following gerund phrases.

1. cleaning my room
2. meeting with the principal
3. calling long distance
4. falling asleep at night
5. driving a car
6. writing quickly
7. flying to Texas
8. getting a suntan
9. doing my homework
10. swimming ten laps

Infinitives

A third kind of verbal is called an *infinitive*. It looks very different from a participle or a gerund because it usually begins with the word *to*.

9e An **infinitive** is a verb form that usually begins with *to*. It is used as a noun, an adjective, or an adverb.

An infinitive can be used in almost all the ways a noun can be used, but an infinitive can also be used as an adjective or an adverb. An adjective modifies a noun or a pronoun. An adverb modifies a verb, an adjective, or another adverb.

NOUN **To succeed** was his only goal. [subject]
They wanted **to eat.** [direct object]

ADJECTIVE That is a big question **to answer.** [*To answer* modifies the noun *question.*]
The book **to read** is a mystery. [*To read* modifies the noun *book.*]

ADVERB She was eager **to study.** [*To study* modifies the adjective *eager.*]
She ran **to catch** the bus. [*To catch* modifies the verb *ran.*]

EXERCISE 11 Finding Infinitives

Write the infinitive in each sentence. Then label it *noun, adjective,* or *adverb.*

1. Do you know the name of the person to see?
2. Jeff just learned to ski.
3. The best way to go would be on Route 62.
4. Your teacher will give you the topic to research.
5. To relax is difficult for some people.
6. The items to sell are on the table.
7. The crossword puzzle is easy to do.
8. Tom is planning to return.
9. Their words were too muffled to understand.
10. The movie to see is showing at the Plaza.

Infinitive or Prepositional Phrase?

Because an infinitive usually begins with the word *to,* it is sometimes confused with a prepositional phrase. Just remember that an infinitive is *to* plus a verb form. A prepositional phrase is *to* plus a noun or a pronoun.

INFINITIVE   I'm finally learning **to drive.** [ends with the verb form *drive*]

PREPOSITIONAL   I'll take this duffel bag **to camp.** [ends
PHRASE   with the noun *camp*]

EXERCISE 12   Distinguishing between Infinitives and Prepositional Phrases

Write the underlined words. Then label them *infinitive* or *prepositional phrase.*

1. Now I would like <u>to speak</u>.
2. Should we take the dog <u>to Tennessee</u> with us?
3. That stereo is too expensive <u>to buy</u>.
4. What do you want <u>to say</u>?
5. The oboe is considered the hardest woodwind instrument <u>to master</u>.
6. Of all brass instruments, the French horn is generally considered the most difficult <u>to play</u>.
7. Let's walk <u>to school</u> today.
8. I need some time <u>to rest</u>.
9. Give that message <u>to Larry</u>.
10. Take this pencil <u>to class</u> with you.

Infinitive Phrases

Like a gerund, an infinitive can be combined with modifiers or a complement to form an *infinitive phrase.*

9f ▶ An **infinitive phrase** is an infinitive with its modifiers and complements—all working together as a noun, an adjective, or an adverb.

131

The following examples show three variations of the infinitive phrase.

INFINITIVE WITH AN ADVERB	We hope **to finish early.**
INFINITIVE WITH A PREPOSITIONAL PHRASE	Tomorrow my family plans **to leave for Utah.**
INFINITIVE WITH A COMPLEMENT	Does he want **to cook dinner?**

Sometimes *to* is omitted when an infinitive follows such verbs as *dare, feel, hear, help, let, make, need, see,* and *watch.*

Did you watch me **play** tennis? [to play]
No one dared **go** without permission. [to go]
Chris helped his uncle **paint** the canoe. [to paint]

EXERCISE 13 Finding Infinitive Phrases
Write the infinitive phrase in each sentence. Then underline the infinitive. Remember that *to* is sometimes omitted.

Facts and Figures

1. Europeans were the first people to use wallpaper.
2. Joseph Lister was the first doctor to use antiseptic methods during surgery.
3. Benjamin Franklin went to Paris to enlist French aid for the American Revolution.
4. In colonial days children helped make candles and soap with their families.
5. Henry Ford was the first employer in America to guarantee a minimum daily wage of five dollars.
6. Warren G. Harding was the first president to speak over the radio from the White House.
7. Until 1937, a referee had to toss a jump ball after every basket.
8. To prevent snow blindness, Eskimos have been wearing sunglasses for 2,000 years.
9. Helene Madison was the first woman to swim 100 yards in one minute.
10. In Baltimore it is a crime to mistreat an oyster.

EXERCISE 14 Finding Infinitive Phrases

Write the infinitive phrase in each sentence. Then label it *noun, adjective,* or *adverb.*

1. My plan is to work every other weekend.
2. We left early to catch the bus.
3. People begin to shrink after the age of 30.
4. Ralph is eager to know his grade on the test.
5. To be on time won't be easy.
6. Dad promised to take us to the rodeo in Salinas.
7. To become a lawyer is one of my ambitions.
8. Until 1944, women were not allowed to vote in France.
9. The Chinese were the first people to use paper money.
10. An old remedy for too many mice is to get a cat.

EXERCISE 15 Writing Sentences

Write a sentence for each of the following infinitive phrases.

1. to complete the report as soon as possible
2. to hear clearly
3. to write a letter to my aunt
4. to play in the school band
5. to win the championship
6. to read the book in one sitting
7. to answer the question correctly
8. to hear from her
9. to make a birthday card for Mom
10. to get there on time

EXERCISE 16 Time-out for Review

Number your paper 1 to 15. Write each verbal or verbal phrase. Then label it *participial, gerund,* or *infinitive.*

A Very
Strong
Man

1. Weighing over 300 pounds, Louis Cyr may have been the strongest man in recorded history.
2. Lifting a full barrel of cement with one arm was an easy task for him.
3. One story, known to everyone in Quebec, tells about his pushing a heavy freight car up an incline.

4. To entertain townspeople, Louis also would lift 588 pounds off the floor — by using only one finger!
5. Pitting himself against four horses in 1891 was, however, his greatest feat.
6. Standing before a huge crowd, Louis was fitted with a special harness.
7. The horses, lined up two on each side, were attached to the harness.
8. Louis stood with his arms on his chest and his feet planted wide.
9. The signal was given, and the horses began to pull.
10. Moving either arm from his chest would disqualify him.
11. The horses strained hard to dislodge him.
12. The grooms urged the slipping horses to pull harder.
13. Not budging an inch, Louis held on.
14. After a few more minutes of tugging, the winner was announced.
15. Louis Cyr bowed before the cheering crowd.

MISPLACED AND DANGLING MODIFIERS

Participial phrases and infinitive phrases can be used as modifiers. As a result, they should be placed as close as possible to the word they modify. Sometimes when they are placed too far away from the word they modify, they become *misplaced modifiers*.

MISPLACED   We saw a bear hiking along with our cameras.

CORRECTED   **Hiking along with our cameras,** we saw a bear.

At other times, verbal phrases that should be acting as modifiers have nothing to describe. These phrases are called *dangling modifiers*.

DANGLING   To enter the contest, a form must be signed.

CORRECTED   **To enter the contest,** you must sign a form.

EXERCISE 17   Correcting Misplaced and Dangling Modifiers

Write the following sentences, correcting the error in each one. To do this, follow one of two steps: (1) Place a verbal phrase closer to the word it modifies, or (2) Add words and change the sentence around so that the phrase has a noun or a pronoun to modify. Remember to use commas where needed.

1. Jack noticed two robins bicycling to school.
2. I came upon an accident turning the corner.
3. Weighed down by our packs, the trail seemed endless.
4. Driving to Miami, our road maps were a big help.
5. Jogging along the street, my ankle twisted.
6. We saw a deer riding along in our car.
7. Turning the pages, my eye noticed the record sale.
8. That gift was given by Eric wrapped in silver paper.
9. After glancing at the clock, the book was closed by Linda.
10. Growing in the garden, I picked some tomatoes.
11. We admired the autumn leaves gliding along in our canoe.
12. Having waited up for the election results, weariness overcame us.
13. Leaping out of the water, the trainer threw a fish to the porpoise.
14. We noticed a stranger at the front door looking out the upstairs window.
15. To avoid any last minute problems, reservations should be made in advance.
16. Driving through town, many traffic lights delayed us.
17. I found the missing sneakers opening the door to the hall closet.
18. Baskets were given to all the children filled with raisins and nuts.
19. While napping, the doorbell awakened me.
20. To participate in the New York Marathon, a place in the lottery has to be won.

DIAGRAMING VERBAL PHRASES

How a verbal phrase is used in a sentence will determine how it is diagramed.

Participial Phrases. Because a participial phrase is always used as an adjective, it is diagramed under the word it modifies. The participle, however, is written in a curve.

Winding through the mountains, the trail was used by many hikers.

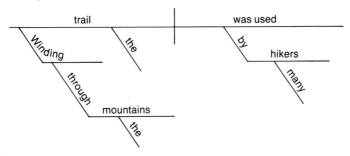

Gerund Phrases. Because a gerund phrase is used as a noun, it can be diagramed in any noun position. In the following example, a gerund phrase is used as a direct object. Notice that a complement and a prepositional phrase are part of the gerund phrase.

José enjoys growing plants in his room.

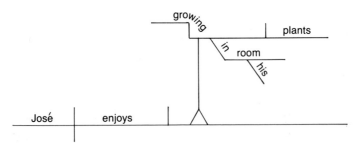

Infinitive Phrases. Because an infinitive phrase may be used as an adjective, an adverb, or a noun, it is diagramed in several ways. The following example shows how an infinitive phrase used as an adjective is diagramed.

136

This is the best place to stop for lunch.

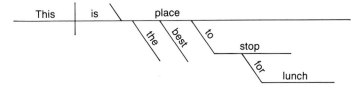

An infinitive phrase used as a noun can be diagramed in any noun position. In the following example, an infinitive phrase is used as the subject of the sentence.

To arrive on time is important.

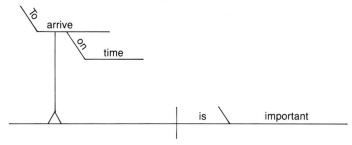

In the following example, the infinitive phrase is used as a direct object. If the *to* of an infinitive is omitted from the sentence, it is diagramed in parentheses.

Do you dare decorate the gym?

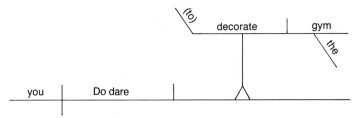

EXERCISE 18   Diagraming Verbal Phrases

Diagram the following sentences or copy them. If you copy them, draw one line under each subject and two lines under each verb. Put parentheses around each verbal phrase. Then label each one *participial, gerund,* or *infinitive.*

1. Sitting on the doorstep, the dog waited for its owner.
2. Spilt by accident, the milk dripped from the counter.

3. No one noticed Sally tiptoeing down the stairs.
4. I enjoy speaking before an audience.
5. The team practiced kicking the football between the goalposts.
6. Eating food in the halls is not permitted.
7. This is the best shovel to use for that job.
8. To rush into a decision is a mistake.
9. Do you dare plan the menu?
10. The uniform to wear to the banquet is the blue one.

Application to Writing

Two short sentences can be combined by changing the information in one sentence into a verbal phrase.

TWO SENTENCES Miguel found the hamster. It was hiding in the closet.

ONE SENTENCE Miguel found the hamster **hiding in the closet.** [participial phrase]

TWO SENTENCES Donald makes his livelihood in Maine. He repairs wood stoves.

ONE SENTENCE Donald makes his livelihood in Maine **by repairing wood stoves.** [gerund phrase]

TWO SENTENCES The director needs Roy. He will construct the scenery.

ONE SENTENCE The director needs Roy **to construct the scenery.** [infinitive phrase]

EXERCISE 19 Combining Sentences with Verbal Phrases
Combine each pair of sentences by changing the information in one sentence into a verbal phrase. Remember to use commas where needed.

1. Melanie saw Jake. He was rehearsing his part for the school play.
2. Lucia has written a report. It is based on the life of Henry Ford.

138

3. The octopus shoots a cloud of black fluid. In this way it conceals itself from enemies.

4. I sleep eight hours a night. This amount of sleep is necessary for me.

5. The pelican flew close to the water. Suddenly it dived for a fish.

6. We should talk with Mavis. We should find out the dates of the games from her.

7. I prepared for the tryouts. I jogged every day for two hours.

8. We tested the water first. Then we jumped in and swam to the boat house.

9. Kate is coming over. She will help me with my science project.

10. The tomatoes tasted delicious. They were canned last August.

11. The experts had studied the unusually large diamond for about six months. Then they were ready to make the first cut.

12. In the salad we used three ripe tomatoes. They were grown in our garden.

13. One creature has 50 joints in each leg. It is known as daddy longlegs.

14. In the backyard we have huge barrels. That is how we catch rainwater.

15. Bloodhounds are trained by the police. Bloodhounds track people who are lost.

16. The Romans believed that onions made men brave. They fed the vegetable to their soldiers.

17. For a few years Samuel Clemens worked as a riverboat pilot on the Mississippi River. Then he became a newspaper reporter and an author.

18. Throughout history a typical village was small. It consisted of 5 to 30 families.

19. Janice carved three pumpkins. She will take them with her to the Halloween party.

20. Mr. Mann makes wooden models of seabirds. This is his hobby.

CHAPTER REVIEW

A. Write each participial phrase in the following sentences.

1. Stopping for a moment, Jill untangled the reins.
2. Steam is simply water expanded 1,600 times its original volume.
3. Discovering the entrance, the boys eagerly explored the cave.
4. The ship, suffering damage to its hull, finally arrived in New York.
5. We could hear the planes circling overhead, waiting for instructions from the control tower.
6. One out of every four human beings living in the world today is Chinese.
7. Traveling due south from Chicago, you would never reach South America.
8. The location of Chicago, situated west of every point in South America, is often misjudged.
9. Walking to the museum, Isabel met a group of friends.
10. Miguel frowned when he discovered the toast burnt to a crisp.

B. Write each gerund phrase in the following sentences.

1. I enjoy riding my bicycle, but Ned prefers using his moped.
2. Cleaning up after the party took Tim three hours.
3. Upon hearing the good news, Marta didn't know what to say to the radio announcer.
4. Performing on the stage is a new experience for me.
5. Forgetting your homework could result in remaining after school.
6. What did you think of José's winning the high jump?
7. Ancient Egyptian boats were constructed by binding together bundles of papyrus stems.
8. Yolanda enjoyed talking with the actors.
9. Rehearsing for the concert is the best part of Erica's day.

10. After arriving at the airport, Mom waited two hours for the plane.

C. Write each infinitive phrase in the following sentences.

1. Our schedule must be changed to accommodate our visitors.
2. It takes about ten seconds to slice six cucumbers in a food processor.
3. Clara hopes to win the golf tournament next weekend.
4. The first apples to reach America arrived from England in 1629.
5. A house cat can be expected to live from 8 to 20 years.
6. To wake up early in the morning is easy for some people.
7. My sister has agreed to paint your portrait.
8. To avoid an accident, Kim drove slowly through the fog.
9. Lee would like to visit Austria someday.
10. To play the piano well requires hours of practice.

MASTERY TEST

Number your paper 1 to 10. Write the verbal phrase in each sentence. Then label it *participial, gerund,* or *infinitive*.

1. Walking along, Meg saw Gordon and spoke to him.
2. Mom likes playing tennis.
3. The plane is scheduled to arrive at six o'clock.
4. Across the room I could see Greg grinning at me.
5. Finding a four-leaf clover isn't easy.
6. Seeing the date, I suddenly remembered your birthday.
7. To sleep soundly all night is a big blessing.
8. Picking blueberries requires care.
9. The hikers found him resting beside a waterfall.
10. I plan to fly a plane by the age of 20.

10

Clauses

DIAGNOSTIC TEST

Number your paper 1 to 10. Write the underlined clause in each sentence. Then label it *independent, adjective, adverb,* or *noun.*

EXAMPLE   <u>When Mom returned from work</u>, she took us swimming.

ANSWER   When Mom returned from work — adverb

1. <u>We'll meet you at six</u> unless it rains.
2. <u>Because we left the game early</u>, we missed the winning touchdown.
3. Give that book to Gladys, <u>who will return it to the library</u>.
4. <u>As long as you're here</u>, you should stay for dinner.
5. Stacy didn't hear <u>what you said</u>.
6. <u>Whichever movie you chose</u> is all right with me.
7. The cereal <u>that I like so much</u> has no sugar in it.
8. Since I have taken skiing lessons, <u>I hardly ever fall</u>.
9. The computer <u>that you want</u> is very expensive.
10. I want a job <u>so that I can save money for college</u>.

In the last chapter you learned that a group of words called a *phrase* can be used as a noun, an adjective, or an adverb. In this chapter you will learn that another group of words, called a *clause,* can also be used as a noun, an adjective, or an adverb.

10a ▶ A **clause** is a group of words that has a subject and a verb.

From the definition of a clause, you can see the difference between a clause and a phrase. A clause has a subject and a verb; a phrase does not have a subject and a verb.

PHRASE We arrived home **after dinner.**
CLAUSE We arrived home **after dinner was finished.**
[*Dinner* is the subject; *was finished* is the verb.]

INDEPENDENT AND SUBORDINATE CLAUSES

There are two kinds of clauses. One kind is called a main clause or an *independent clause.*

10b ▶ An **independent (or main) clause** can stand alone as a sentence because it expresses a complete thought.

An independent clause is called a *sentence* when it stands by itself. However, it is called a *clause* when it appears in a sentence with another clause. In the following example, each subject is underlined once, and each verb is underlined twice.

I will wash the dishes, and you can dry them.

This sentence has two independent clauses. Each clause could be a sentence by itself.

I will wash the dishes. You can dry them.

The second kind of clause is called a dependent clause or a *subordinate clause.*

10c ▸ A **subordinate (or dependent) clause** cannot stand alone as a sentence because it does not express a complete thought.

The subordinate clause in each of the following examples does not express a complete thought — even though it has a subject and a verb.

┌──── subordinate clause ────┐ ┌──── independent clause ────┐
If <u>they</u> <u>win</u> this game, the <u>championship</u> <u>is</u> theirs.

┌── independent clause ──┐ ┌──── subordinate clause ────┐
<u>We</u> <u>bought</u> a clock <u>that</u> <u>chimes</u> every hour.

EXERCISE 1   Distinguishing between Independent and Subordinate Clauses

Write each underlined clause. Then label each one *independent* or *subordinate*.

Hidden
Traits

1. Graphology, <u>which is the study of handwriting</u>, has existed for many years.
2. Many people think <u>that handwriting can reveal personality traits</u>.
3. <u>Because some businesses believe this theory</u>, an applicant's handwriting is analyzed.
4. <u>If your writing slants to the right</u>, you are probably friendly and open.
5. If your writing slants to the left, <u>you may well be a nonconformist</u>.
6. Writing uphill indicates an optimist, and <u>writing downhill suggests a reliable person</u>.
7. Capital letters <u>that are inserted in the middle of a word</u> reveal a very creative person.
8. <u>A circle over an *i* shows an artistic nature</u>, and a correctly dotted *i* indicates a careful person.
9. <u>When an *i* is dotted high above the letter</u>, the writer is thought to be a serious thinker.
10. None of this should be taken too seriously, however, <u>since graphology is not a technical science</u>.

USES OF SUBORDINATE CLAUSES

A subordinate clause can be used in several ways. It can be used as an adverb, an adjective, or a noun.

Adverb Clauses

A subordinate clause can be used like a single adverb or an adverb phrase. When it is, it is called an *adverb clause.*

SINGLE ADVERB   Leroy awoke **early.**

ADVERB PHRASE   Leroy awoke **at dawn.**

ADVERB CLAUSE   Leroy awoke **when the sun rose.**

> **10d**   An **adverb clause** is a subordinate clause that is used like an adverb to modify a verb, an adjective, or an adverb.

An adverb clause answers the adverb question *How? When? Where? How much?* or *To what extent?* An adverb clause also answers the question *Under what condition?* or *Why?*

WHEN?   I will stay on my diet **until I lose 15 pounds.**

UNDER WHAT CONDITION?   **If the train is late,** will you wait for me at the station?

WHY?   I saw the movie **because everyone was talking about it.**

The adverb clauses in the preceding examples all modify verbs. Notice that they modify the whole verb phrase. Adverb clauses also modify adjectives and adverbs.

MODIFYING AN ADJECTIVE   Lynn is happy **whenever she is riding a horse.**

MODIFYING AN ADVERB   The play began later **than it usually does.**

Subordinating Conjunctions. All adverb clauses begin with a *subordinating conjunction.* Keep in mind that *after, as, before, since,* and *until* can also be used as prepositions.

Common Subordinating Conjunctions			
after	as soon as	in order that	until
although	as though	since	when
as	because	so that	whenever
as far as	before	than	where
as if	even though	though	wherever
as long as	if	unless	while

Unless you hear from me, I will meet you at six o'clock. The date was not changed **as far as I know.**

EXERCISE 2 Finding Adverb Clauses

Write the adverb clause in each sentence. Then underline the subordinating conjunction.

1. United States Marines are called leathernecks because their coats once had big leather collars.
2. A tornado once sheared a whole herd of sheep while they grazed.
3. I will exercise as long as you do.
4. Although Columbus made four voyages to the New World, he never discovered the coast of the mainland.
5. Unless I set the alarm, I will sleep until nine o'clock and be late for school.
6. The quality of TV programs declines when summer comes.
7. The Battle of New Orleans was fought after the peace treaty had been signed.
8. As Mother drove, Father studied the road map.
9. If all cod eggs produced live fish, there would be no room left in the ocean for water.
10. We can attend the meeting even though we aren't members.

EXERCISE 3 Supplying Subordinating Conjunctions

Choose an appropriate subordinating conjunction to fill each blank. (Do not use the same subordinating conjunction more than once.) Then write each complete adverb clause.

1. _____ my brother is accepted by Ohio State, he plans to go there.
2. _____ you find the answer, please call me.
3. _____ you complete your term paper, return your books to the library.
4. Jeb is much stronger _____ I am.
5. _____ we put out the sunflower seeds, the cardinals came to the feeder.
6. Terry studied the piano _____ she never plays.
7. _____ it was pouring, we enjoyed ourselves in the picnic shelter.
8. We chose a beagle _____ we wanted a small dog.
9. _____ I won't be finished by seven o'clock, you'll have to go in my place.
10. _____ I know, the track meet was canceled.

EXERCISE 4 Finding Adverb Clauses

Write the adverb clause in each sentence. Then beside each clause, write the word or words it modifies.

1. Meet me in the library before class starts.
2. As far as I know, Suki fed the dog.
3. When one cup of rice is cooked, it expands to three cups.
4. I can type faster than anyone else I know.
5. If you could jump like a grasshopper, you could jump over a house!
6. They acted as if nothing had happened.
7. I cannot leave until I do my homework.
8. Whenever you're ready to go, just tell me.
9. Since cowbirds don't build nests, they lay their eggs in the nests of other birds.
10. This week is colder than the last two weeks have been.

Punctuation with Adverb Clauses

Always place a comma after an adverb clause that comes at the beginning of a sentence.

Since you have finished your chores, you may leave.

Sometimes an adverb clause will interrupt an independent clause. If it does, place a comma before and after the adverb clause.

The schedule, **as far as I can tell,** is excellent.

EXERCISE 5 Writing Sentences

Write sentences that follow the directions below. Then underline each adverb clause. Include commas where needed.

1. Include an adverb clause that begins with *than.*
2. Include an adverb clause that begins with *even though.*
3. Include an adverb clause that begins with *since* at the beginning of a sentence.
4. Include an adverb clause that begins with *because* at the end of a sentence.
5. Include an adverb clause that begins with *unless* and interrupts an independent clause.

Adjective Clauses

A subordinate clause can be used like a single adjective or an adjective phrase. When it is, it is called an *adjective clause.*

SINGLE ADJECTIVE   My uncle has an **antique** chair.

ADJECTIVE PHRASE   My uncle has a chair **with a long history.**

ADJECTIVE CLAUSE   My uncle has a chair **that was built in the 1600s.**

148

10e   An **adjective clause** is a subordinate clause that is used like an adjective to modify a noun or a pronoun.

An adjective clause answers the adjective question *Which one?* or *What kind?*

WHICH ONE?   I know the actor **who has the lead role.**

WHAT KIND?   The only store **that sold cordless phones** just went out of business.

Relative Pronouns. Most adjective clauses begin with a *relative pronoun*. A relative pronoun relates an adjective clause to its antecedent—the noun or pronoun it modifies.

Relative Pronouns				
who	whom	whose	which	that

Yvonne is the person **whom I met yesterday.**

The casserole **that I made for dinner** was very tasty.

NOTE: Sometimes a word such as *where* or *when* can also introduce an adjective clause.

Rhode Island is the place **where I was born.**

Morning is the time **when I most enjoy jogging.**

EXERCISE 6   Finding Adjective Clauses

Write the adjective clause in each sentence. Then underline the relative pronoun.

1. The crocus, which usually flowers in early spring, is a native of Europe and Asia.
2. Cleopatra, who is perhaps the most famous Egyptian queen, was actually of Greek ancestry.

3. Have they tested the purity of the water that comes into your house?
4. Benjamin Franklin, whom we know best for his political activities, was also a scientist and an inventor.
5. Near Los Angeles there is a single wisteria vine that covers an entire acre.
6. Special certificates will be awarded to the freshmen whose scholarship and citizenship are outstanding.
7. Jake handed the net to Ted, whom he mistook for Joe.
8. The impala, which can easily leap 30 feet, is one of the most graceful antelopes.
9. The player who caught the line drive threw the ball to first for a double play.
10. Clyde Beatty, whose life was devoted to the circus, was probably the greatest animal tamer of all time.

EXERCISE 7 Finding Adjective Clauses
Write the adjective clause in each sentence. Then beside each one, write the word it modifies.

The
Titanic

1. In 1912, the *Titanic* was crossing the North Atlantic, where icebergs were a constant threat.
2. The passengers, who felt secure in this great ship, were having a good time.
3. Several iceberg warnings, which should have been heeded, were ignored by the crew.
4. An iceberg, whose size was tremendous, suddenly appeared in front of the ship.
5. A slight impact, which scarcely disturbed the passengers, had actually struck a fatal blow.
6. At first the passengers, who were unaware of their danger, chatted casually about the accident.
7. The lifeboats that were on board could carry only a fraction of the passengers.
8. Boats that were launched quickly were not even filled.
9. The panic that overcame the passengers at the end might have been avoided.
10. The disaster, which resulted in the loss of 1,513 lives, will never be forgotten.

The Functions of a Relative Pronoun. In addition to introducing an adjective clause, a relative pronoun has another function. It can serve as a subject, a direct object, or an object of a preposition within the adjective clause itself. It can also show possession.

SUBJECT	The program, **which begins at eight o'clock,** should be interesting. [*Which* is the subject of *begins.*]
DIRECT OBJECT	The job **that I want** pays very well. [*That* is the direct object of *want,* answering the question *Want what?*]
OBJECT OF A PREPOSITION	The stamp club **of which I am a member** is open to anyone. [*Which* is the object of the preposition *of.*]
POSSESSION	Harvey is the person **whose voice sounds like yours.** [*Whose* shows possession of *voice.*]

Sometimes the relative pronoun *that* is omitted from an adjective clause. Nevertheless, it is still part of the clause and has its function within the clause.

This is the book **I need for my report.** [*That I need for my report* is the adjective clause. *That* (understood) is used as the direct object within the adjective clause.]

EXERCISE 8 Finding Adjective Clauses
Write the adjective clause in each sentence. Then underline each relative pronoun. Remember that the relative pronoun *that* may be omitted from the clause.

1. The Carters, whose dog I walk, will be away for three weeks.
2. Lions that are raised in captivity are surprisingly tame.
3. Are you wearing the raincoat you bought last week at the mall?
4. The longest tunnel through which we drove was about a mile long.

5. Daniel Webster, who became famous for his work in law, never went to law school.
6. The records I gave him dated back to the 1950s.
7. The story, whose author was unknown, was very scary.
8. A rat can gnaw through concrete that is two feet thick.
9. He is the man to whom you must speak.
10. The ostrich, which is the largest of all birds, can outrun a horse.

EXERCISE 9   Determining the Function of a Relative Pronoun

Number your paper 1 to 10. Using the following abbreviations, label the use of each relative pronoun in Exercise 8. If an adjective clause begins with an understood *that,* write *understood* and then write how *that* is used.

subject = *subj.*   object of a preposition = *o.p.*
direct object = *d.o.*   possession = *poss.*

Punctuation with Adjective Clauses

No punctuation is used with an adjective clause that contains information that is essential to identify a person, place, or thing in the sentence. A comma or commas, however, should set off an adjective clause that is nonessential. A clause is nonessential if it can be removed without changing the basic meaning of the sentence.

ESSENTIAL   The radio station **that plays the best music** is WXTR. [No commas are used because the clause is needed to identify which radio station.]

NONESSENTIAL The radio station, **which went on the air in 1947,** broadcasts interviews with recording artists. [Commas are used because the clause could be removed from the sentence.]

Always use the relative pronoun *that* in an essential clause and *which* in a nonessential clause.

EXERCISE 10 Writing Sentences

Write a sentence for each relative pronoun. Then underline each adjective clause. Use commas where needed.

1. who   2. whom   3. whose   4. which   5. that

Misplaced Modifiers

Place an adjective clause as near as possible to the word it modifies. A clause that is too far away from the word it modifies is called a *misplaced modifier*.

MISPLACED   Mark has a computer **who lives across the street.**

CORRECT   Mark, **who lives across the street,** has a computer.

EXERCISE 11 Correcting Misplaced Modifiers

Write the following sentences, correcting each misplaced modifier. Use commas where needed.

1. The birds ignored the dog that chirped in the trees.
2. The present is on the table that I received for my birthday.
3. The bicycle is in the garage that my father bought for me.
4. The movie will be shown in the auditorium which had Antarctica as the setting.
5. My car who is a good friend of mine was repaired by Glenn.
6. We met Mrs. Walker in the park who lives nearby.
7. The note was a reminder to order Pat's birthday cake that was written on the calendar.
8. The record album is in the cabinet that I thought I had lost.
9. The rain flooded our basement which lasted a week.
10. The oak tree provides us with shade that grows in our backyard.

153

Noun Clauses

A subordinate clause can also be used like a single noun. When it is, it is called a *noun clause.*

SINGLE NOUN   I just learned an interesting **fact.**
NOUN CLAUSE   I just learned **that trees can become sunburned.**

10f ▸   A **noun clause** is a subordinate clause that is used like a noun.

A noun clause can be used in all the ways a single noun can be used.

SUBJECT   **Whatever you order** is fine with me.
DIRECT OBJECT   Do you know **when they arrived?**
INDIRECT OBJECT   Give **whoever comes to the party** a paper hat.
OBJECT OF A
PREPOSITION   Terry was confused by **what the clerk said.**
PREDICATE
NOMINATIVE   The science of astronomy is **what interests me most.**

Following is a list of words that often begin a noun clause.

Common Introductory Words for Noun Clauses			
how	whatever	which	whomever
if	when	who	whose
that	where	whoever	why
what	whether	whom	

Keep in mind that the words *who, whom, whose, which,* and *that* may also begin an adjective clause. For this reason, do not rely on the introductory words themselves to identify a clause. Instead, determine how a clause is used in a sentence.

NOUN CLAUSE	**Who is running for office** is common knowledge. [used as a subject]
ADJECTIVE CLAUSE	Sam Johnson, **who is running for office,** is hanging campaign posters. [used to modify *Sam Johnson*]

EXERCISE 12 Finding Noun Clauses

Write the noun clause in each sentence.

1. That Miriam deserved the prize for the best costume was not disputed by anyone.
2. I don't know what you mean.
3. Are you really most concerned with what is best for the school?
4. What you say is true up to a point.
5. Some botanists believe that the cabbage is the most ancient vegetable still grown today.
6. Does Pilar know where she stored the decorations?
7. The parrot speaks to whoever comes into the house.
8. I wondered why the group had gathered at the mall.
9. Some people believe that snake meat is healthful.
10. The police always give tickets to whoever parks in front of a hydrant.

EXERCISE 13 Finding Noun Clauses

Write the noun clause in each sentence.

1. For many years no one knew where tuna spawned.
2. We will go along with whatever you decide.
3. Give whoever calls the directions to our house.
4. I don't know why I said that.
5. How Jerry lost my bicycle is a big mystery.
6. I'll vote for whoever is best qualified.
7. Life is what you make it.
8. Send whoever answers the ad a brochure.
9. The problem is whether he should play in the band or sing in the chorus.
10. Rachel Carson says that some waves may travel thousands of miles before breaking on shore.

EXERCISE 14 Labeling Noun Clauses
Using the following abbreviations, label the use of each
noun clause in Exercise 13.

subject = *subj.*   object of a preposition = *o.p.*
direct object = *d.o.*   predicate nominative = *p.n.*
indirect object = *i.o.*

EXERCISE 15 Supplying Subordinate Clauses
Complete the following skeleton sentences. Then label
each subordinate clause *adverb, adjective,* or *noun.*

EXAMPLE The runner who _____ .
POSSIBLE The runner <u>who came in first</u> is on our team.
ANSWER (adjective)

1. What _____ amazed the entire audience.
2. Since _____ , we were all late for the meeting.
3. Those are the books that _____ .
4. Today's newspaper mentioned that _____ .
5. The actor who _____ .
6. Did you know that _____ ?
7. Because _____ , we left early.
8. That some persons _____ is certainly true.
9. We were not disappointed even though _____ .
10. The pup that _____ .

EXERCISE 16 Time-out for Review
Number your paper 1 to 15. Write each subordinate clause
in the following paragraphs. Then label each one *adverb,
adjective,* or *noun.*

A
Tragic
Start

The Panama Canal, which connects two oceans, is the
greatest constructed waterway in the world. Because it was
completed over 80 years ago, few people can remember the
tragic problems that occurred during its construction. In
1881, a French firm that was headed by Ferdinand de Les-
seps began to dig the canal. Although the work was hard, it
was possible. What wasn't possible was finding a way to
overcome the mosquitoes that infested the whole area.
Within 8 years, nearly 20,000 men died of malaria as they

worked on the canal. The French company that had first built the Suez Canal finally went bankrupt after it had lost $325 million.

After 18 years had passed, some Americans tried their luck. They first found a plan that wiped out the mosquitoes. Their work then proceeded without the hazard that had doomed the French. The construction, which began at both ends, moved inland through the dense jungle. Finally, after 10 billion tons of earth had been removed, the canal was opened in 1914.

KINDS OF SENTENCE STRUCTURE

Once you know the difference between independent and subordinate clauses, you can understand the different kinds of sentence structure. The four kinds of sentences are *simple, compound, complex,* and *compound-complex.*

10g ▶ A **simple sentence** consists of one independent clause.

The subject and the verb in a simple sentence, however, can be compound. In the following examples, each subject is underlined once, and each verb is underlined twice.

The <u>cat</u> <u>slept</u> in the afternoon sun.
<u>Henry</u> and <u>Frank</u> <u>met</u> and <u>walked</u> to school together.

10h ▶ A **compound sentence** consists of two or more independent clauses.

┌────── independent clause ──────┐   ┌────── independent
<u>Mom</u> just <u>baked</u> a cherry pie, and <u>I</u> <u>can</u> hardly <u>wait</u>
clause ──┐
to taste it.

┌────── independent clause ──────┐ ┌────── independent
<u>Pat</u> and <u>I</u> <u>pitched</u> the tent; <u>Barb</u> <u>started</u> the fire
clause ──────┐
and <u>cooked</u> dinner.

157

NOTE: A compound sentence should include only closely related clauses. If two ideas are not related, they should be placed in separate sentences.

COMPOUND SENTENCE	The earth has only one moon, but Jupiter has at least fourteen.
SEPARATE SENTENCES	The earth has only one moon. Jupiter is the largest planet of all.

Punctuation with Compound Sentences

There are several ways to connect the independent clauses in a compound sentence. You can join them with a comma and a conjunction.

The bicycle trip lasted a whole week, **but** everyone enjoyed it.

You also can join independent clauses with a semicolon and no conjunction.

Noreen likes team sports; her sister prefers swimming and jogging.

10i A **complex sentence** consists of one independent clause and one or more subordinate clauses.

┌─── subordinate clause ───┐ ┌─── independent
Since I joined the swim team, I have practiced
clause ──┐
every day.

┌── subordinate clause ──┐ ┌── independent clause ──┐
After the game is over, we will go to Toby's house,
┌─── subordinate clause ───┐
which is near the stadium.

10j A **compound-complex sentence** consists of two or more independent clauses and one or more subordinate clauses.

— independent clause —
My science <u>project</u> <u>isn't</u> <u>required</u> until Friday, but

— independent clause —   — subordinate
<u>I</u> <u>have</u> already <u>turned</u> it in because <u>I</u> <u>finished</u> the

clause —   — subordinate clause —
work sooner than <u>I</u> <u>had expected</u>.

EXERCISE 17 Classifying Sentence Structure
Label each sentence *simple, compound, complex,* or *compound-complex.*

1. Most parakeets are green and yellow, but our parakeet is blue.
2. Terns, which migrate over 10,000 miles each year, are guided by an unerring instinct.
3. You'll have to cross the stream by whatever means you have because the bridge has been washed out.
4. The squirrel comes down a tree head first, but the raccoon prefers to come down tail first.
5. The final game of the series is on Friday, but we'll have to play without Dan because he's out of town.
6. Little skiffs and big sloops raised their sails and started out through the inlet.
7. The frost killed most of the flowers, but one lonely rose near the chimney still lives.
8. The Rh factor in blood is so called because it was discovered in the blood of Rhesus monkeys.
9. Both Mozart and Schubert wrote great music but died quite young.
10. The male fox will choose a mate, and if the female dies, he remains single for the rest of his life.

EXERCISE 18 Classifying Sentence Structure
Label each sentence *simple, compound, complex,* or *compound-complex.*

Burgers

1. The hamburger came from Hamburg, Germany, and the frankfurter came from Frankfurt.
2. The idea of placing meat on a bun, however, came from the United States.

3. When the hamburger first arrived in the United States, it was eaten almost raw.
4. The French still prefer rare meat, but the Germans eat raw hamburger meat.
5. Hamburger first became popular among German immigrants who lived in Cincinnati.
6. Hamburger wasn't placed between halves of a bun until early in this century.
7. Officially, the first hamburger sandwich appeared in 1904 in St. Louis, Missouri, which was also the birthplace of the ice-cream cone.
8. Today the frankfurter is not so popular, but the hamburger is on the rise.
9. Chopped meat now accounts for about 30 percent of all meat sales.
10. Scientists are working on the hamburger, and it may change drastically in the future because it may be made of soybeans or cotton!

EXERCISE 19 Writing Sentences
Write one simple sentence, one compound sentence, one complex sentence, and one compound-complex sentence. Use punctuation where needed.

DIAGRAMING SENTENCES

The simple sentences that you diagramed earlier in this book had only one baseline. In the diagrams for compound, complex, and compound-complex sentences, each clause has its own baseline.

Compound Sentences. These sentences are diagramed like two simple sentences, except that they are joined by a broken line on which the conjunction is placed. The broken line connects the verbs.

Mysteries are interesting, but I prefer biographies.

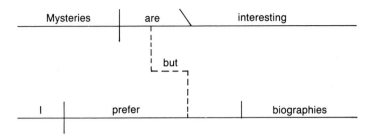

Complex Sentences. In a complex sentence, an adverb clause is diagramed beneath the independent clause. The subordinating conjunction goes on a broken line that connects the verb in the adverb clause to the word the clause modifies.

I read my report after I typed it.

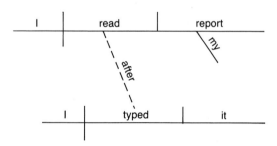

An adjective clause is also diagramed beneath the independent clause. The relative pronoun is connected by a broken line to the noun or pronoun the clause modifies.

This song is one that I will never forget.

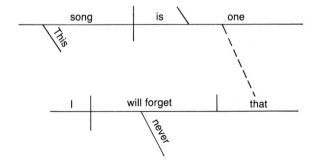

A noun clause is diagramed on a pedestal in the same place a single noun would be placed that has the same function. The noun clause in the following diagram is used as the subject.

What the teacher said pleased Jane.

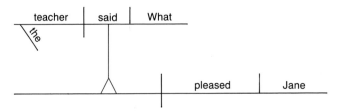

Compound-complex Sentences. To diagram these sentences, just apply what you learned about diagraming compound and complex sentences. In the following diagram, the subordinate clause is a noun clause that is used as a direct object. If an introductory word in the noun clause has no function in the clause, it is written along the pedestal.

The new museum opened, and everyone says that it is beautiful.

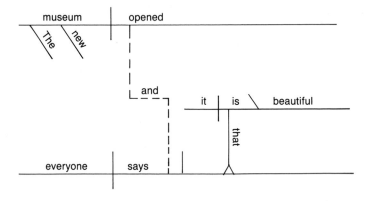

EXERCISE 20 Diagraming Sentences
Diagram the following sentences or copy them. If you copy them, draw one line under each subject and two lines under each verb. Put parentheses around each subordinate clause. Label each clause *adverb, adjective,* or *noun.*

162

1. My homework is done, but I still must walk the dog.
2. My car needs a paint job, but I can't afford it.
3. We drove Justin to college when his vacation ended.
4. We will visit Texas because our friends live there.
5. I like the coat that you gave me.
6. The bird that you just saw is a cardinal.
7. What Tom said surprised me.
8. Reading is what I like best.
9. Everyone said that the movie was great, but I was bored.
10. I know that you have your opinion, but you should listen to mine.

Application to Writing

Good writing style includes sentence variety. To create sentence variety, you can combine related simple sentences into a compound or a complex sentence.

TWO SIMPLE SENTENCES	I wanted to watch television. The set was broken.
A COMPOUND SENTENCE	I wanted to watch television, **but the set was broken.**
TWO SIMPLE SENTENCES	Bianca gave up her paper route. Steve took over for her.
A COMPLEX SENTENCE	**When Bianca gave up her paper route,** Steve took over for her.
TWO SIMPLE SENTENCES	Dennis is captain of the hockey team. He is my cousin.
A COMPLEX SENTENCE	Dennis, **who is my cousin,** is captain of the hockey team.

EXERCISE 21 Combining Sentences

Combine the first five pairs of sentences into compound sentences. Then combine the next five pairs of sentences into complex sentences. Use commas where needed.

1. Wolves may live up to 16 years in captivity. In the wild their lives are much shorter.
2. Insects have six legs. Spiders have eight.

3. Bennett threw the ball to third base. Carlos tagged the runner out.
4. My shoes need new heels. The shoe-repair store is closed today.
5. The Indian rhinoceros has one horn. The African rhinoceros has two.
6. Leo painted our house. He lives next door.
7. Peanuts contain protein. They are a healthful snack.
8. Ann answered the doorbell. Brian answered the phone.
9. Spanish seemed interesting. I studied it.
10. The first Ferris wheel was constructed in 1893. It was 250 feet in diameter.

CHAPTER REVIEW

A. Write the subordinate clause in each sentence. Then label each one *adverb, adjective,* or *noun.*

1. Your jacket, which is too small, should be given to your brother.
2. Some of our friends joined us when we were walking to the subway.
3. Most people see what they want to see.
4. Wood is seasoned before it is used in construction.
5. Although I didn't say anything, I agreed with you.
6. Did you know that Mike reads the newspaper daily?
7. The fifth person who calls this number will win $500.
8. I can't figure out how these pieces fit together.
9. New York was the first state that required the licensing of motor vehicles.
10. Even though I'm tired, I want to go to the concert.

B. Label each sentence *simple, compound, complex,* or *compound-complex.*

1. Many dogs and cats get along very well together.
2. The island of Puerto Rico was originally called San Juan, and the city was called Puerto Rico.

3. Because the books that I need for my report are not available at the library, I will have to find a new topic.
4. Penguins are good swimmers but cannot fly at all.
5. After you left the party, Ken left too, but I stayed for another hour.
6. The children played on the swings while their parents talked.
7. Plants manufacture food in the light, but they absorb their food during the evening hours.
8. Haven't you heard the news on the radio?
9. Dinner was delicious, but I wasn't hungry because I had eaten a pizza just an hour before.
10. I didn't know what I should say to her.

MASTERY TEST

Number your paper 1 to 10. Write the underlined clause in each sentence. Then label it *independent, adjective, adverb,* or *noun.*

1. When I joined the club, <u>I paid my dues</u>.
2. <u>Since it's already ten o'clock</u>, will you have time to finish?
3. I just bought a bicycle, <u>which I paid for out of my savings account</u>.
4. You must explain <u>why you're late</u>.
5. Meg couldn't see the person <u>who was talking</u>.
6. <u>Don't you know</u> which plane you're taking?
7. I played tennis <u>after I had finished the chores</u>.
8. <u>Because I lost the library book</u>, I paid for it.
9. The cat <u>that you found</u> belongs to the Stevensons.
10. Please return this vase to <u>wherever you found it</u>.

11

Sound Sentences

Most of the confusion that comes from written words stems from two basic problems: sentence fragments and run-on sentences. This chapter will help you recognize these problems and show you specific ways to correct them.

SENTENCE FRAGMENTS

One mistake writers sometimes make is to express an incomplete thought as a sentence. These incomplete thoughts are called *sentence fragments*.

11a ▶ A **sentence fragment** is a group of words that does not express a complete thought.

Kinds of Sentence Fragments

There are several kinds of sentence fragments. Each one of them is missing one or more essential elements to make it a sentence.

Phrase Fragments. A phrase does not have a subject and a verb; therefore, it can never stand alone as a sentence. Following are examples of phrase fragments.

PREPOSITIONAL PHRASES	The coach gave us a pep talk. **During halftime in the game against Bolton.**
	Before my usual breakfast of cereal and toast. I like to read the newspaper.
PARTICIPIAL PHRASES	We found the newspaper. **Lying in a mud puddle.**
	Flipping the pancake into the air. Dad caught it with the frying pan.
INFINITIVE PHRASES	The yearbook staff met yesterday. **To elect an editor.**
	To appear friendly. The mayor shook hands with everyone and held a baby.

APPOSITIVE PHRASES   Roberta works at Greyson's. **The dress store on Cornell Street.**

Have you seen my library books? **The ones about solar energy.**

EXERCISE 1   Finding Phrase Fragments

Label each group of words *sentence* or *fragment.* If a group of words is a fragment, add the words necessary to make it a sentence. Use punctuation where needed.

EXAMPLE   During the terrible blizzard of 1985.

ANSWER   fragment — During the terrible blizzard of 1985, we couldn't leave our house for two days.

1. My bicycle can be repaired for 15 dollars.
2. Speaking at the assembly for all ninth graders.
3. To think of something funny to say.
4. Mowing the lawn is my responsibility.
5. Put the groceries away.
6. The director and also the author of the play.
7. At ten o'clock on Friday, the meeting will be held.
8. Slugging the ball with all her might.
9. The library on the corner of Evergreen Street.
10. To answer as promptly as possible.

Clause Fragments. All clauses have a subject and a verb. Only an independent clause, however, can stand alone as a sentence. A subordinate clause is a fragment when it stands alone because it does not express a complete thought. Following are examples of clause fragments.

ADVERB CLAUSES   You could save money. **If you took your lunch to school.**

Because the game went into extra innings. We didn't get home until 11 o'clock.

ADJECTIVE CLAUSES   This is the basketball. **That we bought for Harold.**

Is this the road? **That we should take to get to the civic center.**

EXERCISE 2   Finding Clause Fragments

Label each group of words *sentence* or *fragment*. If a group
of words is a fragment, add the words necessary to make it a
sentence. Use punctuation where needed.

EXAMPLE   Since my brother left.
ANSWER   fragment — Since my brother left, I have been
          very lonesome.

 1. After the painting was framed and hung on the wall.
 2. That the witness told the police after the accident.
 3. Before he left, he spoke with her.
 4. Dry the dishes while you're standing there.
 5. After we know the results of the tests.
 6. Who is the new captain of the football team?
 7. While the weather is still cool.
 8. Until we know, there's nothing to do.
 9. She's the one who told me.
10. Even though we couldn't see well from the second
    balcony.

Other Kinds of Fragments.   Other groups of words can also
be mistakenly thought of as a sentence.

| PART OF A COMPOUND VERB | Will you wait for us? **Or come back to get us?** |
| ITEMS IN A SERIES | We will have to take warm clothes with us. **Coats, wool scarves, and gloves.** |

EXERCISE 3   Finding Sentence Fragments

Label each group of words *sentence* or *fragment*. If a group
of words is a fragment, add the words necessary to make it a
sentence. Use punctuation where needed.

EXAMPLE   And throw away the trash.
ANSWER   fragment — Rake the leaves and throw away the
          trash.

 1. Red, purple, and blue are my favorite colors.
 2. And write as clearly as possible.
 3. Before the voting booths close.

4. A pencil, four sheets of paper, and a ruler.
5. Flying a kite on a windy day.
6. I haven't spoken with him yet.
7. Or take the bus to Haley Street.
8. Light bulbs, a hammer, and some scotch tape.
9. We should leave very shortly.
10. Which falls on a Tuesday this year.

Ways to Correct Sentence Fragments

There are two ways to correct a sentence fragment. First, you can add words to make it into a separate sentence as you have done in the previous exercises. Second, you can attach it to the sentence that is next to it.

SENTENCE AND FRAGMENT	We're going to Kansas City in the spring. **To see our cousins.**
SEPARATE SENTENCES	We're going to Kansas City in the spring. **We're planning to see our cousins.**
ATTACHED	We're going to Kansas City in the spring **to see our cousins.**
SENTENCE AND FRAGMENT	This is Mr. Jefferson. **My last year's math teacher.**
SEPARATE SENTENCES	This is Mr. Jefferson. **He was my math teacher last year.**
ATTACHED	This is Mr. Jefferson, **my last year's math teacher.**

EXERCISE 4   Correcting Sentence Fragments

Write the following sentences, correcting each sentence fragment. Either make the fragment a complete sentence by adding any necessary words, or attach it to the other sentence. Add capital letters and punctuation marks where needed.

1. Tennessee was known as Franklin. Before it was granted statehood in 1796.
2. Hernandez can program computers. To do whatever he wants them to do.

3. We could unload the boxes from the truck. Or unpack them in the store.
4. The chow is the only dog. That has a black tongue.
5. History has had some famous marble players. George Washington, Thomas Jefferson, and John Adams.
6. The first house numbers appeared in 1463. On a street in Paris.
7. Tonight I must go to hockey practice. And write a science report.
8. Aspirin was first marketed in 1899. And was available only by prescription.
9. Did you hear about Jim's new job? Running errands for his neighbors.
10. Amateur astronomers can tell a star from a planet. Because only stars twinkle.
11. Some jets require tremendous amounts of fuel. Eleven thousand gallons an hour.
12. Fortunately, jets can use kerosene. A cheaper fuel than high-octane gasoline.
13. During our trip west, we will stay with my sister. Who lives in Arkansas.
14. Last summer we traveled to Boston. Where we walked the Freedom Trail.
15. Last night I went to the meeting at the school. To learn about the new sports program.
16. On the lawn this morning. I saw the first robin of spring.
17. The jet plane streaked across the sky. Leaving behind a long, thin trail of white vapor.
18. We have always owned at least one pointer. A dog easily trained for hunting.
19. We'll go to the fair on Sunday. Unless it rains.
20. Ponce de León was a famous Spanish adventurer. Who searched for the legendary Fountain of Youth.

EXERCISE 5 Correcting Sentence Fragments

Rewrite the following paragraphs, correcting all sentence fragments. Add capital letters and punctuation marks where needed.

When Jesse Owens graduated from East Technical High School in Cleveland, Ohio. He had established three national high school records in track. At Ohio State University Jesse broke a few more world records. Then in the 1936 Olympic Games at Berlin. He acquired world fame by winning four gold medals!

Jesse's performance on May 25, 1935, at the Big Ten Conference championships, however, will always be remembered. Getting up from a sickbed. Jesse ran the 100-yard dash in 9.4 seconds. To tie the world's record. Ten minutes later in the broad jump. Jesse leaped 26 feet 8¼ inches on his first try. To beat a world's record. When the 220-yard dash was over. Jesse had smashed another world's record. He then negotiated the hurdles in 22.6 seconds. And shattered another record. Within three quarters of an hour. Jesse Owens had established world records in four events.

RUN-ON SENTENCES

The second mistake that some writers make is to combine several thoughts and write them as one sentence. This results in a *run-on sentence*. Generally run-on sentences are written two ways.

WITH A COMMA   John has an extra bat, **mine is lost.**

WITH NO
PUNCTUATION   At camp I will take horseback riding
computer programming sounds like fun.

11b ▶ A **run-on sentence** is two or more sentences that are written as one sentence and are separated by a comma or no mark of punctuation at all.

EXERCISE 6 Finding Run-on Sentences
Label each group of words *sentence* or *run-on*.

1. Armon has several pets they include two turtles.
2. Those earrings are unusual, they are made of jade.

3. The dance will be held at Robinsons' barn, which is just off Old Raven Road.
4. I just took skiing lessons the instructor has been skiing since she was three years old.
5. When you entered the room, did you notice the painting on the wall?
6. I have three favorite subjects they are French, history, and chorus.
7. Just as I was getting comfortable, my mother called me to do the dishes.
8. Have you ever ridden on a roller coaster, my cousin just loves them.
9. I have three brothers two of them are in elementary school.
10. As long as you're going to the kitchen, please get me an apple.

Ways to Correct Run-on Sentences

There are several ways to correct a run-on sentence. You can turn it into separate sentences or turn it into a compound sentence or a complex sentence.

RUN-ON SENTENCE	I was swimming very hard the tide was against me.
SEPARATE SENTENCES	I was swimming very hard. The tide was against me. [separated with a period and a capital letter]
COMPOUND SENTENCE	I was swimming very hard, but the tide was against me. [combined with a comma and a conjunction] I was swimming very hard; the tide was against me. [combined with a semicolon]
COMPLEX SENTENCE	Although I was swimming very hard, the tide was against me. [combined by changing one sentence into a subordinate clause]

EXERCISE 7   Correcting Run-on Sentences

Correct the following run-on sentences. Write them as separate sentences or as compound or complex sentences. Add capital letters and punctuation marks where needed.

1. Vivian heard the strange noise it was coming from the basement.
2. The oldest subway system in the world is in London, it went into service in 1863.
3. Mack won the 100-yard dash this was his second victory of the day.
4. Flamingos are usually pink one variety is bright red.
5. I am taking pottery lessons from Helen Kent she has a small gallery on Evergreen Street.
6. I heard the weather report, it is going to rain.
7. A fly has mosaic eyes, it can see in many directions at the same time.
8. Tim is collecting bottles and redeeming them, the money he earns will go toward a new jacket.
9. My camera is old I'll be glad to loan it to you.
10. Today is Ellen's birthday we are having a party.
11. Something happened to the pitcher in the sixth inning, he walked three batters in a row.
12. Everyone seems to have a hobby, mine is collecting pictures of horses.
13. Amber won the science contest, she had worked very hard on her project.
14. Cheryl is making posters for the dance, can you help?
15. Martin is on the hockey team he skates very well.
16. A short story must have a plot a simple incident or a string of incidents is not a short story.
17. Blue eyes are the most sensitive to light, dark brown eyes are the least sensitive.
18. Up to six or seven months, a child can breathe and swallow at the same time an adult cannot do this.
19. The crocodile is a cannibal, it will occasionally eat another crocodile.
20. A squirrel has no color vision it sees only in black and white.

EXERCISE 8 Correcting Run-on Sentences

Rewrite the following paragraph, correcting all run-on sentences. Add capital letters and punctuation marks where needed.

The
White
White
House

The White House wasn't always white, it started out gray. During the War of 1812, British troops invaded Washington they burned the structure on August 24, 1814. Only a shell was left standing. Under the direction of James Hoban, the original architect, the building was finally restored, the work was completed in 1817. The *White House* did not become its official name until 1902, Theodore Roosevelt adopted it.

EXERCISE 9 Time-out for Review

Write the following sentences, correcting each sentence fragment or run-on sentence. Add capital letters and punctuation marks where needed.

1. I found a squirrel's nest. Hidden in a box that was stored in the basement.
2. Let's study in the library. During our free period.
3. The team practices every afternoon the weather makes no difference.
4. We can eat the bread. After it has cooled for about 15 minutes.
5. George Washington crossed the Delaware River. To attack the British in Trenton.
6. I arrived late, I didn't have a chance to vote.
7. You have to take driver's training, lessons are given at the school.
8. The giraffe is a ruminant it can swallow a meal and chew it later.
9. The chaperon at the dance tonight will be Mrs. Jordan. The wife of the superintendent.
10. The white rhinoceros is not white, it is gray.
11. I have two favorite courses. French and history.
12. When the plane was first invented. Its maximum speed was about 35 miles per hour.

13. The quarterback caught the pass, then he immediately threw the ball over the line of scrimmage.
14. The character of Aunt Polly in *Tom Sawyer* was modeled after Mark Twain's mother. A gentle woman.
15. Bamboo is not a tree, it is a wood grass.
16. The lungfish can live out of water. In a state of suspended animation for three years.
17. Wyoming was the first state. To allow women to vote.
18. The first Secretary of Health, Education and Welfare was Oveta Hobby. Who took office in 1953.
19. Seven men in 100 have some form of color blindness only 1 woman in 1,000 suffers from it.
20. Of all known forms of animal life ever to inhabit the earth. Only about 10 percent still exist today.

Application to Writing

After you finish writing anything—from a letter to a report—reread what you have written. Read your work aloud and look for sentence fragments and run-on sentences. If you find any, correct them.

EXERCISE 10   Editing for Sentence Errors
Rewrite the following paragraphs, correcting all sentence fragments and run-on sentences. Make sure that you correct the errors in a variety of ways. Otherwise, you will have all short, choppy sentences. Add capital letters and punctuation marks where needed.

Making Money

If you owned *Marvel Comics #1.* You would be a rich person. In 1939, it cost a dime today it is worth $15,000! Collecting comic books can pay off. In the future. No one knows exactly which comic books to save. There are, however, a few things. To look for when you're buying them. Buy the first issue of any comic book. And hold onto it. Origin issues are also valuable, they are the issues in which a character is born or comes into being. Cross-over issues can be big money-makers too. In a cross-over issue, one famous comic-book character joins up with another famous comic-book character this happened in *Superman #76*. When Batman visited Superman.

Do you have any old comic books? Lying around the house. You can find out how much they are worth by looking in a book it's called *The Comic Book Price Guide* by Robert Overstreet. It can be found in most public libraries.

CHAPTER REVIEW

Write the following sentences, correcting each sentence fragment or run-on sentence. Use capital letters and punctuation marks where needed.

1. I want Carl on my team he's a terrific pitcher.
2. We have three kinds of trees growing in our yard. Oak, maple, and spruce.
3. *Smith* is a very common name. Appearing in over 40 languages.
4. In 1946, there were 10,000 television sets in the United States, there were 12 million 5 years later.
5. Of all the ore dug in a diamond mine. Only 1 carat in every three tons proves to be a diamond.
6. Yesterday I mowed the lawn. And trimmed the hedges.
7. If the moon were placed on the surface of the United States. It would extend from California to Ohio.
8. The hardiest of all the world's insects is the mosquito, it can even survive at the North Pole.
9. Mom usually flies. Whenever she goes on business trips.
10. We must have loaned the snowblower I can't find it.
11. Alaska has a sand desert. Located in the northwestern part of the state.
12. Many presidents have attended Groton. A prep school in Massachusetts.
13. South American Indians introduced tapioca to the world it comes from the root of a poisonous plant.
14. A large tree had fallen. At the end of the road leading to the lake.

15. About 70 percent of the earth is covered with water only 1 percent of that water is drinkable.
16. Our galaxy has about 100 billion stars, it is estimated that there are a billion other galaxies.
17. Snorkeling is my favorite water sport, I enjoy sailing.
18. Dark clouds covered the sun. Concealing the eclipse.
19. There are more than 300 clubs in the United States. Devoted exclusively to model railroading.
20. There is absolutely no documented proof. That Betsy Ross designed the American flag.

MASTERY TEST

Number your paper 1 to 10. Then label each group of words *sentence, fragment,* or *run-on.*

1. Lucy Hobbs Taylor was the first woman dentist.
2. Stored in a huge box in the cellar.
3. Along the wall on the right side of the driveway.
4. Norman earned some money last week, he deposited it in the bank.
5. Before you storm angrily into the office.
6. An old bicycle with twisted handlebars and a broken seat.
7. Please water the plants and find the newspaper.
8. As a result of John's scream, I stepped back the car missed me by inches.
9. To find just the right shirt to wear with my slacks.
10. My sister tried to make a call the line was dead.

STANDARDIZED TEST ▬▬▬

GRAMMAR

Directions: Decide which description best fits each group of words. In the appropriate row on your answer sheet, fill in the circle containing the same letter as your answer.

SAMPLE   Walking toward the park on Wednesday.

    A fragment   **B** run-on   **C** sentence

ANSWER Ⓐ Ⓑ Ⓒ

1. A long sleek limousine with tinted windows.

   A fragment   **B** run-on   **C** sentence

2. The zoo is closed today.

   A fragment   **B** run-on   **C** sentence

3. Please row faster.

   A fragment   **B** run-on   **C** sentence

4. I received a postcard from Molly, she is in France.

   A fragment   **B** run-on   **C** sentence

5. Because hungry caterpillars were crawling up the tree.

   A fragment   **B** run-on   **C** sentence

6. When the plane landed, the passengers cheered.

   A fragment   **B** run-on   **C** sentence

7. The camel knelt I climbed on clumsily.

   A fragment   **B** run-on   **C** sentence

8. Next to the violinist with the red hair and purple shirt.

   A fragment   **B** run-on   **C** sentence

9. Thick clouds appeared the world turned dark.

   A fragment   **B** run-on   **C** sentence

10. Still running hard, Ty was over the finish line he had won!

    A fragment   **B** run-on   **C** sentence

Directions: Decide which underlined part is the subject in each sentence. On your answer sheet, fill in the circle containing the same letter as your answer.

SAMPLE   The <u>painting</u> <u>showed</u> a family of <u>clowns</u>.
  A   B   C

ANSWER   Ⓐ Ⓑ Ⓒ

11. A <u>mysterious</u> <u>dot</u> appeared on the radar <u>screen</u>.
  A   B   C

12. A <u>bowl</u> of <u>fruit</u> sat on the <u>table</u> in the dining room.
  A   B   C

13. <u>Did</u> <u>you</u> notice the <u>helicopter</u> flying over the highway?
  A   B   C

14. <u>Here</u> comes the winning <u>Kentucky</u> <u>team</u>.
  A   B   C

15. <u>Across</u> the <u>grass</u> slithered a striped <u>snake</u>.
  A   B   C

Directions: Decide which underlined part is the verb in each sentence. On your answer sheet, fill in the circle containing the same letter as your answer.

SAMPLE   The <u>surgeon</u> <u>scrubbed</u> her hands <u>vigorously</u>.
  A   B   C

ANSWER   Ⓐ Ⓑ Ⓒ

16. The crowd <u>cheered</u> the <u>pitcher</u> and the <u>catcher</u>.
  A   B   C

17. My cousin <u>Henry</u> <u>plays</u> the trumpet <u>loudly</u>.
  A   B   C

18. You <u>never</u> <u>will see</u> a sunrise <u>in the west</u>.
  A   B   C

19. <u>Over</u> the door <u>hung</u> a bronze <u>eagle</u>.
  A   B   C

20. <u>Who</u> <u>was nominated</u> <u>for president</u> of the drama club?
  A   B   C

180

Unit 2

Usage

12

Using Verbs

Number your paper 1 to 10. Then write the past or the past participle for each verb in parentheses.

EXAMPLE   Jamie (take) a large bite out of the apple.
 ANSWER   took

1. Have you ever (ride) in a helicopter?
2. The second baseman (throw) the ball over the shortstop's head.
3. My watch strap has (break) again.
4. Victor Mandino is the most unselfish person I have ever (know).
5. Yesterday my mother (bring) me breakfast in bed.
6. My sister's big yellow balloon hit a sharp twig and (burst).
7. Adam (do) a wonderful imitation of Mr. Martin.
8. I (see) a Broadway play when I visited New York City last month.
9. Have you ever (eat) Hungarian goulash?
10. I've (shrink) my socks in the dryer.

This chapter begins a unit on usage. In this unit you will learn how to use the various elements of grammar that you learned in the first five chapters of this book.

In this chapter you will look more closely at verbs. Because verbs have so many forms, people often make mistakes when they use them. Even though verbs can be the most informative words in the language, they can also be the most difficult words to master. This chapter will help you become more familiar with the various forms of the verbs you use each day. It also will show you how the tense of a verb is used to express time.

PRINCIPAL PARTS

Every verb has four basic forms. They are called *principal parts*.

12a   The **principal parts** of a verb are the *present*, the *present participle*, the *past*, and the *past participle.*

The principal parts of the verb *jog* are used in the following examples. Notice that the present participle and the past participle must have a helping verb when they are used as a verb.

PRESENT	I **jog** two miles every day.
PRESENT PARTICIPLE	I was **jogging** early today.
PAST	Today I **jogged** with Bert.
PAST PARTICIPLE	I have **jogged** every day for a year.

Regular Verbs

The past and the past participle of most verbs are formed by adding *-ed* or *-d* to the present. Such verbs are called *regular verbs*.

12b   A **regular verb** forms its past and past participle by adding *-ed* or *—d* to the present.

183

Following are the principal parts of the regular verbs *paint* and *stop*. Notice how the spelling changes when endings are added to the verb *stop*. If you are unsure of the spelling of a verb form, look it up in the dictionary.

PRESENT	PRESENT PARTICIPLE	PAST	PAST PARTICIPLE
paint	painting	painted	(have) painted
stop	stopping	stopped	(have) stopped

EXERCISE 1 Determining the Principal Parts of Regular Verbs

Make four columns on your paper. Label them *present, present participle, past,* and *past participle*. Then write the four principal parts of each of the following regular verbs.

1. ask	5. share	9. taste	13. check	17. call
2. use	6. climb	10. weigh	14. drop	18. talk
3. hop	7. wrap	11. shout	15. cook	19. shop
4. row	8. jump	12. stare	16. gaze	20. look

Irregular Verbs

Some verbs do not form their past and past participle by adding *-ed* or *-d* to the present. These verbs are called *irregular verbs*.

12c An **irregular verb** does not form its past and past participle by adding *-ed* or *-d* to the present.

The following irregular verbs have been divided into six groups according to the way they form their past and past participle.

NOTE: *Have* is not part of the past participle. It has been added, though, to help you remember that a past participle must have a helping verb when it is used as a verb.

184

Group 1

These irregular verbs have the same form for the present, the past, and the past participle.

PRESENT	PRESENT PARTICIPLE	PAST	PAST PARTICIPLE
burst	bursting	burst	(have) burst
cost	costing	cost	(have) cost
hit	hitting	hit	(have) hit
hurt	hurting	hurt	(have) hurt
let	letting	let	(have) let
put	putting	put	(have) put
set	setting	set	(have) set

Group 2

These irregular verbs have the same form for the past and the past participle.

PRESENT	PRESENT PARTICIPLE	PAST	PAST PARTICIPLE
bring	bringing	brought	(have) brought
buy	buying	bought	(have) bought
catch	catching	caught	(have) caught
feel	feeling	felt	(have) felt
find	finding	found	(have) found
get	getting	got	(have) got or gotten
hold	holding	held	(have) held
keep	keeping	kept	(have) kept
lay	laying	laid	(have) laid
lead	leading	led	(have) led
leave	leaving	left	(have) left
lose	losing	lost	(have) lost
make	making	made	(have) made
say	saying	said	(have) said
sell	selling	sold	(have) sold
send	sending	sent	(have) sent
sit	sitting	sat	(have) sat
teach	teaching	taught	(have) taught
tell	telling	told	(have) told
win	winning	won	(have) won

EXERCISE 2 Oral Practice

Read aloud all the forms of the irregular verbs in Groups 1 and 2 to help you remember them.

EXERCISE 3   Using the Correct Verb Form

Write the past or past participle of each verb in parentheses.
Then read each sentence aloud to check your answer.

EXAMPLE   Have they (build) their new garage yet?
 ANSWER   built

1. The left fielder has (hit) his second long, high fly.
2. Deirdre (win) first place in the marathon.
3. After you have (set) the table, call everyone to dinner.
4. Yesterday I (bring) my lunch from home.
5. I have never (find) my watch.
6. Amanda has (leave) her job at the supermarket.
7. The balloon floated into the sky and (burst).
8. My mother has (sell) her first painting.
9. Our coach (lead) the way to the tennis courts.
10. Ralph (keep) the card you sent him.
11. Lai Kim has already (bring) hot dogs and the potato salad.
12. He (sit) backstage during the entire performance.
13. She had (make) tacos for dinner.
14. My mother has (keep) a lock of my baby hair in her locket.
15. The speeding car (hit) the curb.
16. Four large crows had (sit) on the scarecrow's shoulders for 15 minutes.
17. The contractor (lay) the foundation of the house before the cold weather set in.
18. All the soap bubbles have (burst).
19. Has anyone ever (catch) the measles more than once?
20. Woodrow Wilson (teach) at Princeton University for 12 years.
21. Sharon hit the ball over the shortstop's head and (make) a base hit.
22. You should have (buy) a new pair of sneakers yesterday.
23. Thomas (send) a letter to the newspaper and complained about its poor sports coverage.
24. Lucía (get) the majority of the votes.
25. I have (lose) five pounds in the past month.

EXERCISE 4   Using the Correct Verb Form

Write the past or past participle of each verb in parentheses.
Then read each sentence aloud to check your answer.

1. Karen (say) she wants to pursue a career in music.
2. The lifeguard (tell) the swimmers about the strong undertow.
3. A picture was (keep) upside down in the museum for 47 days before anyone noticed.
4. A computer error has (cost) the company much money.
5. Yesterday I (feel) dizzy and chilled.
6. I have already (let) the cat out twice tonight.
7. I just (find) a shorter route to school.
8. What did you do when you (lose) your science book?
9. For one hour yesterday, the store (sell) video recorders at a 20 percent discount.
10. I wasn't (hurt) at all in the accident.
11. The cheerleaders have (teach) us the new cheers.
12. Jasper Wilkins had (lead) in the polls throughout the primaries.
13. Most of the audience (leave) the theater after the first act was over.
14. Have you (put) the lawnmower into the garage?
15. I (catch) a cold from my sister last week.
16. If Randy had made the last field goal, we would have (win) the game.
17. I haven't (buy) Tim's birthday present yet.
18. The crew of the capsized boat (hold) onto its side until help arrived.
19. She had always (say) that he was innocent.
20. The cooler temperatures these past two days have (feel) invigorating.
21. I should have (set) the table before dinner was ready.
22. He must have (get) a second opinion.
23. Have you (send) for the free sample of soap?
24. Our hens have (lay) a record number of eggs this year.
25. He (put) a dish of warm milk down in front of the hungry kitten.

Group 3

These irregular verbs form the past participle by adding *-n* to the past.

PRESENT	PRESENT PARTICIPLE	PAST	PAST PARTICIPLE
break	breaking	broke	(have) broken
choose	choosing	chose	(have) chosen
freeze	freezing	froze	(have) frozen
speak	speaking	spoke	(have) spoken
steal	stealing	stole	(have) stolen

Group 4

These irregular verbs form the past participle by adding *-n* to the present.

PRESENT	PRESENT PARTICIPLE	PAST	PAST PARTICIPLE
blow	blowing	blew	(have) blown
draw	drawing	drew	(have) drawn
drive	driving	drove	(have) driven
give	giving	gave	(have) given
grow	growing	grew	(have) grown
know	knowing	knew	(have) known
rise	rising	rose	(have) risen
see	seeing	saw	(have) seen
take	taking	took	(have) taken
throw	throwing	threw	(have) thrown

EXERCISE 5   Oral Practice
Read aloud all the forms of the irregular verbs in Groups 3 and 4.

EXERCISE 6   Using the Correct Verb Form
Write the past or past participle of each verb in parentheses. Then read each sentence aloud to check your answer.

1. The pond has finally (freeze) over.
2. The team just (choose) a mascot.
3. Pat (steal) three bases in the third inning.
4. My brother (drive) to Boston to see a friend.
5. Mr. Beck has (grow) his own strawberries.
6. The quarterback (throw) a 50-yard pass.

7. Lenore (know) the poem by heart.
8. I had never (speak) to such a large group before last night.
9. Luis might have (break) the record with that jump.
10. I have (know) him for many years.
11. Have you (see) the new exhibit at the museum?
12. Hannah has (take) the dog along with her to the store.
13. I (give) my brother my old bicycle.
14. The wind has (blow) the lawn chairs over.
15. The winner was (choose) last night.
16. The visiting head of state (speak) to a joint session of Congress.
17. Chris Johnson has (steal) more bases than any other player.
18. Before World War II, the United States had (give) the Philippines a guarantee of independence.
19. Yesterday in art class, we (see) slides of paintings by Picasso.
20. My cousin Amir (grow) three inches last year.
21. During the two-day storm, the strong winds (blow) continuously.
22. The center fielder had (throw) the ball to catch the runner at the plate.
23. If we had not (take) a wrong turn, we would have arrived on time.
24. Waiting on that windy corner, we nearly (freeze).
25. Has the committee (draw) up the bylaws yet?

EXERCISE 7   Using the Correct Verb Form

Write the past or past participle of each verb in parentheses. Then read each sentence aloud to check your answer.

1. Until last summer I had never (drive) my grandfather's tractor.
2. Mr. Foster has (grow) his own vegetables for five years.
3. I don't think Dad has ever (rise) later than 7:00 A.M.
4. Our clumsy puppy (break) two lamps already.
5. The cake (rise) above the sides of the pan.
6. He (draw) me a map to the fairgrounds.

7. The judges of the art contest haven't (choose) the winning picture yet.
8. I don't think the wind has ever (blow) harder than it did last night.
9. The McAllisters have always (give) their dog a present on its birthday.
10. Alani insisted she (see) the comet early this morning.
11. The high winds on Saturday (blow) down the sign in front of Raymond's Pharmacy.
12. Max (throw) the baseball over the pitcher's head and allowed two runners to score.
13. I wish I had (take) piano lessons when I was a child.
14. Until Monday's assembly I had never (speak) before a large audience.
15. Have you ever (drive) an outboard motorboat?
16. The lake has never (freeze) to a depth of four inches.
17. Lionel had (throw) the pass 40 yards down the field.
18. Otis has already (break) two school records in track.
19. Who (draw) that picture of Mr. Turner's barn?
20. Three months ago the sun (rise) much later.
21. How long have you (know) about her promotion?
22. Lloyd (speak) very persuasively at the meeting.
23. I have (grow) more confident using the computer.
24. My wallet hadn't been (steal) after all.
25. Who (choose) brown as the color for this room?

Group 5

These irregular verbs form the past and past participle by changing a vowel. The *i* in the present changes to *a* in the past and *u* in the past participle.

PRESENT	PRESENT PARTICIPLE	PAST	PAST PARTICIPLE
begin	beginning	began	(have) begun
drink	drinking	drank	(have) drunk
ring	ringing	rang	(have) rung
shrink	shrinking	shrank	(have) shrunk
sing	singing	sang	(have) sung
sink	sinking	sank	(have) sunk
swim	swimming	swam	(have) swum

Group 6

These irregular verbs form the past and past participle in other ways.

PRESENT	PRESENT PARTICIPLE	PAST	PAST PARTICIPLE
come	coming	came	(have) come
do	doing	did	(have) done
eat	eating	ate	(have) eaten
fall	falling	fell	(have) fallen
go	going	went	(have) gone
lie	lying	lay	(have) lain
ride	riding	rode	(have) ridden
run	running	ran	(have) run
tear	tearing	tore	(have) torn
wear	wearing	wore	(have) worn
write	writing	wrote	(have) written

EXERCISE 8   Oral Practice

Read aloud all the forms of the irregular verbs in Groups 5 and 6.

EXERCISE 9   Using the Correct Verb Form

Write the past or past participle of each verb in parentheses. Then read each sentence aloud to check your answer.

1. The circus finally (come) to town.
2. Sal has (do) the baking for the party.
3. Polly (drink) all the orange juice.
4. Last weekend I (run) errands for my mother.
5. My family has (go) to Disneyland twice.
6. Rehearsals for the play have not (begin) yet.
7. I have just (write) for a summer job at the camp.
8. Cal has (ride) the Ferris wheel three times already.
9. Juan (swim) to shore from the reef.
10. Martin (ride) his bicycle to school today.
11. My sweater has (shrink) two sizes!
12. Has the homeroom bell (ring) yet?
13. Tom (fall) off his skateboard.
14. Who (eat) all the strawberries?
15. I should have (do) my homework earlier.

16. My heart (sink) when I heard the winner's name.
17. Our puppy has just (tear) the Sunday paper to shreds.
18. Until 1875, no one had ever successfully (swim) the English Channel.
19. Tenors have almost always (sing) the heroes' roles in opera.
20. Davy Crockett (begin) in politics at the age of 35.
21. Have you ever (wear) those hiking boots before?
22. Michael (go) to the movies twice this weekend.
23. Two boats (sink) during the storm last night.
24. Their newspapers have (lie) on their doorstep for a week now.
25. By 1778, Ticonderoga had (fall) to the British.

EXERCISE 10   Using the Correct Verb Form

Write the past or past participle of each verb in parentheses. Then read each sentence aloud to check your answer.

1. After the storm the sailboat (lie) on its side four miles from its mooring.
2. The birds have (eat) all the suet we put out.
3. The chorus (sing) several songs by Gilbert and Sullivan.
4. Before his campaign for the presidency of the Student Council, Griffin had never (run) for office.
5. I would have (come) by earlier, but I had to work late.
6. Oh, no! I just (tear) a hole in my new coat.
7. What he (wear) to the dance was most inappropriate.
8. I (write) a description of Taylor Pond.
9. Church bells across the country (ring) when the hostages were released.
10. I have never (drink) goat's milk.
11. The images on the screen gradually (shrink).
12. Caesar's Roman troops first (come) to Britain in 55 B.C.
13. Have you ever (swim) to the island in the middle of the lake?
14. Before the formation of the Republican party, Lincoln (run) for office as a Whig.
15. Sharon has (ride) every horse at the Elmtree Stables.

16. By the time he was 20, Mozart had already (write) some of his greatest compositions.
17. After Mr. Abernathy launched his model boat, it promptly (sink).
18. The coach (do) his best to encourage the team.
19. Yesterday I (go) to school with one black shoe and one brown shoe!
20. We have (ring) every doorbell in the neighborhood during the paper drive.
21. The dollar had (lie) on the floor for several hours before anyone noticed it.
22. The play had already (begin) when we arrived.
23. Today the goats (eat) all the weeds in the field near my house.
24. According to the latest poll, Mayor Goldman's lead over her opponent has (shrink).
25. After Melba (sing), the audience gave her a standing ovation.

EXERCISE 11   Finding Principal Parts in a Dictionary
Look up each of the following irregular verbs in a dictionary. Then write the principal parts of each one.

1. swing	6. arise	11. bend	16. pay
2. strive	7. become	12. forget	17. mean
3. swear	8. weave	13. lend	18. creep
4. spin	9. build	14. meet	19. hold
5. shake	10. sleep	15. fight	20. sweep

EXERCISE 12   Time-out for Review
Number your paper 1 to 10. Then write the past or the past participle of each verb in parentheses. Then read each sentence aloud to check your answer.

Ice
Cream

1. In ancient Rome, Nero had snow (bring) from the nearby mountains.
2. With the snow he (make) the first frozen dessert.
3. He (experiment) with different mixtures of snow, honey, juices, and fruit.

4. No one in Europe, however, had (see) a frozen milk dessert before the thirteenth century.
5. Marco Polo (introduce) an early version of ice cream to Europe.
6. Improvements on this dessert (lead) to the creation of ice cream in the sixteenth century.
7. Ice cream, however, (remain) a treat for only the rich.
8. For years the great chefs had (keep) the secret of ice cream to themselves.
9. After a French café had (begin) serving ice cream, it (become) everyone's favorite.
10. Only a few Americans had (eat) ice cream before 1700.

VERB TENSE

All verbs express time, called the *tense* of a verb. The principal parts of a verb are used to form the six tenses: *present, past, future, present perfect, past perfect,* and *future perfect.* In the following examples, the six tenses of *run* are used to express action at different times.

PRESENT	I **run** a mile every day.
PAST	I **ran** a mile yesterday.
FUTURE	I **will run** a mile tomorrow.
PRESENT PERFECT	I **have run** a mile every day since June.
PAST PERFECT	I **had** not **run** much before that.
FUTURE PERFECT	I **will have run** almost 100 miles before the end of the year.

Conjugation of a Verb

One way to see or study all the tenses of a particular verb is to look at a conjugation of that verb. A *conjugation* is a list of all the singular and plural forms of a verb in its various tenses.

Regular verbs are conjugated like irregular verbs. The only variations result from the differences in the principal parts of the verbs themselves. Following is a conjugation of the irregular verb *ride*. The principal parts of *ride* are *ride, riding, rode,* and *ridden.*

NOTE: The present participle is used to conjugate only the progressive forms of a verb. They are covered on page 196.

Conjugation of *Ride*

Present

This tense expresses action that is going on now.

SINGULAR	PLURAL
I ride	we ride
you ride	you ride
he, she, it rides	they ride

Past

This tense expresses action that took place in the past.

SINGULAR	PLURAL
I rode	we rode
you rode	you rode
he, she, it rode	they rode

Future

This tense expresses action that will take place in the future. It is formed by adding *shall* or *will* to the present.

SINGULAR	PLURAL
I shall/will ride	we shall/will ride
you will ride	you will ride
he, she, it will ride	they will ride

Present Perfect

This tense expresses action that was completed at some indefinite time in the past or action that started in the past and is still going on. It is formed by adding *has* or *have* to the past participle.

SINGULAR	PLURAL
I have ridden	we have ridden
you have ridden	you have ridden
he, she, it has ridden	they have ridden

Past Perfect

This tense expresses action that took place before some other past action. It is formed by adding *had* to the past participle.

SINGULAR	PLURAL
I had ridden	we had ridden
you had ridden	you had ridden
he, she, it had ridden	they had ridden

Future Perfect

This tense expresses action that will be completed by some given time in the future. It is formed by adding *shall have* or *will have* to the past participle.

SINGULAR	PLURAL
I shall/will have ridden	we shall/will have ridden
you will have ridden	you will have ridden
he, she, it will have ridden	they will have ridden

EXERCISE 13   Conjugating a Verb

Using the conjugation of *ride* as a model, write the conjugation of the following verbs.

1. play, playing, played, played
2. know, knowing, knew, known

Progressive Forms.   Each of the six tenses that you have just studied has an additional form called the *progressive form*. It consists of a form of *be* plus the present participle of the verb. The progressive form is used to express continuing action. Following are the progressive forms of *ride*.

PRESENT PROGRESSIVE	am, is, are riding
PAST PROGRESSIVE	was, were riding
FUTURE PROGRESSIVE	shall/will be riding
PRESENT PERFECT PROGRESSIVE	has, have been riding
PAST PERFECT PROGRESSIVE	had been riding
FUTURE PERFECT PROGRESSIVE	shall/will have been riding

EXERCISE 14   Forming the Progressive

Using the model of *ride* above, write the progressive forms of the verbs *play* and *run*.

Conjugation of the Irregular Verb *Be*. Since the principal parts of the verb *be* are highly irregular, the conjugation of that verb is very different from other irregular verbs. The principal parts of *be* are *am, being, was,* and *been.*

Conjugation of *Be*

Present

SINGULAR	PLURAL
I am	we are
you are	you are
he, she, it is	they are

Past

SINGULAR	PLURAL
I was	we were
you were	you were
he, she, it was	they were

Future

SINGULAR	PLURAL
I shall/will be	we shall/will be
you will be	you will be
he, she, it will be	they will be

Present Perfect

SINGULAR	PLURAL
I have been	we have been
you have been	you have been
he, she, it has been	they have been

Past Perfect

SINGULAR	PLURAL
I had been	we had been
you had been	you had been
he, she, it had been	they had been

Future Perfect

SINGULAR	PLURAL
I shall/will have been	we shall/will have been
you will have been	you will have been
he, she, it will have been	they will have been

EXERCISE 15 Using Tenses of the Verb *Be*

For each blank, write the tense of the verb *be* that is indicated in parentheses.

EXAMPLE   Red always _____ (*present perfect*) my favorite color.

ANSWER   has been

1. The bat _____ (*present*) the only mammal that can fly.
2. Some cats who lived 40 million years ago _____ (*past*) 14 feet long.
3. April _____ (*present perfect*) a very rainy month.
4. Kent and Barbara _____ (*future*) our representatives at the conference.
5. No two snowflakes _____ (*present*) exactly alike.
6. Jeff _____ (*past perfect*) my friend before I met Brian.
7. Lady Jane Grey _____ (*past*) Queen of England for only nine days.
8. We _____ (*future perfect*) the only ones to see the election returns before Friday.
9. Lynn _____ (*future*) the captain of the field hockey team for another year.
10. Today _____ (*present perfect*) an unpredictable day!

EXERCISE 16 Time-out for Review

Number your paper 1 to 20. Then write the tense of each underlined verb.

EXAMPLE   I will be ready at six o'clock.

ANSWER   future

1. My brother borrowed Dad's car last night to go to the library.
2. We were eating an early breakfast when the telephone rang.
3. Earl and I have collected baseball cards for more than five years now.
4. Leon was here earlier and will be back from lunch in ten minutes.

5. Your birthday <u>will have passed</u> by the time you <u>receive</u> your present.
6. The pilot <u>told</u> us the plane <u>had landed</u> in Buffalo because of the fog.
7. You <u>will understand</u> my reasons for resigning if you <u>think</u> about them.
8. I <u>had been</u> sick with a head cold for two weeks before I <u>felt</u> better.
9. Harvey <u>had been working</u> at the garage.
10. I <u>will miss</u> dinner because the team <u>will be staying</u> for a meeting after practice.
11. By the time the ambulance <u>came</u>, the lifeguard <u>had revived</u> the swimmer.
12. Matt <u>was</u> my tennis partner in the last match.
13. We <u>have known</u> each other for three years.
14. Mom <u>saw</u> that John <u>had decorated</u> the living room.
15. I <u>took</u> your advice and <u>opened</u> a savings account at the local bank.
16. They <u>are</u> very cooperative and <u>will be</u> glad to help.
17. They <u>have been driving</u> all weekend.
18. Suddenly I <u>realized</u> that I <u>had left</u> the package on the subway.
19. You <u>have been</u> absent before, I <u>believe</u>.
20. By January they <u>will have been planning</u> the fair for one year.

Shifts in Tense

As you already know, the tense of a verb indicates when an action takes place. When you write, it is important to keep your tenses as consistent as possible. For example, if you are telling a story that took place in the past, use the past tenses of verbs. If you suddenly shift to the present, your reader might not understand the sequence of events.

12d Avoid shifting tenses when relating events that occur at the same time.

A shift in tense can occur incorrectly within a sentence or within related sentences.

INCORRECT   We **opened** ⌐past⌐ the closet door, and suddenly something **flies** ⌐present⌐ past us.

CORRECT   We **opened** ⌐past⌐ the closet door, and suddenly something **flew** ⌐past⌐ past us.

INCORRECT   When everyone **had finished**, ⌐past perfect⌐ our teacher **collected** ⌐past⌐ the tests. Then she **dismisses** ⌐present⌐ the class.

CORRECT   When everyone **had finished**, ⌐past perfect⌐ our teacher **collected** ⌐past⌐ the tests. Then she **dismissed** ⌐past⌐ the class.

EXERCISE 17 Correcting Shifts in Tense

Number your paper 1 to 10. If the sentence contains a shift in tense, write the second verb in the correct tense. If a sentence is correct, write *C* after the number.

EXAMPLE   After Doreen spent the day at the beach, she suffers from a terrible sunburn.

ANSWER   suffers — suffered

1. The boat slows down before it stopped at the dock.
2. Chris walked bravely to the front of the room and faces his classmates.
3. The kitten stalked into the room and pounces on the rubber mouse.
4. After I had begun to mow the lawn, the rain starts.
5. The sight-seeing boat leaves at noon and returned at three o'clock.
6. The halfback lost his balance but hung onto the ball.
7. Huge jets always pass over our house and headed west.

8. When Cider ran away, Ken searches everywhere.
9. I had played the video game before I order it.
10. After I had seen the movie, I told everyone about it.

EXERCISE 18 Correcting Shifts in Tense
Rewrite the following paragraph, correcting any shifts in tense. Then underline each verb you changed.

The
Early
Days

Modern baseball was once named town ball. It first become popular in the United States in the 1830s. Wooden stakes are the bases, and the playing field is square. A pitcher is called a feeder, and a batter was called a striker. After a batter hits the ball, he runs clockwise. After a fielder catches the ball, he tried to get a runner out by hitting him with the ball. In the early days of baseball, balls are soft and are made by winding yarn around a piece of rubber.

ACTIVE AND PASSIVE VOICE

In addition to tense, a verb has *active voice* or *passive voice.*

12e ▶ The **active voice** indicates that the subject is performing the action.

12f ▶ The **passive voice** indicates that the action of the verb is being performed upon the subject.

In the following examples, the same verb is in the active voice in one sentence and in the passive voice in the other. The verb in the active voice has a direct object. The verb in the passive voice does not have a direct object.

ACTIVE VOICE   Everyone **enjoyed** the concert. [*Concert* is the direct object.]

PASSIVE VOICE   The concert **was enjoyed** by everyone. [There is no direct object.]

EXERCISE 19   Recognizing Active and Passive Voice
Write the verb in each sentence. Then label it *active* or *passive*.

1. Ancient ruins have been discovered in our backyard.
2. The White House has 132 rooms.
3. Some businesses are guarded at night by watchdogs.
4. Jupiter's moons can be seen with good binoculars.
5. Dry the dishes with that towel.
6. The Gulf Stream warms the west coast of Europe.
7. The dog left a track of muddy footprints.
8. Jade can be shattered by a sharp blow.
9. Tonight I must write a report for science.
10. Computers were used to predict the monthly rainfall over the next five years.
11. Jim is always called J.J. by his family.
12. Did you plant those tulips yourself?
13. The lead part was played by Jayne.
14. My report on solar energy will be finished soon.
15. A terrible thunderstorm followed the rain.
16. Bart found two dimes under the cushions of the sofa.
17. The wedding vows were written by the couple.
18. Many deer chew the bark on our trees.
19. Joshua made a lamp for his mother.
20. The kitchen window was broken this afternoon.

Forming the Passive Voice

Only transitive verbs — verbs that take direct objects — can be used in the passive voice. When an active verb is changed to the passive, the direct object of the active verb becomes the subject of the passive verb. The subject of the active verb is then used in a prepositional phrase.

ACTIVE VOICE   Ned gave a wonderful **speech.**

PASSIVE VOICE   A wonderful **speech** was given by Ned.

A verb in the passive voice consists of a form of the verb *be* plus a past participle.

Old newspapers **were collected** by the club members.
Awards **will be presented** at dinner.

Use the active voice as much as possible. It adds more directness and forcefulness to your writing. However, you should use the passive voice when the doer of the action is unknown or unimportant. Use it also when you want to emphasize the receiver of the action.

Collies are still used as sheep dogs in Scotland. [The doer is unknown.]
The leaking faucet was repaired today by the plumber. [Emphasis is on the receiver.]

EXERCISE 20   Using the Active Voice
Number your paper 1 to 10. Then write each sentence, changing the passive voice to the active voice if appropriate. If any sentence is better in the passive voice, write *C* after the number.

1. Orchids are grown as a hobby by my science teacher.
2. Wild horses are still found in the Southwest.
3. His trip to Atlanta will never be forgotten by Dana.
4. More than 100 different types of dogs are bred in the United States.
5. A diary was kept by Admiral Byrd during his expedition to the South Pole.
6. North American white oaks have never been successfully transplanted to Europe.
7. A film about space travel will be shown by the science club.
8. Great interest in conservation has been shown lately by Americans.
9. Religious freedom was promised to the settlers by William Penn.
10. A sturdy bicycle rack was made for me by my uncle.

Application to Writing

Looking for errors in the use of verbs should always be a part of the editing you do when you finish writing.

EXERCISE 21 Editing for Verb Errors

Edit the following paragraph. Check for (1) incorrect verb forms, (2) shifts in tense, and (3) the inappropriate use of the passive voice. Then rewrite the paragraph to include your changes.

Mozart | Mozart's father play in a string quartet. One day the quartet had planned to practice at his home. When the second violinist didn't appear, Mozart takes his place. Even though he had never saw the music before, Mozart plays it perfectly. He was only five years old at the time! Three years later Mozart's first complete symphony was wrote by him. No one has ever doubted that Mozart is the greatest musical genius of his time.

CHAPTER REVIEW

A. Write the past or the past participle of each verb in parentheses.

1. Ten minutes after the downpour, the sun (come) out.
2. How long have you (know) about the party?
3. The sun (rise) at 5:36 A.M. yesterday.
4. Lake Erie has never (freeze) over completely.
5. My sister has (sing) twice on television.
6. Have you (write) your history report yet?
7. Who (do) the screenplay for that movie?
8. The telephone hasn't (ring) all day.
9. You should have (go) to the dance last night.
10. Have you ever (swim) out to the raft and back?

B. Number your paper 1 to 10. Then write the tense of each underlined verb.

1. I <u>am</u> <u>going</u> to the library.
2. Lenny <u>has</u> <u>seen</u> Sarah somewhere before.
3. On Monday Mrs. Saunders <u>will</u> <u>announce</u> the names of the new class officers.
4. Tim <u>was</u> enthusiastic about the project.
5. I <u>have</u> <u>been</u> <u>practicing</u> for my recital every night for a month.
6. Next year will be the third year he <u>will</u> <u>have</u> <u>played</u> for the soccer team.
7. Laura <u>discovered</u> that she <u>had</u> <u>left</u> the theater tickets at home.
8. Pilar <u>knows</u> that we <u>will</u> <u>be</u> <u>working</u> together on the dance committee.
9. Marie <u>has</u> <u>been</u> happy ever since she <u>won</u> the stereo in the contest.
10. Susan and Greg <u>were</u> <u>riding</u> the bus when they first <u>met</u> each other.

MASTERY TEST

Number your paper 1 to 10. Then write the past or the past participle of each verb in parentheses.

1. I (see) the figure-skating championships last year.
2. Our puppy has (grow) eight inches in two months.
3. Mandy (begin) her research paper for history.
4. We (go) to Mobile, Alabama, last August.
5. Dad (drive) our new car to San Francisco.
6. The police officer (give) us directions to the new stadium.
7. Cocker spaniels have (fall) from first place as the favorite breed in the United States.
8. Juan (write) invitations to his party last night.
9. Steve (run) the bases for a home run.
10. The mail carrier (ring) the bell impatiently.

13

Using Pronouns

Number your paper 1 to 10. Then write the correct form of the pronoun in parentheses.

EXAMPLE   Anna and (I, me) decided to have a tag sale.
ANSWER   I

1. Jonah asked Andy and (she, her) to bring suntan lotion and beach towels.
2. (We, Us) science lovers also like science fiction.
3. To (who, whom) did you give the award?
4. The coach gave Nels and (they, them) some help.
5. Do you know if (them, their) skiing has improved since last winter?
6. Sally and (he, him) will be our debaters.
7. Carl divided the duties between Aaron and (he, him).
8. The finalists in the diving competition were Alani and (she, her).
9. I think Bert is a better batter than (he, him).
10. Peter is the only person (who, whom) was absent from choir practice.

If you spoke German, you would know that the word for *children* changes its form, depending upon how it is used in a sentence. You would say *kinder* if *children* was the subject, but *kindern* if *children* was the indirect object. This happens because all nouns and pronouns have *case*.

13a ▶ **Case** is the form of a noun or a pronoun that indicates its use in a sentence.

THE CASES OF PERSONAL PRONOUNS

There are three cases in English: the *nominative case,* the *objective case,* and the *possessive case.* Unlike nouns in German, nouns in English change form only in the possessive case. For example, *Mary* is the nominative form and is used as a subject. *Mary* is also the objective form and is used as an object. *Mary's,* though, is the possessive form and is used to show that Mary has or owns something. However, pronouns usually change form for each of the three cases.

Nominative Case

(Used for subjects and predicate nominatives)

SINGULAR   I, you, he, she, it
PLURAL   we, you, they

Objective Case

(Used for direct objects, indirect objects, and objects of a preposition)

SINGULAR   me, you, him, her, it
PLURAL   us, you, them

Possessive Case

(Used to show ownership or possession)

SINGULAR   my, mine, your, yours, his, her, hers, its
PLURAL   our, ours, your, yours, their, theirs

EXERCISE 1 Determining Case

Number your paper 1 to 10. Write the pronouns in each sentence. Then write the case of each one: *nominative, objective,* or *possessive.*

1. Why wasn't he invited to your party?
2. I hope Sally left me some paper.
3. Mother will pick us up at the airport.
4. Did my brother go with them to the game?
5. We don't know whether the record is his or hers.
6. They often speak of their love of horses.
7. Our dog likes to be at your house rather than ours.
8. You should speak to him about a job.
9. She knew that the lost watch was mine.
10. Are the cassettes yours or theirs?

The Nominative Case

The personal pronouns in the nominative case are *I, you, he, she, it, we,* and *they.*

13b ▶ The **nominative case** is used for subjects and predicate nominatives.

Remember that a predicate nominative is a word that follows a linking verb and identifies or renames the subject. *(See page 43 for a list of linking verbs.)*

SUBJECTS **She** and **I** are applying for the job.
If **they** are late, **he** will go alone.

PREDICATE NOMINATIVES The highest scorer on the team was **he.**
That was **she** with Tony last night.

In everyday conversation, people do not always use the nominative case for predicate nominatives. It is common to hear someone say, "It's *me*" instead of "It is *I,*" or "That's *him*" instead of "That is *he.*" As common as this usage is in conversation, it should be avoided when you write.

A pronoun that is used as a subject or a predicate nominative can have a noun appositive. An *appositive* is a word that comes right after the pronoun and identifies or renames it. The appositive in the following sentence is underlined.

We members must work very hard on the drive.

An appositive, however, will never affect the case of a pronoun. In fact, you can check to see if you have used the correct pronoun by dropping the appositive.

We must work very hard on the drive.

EXERCISE 2   Supplying Pronouns in the Nominative Case
Complete each sentence by writing an appropriate pronoun in the nominative case. (Do not use *you* or *it*.) Then write how the pronoun is used — *subject* or *predicate nominative*.

EXAMPLE   Did _____ do well on the test?
POSSIBLE ANSWER   I — subject

1. Don't make a decision until _____ give their side of the story.
2. The only ones voting will be _____ students.
3. The person who answered the ad was _____.
4. _____ had to wait at the airport for an hour.
5. The two most popular performers are _____.
6. Neither my mother nor _____ can attend the next meeting.
7. No one remembers what _____ did next.
8. If _____ are patient, a solution will be found.
9. The project leader will be _____.
10. _____ reporters must remain objective.

Compound Subjects and Predicate Nominatives.   Choosing the right case for a single subject or a predicate nominative does not usually present any problem. Errors occur more frequently, however, when the subject or predicate nominative is compound. For compound subjects there is a test that will help you check your answer.

Brenda and (I, me) are cooking dinner tonight.

To find the correct answer, say each choice separately.

I am cooking dinner tonight.
Me is cooking dinner tonight.

The nominative case *I* is the correct form to use.

Brenda and **I** are cooking dinner tonight.

Also use this test if both parts of a compound subject are pronouns.

EXERCISE 3 Oral Drill
Read each of the following sentences aloud.

1. He and I have parts in the school musical.
2. The award winners were we reporters.
3. My best friends are she and Hank.
4. She and Jim have the same homeroom.
5. Are you and he going to the football game?
6. Frances and they volunteered their help.
7. Is that he on the palomino?
8. We swimmers have to practice every day.
9. In my opinion, the best performers were they.
10. The fastest runners on the team are she and I.

EXERCISE 4 Using Pronouns in the Nominative Case
Number your paper 1 to 10. Then write the correct form of the pronoun in parentheses.

1. (She, Her) and Naomi will be the hostesses at the open house.
2. The leads in the play were Pepe and (he, him).
3. (They, Them) and the Wallaces have gone to the rodeo.
4. (She, Her) and (I, me) were born on a farm.
5. Is that (he, him) or Tony on the pitcher's mound?

6. Neither the Andersons nor (we, us) can attend the meeting.
7. Was that (she, her) or Janice with Alison?
8. The announcer will be either (he, him) or (I, me).
9. The audience and (we, us) reviewers enjoyed the play.
10. (They, Them) and their old friends met for a reunion.

EXERCISE 5 Writing Sentences

Write two sentences for each of the following groups of words. In the first sentence, use the words as subjects. In the second sentence, use them as predicate nominatives.

1. Jeff and I
2. Nancy and they
3. he and she
4. we or they
5. we winners

The Objective Case

The personal pronouns in the objective case are *me, you, him, her, it, us,* and *them.*

The **objective case** is used for direct objects, indirect objects, and objects of a preposition.

A direct object answers the question *What?* or *Whom?* after a verb. An indirect object answers the questions *To* or *for whom?* or *To* or *for what?* A sentence cannot have an indirect object unless it has a direct object. The object of a preposition is always part of a prepositional phrase.

DIRECT OBJECTS	Lana will join **us** after the game.
	Mom took **him** to the dentist.
INDIRECT OBJECTS	Mr. Kent showed **me** the new lab equipment.
	Please give **her** some sweet potatoes.
OBJECTS OF PREPOSITIONS	This agreement is between Pat and **me.**
	People like **him** are handy to have around.

Pronouns in the objective case can also have appositives.

Today's practice really helped **us** violinists.

EXERCISE 6 Supplying Pronouns in the Objective Case
Complete each sentence by writing an appropriate pronoun in the objective case. (Do not use *you* or *it*.) Then write how the pronoun is used — *direct object, indirect object,* or *object of a preposition*. Read each sentence aloud to check your answer.

1. Mrs. Martinson gave _____ good advice.
2. The award came as a big surprise to _____.
3. Uncle Fred drove _____ to the movies.
4. Please take _____ with you.
5. Did you send _____ a birthday card?
6. Mr. White gave _____ our marks.
7. The class elected _____ unanimously.
8. I want to talk to _____ after school.
9. Dad gave _____ a lesson on changing a tire.
10. Have you called _____ yet?
11. There is disagreement about the date of the dance among _____ students.
12. For getting things done, there's no one like _____.
13. The waitress brought _____ a big piece of honeydew.
14. Meet _____ in the library after school.
15. Tell _____ curious friends about your trip.
16. To their surprise, Cora invited _____ to the party.
17. Jaime will spend a week with _____ at the lake.
18. My parents bought _____ a watch for my birthday.
19. Will you send _____ a postcard during your vacation in Germany?
20. Do you expect a telephone call from _____ in the next few hours?

Compound Objects. If an object is compound, use the same test you used for compound subjects. Say each pronoun separately.

Isn't Marta going with Greg and (I, me)?
Isn't Marta going with **I?**
Isn't Marta going with **me?**

The objective form *me* is the correct form to use.

EXERCISE 7   Oral Drill
Read each of the following sentences aloud.

1. I want to be like her someday.
2. The prize money was divided among us winners.
3. Did you receive any postcards from Sam and him?
4. Give Ed and her another helping of roast beef.
5. The club elected me and them to the executive board.
6. This is strictly between you and me.
7. Kevin built a fire for us.
8. Mr. Mosley gave us students good advice about part-time jobs.
9. Tell Dad and me your side of the story.
10. Aunt Kate told them about her trip to California.

EXERCISE 8   Using Pronouns in the Objective Case
Number your paper 1 to 20. Then write the correct form of the pronoun in parentheses. Read each sentence aloud to check your answer.

1. A package just arrived for my brother and (I, me).
2. The mayor praised the police and (we, us) scouts.
3. Who is sitting between Derek and (he, him)?
4. Bring Sam and (she, her) a glass of milk.
5. The lifeguard warned (I, me) and (he, him) of the strong undertow.
6. Greta sent Peg and (she, her) pictures from Texas.
7. The principal assigned (he, him) and (she, her) the same homeroom.
8. Mrs. Grey took the twins and (they, them) to the circus.
9. Athletes like you and (I, me) need to exercise regularly.
10. Gloria's parents invited the coaches and (we, us) team members to their house after the game.
11. Mr. Ames sent Paula and (he, him) to talk with the vocational counselor.
12. My parents planned a barbecue for (I, me) and my friends.
13. Arnie shouted at Wayne and (we, us) from the other side of the pool.

14. Nearsighted people like you and (I, me) probably need glasses.
15. I'll send Otis and (she, her) a letter this weekend about my graduation.
16. Seat Mike and (he, him) beside their parents.
17. For help when you really need it, there is no one like Gwen or (he, him).
18. The bill should be divided between (they, them) and (we, us).
19. Give Lian and (I, me) the tickets to the play.
20. Follow (she, her) and (I, me) to Pat's house.

EXERCISE 9 Writing Sentences
Write five sentences that follow the directions below.

1. Use *him* and *me* as a compound direct object.
2. Use *the Smiths* and *them* as a compound indirect object.
3. Use *Grandmother, Grandfather,* and *me* as a compound object of a preposition.
4. Use *us students* as a direct object with an appositive.
5. Use *you* and *us* as a compound object of a preposition.

The Possessive Case

The personal pronouns in the possessive case are *my, mine, your, yours, his, her, hers, its, our, ours, their,* and *theirs.*

13d	The **possessive case** is used to show ownership or possession.

Some possessive pronouns can be used to show possession before a noun or before a gerund. Others can be used by themselves.

BEFORE A NOUN Pat shared **her** dessert with Laura.
BEFORE A GERUND Jerry takes **his** writing seriously.
BY THEMSELVES This pencil could be **mine.**

Personal possessive pronouns do not take an apostrophe. Sometimes an apostrophe is incorrectly used because possessive nouns are written with an apostrophe.

POSSESSIVE NOUN   **Rob's** bike is in the garage.
POSSESSIVE PRONOUN   The bike is **hers.** [not *her's*]

Also, do not confuse a contraction with a possessive pronoun. *Its, your,* and *their* are possessive pronouns. *It's, you're,* and *they're* are contractions.

POSSESSIVE PRONOUN   The cat drank all **its** milk.
CONTRACTION   **It's** [it is] time to go.

EXERCISE 10   Using Pronouns in the Possessive Case
Write the correct word in parentheses.

1. Are (their, they're) shoes dry yet?
2. (Your, You're) report is due tomorrow.
3. The box of old baseball cards is (hers, her's).
4. (Me, My) exercising has slimmed my waist.
5. Has Lisa borrowed (your, you're) notebook?
6. I think the radio is (hers, her's).
7. Was the cat interested in (it's, its) new toy?
8. We thought that car was (ours, our's).
9. Do you know whether these are (their, they're) coats?
10. Dad spoke about (me, my) spending more time on homework assignments.

EXERCISE 11   Using Pronouns in All Cases
Number your paper 1 to 10. Then write the correct form of the pronoun in parentheses. Read each sentence aloud to check your answers.

1. Harry and (I, me) showed Pearl and (she, her) Daniel Webster's birthplace.
2. (He, Him) and Steve led (we, us) deeper into the cave.
3. For (their, them) anniversary (we, us) took Howard and (she, her) out to dinner.

4. Was that (he, him) with Lola and (she, her)?
5. Between you and (I, me), (they, them) will never make the track team.
6. If (we, us) try out for the football team, will you go with (we, us)?
7. (She, Her) blamed (we, us) ballplayers for the ruined hedges.
8. (They, Them) played tennis with Carlos and (I, me).
9. (She, Her) brought Grace and (he, him) sweaters from Ireland.
10. Did (he, him) mention (my, me) working after school with (they, them)?

EXERCISE 12   Supplying Pronouns in All Cases

Number your paper 1 to 10. Then complete each sentence by writing appropriate pronouns. (Do not use *you* or *it*.)

1. Tell _____ and _____ the story.
2. _____ sat with _____ and Joe.
3. _____ watched the bird build _____ nest.
4. _____ sent for Meg and _____.
5. Pat showed _____ and _____ the poster.
6. _____ was skating with Carl and _____.
7. _____ went camping with _____.
8. _____ invited Rose and _____ to go with _____.
9. The Taylors took _____ dog with _____.
10. Did _____ take _____ to the movies?

EXERCISE 13   Time-out for Review

Number your paper 1 to 20. Find and write each pronoun that is in the wrong case. Then write each one correctly. If a sentence is correct, write *C* after the number. Read each sentence aloud to check your answer.

EXAMPLE   Mr. Dale blamed we boys for the broken window.
ANSWER   we — us

1. Without you and he, the party would have been boring.
2. My grandfather told Judy and I amusing stories about his childhood in Rome.

3. Last summer we campers went on a four-day backpacking trip.
4. You and me have been invited to the surprise party for Christine.
5. Divide the rest of the melon between you and him.
6. Maureen invited we three to dinner.
7. The welcoming committee was formed by Ryan and her last year.
8. Ellen and me are planning a trip to Wyoming.
9. Mr. Trapani took Joe and I to a soccer game.
10. Are those tennis shoes yours?
11. Divide the assignments among Kate, you, and her.
12. The instructor gave we divers some good tips.
13. Last summer he and I climbed Mount Hood.
14. With Jed and he for guides, we arrived earlier than planned.
15. Toby and me biked out to Farmington yesterday.
16. Between you and I, we can't fail.
17. Ms. Leonard sent him and I along with them.
18. Is that him with your parents?
19. Aunt Fran always sends them and us taffy from Atlantic City.
20. Last Wednesday him and I explored Robert Lewis's old barn.

EXERCISE 14 Writing Sentences

Write ten sentences that use the following expressions correctly. Then write the case of the pronouns you use.

EXAMPLE her and Joel
POSSIBLE ANSWER Give the *TV Guide* to her and Joel. — objective

1. Corey and I
2. us students
3. him and me
4. she and Jan
5. Don and he
6. you and me
7. we players
8. Mom, Dad, and I
9. she and I
10. Alex or her

PRONOUN PROBLEMS

Pronoun choice can be a problem. Should you say, "Who is calling?" or "Whom is calling?" Should you say, "Is Jim taller than I?" or "Is Jim taller than me?"

Who or Whom

Who is a pronoun that changes its form depending on how it is used in a sentence.

NOMINATIVE CASE   who, whoever
OBJECTIVE CASE   whom, whomever
POSSESSIVE CASE   whose

Who and its related pronouns are used in questions and in subordinate clauses.

13e ▸ The correct case of *who* is determined by how the pronoun is used in a question or a clause.

In Questions. Forms of *who* are often used in questions. The form you choose depends upon how the pronoun is used.

NOMINATIVE CASE   **Who** is coming to the party? [subject]
OBJECTIVE CASE   **Whom** did you call? [direct object]
  To **whom** is the letter addressed? [object of the preposition *to*]

When deciding which form to use, turn a question around to its natural order.

QUESTION   **Whom** did you ask?
NATURAL ORDER   You did ask **whom.**

EXERCISE 15   Using Forms of *Who* in Questions
Write the correct form of the pronoun in parentheses. Then using the following abbreviations, write how each pronoun is used in the question.

subject = *subj.*   object of the preposition = *o.p.*
direct object = *d.o.*

1. (Who, Whom) is on the phone?
2. (Who, Whom) did you meet on the way to school this morning?
3. With (who, whom) did Lee eat lunch?
4. (Who, Whom) will address the students at the computer workshop?
5. From (who, whom) did you get my name?
6. (Who, Whom) sent that package to you?
7. (Who, Whom) will you choose for your partner for the mountain hike?
8. (Who, Whom) is your best friend?
9. (Who, Whom) has the lead in the play?
10. With (who, whom) did you go to the dance?

In Clauses. Forms of *who* can be used in both adjective clauses and noun clauses. The form you use depends upon how the pronoun is used within the clause—not by any word outside the clause. The following examples show how *who* and *whom* are used in adjective clauses.

NOMINATIVE CASE She is the doctor **who spoke at the assembly.** [*Who* is the subject of *spoke*.]

OBJECTIVE CASE Mr. Rowland is the man **whom I met yesterday.** [I met whom yesterday. *Whom* is the direct object of *met*.]

Have you met Mr. Keats **from whom I take piano lessons?** [I take piano lessons from whom. *Whom* is the object of the preposition *from*.]

The following examples show how forms of *who* are used in noun clauses.

NOMINATIVE CASE Our dog will obey **whoever will feed it.** [*Whoever* is the subject of *will feed*.]

Do you know **who the winners are?** [The winners are who. *Who* is a predicate nominative.]

219

OBJECTIVE CASE	Invite **whomever Betsy wants.** [Betsy wants whomever. *Whomever* is the direct object of *wants.*]
	I don't know **to whom I should address the envelope.** [*Whom* is the object of the preposition *to.*]

EXERCISE 16   Using Forms of *Who* in Clauses

Number your paper 1 to 15. Write the correct form of the pronoun in parentheses. Then, using the following abbreviations, write how each pronoun is used in the clause.

subject = *subj.*   object of a preposition = *o.p.*
predicate nominative = *p.n.*   direct object = *d.o.*

1. Melba didn't know (who, whom) sent the flowers.
2. The club accepts (whoever, whomever) wants to join.
3. Sam couldn't tell to (who, whom) she was referring.
4. (Whoever, Whomever) answers the phone should take messages.
5. Did Gene know (who, whom) the judge was?
6. The person (who, whom) they select will get a free screen test.
7. (Whoever, Whomever) is the sixth caller wins $100.
8. No one questioned (who, whom) made that decision.
9. Everyone admires the person (who, whom) you are.
10. This is Willie Foster to (who, whom) all the credit must be given.
11. The parade was led by two drum majors (who, whom) were dressed in white and gold.
12. Glenn Carlson, (who, whom) is the team's best runner, sprained his ankle.
13. Two men, one of (who, whom) dove into the icy water, are responsible for saving the boy's life.
14. Take (whoever, whomever) you need to get the job done.
15. I spoke with the people from (who, whom) I had received the invitation.

220

EXERCISE 17 Time-out for Review

Write the correct form of the pronoun in parentheses. Then, using the following abbreviations, write how each pronoun is used in the question or the clause.

subject = *subj.*   object of a preposition = *o.p.*
predicate nominative = *p.n.*   direct object = *d.o.*

1. (Whoever, Whomever) is best qualified will get the job.
2. Did the police find out (who, whom) the burglars are?
3. They (who, whom) need advice most like it least.
4. The person from (who, whom) you'll get all the answers is Mrs. Chin.
5. (Who, Whom) called me last night?
6. Isn't Ray the one (who, whom) you recommend?
7. Send (whoever, whomever) answers the ad a brochure.
8. (Who, Whom) did you meet at the conference?
9. I'd like to know for (who, whom) you're substituting.
10. Is he the child (who, whom) you found?

Elliptical Clauses

Over the years writers have introduced shortcuts into our language. One such shortcut is an *elliptical clause*. This is a subordinate clause in which words are omitted but are understood to be there. Elliptical clauses begin with *than* or *as*.

Peter takes more courses **than I.**
Wade weighs as much **as I.**

13f ▶ In an elliptical clause, use the form of the pronoun you would use if the clause was completed.

In the following examples, both of the expressions in heavy type are elliptical clauses. They are also both correct because they have two different meanings.

Nancy is with us more **than he.**
Nancy is with us more **than him.**

He is correct in the first example because it is used as the subject of the elliptical clause.

Nancy is with us more **than *he* is with us.**

Him is correct in the second example because it is used as an object of a preposition.

Nancy is with us more **than she is with *him*.**

Because the meaning of a sentence with an elliptical clause sometimes depends upon the case of a pronoun, you must be careful to choose the correct case. One way to do this is to complete the elliptical clause mentally. Then choose the form of the pronoun that expresses the meaning you want.

Ted cares for her as much as (I, me).
Ted cares for her as much **as I care for her.**
Ted cares for her as much **as he cares for me.**

In the example above, decide which meaning you want. Then choose either *I* or *me.*

EXERCISE 18 Using Pronouns in Elliptical Clauses
Write each sentence, completing the elliptical clause. Be sure to choose the pronoun that correctly completes each clause. Then underline the pronoun you chose.

EXAMPLE   Ronald is a better storyteller than (he, him).
ANSWER   Ronald is a better storyteller than <u>he</u> is.

1. Greg spends more time with them than (I, me).
2. Do you think I'm as tall as (he, him)?
3. Our teacher didn't review the test with us as much as (they, them).
4. Is Toby as old as (she, her)?
5. I studied longer than (he, him).
6. The tennis tournament was enjoyed more by them than (we, us).
7. Helmut lifts as many weights as (he, him).

8. I think Marvin is a better singer than (she, her).
9. Our cat means more to Shelby than (I, me).
10. Hayes likes hot weather as much as (they, them).

PRONOUNS AND THEIR ANTECEDENTS

In Chapter 2 you learned that a pronoun takes the place of a noun. That noun is called the pronoun's *antecedent*. In the following sentence, Ralph is the antecedent of *his*.

Ralph left **his** notebook in the band room.

There must be agreement between a pronoun and its antecedent in both number and gender.

13g A pronoun must agree in number and gender with its antecedent.

Number is the term used to indicate whether a noun or a pronoun is *singular* or *plural*. Singular indicates one, and plural indicates more than one. *Gender* is the term used to indicate whether a noun or a pronoun is *masculine, feminine,* or *neuter.*

Masculine	Feminine	Neuter
he, him, his	she, her, hers	it, its

NOTE: The pronouns *I, you,* and *they* do not show gender because they can be either masculine or feminine.

If the antecedent of a pronoun is one word, there usually is no problem with agreement.

Our **dog** likes **its** new house.

Kate just sang in **her** first concert.

If the antecedent of a pronoun is more than one word, there are two rules you should remember.

13h ▶ If two or more singular antecedents are joined by *or, nor, either/or,* or *neither/nor,* use a singular pronoun to refer to them.

These conjunctions indicate a choice. In the following example only *one* person should read a story. Maud should read her story, or Rosa should read her story.

Either **Maud** or **Rosa** should read **her** story.

13i ▶ If two or more singular antecedents are joined by *and* or *both/and,* use a plural pronoun to refer to them.

These conjunctions always indicate more than one. In the following example, Anthony and Martin — together — volunteered *their* help.

Both **Anthony** and **Martin** volunteered **their** help.

Sometimes you will not know whether an antecedent is masculine or feminine. Standard English solves this agreement problem by using *his* or *his or her* to refer to such vague antecedents.

Each **worker** will donate two hours of **his** time.

Each **worker** will donate two hours of **his** or **her** time.

You can avoid this problem completely if you rewrite such sentences, using the plural form.

All **workers** will donate two hours of **their** time.

EXERCISE 19   Making Pronouns and Antecedents Agree
Write the pronoun that correctly completes each sentence. Make sure that the pronoun agrees in both number and gender with its antecedent.

1. Either Bart or Joe left _____ lunch in the library.
2. All camera-club members should choose five of _____ best pictures for the exhibit.
3. Otis and Roy will give _____ speeches tomorrow.
4. Neither Ruth nor Virginia remembered _____ key.
5. Nathan took five suitcases with _____ to Florida.
6. All players were responsible for _____ own uniforms.
7. After the Brennans bought the house, _____ painted it blue.
8. Dad brought the groceries from the car and put _____ on the table.
9. A robin built _____ nest near the back porch.
10. Either Kate or Sue will play _____ own original composition at the recital.

Indefinite Pronouns as Antecedents

Sometimes an indefinite pronoun is the antecedent of a personal pronoun. Making the personal pronoun and the indefinite pronoun agree can be confusing because some singular indefinite pronouns suggest a plural meaning. Other indefinite pronouns can be either singular or plural.

The following lists break the common indefinite pronouns into three groups. A personal pronoun, for example, should be singular if its antecedent is one of the indefinite pronouns in the first group.

Singular Indefinite Pronouns			
anybody	either	neither	one
anyone	everybody	nobody	somebody
each	everyone	no one	someone

One of the girls left **her** purse on the table.

Neither of the men can loan you **his** car.

The gender of a singular indefinite pronoun sometimes is not indicated in a sentence. Standard English solves this problem by using *his* or *his or her*.

Everyone must bring **his** own tennis racket.

Everyone must bring **his** or **her** own tennis racket.

Plural Indefinite Pronouns

both   few   many   several

Few of my neighbors have **their** own garage.

Several of the tourists lost **their** way.

Singular or Plural Indefinite Pronouns

all   any   most   none   some

Agreement with one of these indefinite pronouns depends upon the number and the gender of the object of the preposition that follows it.

Some of the **crystal** has lost **its** shine.

Most of the **performers** played **their** own music.

EXERCISE 20 Making Personal Pronouns Agree with Indefinite Pronouns

Write the pronoun that correctly completes each sentence.

1. Each of the girls won _____ school letter.
2. All of the trees in our yard have lost _____ leaves.
3. No one on the girls' team likes _____ uniform.
4. Many of the citizens cast _____ votes early.
5. Some of the cheese has lost _____ flavor.

6. Neither of the girls received _____ driver's license.
7. Several of the employees bring _____ lunches.
8. Someone in the boys' choir had forgotten _____ part.
9. One of the bridesmaids lost _____ bouquet.
10. Both of the twins jog on the path near _____ home.

Application to Writing

   When you edit your writing, check each pronoun to be sure it is in the proper case and has the correct number and gender. In addition, check for pronoun shifts and missing antecedents. For example, did you shift to the pronoun *you* when you should have used another pronoun to agree with its antecedent? Is the antecedent of a pronoun missing or confusing?

PRONOUN SHIFT	Tim applied for the job but was told that **you** should wait a week.
CORRECT	Tim applied for the job but was told that **he** should wait a week.
MISSING ANTECEDENT	We tried to call Joanne, but **it** was busy.
CORRECT	We tried to call Joanne, but **the line** was busy.
VAGUE ANTECEDENT	Ellen filed the letter in the briefcase, but she can't find **it.**
CORRECT	Ellen can't find **the letter** that she filed in the briefcase.
CORRECT	Ellen can't find **the briefcase** in which she put the letter.

EXERCISE 21   Editing Pronoun Errors
Rewrite each sentence to make its meaning clear.

1. When the teacher gives you the reading assignment, open it at once to the right page.
2. All people can learn to swim if you try hard enough.

3. Remove the bandage from your arm and throw it away.
4. Almost everyone likes to read if it is interesting.
5. Ants attacked the sandwiches before we could eat them.
6. I like sailing because you get plenty of sun.
7. Although I never make a goal, I like it anyway.
8. The next time the children come home with wet sweaters, don't hang them up by their necks.
9. Al and his brother like to jog, but you get really tired.
10. Henry took the rugs off the floors and cleaned them.

CHAPTER REVIEW

A. Write the correct form of the pronoun in parentheses.

1. Neither Dina nor Candy has had (her, their) turn at bat.
2. Will someone lend me (his, their) pen?
3. Please explain to (we, us) students how the computer works.
4. To (who, whom) should I send the invitations?
5. Do other students study as hard as (we, us)?
6. (They, Them) made a delicious dinner for us.
7. Sandra went to the movies with David and (I, me).
8. Both Raul and Ted forgot (his, their) skates.
9. Our debaters will be Hans and (he, him).
10. It was (she, her) who won the local marathon.
11. Jessica and (he, him) went to the game with us.
12. (Whoever, Whomever) picks the most apples will win a prize.
13. That was quick thinking for an inexperienced quarterback like (he, him).
14. There is no one who is as fast as (she, her) on the typewriter.
15. Between you and (I, me), we're never going to get there on time.
16. She is the only person (who, whom) arrived early.
17. (We, us) joggers need to pay special attention to the traffic lights.

18. I think that's (she, her) in the blue coat.
19. Yes, I think she dives as well as (I, me).
20. I think Mr. Pentose is someone (who, whom) we met in Florida last year.

B. Write the personal pronoun that correctly completes each sentence.

1. Either Tim or Morris will bring _____ guitar.
2. One of my brothers just received _____ diploma.
3. Both Heidi and Irene turned _____ reports in early.
4. The tire has lost most of _____ air.
5. All students will be assigned to _____ homerooms.
6. Several of my friends want to add mechanics to _____ schedules.
7. Both of the girls think that _____ will compete.
8. Anton or Elroy should drive _____ car to the fair.
9. After we painted the posters, we hung _____ in the halls.
10. Either Claire or Erica will have _____ camera.

MASTERY TEST

Number your paper 1 to 10. Then write the correct form of the pronoun in parentheses.

1. Please loan (we, us) would-be campers a tent.
2. Send an application to (whoever, whomever) calls.
3. Neither my mother nor (I, me) can ski.
4. It's between Marco and (she, her).
5. Travel is more important to Shirley than (I, me).
6. Mr. Hanson is the only teacher (who, whom) I visit after school.
7. The man in the tuxedo is (he, him).
8. Hard workers like you and (I, me) need to relax more.
9. (Who, Whom) is the best candidate?
10. Rick and (I, me) mow lawns for extra money.

14

Subject and Verb Agreement

DIAGNOSTIC TEST

Number your paper 1 to 10. Write the subject in each sentence. Then next to each one, write the form of the verb in parentheses that agrees with the subject.

EXAMPLE   Where (is, are) the bananas for breakfast?
ANSWER   bananas — are

1. (Was, Were) you at the class picnic on Saturday?
2. Carl (doesn't, don't) remember the combination.
3. Either the battery or the bulb in my flashlight (has, have) just failed.
4. There (is, are) only a few swimmers entered in the 100-meter race.
5. Two students from our school (was, were) sent to a press conference in Washington.
6. Brad, as well as Dee, (is, are) running for office.
7. (Does, Do) a warm day and a cool evening cause foggy weather?
8. In Vermont there (is, are) several big ski resorts.
9. Not one of the climbers (was, were) able to reach the summit.
10. A compass and a pocketknife (is, are) standard equipment for every hiker.

Language is very much like a jigsaw puzzle. You must put all the pieces of a jigsaw puzzle together correctly to end up with a completed picture. You must also fit all the parts of a sentence together correctly in order to communicate clearly. For example, some subjects and verbs fit together, while others may seem to, but don't. In English when a subject and a verb fit together, a sentence is said to have *agreement*. This chapter will show you how to make subjects and verbs agree so that your writing will communicate a complete, clear picture to your reader.

AGREEMENT OF SUBJECTS AND VERBS

One basic rule applies to this entire chapter.

14a A verb must agree with its subject in number.

Number

In the last chapter, you learned that *number* refers to whether a noun or a pronoun is singular or plural. *Singular* indicates one, and *plural* indicates more than one. In this chapter you will learn that verbs also have number, and the number of a verb must agree with the number of its subject.

Number of Nouns and Pronouns. In English the plural of most nouns is formed by adding *-s* or *-es* to the singular form. However, some nouns form their plural in other ways. You should always check a dictionary to see whether a noun has an irregular plural.

SINGULAR floor tax child
PLURAL floors taxes children

In the last chapter, you also learned that pronouns have singular and plural forms. For example, *I, he, she,* and *it* are singular, and *we* and *they* are plural. (*See page 207 for a list of these forms.*)

EXERCISE 1 Determining Number of Nouns and Pronouns

Write each word and label it *singular* or *plural*.

1. Jessica	6. hats	11. they	16. bike
2. everyone	7. mice	12. both	17. he
3. children	8. rakes	13. women	18. Dennis
4. several	9. anyone	14. cap	19. it
5. schools	10. lights	15. we	20. radio

Number of Verbs. The singular and plural forms of nouns and pronouns are fairly easy to recognize. You can easily see, for example, that *eagle* and *it* refer to only one, while *eagles* and *they* refer to more than one.

The number of verbs, however, is not so easy to recognize. The form of the verb is the only indication of its number. Most verbs form their singular and plural in exactly the opposite way nouns form their singular and plural. Most verbs in the present tense add *-s* or *-es* to form the singular. Plural forms of verbs in the present tense drop the *-s* or *-es*.

SINGULAR

The eagle { soars. swoops. flies. }

PLURAL

The eagles { soar. swoop. fly. }

NOTE: Most verbs have the same form for both the singular and the plural when they are used in the past tense.

SINGULAR   The eagle **soared.**
  PLURAL   The eagles **soared.**

The irregular verb *be* shows number differently from most verbs. The singular is not formed by adding *-s* or *-es*.

Forms of *Be*	
SINGULAR FORMS	am is was has been
PLURAL FORMS	are were have been

SINGULAR   The eagle **is** a majestic bird.
  PLURAL   Eagles **are** majestic birds.

NOTE: Review the conjugations of *ride* and *be* on pages 195 and 197. Notice how these verbs change form to indicate singular and plural.

EXERCISE 2 Determining Number of Verbs

Write each verb and label it *singular* or *plural*.

1. breaks	6. works	11. is	16. swim
2. freezes	7. was	12. tear	17. see
3. are	8. reads	13. look	18. speak
4. have been	9. am	14. sings	19. were
5. keep	10. has	15. walk	20. barks

Singular and Plural Subjects

Because a verb must agree in number with its subject, you must remember two rules.

14b   A singular subject takes a singular verb.

14c   A plural subject takes a plural verb.

To make a verb agree with its subject, ask yourself two questions: *What is the subject?* and *Is the subject singular or plural?* Then choose the correct verb form.

SINGULAR   A large shrub **grows** in the front yard.
  PLURAL   Large shrubs **grow** in the front yard.
SINGULAR   She **types** rapidly.
  PLURAL   They **type** rapidly.
SINGULAR   That light **is** very bright.
  PLURAL   Those lights **are** very bright.
SINGULAR   He **was** very talkative at the meeting.
  PLURAL   They **were** very talkative at the meeting.

The pronouns *you* and *I* are the only exceptions to these rules for agreement between subjects and verbs. The pronoun *you*, whether singular or plural, always takes a plural verb.

SINGULAR   You **sing** the solo.   You **are** the captain.
 PLURAL   You **sing** the duet.   You **are** the teammates.

The pronoun *I* also takes a plural verb — except when it is used with a form of *be*.

SINGULAR   I **am** the owner.   I **was** his assistant.
 PLURAL   I **like** that one.   I **have** the key.

EXERCISE 3   Making Subjects and Verbs Agree

Write the subject in each sentence. Then next to each one, write the form of the verb in parentheses that agrees with the subject. Read each sentence aloud to check your answer.

EXAMPLE   My history report (was, were) in my notebook.
 ANSWER   report — was

1. Butterflies (tastes, taste) with their hind feet.
2. My brother (knows, know) her address.
3. Sight (accounts, account) for 90 to 95 percent of all sensory perceptions.
4. I (takes, take) my lunch to school every day.
5. The bananas (seems, seem) ripe.
6. You (is, are) now the club's new president.
7. The hippopotamus (is, are) a close relative of the pig.
8. One 75-watt bulb (gives, give) more light than three 25-watt bulbs.
9. These chairs (needs, need) repairing.
10. I (was, were) busy at the time.
11. Normally, a whale's heart (beats, beat) only nine times per minute.
12. The right lung (takes, take) in more air than the left lung.
13. I (has, have) been here all the time.

14. Carrots (contains, contain) vitamin A.
15. Flamingos (is, are) not naturally pink.
16. You (walks, walk) too slow for me.
17. A cat's eyes (shines, shine) in the dark.
18. They (freezes, freeze) many of their own vegetables.
19. I (likes, like) spring more than autumn.
20. The Empire State Building (exceeds, exceed) the height of the Eiffel Tower by only 265.5 feet.
21. The human body (has, have) 45 miles of nerves.
22. You (appears, appear) tired today.
23. Houdini (was, were) the first man to fly an airplane solo in Australia.
24. The violinists (sits, sit) in the front of the orchestra.
25. I (am, are) responsible for the team's uniforms.

Agreement with Verb Phrases. If a sentence contains a verb phrase, make the first helping verb agree with the subject.

14d The helping verb must agree in number with the subject.

Ralph <u>was working</u> on the committee. [*Ralph* is singular, and *was* is singular.]

They <u>were working</u> on the committee. [*They* is plural, and *were* is plural.]

The following chart shows the singular and plural forms of common helping verbs.

Common Helping Verbs	
Singular	Plural
am, is, was, has, does	are, were, have, do

SINGULAR Lynn **is** making the dessert.
The actor **does** answer his mail.
PLURAL The biscuits **are** burned on the bottom.
Our library books **have** been returned.

EXERCISE 4   Making Subjects and Verb Phrases Agree
Write the subject in each sentence. Then next to each one, write the form of the verb in parentheses that agrees with the subject. Read each sentence aloud to check your answer.

1. They (has, have) finished their science projects.
2. Italian (is, are) spoken by both of Donato's grandparents at family gatherings.
3. You (was, were) really missed at the dance.
4. The magazine subscription (has, have) run out.
5. A hippopotamus (is, are) born underwater.
6. Oak trees (is, are) often struck by lightning.
7. Kevin (has, have) applied for a job at the bank.
8. The invitations (was, were) mailed on Monday.
9. I (was, were) just leaving when you called.
10. Goat's milk (is, are) used more widely throughout the world than cow's milk.
11. Those daisies (does, do) make a beautiful centerpiece.
12. Battleships (is, are) always named after states.
13. The menu (has, have) changed since last month.
14. Camels (was, were) used as pack animals in Nevada and Arizona as late as 1870.
15. The milk (does, do) taste sour to me.
16. The oboe (is, are) considered the most difficult of all woodwind instruments to play correctly.
17. Tammy (does, do) want to go to the movies with us.
18. Before 1941, fingerprints (was, were) not accepted as evidence in court.
19. The Kenmores (does, do) know the way to your home.
20. The best diamonds (is, are) colored blue-white.

Agreement and Interrupting Words.   If the subject is separated from the verb by a phrase or a clause, a mistake in agreement is easy to make. The reason for this is that the object of a preposition or some other word is closer to the verb than the subject. Agreement of the verb may then be incorrectly made with that word—rather than with the subject.

14e

> The agreement of a verb with its subject is not changed by any interrupting words.

In the following examples, notice how the subjects and the verbs agree in number—in spite of the words that come between them. Each subject is underlined once, and each verb is underlined twice.

A bouquet of roses was given to the prom queen. [*Was* agrees with the singular subject *bouquet.* The verb does not agree with *roses,* the object of the preposition— even though *roses* is closer to the verb.]

The engine together with the first three cars was derailed. [*Was* agrees with the subject *engine*—not with the object of the preposition *cars.*]

The paintings that hang in the museum are insured for millions of dollars. [*Are* agrees with the subject *paintings*—not with the object of the preposition *museum.*]

EXERCISE 5   Making Interrupted Subjects and Verbs Agree

Write the subject in each sentence. Then next to each one, write the form of the verb in parentheses that agrees with the subject.

1. The channel between the two islands (is, are) marked by buoys.
2. Every Sunday many people who live on Pine Street (organizes, organize) a baseball game.
3. Flags of France, Spain, and England (has, have) flown over areas of Mississippi.
4. The craters of the moon (is, are) visible through a low-powered telescope.
5. One of Sumi's sisters (goes, go) to Wheaton College.
6. The election of the Student Council officers (was, were) held last week.
7. A town in the Dutch West Indies (is, are) located in an extinct volcano.

237

8. Shape, as well as size, (helps, help) determine the value of a pearl.
9. Three people in our group (was, were) swimming in the ocean.
10. Ammonia, which is used in household cleaners, (is, are) poisonous.
11. One of the New England states (was, were) admitted to the Union in 1820.
12. That tree, including branches and leaves, (weighs, weigh) 100 tons.
13. The front tires of the car (was, were) worn smooth.
14. Until the 19th century, solid blocks of tea (was, were) used as money in Siberia.
15. A representative of several colleges (is, are) visiting our school.
16. Severe weather, including snowstorms, (has, have) never interrupted our mail delivery.
17. Many stories about Lassie (has, have) been written.
18. A total of 63 errors (was, were) made in the 1886 World Series.
19. The hands of the mole (is, are) very much like our own hands.
20. The manufacture of zippers and buttons (is, are) an important industry.

EXERCISE 6   Time-out for Review

Number your paper 1 to 20. Find and write the verbs that do not agree with their subjects. Then write them correctly. If a sentence is correct, write *C* after the number.

EXAMPLE   Two sheets of that color is enough.
ANSWER   is — are

1. My dog, Muscles, chase toads in the backyard.
2. You needs a new alarm clock.
3. The location of the volcanic islands are not marked on that map.
4. The roses in our garden smells very fragrant.

5. Each year many people, mostly fans of country music, go to Opryland in Nashville.
6. I were the only person there on time.
7. A new display of sports photographs have been hung on the gym bulletin board.
8. At one time helicopters was considered impossible.
9. The apples that are on the table is for a pie.
10. The runways at the airport is covered with ice.
11. You is perfect for the job.
12. Summer nights in Denver are usually cool.
13. A person who is dressed in bright colors look larger than a person in dark colors.
14. A group of lions is known as a *pride*.
15. Four rows of plants in the front is enough.
16. A good milking cow gives nearly 6,000 quarts of milk every year.
17. Four people on our team was late for practice.
18. Two important methods of preserving food is canning and freezing.
19. Earthworms in Australia reach a length of as much as ten feet.
20. The steps on the old porch are hazardous.

Compound Subjects

Agreement between a verb and a compound subject can sometimes be confusing. The following two rules will help you avoid errors of agreement.

14f When subjects are joined by *or, nor, either/or,* or *neither/nor,* the verb agrees with the closer subject.

This rule applies even when one subject is singular and the other subject is plural.

Either <u>brown</u> or <u>orange</u> <u>is</u> a good color for the poster. [The verb is singular because the subject closer to it is singular.]

<u>Winds</u> or rising <u>temperatures</u> <u>dispel</u> fog. [The verb is plural because the subject closer to it is plural.]

Neither my <u>brother</u> nor my <u>parents</u> <u>are</u> eating at home tonight. [The verb is plural because the subject closer to it is plural — even though the other subject, *brother*, is singular.]

The conjunctions *and* or *both/and* may also be used to form a compound subject. Because these conjunctions always indicate more than one, a plural verb is used.

14g ▶ When subjects are joined by *and* or *both/and*, the verb is plural.

With *and* or *both/and*, the verb should be plural — whether the subjects are singular, plural, or a combination of singular and plural.

Both the <u>desk</u> and the <u>chair</u> in Carol's room <u>are painted</u> yellow. [Two things — the *desk* and the *chair* — *are painted* yellow. The verb must be plural to agree.]

<u>Clara</u> and the other <u>cheerleaders</u> at school <u>have learned</u> a new cheer. [Even though one subject is singular, the verb is still plural because *Clara* and the *cheerleaders* — together — are more than one.]

There are two exceptions to the second rule. Sometimes two subjects that are joined by *and* refer to only one person or thing. Then a singular verb must be used.

The co-captain and quarterback **is** Bert Roberts. [one person]
Bread and butter **is** served with every meal. [one dish]

The other exception occurs when the word *every* or *each* comes before a compound subject whose parts are joined by *and*. Since each subject is being considered separately in these sentences, a singular verb is called for.

Every pot and pan **has** been packed already.
Each girl and boy **is** allowed to bring one guest.

240

EXERCISE 7 Making Verbs Agree with Compound Subjects

Write the correct form of the verb in parentheses.

1. The plans and arrangements for the picnic (has, have) not been finalized yet.
2. Either Jennie or her brothers (delivers, deliver) the Sunday newspapers.
3. Ham and cheese (is, are) my favorite sandwich.
4. Every student and teacher (was, were) present at the special assembly.
5. Neither Mars nor Jupiter (is, are) as bright as Venus.
6. Each pencil and pen (was, were) marked with Karen's name.
7. Moisture and warm air (is, are) needed to raise orchids.
8. Mums or carnations (was, were) requested for the centerpiece on the table.
9. My softball coach and Spanish teacher (is, are) Mrs. Gomez.
10. Strawberries and cream still (remains, remain) my favorite dessert.
11. Red, white, and blue (is, are) the colors in many flags.
12. After more than 30 years, rock and roll (is, are) still a popular kind of music.
13. Either Pat or Cathy (has, have) the key to the costume room.
14. Earthquakes and volcanoes (has, have) caused cities to sink beneath the sea.
15. Some tape or nails (is, are) needed to hang this poster.
16. The passenger and driver of the truck (was, were) not hurt in the accident.
17. Today, great ice caps and glaciers (covers, cover) one tenth of the earth's surface.
18. Both Paul Bunyan and Pecos Bill (is, are) legendary heroes in American folklore.
19. Every bicycle and car in the parade (was, were) decorated with streamers and balloons.
20. Neither the President nor his aides (was, were) prepared for such a warm welcome.

EXERCISE 8 Oral Practice

Read aloud the following items, adding *is* or *are* after each one. Then repeat the exercise using *was/were* and *has/have*.

1. she
2. you
3. they
4. the horse
5. the old cars
6. either Howard or Tom
7. the box of walnuts
8. bacon and eggs
9. Jay and his brother
10. Deanna with her friends

EXERCISE 9 Writing Sentences

Write a sentence for each item in Exercise 8, using only present tense verbs. Make sure each verb agrees with its subject.

EXERCISE 10 Time-out for Review

Number your paper 1 to 20. Find and write the verbs that do not agree with their subjects. Then write them correctly. If a sentence is correct, write *C* after the number.

1. *Animal Farm* and *1984* were written by George Orwell.
2. The collie, as well as many other dogs, were originally raised as a work animal.
3. Neither the king snake nor the water snake is harmful.
4. Spaghetti and meatballs are my favorite dinner.
5. The leaves of the ginkgo tree looks like tiny fans.
6. Limestone and sandstone is easily split into sheets.
7. The king penguins of the Antarctic is over three feet tall.
8. Snow or showers is predicted for tomorrow.
9. Every box and trash can were filled by the cleanup committee.
10. The number of atoms in a pound of iron is nearly five trillion trillion.
11. The votes for the position of secretary is being counted.
12. Ham and eggs are a favorite Sunday breakfast at our house.
13. Each performer and guest were given an entrance pass.
14. Neither the canoe nor the rowboats was damaged by the storm.

15. Both intensive training and a thorough knowledge of anatomy is required in judo.
16. The captain and the first baseman this year are Ike Saunders.
17. The fastest passenger elevators in the world is located in the Sears Tower in Chicago.
18. An island or a reef is barely visible near the horizon.
19. In 1610, the population of all the American colonies were 350.
20. My uncle, aunt, and cousin from Texas are staying with us for a week.

Special Agreement Problems

Some subjects create special agreement problems.

Indefinite Pronouns as Subjects. In the last chapter, you learned that all indefinite pronouns do not have the same number.

Common Indefinite Pronouns

SINGULAR	anybody, anyone, each, either, everybody, everyone, neither, nobody, no one, one, somebody, someone
PLURAL	both, few, many, several
SINGULAR/PLURAL	all, any, most, none, some

A verb must agree in number with an indefinite pronoun that is used as a subject. The number of an indefinite pronoun in the last group in the box is determined by the object of the preposition that follows the pronoun.

14h ▶ A verb must agree in number with an indefinite pronoun used as a subject.

SINGULAR <u>Everyone</u> in the room <u>is</u> a member of the debate team.

PLURAL <u>Many</u> of the students <u>want</u> shorter homeroom periods.

SINGULAR <u>Most</u> of the money <u>has</u> been collected.
OR PLURAL [Since *money* is singular, *has* is also singular.]

<u>Most</u> of the tomatoes <u>are</u> ripe now. [Since *tomatoes* is plural, *are* is also plural.]

EXERCISE 11 Making Indefinite Pronoun Subjects and Verbs Agree

Write the subject in each sentence. Then next to each one, write the correct form of the verb in parentheses that agrees with the subject.

1. Several of my pictures (was, were) hung in the art room.
2. Each of you (is, are) asked to bring something to the party.
3. Some of the broken glass (is, are) still on the floor.
4. One of the eggs in the carton (was, were) cracked.
5. Many of the bags (contains, contain) old clothes.
6. None of the lights (was, were) on in the house.
7. Nobody (remembers, remember) what time rehearsal begins tonight.
8. Both of the twins usually (eats, eat) at the same table in the cafeteria.
9. Most of the snow (has, have) melted.
10. Either of the books (is, are) interesting to read.

Subjects in Inverted Order.   A verb must agree in number with the subject, regardless of whether the subject comes before or after the verb.

14i The subject and the verb of an inverted sentence must agree in number.

There are several types of inverted sentences. *(See pages 16 – 18.)* To find the subject in an inverted sentence, turn the sentence around to its natural order, placing the subject first.

INVERTED ORDER	At the bottom of the trunk <u>were</u> my father's <u>medals</u>. [My father's <u>medals</u> <u>were</u> at the bottom of the trunk.]
QUESTIONS	<u>Have</u> the <u>birds</u> been fed yet? [The <u>birds</u> <u>have been fed</u>.]
SENTENCES BEGINNING WITH *HERE* or *THERE*	There <u>are</u> three <u>men</u> waiting to see you. [Three <u>men</u> <u>are waiting</u> to see you.]

EXERCISE 12   Making Subjects in Inverted Order and Verbs Agree

Write the subject in each sentence. Then next to each one, write the form of the verb in parentheses that agrees with the subject.

1. There (is, are) 2,500,000 rivets in the Eiffel Tower.
2. In the newspaper (was, were) two ads for collies.
3. (Does, Do) rings really tell the age of a tree?
4. At the head of the parade (was, were) two bands.
5. There (is, are) two fullbacks on a soccer team.
6. In the basket (was, were) apples, pears, and grapes.
7. Here (is, are) the photos of the class party.
8. (Was, Were) you able to find the book in the library?
9. At the foot of the dock (was, were) two old rowboats.
10. (Is, Are) there any good remedies for poison ivy?

***Doesn't* and *Don't*.**   These contractions and other contractions often present agreement problems. When you write a contraction, always say the two words that make up the contraction. Then check for agreement with the subject.

14j ▸ The verb part of a contraction must agree in number with the subject.

Doesn't, isn't, wasn't, and *hasn't* are singular and agree with singular subjects. *Don't, aren't, weren't,* and *haven't* are plural and agree with plural subjects.

He <u>doesn't</u> <u>know</u> the address. [He *does* (not).]
<u>Don't</u> <u>they</u> <u>know</u> the address either? [They *do* (not).]

EXERCISE 13 Making Subjects and Contractions Agree

Write the subject in each sentence. Then next to each one, write the contraction in the parentheses that agrees with the subject.

1. The Chihuahua (doesn't, don't) like dogs of other breeds.
2. (Wasn't, Weren't) they told about the meeting?
3. (Doesn't, Don't) plants give off oxygen?
4. The glass animals on the mantle (hasn't, haven't) been dusted yet.
5. (Doesn't, Don't) you want to join the softball team?
6. (Isn't, Aren't) they joining us for dinner?
7. That (doesn't, don't) sound like a normal jet.
8. (Doesn't, Don't) your neighbors own a Siamese cat?
9. These (isn't, aren't) the books I wanted.
10. I (doesn't, don't) have the information you need.

EXERCISE 14 Time-out for Review

Number your paper 1 to 20. Find and write the verbs that do not agree with their subjects. Then write them correctly. If a sentence is correct, write *C* after the number.

1. Here comes three buses all at once.
2. In this container is the refreshments for tonight's party.
3. Through the efforts of the fire fighters, everyone in the burning buildings were rescued.
4. Many of my friends has part-time jobs.
5. Are there more telephones in America than in any other country?
6. Some of the blueberries was kept for you.
7. Was you going for a swim with Darrell and me?
8. None of the tomatoes is ripe.

9. Until the mid-1880s, there was no difference between right and left shoes.
10. Someone in the bleachers was waving a flag.
11. He don't understand the question.
12. On a football team there are 11 players.
13. Most of the candidates is advertising on TV.
14. In 1921, there were a 76-inch snowfall in 24 hours at Silver Lake, Colorado.
15. Was you afraid of the huge waves?
16. In the center of the table was red and yellow tulips.
17. The penguin don't use its flipperlike wings for flight.
18. No one in the pictures were smiling.
19. Don't he know his lines for the second act yet?
20. There is several cold, snowy mountain peaks right on the equator.

Collective Nouns. In Chapter 2 you learned that a *collective noun* names a group of people or things. Words such as *group, flock, audience,* and *family* are collective nouns.

14k Use a singular verb with a collective-noun subject that is thought of as a unit. Use a plural verb with a collective-noun subject that is thought of as individuals.

The <u>committee</u> <u>is</u> planning to hire a band. [The committee is working as a single unit. Therefore, the verb is singular.]

The <u>committee</u> <u>are</u> unable to agree on a band. [The individuals on the committee are acting separately. Therefore, the verb is plural.]

Words Expressing an Amount. Words that express an amount of time or money or that express a measurement or weight are usually considered singular.

14l A subject that expresses an amount, a measurement, or a weight is usually singular and takes a singular verb.

247

Words expressing an amount can be confusing because they are sometimes plural in form.

> Twelve dollars <u>was</u> all Jody could spend. [one sum of money]
> Nine tenths of Pat's spare time <u>is spent</u> reading. [one part of her time]

Once in a while, an amount is thought of in individual parts. When this happens, a plural verb must be used to agree with the subject.

> Twelve dollars of her salary <u>were put</u> aside for a new coat.

Singular Nouns That Have a Plural Form. Words such as *measles, mathematics, economics,* and *news* all end in *-s,* but they name single things, such as one disease or one area of knowledge.

14m ▶ Use a singular verb with certain subjects that are plural in form but singular in meaning.

> <u>Mathematics</u> <u>is</u> Gail's favorite subject.
> The <u>news</u> of her award <u>delights</u> all of us.

Subjects with Linking Verbs. Sometimes a sentence will have a subject and a predicate nominative that do not agree in number.

14n ▶ A verb agrees with the subject of a sentence, not with the predicate nominative.

In the following examples, notice that the number of the predicate nominative does not affect the number of the verb.

> One <u>problem</u> in our town <u>is</u> huge potholes.
> <u>Problems</u> in the cafeteria <u>are</u> one issue that will be discussed at the school-board meeting.

248

Titles. Titles may have many words in them, and some of those words may be plural. Nevertheless, a title is the name of only one book or one work of art.

14o ▶ A title is singular and takes a singular verb.

Wuthering Heights by Emily Brontë <u>was dramatized</u> on public television last fall.
Three Musicians by Picasso <u>was</u> on display at the art museum.

EXERCISE 15 Making Subjects and Verbs Agree
Write the correct form of the verb in parentheses.

1. Those singers (is, are) a big hit now.
2. My pottery class (is, are) learning about glazes.
3. *Thirteen Days* (is, are) a book by Robert Kennedy.
4. Computers (is, are) a learning tool in many schools today.
5. Eight miles of the River Seine (is, are) inside the city of Paris.
6. Economics (is, are) the subject I enjoy most this year.
7. Nearly three fourths of the earth's surface (is, are) covered by salt water.
8. One result of inflation (is, are) higher interest rates.
9. *The Cardsharps* (was, were) painted about 1590.
10. A ship's crew (drinks, drink) lemon juice to prevent scurvy.
11. Twenty dollars (was, were) donated to the fund by our homeroom.
12. Three days (was, were) spent studying for final exams.
13. The athletic club (is, are) holding a fund-raising drive next week.
14. (Is, Are) mathematics one of your favorite subjects?
15. (Has, Have) the family agreed about what to do over the weekend?
16. *Gulliver's Travels* first (tells, tell) about Gulliver's voyage to Lilliput.

17. The main attraction at the zoo (is, are) the monkeys.
18. Ninety-seven percent of the world's water (is, are) in the ocean.
19. The entertainment committee (is, are) hiring a band for the dance.
20. *The Book of Lists* (is, are) a very informative book.

EXERCISE 16   Oral Practice
Read aloud the following items, adding *is* or *are* after each one. Then repeat the exercise using *doesn't/don't* and *was/were*.

1. ten dollars
2. both of them
3. the club
4. one half
5. measles

6. none of the apples
7. mathematics
8. neither of the tapes
9. one complaint
10. two tons

EXERCISE 17   Writing Sentences
Write a sentence for each item in Exercise 16, using only present tense verbs. Make sure each verb agrees with its subject.

EXERCISE 18   Time-out for Review
Number your paper 1 to 10. Find and write the verbs that do not agree with their subjects. Then write them correctly. If a sentence is correct, write *C* after the number.

They
Can
Tell

1. The groundhog for years have been used to predict the arrival of spring.
2. The fuzz on woolly caterpillars are used to determine how hard a winter will be.
3. Neither a groundhog nor caterpillars is really dependable for forecasting though.
4. Many of the predictions are wrong.
5. There are reports, however, that some animals can predict disasters.
6. Ten catfish in a laboratory was observed for two years.
7. During that time, 20 earthquakes was experienced.

8. Most of the earthquakes was inaccurately forecast by humans.
9. Seventeen of the tremors, nevertheless, were predicted by the fish.
10. Catfish doesn't talk, of course, but they wiggled their whiskers just before the quakes struck.

Application to Writing

One of the most important steps in editing your writing is to check for correct subject and verb agreement.

EXERCISE 19   Editing for Subject and Verb Agreement
Find each verb that does not agree with its subject. Then write the correct form of the verb and its subject.

The
Wolf

Everyone have read fairy tales about cunning wolves. Movies have shown wolves attacking people. Is all these stories about wolves really true? According to Boye Rensberger, they aren't. He says that a wolf don't like to fight. In fact, wolves often go out of their way to avoid harming humans. Rensberger goes on to say that a wolf pack are a tightly knit family. Both males and females raise the young. When both of the parents goes out to hunt, another wolf baby-sits for the pups.

CHAPTER REVIEW

A. Write the subject in each sentence. Then next to each one, write the form of the verb in parentheses that agrees with the subject.

1. (Isn't, Aren't) these loaves of bread enough for the stuffing?
2. There (is, are) still horse ranches within the city limits of San Diego.
3. Neither of the loudspeakers (was, were) working.

4. Two members of the golf team (was, were) able to finish the course at five under par.
5. Off the coast of Maine (is, are) many rocky islands.
6. Ten dollars (was, were) a fair price for the used tennis racket.
7. My height and weight (is, are) average for my age.
8. (Doesn't, Don't) you think we can win?
9. The team (was, were) fighting among themselves over the choice of a new captain.
10. *Incredible Athletic Feats* (is, are) an interesting book by Jim Benagh.
11. Every student and teacher (was, were) at the dedication ceremony.
12. Both Ellen's sister and my sister (is, are) at the University of Wisconsin.
13. One fourth of the world's population (lives, live) on less than two thousand dollars a year.
14. (Wasn't, Weren't) you able to solve the math problem?
15. One of our best pitchers (was, were) unable to play in the county championships.
16. Either Amanda or Mary (is, are) sure to win the race.
17. My friends from school (doesn't, don't) ride the bus.
18. Some of the pages in this book (is, are) missing.
19. The two longest rivers in the world (is, are) the Nile and the Amazon.
20. Many of the participants (has, have) already arrived.

B. Number your paper 1 to 10. Find and write the verbs that do not agree with their subjects. Then write them correctly. If a sentence is correct, write *C* after the number.

1. Was you able to find Les in the crowd after the football game?
2. In the picnic basket were two sandwiches for every person.
3. Fifty dollars were contributed by me and my friends to the fire victims.
4. Crackers and cheese are my favorite snack.
5. Either red or green looks good on you.

6. Every actor and dancer were dressed in a colorful costume.
7. Don't that dripping faucet bother you?
8. There are few poisonous snakes in northern regions.
9. Each of the members are assigned to a committee.
10. Is your father and mother at home this evening?

MASTERY TEST

Number your paper 1 to 10. Write the subject in each sentence. Then next to each one, write the form of the verb in parentheses that agrees with the subject.

1. (Doesn't, Don't) you have your driver's license yet?
2. The food, tents, and supplies (is, are) on the truck.
3. My family (is, are) planning to drive to Florida during spring break.
4. On Dale's workbench (was, were) several unfinished boat models.
5. Some of the old photos (has, have) lost their color.
6. A big breakfast including home fried potatoes and biscuits (was, were) eaten by everyone.
7. Neither Madison nor the nearby towns (was, were) touched by the tornado.
8. Every glass and cup in the house (was, were) sitting in the sink.
9. Three fourths of the crop (was, were) damaged by the storm.
10. One of the algebra problems (is, are) too hard.

15

Using Adjectives and Adverbs

DIAGNOSTIC TEST

Number your paper 1 to 10. Then write the correct form of the modifier in parentheses.

EXAMPLE   Pearl is the (friendlier, friendliest) member of the group.

ANSWER   friendliest

1. Which of the three routes to Manchester is the (shorter, shortest)?
2. Of the three, Sal can whistle (louder, loudest).
3. Which is (heavier, heaviest), a ton of bricks or a ton of feathers?
4. Of the three trails up Mount Keating, which one is the (more, most) scenic?
5. I don't know which is (worse, worst), having a tooth filled or thinking about having it filled.
6. Of all the sprinters, Phyllis wins races (more, most) consistently.
7. Jesse was the (older, oldest) of the two James brothers.
8. Which twin made the (better, best) grades?
9. Of the ten problems, this one was (easier, easiest).
10. Do you think Martha, Jane, or Zelda has the (less, least) chance of getting the job?

If you are going to buy a bicycle, you should do some comparison shopping first. You might find out, for example, that one make of bicycle is a *good* buy. A second make, however, is a *better* buy, but a third make is the *best* buy of all. This example shows that different forms of a modifier are used to show comparison.

COMPARISON OF ADJECTIVES AND ADVERBS

Most adjectives and adverbs have three forms. These forms are used to show differences in degree or extent.

15a Most modifiers show degrees of comparison by changing form.

The three degrees of comparison are the *positive,* the *comparative,* and the *superlative.* The *positive* degree is the basic form of an adjective or an adverb. It is used when no comparison is being made.

Eric is a **tall** basketball player.

The *comparative* degree is used when two people, things, or actions are being compared.

Eric is **taller** than Bruce.

The *superlative* degree is used when more than two people, things, or actions are being compared.

Eric is the **tallest** player on the team.

Following are additional examples of the three degrees of comparison.

POSITIVE	Today is a **hot** day. [adjective]
	Hugh exercises **often.** [adverb]
COMPARATIVE	Today is **hotter** than yesterday.
	Hugh exercises **more often** than Pat.

SUPERLATIVE   Today is the **hottest day** of the year.
Hugh exercises the **most often** of all the
team members.

NOTE: Some adverbs, such as *too, somewhere, very,* and
never, cannot be compared.

EXERCISE 1   Determining Degrees of Comparison
Write each underlined modifier in the following sentences.
Then label its degree of comparison *positive, comparative,*
or *superlative.*

EXAMPLE   Pepper is <u>friendlier</u> than Muffin.
ANSWER   friendlier — comparative

1. Which is <u>longer</u>, a yard or a meter?
2. Of all the states east of the Mississippi, Georgia is the
<u>largest</u>.
3. Quartz is <u>harder</u> than feldspar.
4. Mario made his bed <u>hurriedly</u>.
5. Who can run <u>faster</u>, Carl or Ellen?
6. That was the <u>funniest</u> movie I have ever seen.
7. It is <u>easier</u> to make biscuits than it is to make bread.
8. Who is the <u>most</u> <u>considerate</u>, Larry, Meg, or Glen?
9. Today was a <u>wonderful</u> day!
10. Hematite is the <u>most</u> <u>important</u> of all iron ores.

Regular and Irregular Comparison

Most modifiers form the comparative and superlative
degrees regularly, but a few modifiers form the comparative and superlative degrees irregularly.

Regular Comparison.   The number of syllables in a modifier
will determine how it forms its comparative and superlative
degrees.

15b Add *-er* to form the comparative degree and *-est* to form the
superlative degree of one-syllable modifiers.

POSITIVE	COMPARATIVE	SUPERLATIVE
brave	braver	bravest
kind	kinder	kindest
soon	sooner	soonest

The comparative and superlative degrees of many two-syllable modifiers are formed the same way. However, some two-syllable modifiers sound awkward when *-er* or *-est* is added. For these modifiers, *more* or *most* should be used to form the comparative and superlative degrees.

15c ▶ Use *-er* or *more* to form the comparative degree and *-est* or *most* to form the superlative degree of two-syllable modifiers.

NOTE: *More* and *most* are always used with adverbs that end in *-ly*.

POSITIVE	COMPARATIVE	SUPERLATIVE
happy	happier	happiest
helpful	more helpful	most helpful
quickly	more quickly	most quickly

When deciding whether to add *er/est*, or to use *more/most* with a two-syllable modifier, let your ear be your guide. If adding *-er* or *-est* makes a word difficult to pronounce, use *more* or *most* instead. Your ear should tell you, for example, to avoid comparisons such as "helpfuler," "harmlesser," and "faithfuler."

The comparative and superlative degrees of modifiers with three or more syllables are always formed by using *more* and *most*.

15d ▶ Use *more* to form the comparative degree and *most* to form the superlative degree of modifiers with three or more syllables.

POSITIVE	COMPARATIVE	SUPERLATIVE
trivial	more trivial	most trivial
serious	more serious	most serious
vigorously	more vigorously	most vigorously

Since *less* and *least* mean the opposite of *more* and *most,* use these words to form negative comparisons.

trivial	less trivial	least trivial
serious	less serious	least serious
vigorously	less vigorously	least vigorously

EXERCISE 2   Forming the Comparison of Regular Modifiers

Number your paper 1 to 20. Write each modifier. Then write its comparative and superlative forms.

1. difficult	6. quick	11. safe	16. slow
2. colorful	7. sure	12. high	17. seasick
3. eagerly	8. muddy	13. lively	18. dark
4. swiftly	9. hastily	14. loudly	19. easily
5. abrupt	10. heavy	15. fast	20. frisky

EXERCISE 3   Forming the Negative Comparison of Modifiers

Number your paper 1 to 5. Write the first five modifiers in Exercise 2. Then write the negative comparison of each one by using *less* and *least.*

Irregular Comparison.   The following adjectives and adverbs are compared irregularly. The comparative and superlative forms of these modifiers should be memorized.

POSITIVE	COMPARATIVE	SUPERLATIVE
bad/badly/ill	worse	worst
good/well	better	best
little	less	least
many/much	more	most

Do not add the regular comparison endings to the comparative and superlative degrees of these irregular modifiers. For example, *worse* is the comparative form of *bad.* You should never use "worser."

EXERCISE 4   Forming the Comparison of Irregular Modifiers

Number your paper 1 to 5. Write the comparative and superlative forms of the underlined modifier.

1. That movie was really <u>bad</u>.
   It was _____ than the movie I saw last week.
   In fact, it was the _____ movie I have ever seen.
2. Frank shows <u>little</u> concern about the pollution in our neighborhood.
   Betty shows even _____ concern than Frank.
   Amazingly, Paula shows the _____ concern of all.
3. <u>Many</u> households have a cat.
   _____ households have a dog.
   However, _____ households have more than one pet.
4. Your corn muffins are <u>good</u>.
   They certainly are _____ than your first ones.
   In fact, they are the _____ you have ever made.
5. My brother is <u>ill</u>.
   He was _____ yesterday.
   Three days ago he was the _____.

EXERCISE 5   Writing Sentences

Write five sentences, using a noun in Group A and a modifier in Group B. Remember that the comparative form is used when two people or things are being compared. The superlative form is used when three or more people or things are being compared.

EXAMPLE   program, worst
POSSIBLE ANSWER   That program was the worst I have seen all week.

GROUP A		GROUP B	
performance	car	most special	worst
sister	man	most handsome	kinder
assignment	help	colorful	older
costume	star	loudest	faster
program	room	more generous	less

259

EXERCISE 6   Time-out for Review

Number your paper 1 to 20. Find and write each incorrect modifier. Then write it correctly. If a sentence is correct, write *C* after the number.

EXAMPLE   Which will live longest, a turtle or a goldfish?
 ANSWER   longest — longer

1. The thinnest twin is Roberta.
2. Norman Rockwell was one of America's best-known illustrators.
3. Colleen is the youngest of the two Compton sisters.
4. Of the three finalists, Greg has the least chance of winning.
5. Rebecca thinks spring is the more beautiful season of the year.
6. Of all the mountains in the Andes, which is the higher?
7. Tony can mow the lawn and weed the garden faster than his brother.
8. Which way of going downtown is quickest, by bus or by subway?
9. Yesterday was the happiest day of my life!
10. Of the two movies, I enjoyed this one most.
11. Betsy is the more considerate of the two girls.
12. Of the three buildings facing the square, the post office is the larger.
13. There is least traffic on Route 4 than on the Meriden Turnpike.
14. Who is the best actor, Chris or Willie?
15. Of the two biographies, I have enjoyed reading this one most.
16. I have seen four jackets so far, and I like this one less of all.
17. Which city has the larger population, Detroit or Los Angeles?
18. Which of the two pairs of scissors is better for cutting paper?
19. Friday's snowstorm was the worst of the year.
20. Which of these three boxes is stronger?

Problems with Modifiers

A few special problems can arise when you use modifiers.

Double Comparisons. Use only one method of forming the comparative or superlative degrees of a modifier.

15e Do not use both *-er* and *more* to form the comparative degree, or both *-est* and *most* to form the superlative degree.

DOUBLE COMPARISON	Joan is **more kinder** than Greta.
CORRECT	Joan is **kinder** than Greta.
DOUBLE COMPARISON	This is the **most violentest** storm I have ever seen.
CORRECT	This is the **most violent** storm I have ever seen.

Other and Else in Comparisons. Be sure that you do not make the mistake of comparing one thing with itself when it is part of a group. You can avoid this by adding *other* or *else* to your comparison.

15f Add *other* or *else* when comparing a member of a group with the rest of the group.

In the first sentence below, the television tower is supposedly being compared with the *other* structures in the city. However, without the word *other* added, the tower is also being compared with itself. It is a structure in the city.

INCORRECT	The television tower is taller than any structure in the city.
CORRECT	The television tower is taller than any **other** structure in the city.
INCORRECT	Edgar runs faster than anyone on the track team.
CORRECT	Edgar runs faster than anyone **else** on the track team.

EXERCISE 7 Correcting Mistakes in Comparisons

Write the following sentences, correcting each mistake.

EXAMPLE Leo is paid more than anyone in the store.
ANSWER Leo is paid more than anyone else in the store.

1. Diagrams help make explanations more clearer to a reader.
2. The sperm whale has a heavier brain than any animal.
3. More turkeys are raised in California than in any state in the United States.
4. Frank is the most strongest student in our class.
5. You are the most happiest person I have ever known.
6. Wanda, the captain of the team, can swim faster than anyone on the team.
7. We need to walk more faster if we're going to get there on time.
8. Greyhounds have better eyesight than any breed of dog.
9. I think this was the most hardest test I have ever taken in my life.
10. Florida is more farther south than any state except Hawaii.

Double Negatives. Words such as *but* (when it means "only"), *hardly, never, no, nobody, not,* (and its contraction *n't*), *nothing, only,* and *scarcely* are all negatives. Two negatives should not be used to express one negative meaning.

15g Avoid using a double negative.

A double negative often cancels itself out, leaving you with a positive statement. For example, if you say, "There isn't no more time," you are really saying, "There is more time."

DOUBLE NEGATIVE I don't have **no** homework tonight.
CORRECT I don't have **any** homework tonight.

DOUBLE NEGATIVE There are**n't hardly** any apples left.
CORRECT There are **hardly** any apples left.

DOUBLE NEGATIVE   **Don't never** scare me like that again!

CORRECT   **Don't ever** scare me like that again!

CORRECT   **Never** scare me like that again!

EXERCISE 8 Correcting Double Negatives

Write the following sentences, correcting each mistake.

1. I didn't go nowhere near the beach today.
2. She was so sleepy she couldn't hardly stay awake.
3. Uncle Al can't hardly wait to see the Colts play again.
4. Pam hasn't done nothing about getting us tickets.
5. Because of fog, we couldn't scarcely see the road.
6. Don't tell nobody what I just told you.
7. Cheryl didn't say nothing about the invitation.
8. I can't hardly wait for summer vacation.
9. I'm never going to walk in no more poison ivy again.
10. The fire fighters couldn't do nothing to save the house.

EXERCISE 9 Time-out for Review

Number your paper 1 to 20. Write the following sentences correcting each mistake. If a sentence is correct, write *C* after the number.

1. The Dead Sea forms part of the most deepest chasm on the earth's surface.
2. Which is more fiercer, the leopard or the lion?
3. Sometimes my grandfather is livelier than I am.
4. Notre Dame is more famous than any church in France.
5. Don't feed Bruno nothing before his dinner.
6. Is there an animal more smarter than the beaver?
7. Pam draws better than anyone I know.
8. Don't never answer in that tone of voice.
9. I like this job better than any job I have ever had.
10. We couldn't hardly recognize Nora.
11. There weren't no seats left by the time we got there.
12. The Folger Library in Washington has more books on Shakespeare than any library in the country.
13. Of these three shirts, which do you like more?
14. I think our phone is the most busiest in town.

15. I've never seen a more larger dog.
16. We couldn't scarcely see the eclipse.
17. I like fish much more better than steak.
18. Mount Aconcagua in Argentina is higher than any other mountain in the Western Hemisphere.
19. We didn't have no time to make other plans.
20. This winter was colder than last winter.

Application to Writing

Factual writing often contains comparisons. When you edit a report, always check to see if you have used the correct form of comparison.

EXERCISE 10   Editing for the Correct Use of Modifiers
Rewrite the following paragraph, correcting each mistake.

The Best Event

The Olympic decathlon is held in greater esteem than any event in sports. The champion of this event is generally considered the most greatest athlete in the world. The performances in the decathlon are watched more than any Olympic event. A decathlon performer must be able to jump the highest, run the fastest, and throw the javelin the most farthest. The winner must be the bestest.

CHAPTER REVIEW

Number your paper 1 to 20. Then write the following sentences, correcting each mistake. If a sentence is correct, write *C* after the number.

1. For its size, the honeybee is much more stronger than a person.
2. Paul hasn't done nothing yet about the garden.
3. Rainbow Bridge in Utah is larger than any other natural arch.
4. Woodworking is the bestest class I have this year.

264

5. Sean hasn't never seen *Star Wars*.
6. English contains more words than any language.
7. There isn't no more hamburger for the picnic.
8. The Great Dane is among the most largest of all dogs.
9. I think Molly is smarter than anyone in her class.
10. The copies seem brightest than the originals.
11. Which is hardest, ice-skating or roller skating?
12. Do people in the United States have a higher standard of living than anyone in the world?
13. Nobody knew nothing about the defective fuse.
14. The flood last week was the worst yet.
15. That was the less expensive gift I could find.
16. Even an expert could hardly tell the difference between the real and the counterfeit bill.
17. Lee plays the drums better than anyone in his band.
18. Of Sarah's parents, her dad is the most easygoing.
19. Tulips haven't never done well on that side of the house.
20. Of the two finalists, Carl has the best chance of winning.

MASTERY TEST

Number your paper 1 to 10. Then write the correct form of the modifier in parentheses.

1. Who is (taller, tallest), Vincent or Tom?
2. Of all the routes, this way is the (longer, longest).
3. Which do you consider (sweeter, sweetest), honey or maple syrup?
4. The (younger, youngest) of the girls is very tall.
5. Of the three pups, I like this one (more, most).
6. Kent is the (stronger, strongest) in our family.
7. I felt (worse, worst) yesterday than today.
8. Which of the two cars is (more, most) economical?
9. Of the three brothers, Bart gave the (less, least) support.
10. Lightning is the (shyer, shyest) of the two colts.

Glossary
of Usage

In the last four chapters, you covered all the fundamental elements of usage. The Glossary of Usage will present some specific areas of usage that were not covered in those chapters. Because this section is intended to be a reference tool, the 50 items in the glossary are listed alphabetically. This arrangement will help you find the information you need easily and quickly.

References in this section will be made to "standard English" and "nonstandard English." *Standard English* refers to the rules and the conventions of usage that are accepted and used most widely by English-speaking people throughout the world. *Nonstandard English* has many variations because it is influenced by regional differences and dialects, as well as by current slang. Since nonstandard English lacks uniformity, you should always use standard English when you write.

a, an.   Use *a* before words beginning with consonant sounds and *an* before words beginning with vowel sounds.

Did you buy **a** new record?

No, it was given to me as **an** early birthday gift.

accept, except.   *Accept* is a verb that means "to receive with consent." *Except* is usually a preposition that means "but" or "other than."

Everyone **except** Bernie **accepted** the news calmly.

advice, advise. *Advice* is a noun that means "a recommendation." *Advise* is a verb that means "to recommend."

I usually follow Marvin's **advice.**

My doctor **advised** me to exercise more often.

affect, effect. *Affect* is a verb that means "to influence" or "to act upon." *Effect* is usually a noun that means "a result" or "an influence." As a verb, *effect* means "to accomplish" or "to produce."

Does the weather **affect** your mood?

No, it has no **effect** on me.

The medicine **effected** a change in his condition.

ain't. This contraction is nonstandard English. Avoid it in your writing.

NONSTANDARD   Ken **ain't** here yet.

STANDARD   Ken **isn't** here yet.

all ready, already. *All ready* means "completely ready." *Already* means "previously."

We were **all ready** to go by seven o'clock.

By the time he called, I had **already** left.

all together, altogether. *All together* means "in a group." *Altogether* means "wholly" or "thoroughly."

Let's try to sing **all together** for a change.

This cereal is **altogether** too sweet.

a lot. People very often write these two words incorrectly as one. There is no such word as "alot." *A lot,* however, should be avoided in formal writing.

INFORMAL   Famous movie stars usually receive **a lot** of fan mail.

FORMAL   Famous movie stars usually receive **a large quantity** of fan mail.

among, between. These words are both prepositions. *Among* is used when referring to three or more people or things. *Between* is used when referring to two people or things.

Put your present **among** the others.

Then come and sit **between** Judith and me.

amount, number. *Amount* refers to a singular word. *Number* refers to a plural word.

Although there were a **number** of rainy days this month, the total **amount** of rain was less than usual.

EXERCISE 1 Determining the Correct Word

Write the word in parentheses that correctly completes each sentence.

1. Have you finished your homework (all ready, already)?
2. The choice is (between, among) these two ties.
3. There will be (a, an) evening meeting on Tuesday.
4. Did you (accept, except) the job?
5. How did the hurricane (affect, effect) your town?
6. I don't think I'm in a position to (advice, advise) him.
7. The (amount, number) of rainfall has decreased.
8. We met (all together, altogether) before the meeting.
9. I can't tell you (a lot, much) about the accident.
10. This (ain't, isn't) the right road.

anywhere, everywhere, nowhere, somewhere. Do not add -*s* to any of these words.

I looked **everywhere**, but could not find my keys.

at. Do not use *at* after *where*.

NONSTANDARD Do you know **where** we're **at**?

STANDARD Do you know **where** we are?

a while, awhile. *A while* is an article and a noun that is used mainly after a preposition. *Awhile* is an adverb that stands alone and means "for a short period of time."

We can stay for **a while.**

After we work **awhile,** we can take a break.

beside, besides. *Beside* is always a preposition that means "by the side of." As a preposition, *besides* means "in addition to." As an adverb, *besides* means "also" or "moreover."

I want Grandfather to sit **beside** me. [by the side of]

Besides Mom, Aunt Peg was there. [in addition to]

Some other relatives are coming **besides.** [also]

bring, take. *Bring* indicates motion toward the speaker. *Take* indicates motion away from the speaker.

Bring me the stamps.

Now please **take** this letter to the post office.

can, may. *Can* expresses ability. *May* expresses possibility or permission.

I **can** baby-sit for you tonight.

May I watch TV after Kenny is asleep?

doesn't, don't. *Doesn't* is singular and must agree with a singular subject. *Don't* is plural and must agree with a plural subject.

This article **doesn't** make sense to me.

These articles **don't** make sense to me.

double negative. Words such as *but* (when it means "only"), *hardly, never, no, none, no one, nobody, not,* (and its contraction *n't*), *nothing, nowhere, only, barely,* and *scarcely* are all negatives. Do not use two negatives to express one negative meaning.

NONSTANDARD   I **hardly never** see you anymore.

STANDARD   I **hardly** see you anymore.

STANDARD   I **never** see you anymore.

etc. *Etc.* is an abbreviation for a Latin phrase that means "and other things." Never use *and* with *etc.* If you do, what you are really saying is "and and other things." It is best, however, not to use this abbreviation at all in formal writing.

INFORMAL   We had to pack our clothes, books, records, **etc.**

FORMAL   We had to pack our clothes, books, records, **and other belongings.**

fewer, less. *Fewer* is plural and refers to things that can be counted. *Less* is singular and refers to quantities and qualities that cannot be counted.

There seem to be **fewer** hours in the day.

I seem to have **less** time to get everything done.

EXERCISE 2   Determining the Correct Word

Write the word in parentheses that correctly completes each sentence.

1. That shade of red (doesn't, don't) look good on you.
2. During the year there are (fewer, less) lunar eclipses than solar eclipses.
3. Let's stop for (a while, awhile) and rest.
4. Don't put the bag of ice (beside, besides) the hot stove.
5. He can't bear to give money to (anyone, nobody) except his friends.
6. I haven't been able to find the directions to their house (anywhere, anywheres).
7. (Can, May) I help you with those packages?
8. I have (fewer, less) free time now that I'm working after school.
9. We didn't have (anything, nothing) to keep us dry in the rain.
10. Please (bring, take) this note to your teacher.

good, well.   *Good* is an adjective and often follows a linking verb. *Well* is an adverb and often follows an action verb. However, when *well* means "in good health," "attractive," or "satisfactory," it is used as an adjective.

The biscuits smell **good.** [adjective]
Janice cooks **well.** [adverb]
I feel quite **well** now. [adjective — "in good health"]

have, of.   Never substitute *of* for the verb *have.* When speaking, many people make a contraction of *have.* For example, they might say, "We should've gone." Because *'ve* sounds like *of, of* is often substituted for *have* when written.

NONSTANDARD   We should **of** started earlier.
STANDARD   We should **have** started earlier.

hear, here.   *Hear* is a verb that means "to perceive by listening." *Here* is an adverb that means "in this place."

I can't **hear** the music from **here.**

hole, whole. A *hole* is an opening. *Whole* means "complete" or "entire."

Have you noticed the **hole** in your coat?

Did you see the **whole** movie twice?

in, into. Use *into* when you want to express motion from one place to another.

Is the money **in** your coat pocket?

Be careful that you don't walk **into** those glass doors.

knew, new. *Knew,* the past tense of the verb *know,* means "was acquainted with." *New* is an adjective that means "recently made" or "just found."

Michael's sneakers are so clean and white, I **knew** they were **new.**

learn, teach. *Learn* means "to gain knowledge." *Teach* means "to instruct" or "to show how."

I just **learned** how to use the word processor.

I can **teach** you how to use the word processor.

leave, let. *Leave* means "to depart" or "to go away from." *Let* means "to allow" or "to permit."

NONSTANDARD   **Leave** me help you with those packages.

STANDARD   **Let** me help you with those packages.

STANDARD   Don't **leave** before you help me.

lie, lay. *Lie* means "to rest or recline." *Lie* is never followed by a direct object. Its principal parts are *lie, lying, lay,* and *lain. Lay* means "to put or set (something) down." *Lay* is usually followed by a direct object. Its principal parts are *lay, laying, laid,* and *laid.*

LIE   Our dogs always **lie** near the fireplace.

They are **lying** there now.

They **lay** there all last evening.

They have **lain** there now for an hour.

LAY   **Lay** the mat on the floor. [*Mat* is the direct object.]

George is **laying** the mat on the floor.

Melvin **laid** the mat on the floor the last time.

Most of the time Gert has **laid** the mat on the floor.

like, as. *Like* is a preposition that introduces a preposi- tional phrase. *As* is usually a subordinating conjunction that introduces an adverb clause.

STANDARD   Betty talks exactly **like** her mother.
            [prepositional phrase]
NONSTANDARD   Betty usually does **like** she is told. [clause]
STANDARD   Betty usually does **as** she is told.

EXERCISE 3   Determining the Correct Word

Write the word in parentheses that correctly completes each sentence.

1. The seal slipped through the (hole, whole) in the ice and disappeared.
2. Chico is (learning, teaching) me Spanish.
3. No one could (have, of) known about the secret key.
4. That hot chocolate tastes unusually (good, well).
5. Put the packages down (hear, here).
6. We should go to the party just (like, as) we are.
7. You should (have, of) mowed the lawn before the rain.
8. Candace dove (in, into) the pool.
9. Skydiving was a (knew, new) experience for me.
10. My parents (leave, let) me choose my own clothes.

EXERCISE 4   Using *Lie* and *Lay* Correctly

Complete each sentence by writing the correct form of *lie* or *lay*.

1. The blame should not be _____ entirely on Pete.
2. For 50 years this guitar _____ in the attic.
3. _____ the new blanket at the bottom of the bed.
4. The huskies turned around three times and _____ down in the snow to sleep.
5. Trash was _____ all over the sidewalk.
6. The President _____ a wreath at the monument.
7. The Murphys are _____ a new floor in their kitchen.
8. The rotten apples had _____ on the ground for weeks.
9. Duke, _____ down.
10. Sally _____ the kittens beside their mother.

passed, past. *Passed* is the past tense of the verb *pass*. As a noun *past* means "a time gone by." As an adjective *past* means "just gone" or "elapsed." As a preposition *past* means "beyond."

In the **past** I have easily **passed** all math tests. [*past* as a noun]

I have walked **past** that store for the **past** few days without noticing its new name. [*past* as a preposition and then as an adjective]

rise, raise. *Rise* means "to move upward" or "to get up." *Rise* is never followed by a direct object. Its principal parts are *rise, rising, rose,* and *risen. Raise* means "to lift (something) up," "to increase," or "to grow something." *Raise* is usually followed by a direct object. Its principal parts are *raise, raising, raised,* and *raised.*

The sun will **rise** at 6:23 A.M.

Raise the blinds. [*Blinds* is the direct object.]

shall, will. Formal English uses *shall* with first person pronouns and *will* with second and third person pronouns. Today, however, *shall* and *will* are used interchangeably with *I* and *we,* except that *shall* is still used with I and we for questions.

Shall I invite her to join the club?

I **will** ask her tonight.

sit, set. *Sit* means "to rest in an upright position." *Sit* is never followed by a direct object. Its principal parts are *sit, sitting, sat,* and *sat. Set* means "to put or place (something)." *Set* is usually followed by a direct object. Its principal parts are *set, setting, set,* and *set.*

After you have **set** the table, everyone should **sit** down.

[*Table* is the direct object.]

so. Because *so* is a conjunction, it should not be used to begin a sentence.

NONSTANDARD   **So** after the game we celebrated.

STANDARD   The rain stopped, **so** we finished our picnic.
[coordinating conjunction]

than, then. *Than* is a subordinating conjunction and is used for comparisons. *Then* is an adverb and means "at that time" or "next."

NONSTANDARD   Jupiter is much larger **then** Saturn.

STANDARD   After learning that Jupiter is much larger **than** Saturn, we **then** learned some other interesting facts about the solar system.

that, which, who. As relative pronouns, *that* refers to people, animals, or things; *which* refers to animals or things; and *who* refers to people.

The books **that** I found in the attic were very old.

We watched the baby goats, **which** were in the field.

The stewardess **who** was on our flight seemed tired.

their, there, they're. *Their* is a possessive pronoun. *There* is usually an adverb, but sometimes it also begins an inverted sentence. *They're* is a contraction for *they are*.

Tell them to take **their** time.

There were many reporters **there**.

They're meeting at seven o'clock.

theirs, there's. *Theirs* is a possessive pronoun. *There's* is a contraction for *there is*.

These are ours; those are **theirs**.

There's a message for you in the office.

them, those. Never use *them* as a subject or a modifier.

NONSTANDARD   **Them** are freshly picked tomatoes. [subject]

STANDARD   **Those** are freshly picked tomatoes.

NONSTANDARD   Did you like **them** tomatoes? [adjective]

STANDARD   Did you like **those** tomatoes?

EXERCISE 5   Determining the Correct Word

Write the word in parentheses that correctly completes each sentence.

1. Did you see the car that just (passed, past)?
2. These gloves are warmer (than, then) those gloves.

3. I didn't see them (their, there, they're).
4. (Shall, Will) we ask him to join us?
5. The people (which, who) attended the meeting were interested in solar energy.
6. (Them, Those) are the best peaches.
7. Did they find (their, there, they're) coats?
8. (Theirs, There's) nothing to do but wait.
9. They said (their, there, they're) leaving around nine o'clock.
10. He often talks about the (passed, past).

EXERCISE 6 Using *Rise/Raise* and *Sit/Set* Correctly
Complete each sentence by writing the correct form of *rise/raise* or *sit/set*.

1. During the performance we _____ in the balcony.
2. By ten o'clock the tide had come in, and the water had _____ ten feet.
3. After dinner everyone _____ around the campfire.
4. Who _____ the tool box on the table?
5. People _____ and applauded.
6. Is there any steam _____ from the kettle?
7. How long have you been _____ here?
8. I have _____ the flower pots on the bench.
9. Steve _____ tomatoes every year.
10. The bread dough _____ on top of the stove.

this here, that there. Avoid using *here* or *there* in addition to *this* or *that*.
NONSTANDARD **That there** chair is very comfortable.
STANDARD **That** chair is very comfortable.

threw, through. *Threw* is the past tense of the verb *throw*. *Through* is a preposition that means "in one side and out the other."
Denny **threw** the ball to first base.
Have you ever looked **through** a high-powered telescope before?

to, too, two. *To* is a preposition. *To* also begins an infinitive. *Too* is an adverb that modifies a verb, an adjective, or another adverb. *Two* is a number.

Keith went **to** the gym **to** practice.

Two of the members were **too** late to vote.

Jim was invited, but Greg came **too.**

way, ways. Do not substitute *ways* for *way* when referring to a distance.

NONSTANDARD　We have gone a long **ways** since noon.

STANDARD　We have gone a long **way** since noon.

weak, week. *Weak* is an adjective that means "not strong" or "likely to break." *Week* is a noun that means "a period of seven days."

That chair is too **weak** to hold you.

School will be closed all next **week.**

when, where. Do not use *when* or *where* directly after a linking verb in a definition.

NONSTANDARD　A *presbyope* is **when** a person is farsighted.

STANDARD　A *presbyope* is a farsighted person.

NONSTANDARD　A *domicile* is **where** people live.

STANDARD　A *domicile* is a place where people live.

where. Do not substitute *where* for *that.*

NONSTANDARD　I heard **where** crime rates are going down.

STANDARD　I heard **that** crime rates are going down.

who, whom. *Who,* a pronoun in the nominative case, is used as a subject or a predicate nominative. *Whom,* a pronoun in the objective case, is used as a direct object, an indirect object, or an object of a preposition. *(See page 218.)*

Who is coming to your party? [subject]

Whom did you choose? [direct object]

whose, who's. *Whose* is a possessive pronoun. *Who's* is a contraction for *who is.*

Whose bicycle did you borrow?

Who's living next door to you?

your, you're. *Your* is a possessive pronoun. *You're* is a contraction for *you are.*

Are these **your** gloves?

You're the one we want for president of the class.

EXERCISE 7   Determining the Correct Word

Write the word in parentheses that correctly completes each sentence.

1. The action in that movie was much (to, too, two) slow for me.
2. *Pioneer 10* passed (threw, through) the solar system and out into deep space.
3. The signals from Channel 4 are too (weak, week) for us to receive clearly.
4. Why aren't you taking (your, you're) tent with you?
5. You have a long (way, ways) to go before you will be finished.
6. (Who, Whom) was in the car with her?
7. I read in a magazine (where, that) more foreign aid is being requested.
8. (This, This here) is the one that I want.
9. (Whose, Who's) driving you to the mall?
10. I need (to, too, two) study for the test tonight.

GLOSSARY REVIEW

Write the word in parentheses that correctly completes each sentence.

1. Please (bring, take) the hammer to your brother.
2. My uncle (learned, taught) me how to bait a hook.
3. The operator asked if I would (accept, except) the charges.
4. Will Mr. Ames (leave, let) you use his computer?

5. William went (in, into) the restaurant to use the telephone.
6. She has gone just about (everywhere, everywheres), it seems.
7. The full moon has already (raised, risen).
8. Because of the dry weather, there are (fewer, less) mosquitoes this year.
9. Bud dances better (than, then) Mickey.
10. Mom divided the strawberries (among, between) her and me.
11. The magazine you want is (lying, laying) on the coffee table.
12. I should (have, of) followed your suggestion.
13. What (affect, effect) did the eruption of Mount St. Helens have on the climate of the United States?
14. The quarterback (threw, through) the football nearly 50 yards down the field.
15. I thought you (knew, new) that Jon moved to Phoenix.
16. Will you swap (a, an) apple for this banana?
17. Be sure that your hiking boots fit (good, well).
18. How long will it take for (them, those) men to mark off the foul lines?
19. Haven't they found (a, no) place to meet yet?
20. Jennifer gave me some very good (advice, advise) the other day.
21. (Their, There, They're) still waiting for you.
22. We won't be leaving for (a while, awhile).
23. I have seen (this, this here) movie before.
24. Wayne has (all ready, already) had his physical.
25. Your new cat looks exactly (like, as) your other one.

STANDARDIZED TEST

USAGE

Directions: Choose the word or words that best complete each sentence. In the appropriate row on your answer sheet, fill in the circle containing the same letter as your answer.

SAMPLE   The balloon _____ when Jerry sat on it.

      A burst   **B** bursted   **C** bursts

ANSWER Ⓐ Ⓑ Ⓒ

1. The outfielder _____ the ball quickly to second base.

   A throwed   **B** throw   **C** threw

2. Although today is still cold, it feels _____ than yesterday.

   A warmer   **B** warmest   **C** more warmer

3. By the time I finished raking, more leaves had _____.

   A fell   **B** fallen   **C** falled

4. The red shirt _____ when Toby washed it in hot water.

   A shrinked   **B** shrank   **C** shrunk

5. Which is _____, an elephant or a rhinoceros?

   A biggest   **B** bigger   **C** more bigger

6. For me winter is the _____ season of the year.

   A most enjoyable   **B** enjoyablest   **C** more enjoyable

7. When the curtain finally rose, the audience _____.

   A cheered   **B** cheers   **C** is cheering

8. The calf is still ill, but it isn't getting _____.

   A worser   **B** iller   **C** worse

9. Although everyone had heard the bell, no one _____.

   A moves   **B** move   **C** moved

10. My right eye is _____ than my left eye.

   A strongest   **B** stronger   **C** more strong

Directions: Decide which underlined part in each sentence contains an error in usage. On your answer sheet, fill in the circle containing the same letter as the incorrect part. If there is no error, fill in *D*.

SAMPLE   He <u>accompanies</u> Pat and <u>I</u> on the guitar.   <u>No errors</u>
         A   B   C   D

ANSWER   Ⓐ Ⓑ Ⓒ Ⓓ

11. <u>Us</u> computer fans <u>are</u> <u>forming</u> a club.   <u>No errors</u>
   A   B   C   D

12. <u>Its</u> <u>another</u> victory for <u>our</u> team!   <u>No errors</u>
   A B   C   D

13. Writers like Lynn and <u>him</u> <u>submit</u> <u>their</u> work to the
                         A   B   C
    student newspaper.   <u>No errors</u>
                   D

14. <u>Each</u> of the girls <u>brought</u> <u>their</u> umbrella.   <u>No errors</u>
   A   B   C   D

15. Both Mike and Leon <u>has</u> <u>finished</u> <u>their</u> work.   <u>No errors</u>
                    A   B   C   D

16. Neither the ant nor the mosquito <u>have</u> <u>found</u> <u>its</u>
                                 A   B C
    supper yet.   <u>No errors</u>
               D

17. Lauren and <u>I</u> <u>are</u> wondering <u>whom</u> will win.   <u>No errors</u>
             A B   C   D

18. <u>Your</u> photographs <u>has been chosen</u> by the newspaper
   A   B
    editor <u>whom</u> you met yesterday.   <u>No errors</u>
         C   D

19. <u>Besides</u> Ira and <u>I</u>, there <u>are</u> ten people signed
   A   B   C
    up.   <u>No errors</u>
       D

20. <u>Do</u> Karen and <u>she</u> know where the books <u>are at</u>?   <u>No errors</u>
   A   B   C   D

Unit 3

Mechanics

16

Capital Letters

DIAGNOSTIC TEST

Number your paper 1 to 10. Then write each word that should begin with a capital letter.

EXAMPLE   i would like to spend the winter in florida.
ANSWER   I, Florida

1. i baby-sit for mrs. martha anderson every tuesday night.
2. my brother bill just moved to houston, texas.
3. does labor day fall on september 3 this year?
4. the senator from ohio is running for reelection.
5. has washington, d.c., always been the capital of the united states?
6. everyone in my science class enjoyed the american museum of natural history.
7. henderson high school is the largest school in butler county.
8. have you ever read the book *the call of the wild* by jack london?
9. next year i plan to take english, french, art, biology, european history, and advanced math II.
10. on our trip to the south, we flew into atlanta, georgia, on delta airlines.

Written English is a bit like a detective story. It is filled with many clues that help readers understand an author's message. Capital letters and punctuation are two such clues. If some of the clues are missing, the message can easily become confused and misleading.

RULES FOR CAPITAL LETTERS

By now you probably know most of the rules for capital letters. This chapter, however, can serve as a review—especially since capital letters are such important clues to the meaning of your writing.

First Words

A capital letter signals the beginning of a new idea or a new line in a poem.

16a ▶ Capitalize the first word in a sentence or a line of poetry.

SENTENCE **A** lone rose stood in the vase.
LINES OF **W**ater, water, everywhere,
POETRY **N**or any drop to drink.
—SAMUEL TAYLOR COLERIDGE

NOTE: A few modern poets deliberately misuse or eliminate capital letters. If you are quoting such a poem, copy it exactly as the poet has written it.

I and O

Some words are always capitalized.

16b ▶ Capitalize the pronoun *I*, both alone and in contractions. Also capitalize the interjection *O*.

I **I** hope **I**'ve heard the last of that story.
O "Build thee more stately mansions, **O** my soul."

NOTE: The interjection *oh* is not capitalized unless it comes at the beginning of a sentence.

Proper Nouns

A proper noun is the name of a particular person, place, or thing.

16c ▸ Capitalize proper nouns and their abbreviations.

Names of Persons and Animals. Capitalize the names of particular persons and animals.

PERSONS   Grant, Lisa Ann Thompson, Susan B. Anthony, James Foster, T. H. Murphy, Jr., Timmy

ANIMALS   Rover, Muffin, Morris, Lightning, Peppy

EXERCISE 1   Using Capital Letters

Number your paper 1 to 10. Then write each word that should begin with a capital letter.

1. why did you name your dog roger?
2. with one blow of his ax, paul bunyan toppled an oak.
3. what did carol t. haver say at the conference?
4. exult o shores, and ring o bells!
   but i with mournful tread,
       walk the deck my Captain lies,
       fallen cold and dead.
             — WALT WHITMAN
5. i went to the play, but oh, how bored i was!
6. sean connery starred in the first six movies about james bond.
7. if i find the book, i'll call you.
8. between 1890 and 1895, george w. vanderbilt II had a 280-room house built for him.
9. with only $28,000 henry ford began his motor company in 1903.
10. my mother named her cats charlie and esther.

16c

Geographical Names. Capitalize particular places and bodies of water.

STREETS, HIGHWAYS	Maple Avenue, Pennsylvania Turnpike, Marcy Boulevard, Route 30, Forty-second Street [The second part of a hyphenated numbered street is not capitalized.]
TOWNS, CITIES	Canton, San Francisco, Memphis
COUNTIES, TOWNSHIPS	Pike County, Franklin Township
STATES	Ohio, North Carolina, Arizona
COUNTRIES	Canada, United States, France
SECTION OF A COUNTRY	the Midwest, the Southwest, the East [Compass directions do not begin with a capital letter. *Go east on Route 4.*]
CONTINENTS	Europe, Asia, North America
ISLANDS	Hawaiian Islands, Long Island
MOUNTAINS	Rocky Mountains, Appalachian Mountains, Mount McKinley
PARKS	Yosemite National Park, the Grand Canyon, Elizabeth Park
BODIES OF WATER	Missouri River, the Great Lakes, the Pacific Ocean, Niagara Falls

NOTE: Words such as *street, lake, ocean,* and *mountain* are capitalized only when they are part of a proper noun.

Which is the smallest lake of the Great Lakes?

EXERCISE 2   Capitalizing Geographical Names
Write the following geographical names, adding capital letters only where needed.

1. new delhi, india
2. munroe falls
3. thirty-third street
4. a river in georgia
5. fort lauderdale
6. north dakota

7. great smoky mountains
8. lake michigan
9. south america
10. central park
11. north on route 20
12. el paso, texas
13. dawson county
14. the south
15. antarctica
16. the indian ocean
17. saudi arabia
18. catalina island
19. mount rushmore
20. memorial highway

EXERCISE 3   Using Capital Letters

Number your paper 1 to 10. Then write each word that should begin with a capital letter.

Trivia
Time

1. the capital of manitoba, canada, is winnipeg.
2. lake titicaca in south america is the highest large lake above sea level.
3. the first pay telephone was installed in hartford, connecticut, in 1889.
4. located in california, mount whitney towers 14,494 feet above sea level.
5. christopher columbus discovered the virgin islands.
6. leather money was used in the soviet union until the seventeenth century.
7. the first straw hat was produced in america in 1798 by a 12-year-old girl from rhode island.
8. the city of paris, france, is over 2,000 years old.
9. louis blériot became the first man to fly across the english channel.
10. brazil is the most populous country in latin america.

EXERCISE 4   Writing Sentences

Write five or six sentences that describe a place you have visited, read about, or seen on television. Mention its location and points of interest. Be sure to capitalize all geographical names.

Nouns of Historical Importance.   Capitalize the names of historical events, periods, and documents.

EVENTS	World War II, the Battle of Bull Run
PERIODS	the Renaissance, the Middle Ages, the Industrial Revolution, the Ice Age
DOCUMENTS	the Declaration of Independence, the Constitution, the Treaty of Versailles

NOTE: Prepositions are not capitalized.

Names of Groups and Businesses. Capitalize the names of organizations, businesses, institutions, government bodies, and political parties.

ORGANIZATIONS	the American Red Cross, the United Nations, the Boston Red Sox
BUSINESSES	the Ford Motor Company, the Xerox Corporation, Lexington Lumber
INSTITUTIONS	the University of Chicago, Emerson High School, Memorial Hospital [Words such as *university, high school,* and *hospital* are not capitalized unless they are a part of a proper noun. *Where is the nearest hospital?*]
GOVERNMENT BODIES	Congress, the State Department, the Bureau of Labor Statistics
POLITICAL PARTIES	Democratic Party, Republican Party, a Democrat, a Republican

Specific Time Periods and Events. Capitalize days of the week, months of the year, civil and religious holidays, and special events.

DAYS, MONTHS	Tuesday, Sunday, February, June
HOLIDAYS	Valentine's Day, New Year's Day, Labor Day, Fourth of July
SPECIAL EVENTS	the Orange Bowl Parade, the New York Marathon, the Junior Prom

NOTE: Do not capitalize the seasons of the year unless they are part of a proper noun.

I like **w**inter best.   Did you go to the **W**inter Fair?

EXERCISE 5 Capitalizing Proper Nouns

Write the following items, adding capital letters only where needed.

1. world war I
2. thanksgiving
3. summer
4. olympic games
5. the senate
6. december
7. the stone age
8. veterans day
9. monday
10. the united way
11. a hospital in new jersey
12. fourth of july parade
13. raytheon company
14. rock island railroad
15. a high school in detroit
16. the monroe doctrine
17. national security council
18. the library of congress
19. the treaty of paris
20. the republican party

EXERCISE 6 Using Capital Letters

Number your paper 1 to 10. Then write each word that should begin with a capital letter.

1. many students in school must memorize the preamble to the constitution of the united states.
2. next year memorial day falls on the last monday in may.
3. william c. potts of the detroit police department is credited with the invention of traffic lights.
4. the treaty of paris ended the american revolution.
5. two religious holidays are christmas and hanukkah.
6. my report about the united nations focused on the general assembly and the security council.
7. many years ago the george b. carpenter company sold tents for $6.85 each.
8. the symbol of the democratic party is a donkey.
9. the truman doctrine marked a turning point in the foreign policy of the united states.
10. last winter i took a tour through the senate and the house of representatives.

EXERCISE 7   Writing Sentences
Write four or five related facts about an historical event. Be sure to capitalize each proper noun.

Nationalities, Races, and Languages.   Capitalize the names of nationalities, races, and languages.

NATIONALITIES   an **A**merican, a **C**anadian, a **M**exican
RACES   **C**aucasian, **O**riental, **A**fro-American
LANGUAGES   **S**panish, **G**erman, **I**talian, **R**ussian

Religions and Religious References.   Capitalize the names of religions and names referring to the Deity, the Bible, and divisions of the Bible. Also capitalize pronouns that refer to the Deity.

RELIGIONS   **C**hristianity, **J**udaism, **B**uddhism
RELIGIOUS   **J**ehovah, the **L**ord, **G**od and **H**is children,
REFERENCES   the **B**ible, **E**xodus, the **S**criptures

NOTE: The word *god* is not capitalized when it refers to mythological gods.

Neptune was the god of the sea.

Names of Stars, Planets, and Constellations.   Capitalize the names of the stars, planets, and constellations.

STARS   the **D**og **S**tar, **C**anopus, the **N**orth **S**tar
PLANETS   **M**ars, **S**aturn, **V**enus, **P**luto, **J**upiter
CONSTELLATIONS   the **M**ilky **W**ay, the **B**ig **D**ipper

NOTE: The words *sun* and *moon* are not capitalized. *Earth* is not capitalized if it is preceded by the word *the.*

Other Proper Nouns.   Other proper nouns should also begin with a capital letter.

AIRCRAFT, SPACECRAFT   the *Concorde, Titan II*
AWARDS   the **N**obel **P**rize, an **O**scar, an **E**mmy, the **H**eisman **T**rophy

289

BRAND NAMES	**P**rell shampoo, **C**amay soap [The product itself is *not* capitalized.]
MONUMENTS, MEMORIALS	the **W**ashington **M**onument, the **L**incoln **M**emorial
BUILDINGS	the **E**mpire **S**tate **B**uilding, the **E**iffel **T**ower, **F**irst **N**ational **B**ank
SHIPS, TRAINS	the *Mayflower,* the *Chesapeake*
NAMES OF COURSES	**H**istory 1A, **A**rt II, **L**atin, **E**nglish

NOTE: Do not capitalize the name of an unnumbered course such as *history, math,* or *biology,* unless it is the name of a language.

Last year I studied **h**istory, **a**rt, and **J**apanese.

Also, do not capitalize class names such as *freshman* and *senior* unless they are part of a proper noun.

Eighty percent of the **s**eniors are going to the **S**enior Prom.

EXERCISE 8   Capitalizing Proper Nouns

Write the following items, adding capital letters only where needed.

1. typing and spanish
2. kraft cheese
3. the new testament
4. nine lives cat food
5. god and his kingdom
6. the vietnam memorial
7. advanced geometry II
8. the pulitzer prize
9. judaism
10. *spirit of st. louis*
11. the sun and mars
12. polish and russian
13. presbyterian
14. the *hindenberg*
15. a canadian
16. statue of liberty
17. a methodist
18. the war of 1812
19. the world trade center
20. sirius and other stars

EXERCISE 9   Using Capital Letters

Number your paper 1 to 10. Then write each word that should begin with a capital letter.

1. like venus, jupiter has a thick cloud cover.
2. twenty-one million americans now play the piano.
3. the greatest concentration of catholics in the united states is in rhode island.
4. is exodus the second book in the old testament?
5. in 1976, *viking 1* landed on mars.
6. after the thirty years' war, the french, not the germans, became the leading watchmakers.
7. at night, north can be determined almost exactly by locating the position of polaris, the north star.
8. three out of four people living in utah are mormon.
9. the diameter, density, and gravity of venus are similar to those of the earth.
10. the lincoln memorial in washington, d.c., is the work of daniel chester french.

EXERCISE 10 Writing Sentences

Write one sentence that names each course that you are studying this year. Be sure to capitalize languages, names of numbered courses, and any other proper nouns that you may use.

EXERCISE 11 Time-out for Review

Number your paper 1 to 20. Then write each word that should begin with a capital letter.

Who's Who

1. was william sherman a general in the american revolution or the civil war?
2. who wrote the declaration of independence?
3. who carried the message that the british were coming through massachusetts?
4. is andrew wyeth a painter or a member of the united states senate?
5. who were the two explorers that led an expedition from st. louis, missouri, to the pacific ocean in 1804?
6. is george c. scott a composer or the winner of an oscar?
7. who was the couple that tried to rule the roman empire from the nile river?

8. what famous person's address is 1600 pennsylvania avenue, washington, d.c.?
9. is sara lee a winner in the olympics or a brand name?
10. did captain james kirk or captain bligh command the *starship enterprise?*
11. who joined the boston bruins at age 18 and led the team to win the stanley cup?
12. who was the first american to set foot on the moon?
13. who flew across the atlantic ocean in the *spirit of st. louis?*
14. who paid for the statue of liberty in new york by giving donations, the french or the americans?
15. did thomas edison or george eastman invent the first kodak camera?
16. who delivered the gettysburg address to the nation during the civil war?
17. who painted the ceiling of the sistine chapel in the vatican in rome?
18. washington, jefferson, lincoln, and who else are part of the mount rushmore memorial?
19. who was the fictitious character who lived on baker street in london, england?
20. who led his troops across the delaware river to attack the british during the american revolution?

Proper Adjectives

Proper adjectives are formed from proper nouns. Like proper nouns, proper adjectives begin with a capital letter.

16d Capitalize most proper adjectives.

PROPER NOUNS	PROPER ADJECTIVES
France	French doors
Rome	Roman numeral
Alaska	Alaskan oil
Boston	Boston baked beans

NOTE: Some adjectives that originated from proper nouns are so common that they are no longer capitalized.

Be careful not to drop the **c**hina plate.

EXERCISE 12 Capitalizing Proper Adjectives

Write the following items, adding capital letters only where needed.

1. a chinese restaurant
2. a british naval officer
3. a former french colony
4. an ancient egyptian tomb
5. irish stew
6. new england weather
7. a german clock
8. a turkish towel
9. maine lobster
10. a swedish ship

Titles

Capital letters indicate the importance of titles of people, written works, and other works of art.

16e Capitalize certain titles.

Titles Used with Names of People. Capitalize a title showing office, rank, or profession when it comes directly before a person's name.

BEFORE A NAME Have you met **D**r. Anna Richman?
AFTER A NAME Jennifer Kemp is also a **d**octor.

BEFORE A NAME Did you vote for **G**overnor Harper?
AFTER A NAME Did you think George Harper would be elected **g**overnor?

Titles Used Alone. Capitalize a title that is used alone when the title is being substituted for a person's name in direct address.

USED AS A NAME Please, **D**octor, may I speak with you?
I didn't see the sign, **O**fficer.

293

Titles of high government officials, such as *President, Vice-President, Chief Justice,* and *Queen of England,* are almost always capitalized when they stand alone.

The **P**resident made a trip to China.

NOTE: *President* and *vice-president* are capitalized when they stand alone only if they refer to the current president or vice-president.

Titles Showing Family Relationships. Capitalize a title showing family relationship when it comes directly before a person's name, when it is used as a name, or when it is being substituted for a person's name in direct address.

BEFORE A NAME   Did you call **A**unt **H**arriet?
USED AS A NAME   May we watch the late movie, **M**om?

Do not capitalize titles showing family relationship when they are preceded by a possessive noun or pronoun — unless the titles are considered part of a person's name.

Have you met Ted's **a**unt?
Have you met Ted's **A**unt Katherine?

EXERCISE 13   Capitalizing Titles of People
Number your paper 1 to 10. Then write each word that should begin with a capital letter. If a sentence is correct, write *C* after the number.

1. My uncle is coming for a visit.
2. The president of the united states and the queen of england met for the first time recently.
3. My aunt ruth is going to marry senator tobin.
4. Thanks, sis, for helping me with the dishes.
5. My brother jeff is running for president of our club.
6. The senators from our state will visit our school.
7. Could I make a suggestion, coach?
8. When did you decide to become a dentist?
9. Who is the superintendent of your school district?
10. The pastor of our church knows ambassador lang.

Titles of Written Works and Other Works of Art. Capitalize the first word, the last word, and all important words in the titles of books, newspapers, periodicals, stories, poems, movies, plays, musical compositions, and other works of art. Do *not* capitalize a preposition, a conjunction, or an article (*a, an,* and *the*) — unless it is the first word of a title.

BOOK AND CHAPTER TITLES	I just finished reading a chapter called "**The M**an on the **T**or" in the book *The Hound of the Baskervilles.*
NEWSPAPERS, PERIODICALS	My family subscribes to the *Chicago Tribune* and to *Field and Stream.* [Generally, do not capitalize *the* as the first word of a newspaper or a periodical title.]
MOVIES	I have seen both *Star Wars* and *E.T.* three times.
MUSICAL WORKS	My favorite song from Willie Nelson's album *Always on My Mind* is "**A W**hiter **S**hade of **P**ale."
WORKS OF ART	When I was at the museum, I especially enjoyed the paintings *The Sleeping Gypsy* and *Fur Traders on the Missouri.*

EXERCISE 14 Capitalizing Titles of Things
Number your paper 1 to 10. Then write each word that should begin with a capital letter.

1. My sister is a reporter for the *washington post.*
2. The best song in the play *cats* is "memory."
3. Do you know who wrote the book *sawdust in his shoes?*
4. Yesterday I memorized the poem "casey at the bat."
5. Probably everyone has seen a picture of the famous statue *the thinker.*
6. My favorite short story is "to build a fire."
7. Many paintings, such as *the ceiling of saint matthew,* have religious themes.

8. I read an article called "solar energy."
9. I just saw a local production of *the pirates of penzance.*
10. Isn't the song "somewhere over the rainbow" from *the wizard of oz?*

Letters

When you write a letter, keep in mind all of the rules that you have learned in this chapter—plus one more.

16f ▶ Capitalize the first word and all nouns in a salutation and the first word in the closing of a letter.

SALUTATIONS **D**ear **H**arvey,   **D**ear **S**ir:
CLOSINGS **Y**our friend,   **S**incerely,

NOTE: A comma comes after the salutation in a friendly letter, but a colon follows the salutation in a business letter. A comma always follows the closing of a letter.

EXERCISE 15   Using Capital Letters in a Letter
Write the letter below using capital letters where needed.

136 willow road
winfield, wisconsin 53711
april 26, 1986

rogers sporting goods company
1781 south olympia avenue
chicago, illinois 60657

dear sir or madam:
   in your regular mail-order catalog, you list a number of specialized booklets which you invite your customers to order. I would like the <u>boating and fishing catalog</u>.
   I am looking forward to hearing from you.

very truly yours,

Kevin Murphy

kevin murphy

EXERCISE 16   Time-out for Review

Number your paper 1 to 20. Then write each word that should begin with a capital letter.

1. what are the names of the stars in the movies *duck soup* and *a night at the opera?*
2. what are the seven roman numerals?
3. what god in greek mythology held the world on his shoulders?
4. an old form of what sport takes place in the story "rip van winkle"?
5. what is the name of the fictional reporter who worked on the *daily planet* in the city of metropolis?
6. what is the name of the movie in which a giant ape, fay wray, and the empire state building were featured?
7. what is the name of the captain of the *nautilus* in the film *20,000 leagues under the sea?*
8. what is the motto of the boy scouts of america?
9. what does the initial stand for in president john f. kennedy's name?
10. what is the name of the football team in dallas, texas, the cowboys or the broncos?
11. what was the name of the president of the confederacy during the civil war?
12. what are the chief ingredients of english muffins?
13. what group recorded "i want to hold your hand"?
14. what television series has run longer, *meet the press* or *search for tomorrow?*
15. what is the name of the author of the novel *the red badge of courage?*
16. in the united states, what is the first monday after the first tuesday in september called?
17. what is the lower priced property in monopoly, baltic avenue or mediterranean avenue?
18. in what art museum does the *mona lisa* hang?
19. what is the name of the first american writer to win the nobel prize?
20. in what book is captain ahab a character, *two years before the mast* or *moby dick?*

Application to Writing

After you write, always edit for proper capitalization.

EXERCISE 17   Editing for Capital Letters

Write all the words in the following paragraphs that should have a capital letter. Do not include words that are already capitalized.

A
Mighty
River

High in the lofty snow-covered andes mountains the amazon river begins. It runs eastward across the continent of south america, flowing through the jungles of brazil. Finally it empties into the atlantic ocean.

The mighty amazon river has more water flowing through it than north america's mississippi, egypt's nile, and china's yangtze river—all put together! The reason for this fact is that the drainage basin of the giant south american river lies in one of the rainiest regions of the world.

CHAPTER REVIEW

Number your paper 1 to 20. Then write each word that should begin with a capital letter.

1. the world's largest church is st. peter's in rome.
2. the *voyager* missions studied jupiter and saturn.
3. the soviet union is the largest country in the world.
4. during thanksgiving vacation i read about the *titanic*.
5. required courses for juniors are english, math II, biology, and american history.
6. in his novel *the grapes of wrath*, john steinbeck tells about the problems of the poor in oklahoma.
7. the houston oaks hotel is in the southwest.
8. last fall my aunt pat flew to athens on world airways.
9. did michigan ever beat nebraska in the cotton bowl?
10. yes, senator parks will speak at logan high school.
11. have you read the book *dr. jekyll and mr. hyde?*

12. the west indies form an island arc in the atlantic ocean.
13. the irish potato originated in south america.
14. the *orient express* train ran from france to turkey.
15. the snake river flows from wyoming to washington.
16. the university of utah was founded in 1850.
17. pasta appeared in italy after the renaissance.
18. the nickname for utah is the beehive state.
19. the treaty of versailles ended world war I.
20. the *apollo 16* carried a special camera to take pictures of the moon.

MASTERY TEST

Number your paper 1 to 10. Then write each word that should begin with a capital letter.

1. last monday we ate in an italian restaurant in new haven.
2. would it be all right, mom, if i invited mrs. reese to dinner?
3. the mississippi river flows from minnesota to the gulf of mexico.
4. a museum in vermont is closed on mondays during the winter months.
5. the elizabethan era was named after queen elizabeth I of england.
6. during the american revolution the battle of bunker hill was actually fought on breed's hill.
7. our new ambassador to turkey was formerly a senator from new mexico.
8. an english army defeated a much larger french army at the battle of agincourt in 1415.
9. *christina's world* is a painting by andrew wyeth.
10. from earth the andromeda galaxy is faintly visible to the eye.

17

End Marks and Commas

Number your paper 1 to 10. Write each sentence, adding commas where needed. Then write an appropriate end mark.

EXAMPLE   Yes Paul was born in Des Moines Iowa
ANSWER   Yes, Paul was born in Des Moines, Iowa.

1. Mrs Burns my sixth grade teacher just got married
2. Jeffrey does not play baseball tennis or hockey
3. Sandy did Sue move to Phoenix Arizona
4. Write to Harold Fox 950 Ridley Avenue Folsom Pennsylvania 19033 for more information
5. When Arlene first entered the contest did she have any hope of winning
6. Roberta has such a playful friendly puppy
7. Well I never saw two people do the dishes so quickly
8. The peas not the lima beans should have been picked
9. Ida and Lee however are the two best science students
10. I was born on September 3 1974 in a small town

Imagine New York City without any traffic lights or stop signs. There would be utter confusion. The result of writing without end marks or commas would be very much the same.

In this chapter you will review the three different end marks and the four different types of sentences to which those end marks are added. In addition, you will review the use of the period with abbreviations and the uses of the comma.

KINDS OF SENTENCES AND END MARKS

A sentence may have one of four different purposes or functions. The purpose of a sentence determines the punctuation mark that goes at the end. A sentence may be *declarative, imperative, interrogative,* or *exclamatory.*

One purpose of a sentence is to make a statement or to express an opinion.

17a > A **declarative sentence** makes a statement or expresses an opinion and ends with a period.

Following are two examples of declarative sentences. Notice that the second sentence makes a statement, even though it contains an indirect question.

Modern highways go around cities, not through them.

I asked them what time they were leaving. [A direct question would be *What time are they leaving?*]

A second purpose of a sentence is to give directions, make requests, or give commands. The subject of these kinds of sentences is usually an understood *you.*

17b > An **imperative sentence** gives a direction, makes a request, or gives a command. It ends with either a period or an exclamation point.

Although all of the following examples are imperative, two are followed by a period, and one is followed by an exclamation point.

Turn left.

Please answer the phone.

Call the fire department! [This command would be stated with great excitement or emphasis.]

Sometimes an imperative sentence is expressed as a question, but no reply is expected. Because the purpose of the sentence still remains to request or command, the sentence is followed by a period or an exclamation point — not by a question mark.

May I please have your attention.

A third purpose of a sentence is to ask a question.

17c An **interrogative sentence** asks a question and ends with a question mark.

Following are two examples of interrogative sentences. Notice that the second example is phrased as a statement, but it is intended as a question.

What is the capital of Illinois?
You've been here for 20 minutes?

NOTE: Some questions are not expressed completely; nevertheless, they are followed by a question mark.

You didn't return my call. Why not?

A fourth purpose of a sentence is to express a feeling such as excitement, joy, anger, fear, or surprise.

17d An **exclamatory sentence** expresses strong feeling or emotion and ends with an exclamation point.

I should have thought of that myself!
It's too late now!

Use exclamatory sentences sparingly when you write. They lose their impact when they are used too often.

NOTE: Remember that an exclamation point also follows an interjection. *(See page 75.)*

Wow! That was a wonderful surprise.

EXERCISE 1 Classifying Sentences

Number your paper 1 to 20. Write an appropriate end mark for each sentence. Then label each sentence *declarative, imperative, interrogative,* or *exclamatory.*

1. How far north do palm trees grow
2. I just won ten thousand dollars
3. Would everyone please follow me
4. After you mow the lawn, rake up the clippings
5. Reno, Nevada, is farther west than Los Angeles
6. Which planet is closest to Earth
7. Only rarely do whooping cranes breed in captivity
8. Mother asked why you didn't empty the rubbish can
9. Go to bed right this minute
10. Two professional sports many people watch regularly are baseball and basketball
11. I need to find out what time rehearsal starts
12. Can your dog do any tricks
13. You should do warm-up exercises before jogging
14. Answer the doorbell for me
15. The water in the basement is getting higher and higher
16. Don't go near that burning building
17. Abraham Lincoln wrote over 500 musical pieces
18. How much does a ten-gallon hat really hold
19. I just saw a shark swim by
20. Write your name at the top of the test

EXERCISE 2 Writing Sentences

Write four sentences about space travel in the future. One sentence should be declarative, one imperative, one interrogative, and one exclamatory. Label each sentence according to its purpose.

PERIODS WITH ABBREVIATIONS

Using abbreviations when you write can help you save time. They are useful when you take notes in class or write a quick message. However, most abbreviations should be avoided in formal writing.

17e Use a period after most abbreviations.

Following are a few examples of abbreviations that are acceptable in formal writing. For a listing of other abbreviations, check the dictionary.

| TITLES WITH NAMES | Mr. | Ms. | Rev. | Sgt. | Jr. |
| | Mrs. | Dr. | Gen. | Lt. | Sr. |

TITLES WITH NAMES [*Miss* is not an abbreviation; it has no period.]

TIMES WITH NUMBERS
A.M. (*ante meridiem* — before noon)
P.M. (*post meridiem* — after noon)
B.C. (before Christ)
A.D. (*anno Domini* — in the year of the Lord)

If an abbreviation is the last word of a statement, only one period is necessary. However, if an abbreviation comes at the end of a question, both a period and a question mark are needed. Two marks are also needed when a sentence ends with an abbreviation and an exclamation point.

I'd like to introduce you to Ronald Franklin, Jr.
Should I meet you at 10:00 P.M.?

NOTE: A few special abbreviations are used without periods. Following are some examples.

UN   CIA   FM   TV   IBM   TWA   TX   NY

EXERCISE 3   Writing Abbreviations
Write the abbreviations that stand for the following items. Be sure to include periods where needed. If you are unsure of the spelling or the punctuation of a particular abbreviation, look it up in the dictionary.

1. before Christ
2. mister
3. United States
4. Rhode Island
5. October
6. incorporated
7. Wednesday
8. United Kingdom
9. Bachelor of Arts
10. National Football League

11. association
12. miles per hour
13. boulevard
14. latitude
15. dozen
16. major
17. ounce
18. Fahrenheit
19. mountain
20. *post meridiem*

COMMAS

Although there may seem to be many uses for the comma, there are basically only two. Commas are used to separate items and to enclose items.

Commas That Separate

Commas are used to prevent confusion and to keep items from running into one another. Following are some specific rules for commas that are used to separate items.

Items in a Series. Three or more similar items together form a series. A series can be composed of words, phrases, or clauses.

17f Use commas to separate items in a series.

WORDS Blackberries, raspberries, and strawberries are all members of the rose family. [nouns]
Anita will sing, dance, or tell jokes. [verbs]
We were tired, dirty, and wet. [adjectives]

PHRASES The cat could be in the closet, under the bed, or behind the couch.

CLAUSES We don't know when we are leaving, where we are going, or what we should take.

When a conjunction connects the last two items in a series, some writers omit the last comma. Although this is acceptable, it can be confusing. Therefore, it is always better to include the comma before the conjunction.

CONFUSING   I had juice, bacon and corn pancakes.
    CLEAR   I had juice, bacon, and corn pancakes.

When conjunctions connect all the items in a series, no commas are needed.

> We pushed **and** shoved **and** fought our way out of the toy department. [no commas]

NOTE: Some pairs of words, such as *bacon and eggs*, are thought of as a single item. If one of these pairs of words appears in a series, consider it one item.

> For dinner you could have franks and beans, fish and chips, or pork and sauerkraut.

EXERCISE 4   Using Commas in a Series

Number your paper 1 to 20. Then write each sentence, adding commas where needed. If a sentence does not need any commas, write *C* after the number.

1. The longest known sentence ever written contains 823 words 93 commas 51 semicolons and 4 dashes.
2. Among the strangest names of towns in the United States are Accident Soso Helper and Battiest.
3. Could you tell me when the library opens where it is and how I can get there?
4. The *H* in 4-H Club stands for head heart hands and health.
5. Tadpoles develop hind legs first grow front legs next and finally lose their tails.
6. Two Adamses and two Harrisons and two Roosevelts have been president.
7. A minuet is slow stately and dignified.
8. Interstate 95 goes from New England around Washington and into Florida.

9. How did you get your jacket shoes socks and slacks so muddy?
10. Did you know that harvesting machines reap the grain thresh it and clean it?
11. My cousin Shawn practices the tuba in the morning during the late afternoon and at night.
12. Somerset Maugham Leo Tolstoy and Michelangelo were all working at age 80.
13. The graphite and clay in pencil lead are ground together pressed into thin sticks and baked.
14. Do you like raisin and nut apple and cinnamon or peanut butter and oatmeal granola bars?
15. Did Thomas Edison invent the phonograph in 1833 or in 1877 or in 1903?
16. At Sun Valley we will ski practice our skating and have fun in the snow.
17. Alan Shepard John Glenn and Sally Ride are famous American astronauts.
18. Tell me where I should stand on the stage what I should do and what I should say.
19. News broadcasts soap operas and situational comedies are usually recorded on videotape.
20. Down coats are lightweight extremely warm but somewhat bulky.

EXERCISE 5 Writing Sentences

Write each sentence, filling the blank with a series of three or more appropriate items. Then add commas where needed.

1. On his hamburger Jerry put _____.
2. This year in school I am studying _____.
3. My favorite foods are _____.
4. The birds _____ outside my window every morning.
5. Before leaving for school in the morning, I _____.
6. The weather yesterday was _____.
7. Look for the suitcase _____.

8. The old car _____ up the hill.
9. _____ are my favorite sports.
10. A _____ tree stood on the edge of the cliff.

Adjectives before a Noun. If a conjunction is missing between two adjectives that come before a noun, a comma is sometimes used to take its place.

The rabbits disappeared into the tall, dry grass.

17g Use a comma sometimes to separate two adjectives that precede a noun and are not joined by a conjunction.

There is a test that can help you decide if a comma is needed between two adjectives. If the sentence reads sensibly with *and* between the adjectives, a comma is needed.

COMMA NEEDED   Today was a damp, dismal day. [*A damp and dismal day* reads well.]

COMMA NOT NEEDED   Today was a damp spring day. [*A damp and spring day* does not read well.]

EXERCISE 6   Using Commas with Adjectives
Number your paper 1 to 20. Then write each sentence, adding commas where needed. If a sentence does not need any commas, write *C* after the number.

1. Zip is the biggest strongest dog on the block.
2. Some cacti produce beautiful delicate flowers.
3. My mother just bought a musical German clock.
4. My uncle's house is surrounded by small green shrubs.
5. My father couldn't read the torn wet newspaper.
6. We store tools in a sturdy wooden box.
7. The loud piercing alarm awoke us.
8. The bright clear colors of the old photographs were amazing.
9. The large white house on Baker Street has been sold.
10. Mr. Roberts is the tall dignified man in the blue suit.
11. Last year the ice bent to the ground the oldest most beautiful birch in our garden.

12. Sardines are actually any of a number of small thin-boned fish.
13. The sparkling blue sapphire is the birthstone for the month of September.
14. Brad is the tall good-looking boy on the stage.
15. Young growing spiders can regenerate missing legs and parts of legs.
16. Who lives in that tall brick house?
17. Their quiet peaceful home was never the same after the arrival of the two frisky kittens.
18. The 1500-pound leatherback turtle carries a shell as big as a king-sized bed.
19. The banana is an inexpensive versatile fruit.
20. Black-and-white dairy cows are Holsteins.

Compound Sentences. A comma is usually used to separate the independent clauses in a compound sentence.

17h Use a comma to separate the independent clauses of a compound sentence if the clauses are joined by a conjunction.

A coordinating conjunction most often combines a compound sentence.

Coordinating Conjunctions						
and	but	for	nor	or	so	yet

Notice in the following examples that the comma comes before the conjunction.

Don't tease the dog, or it may bite you.
I play the flute, and my sister plays the cello.

A comma is not needed in a very short compound sentence.

Otis left but I stayed.

NOTE: Be careful that you do not confuse a compound sentence with a sentence that has a compound verb. No comma comes between the parts of a compound verb unless there are three or more verbs.

COMPOUND SENTENCE	We waited for ten minutes**,** but Ben never came. [A comma is needed.]
COMPOUND VERB	We waited for ten minutes and then left. [No comma is needed.]

NOTE: A compound sentence can also be joined by a semicolon. *(See page 158.)*

EXERCISE 7   Using Commas with Compound Sentences
Number your paper 1 to 20. Then write each sentence, adding commas where needed. If a sentence does not need any commas, write *C* after the number.

1. Most animals remain on land but a few are equipped for gliding.
2. Terry caught the fish and Bryan cooked them.
3. The squirrel ran up and darted across the roof.
4. Palm trees are desert trees but they have been transplanted to other areas.
5. The gorilla looks fierce but it is a rather gentle animal.
6. Gourds are hard-shelled and may be used as cups.
7. You wash and I'll dry.
8. A schooner has at least two masts but a sloop has one.
9. The skink looks like a snake but has very tiny legs.
10. Either the rain soaked the mats or someone spilled water on them.
11. I want to go to the movies yet I have homework to do.
12. New York City has an average annual rainfall of 43 inches but a city in India gets 36 feet annually.
13. There is little green in Greenland for the island is covered with ice and snow most of the year.
14. The Australian earthworm grows four feet long and lays eggs the size of olives.
15. Poison ivy is dangerous but it is easily recognized.

16. Decide on a color for your room for I'd like to buy the paint this afternoon.
17. Bryan didn't mention your telephone call nor did he leave me a message.
18. Drifting snow can stall an automobile and bury it in a very short period of time.
19. Canadian football and American football have different rules but have many similar features.
20. I asked Ed to help me yet he did not help me willingly.

EXERCISE 8   Writing Sentences
Write one compound sentence for each of the following subjects. Make sure that the clauses in each compound sentence are related. Add commas where needed.

1. food   2. hobbies   3. friends   4. jobs   5. sports

Introductory Elements.   Some words, phrases, and clauses at the beginning of a sentence need to be separated from the rest of the sentence by a comma.

17i ▶   Use a comma after certain introductory elements.

Following are examples of introductory elements that should be followed by a comma.

WORDS	**No,** I cannot attend the meeting. [Other words include *now, oh, well, why,* and *yes*—except when they are part of the sentence. *Why did you do that?*]
PREPOSITIONAL PHRASE	**After the earthquake in town,** we all helped each other. [A comma comes after two or more prepositional phrases or a single phrase of four or more words. A comma does not come after a short prepositional phrase. Also, a comma does not come after a phrase or phrases that are followed by a verb. *To the bottom of the sea sank the ship.*]

311

PARTICIPIAL PHRASE   **Hearing the noise outside,** I rushed to the window.

ADVERB CLAUSE   **As Toby walked closer,** the cat hissed at him.

OTHERS   **In Room 47,** 35 students were studying. **In the road,** blocks of wood were a traffic hazard. [The commas in these sentences prevent a reader from becoming confused.]

EXERCISE 9   Using Commas with Introductory Elements
Number your paper 1 to 20. Then write each sentence, adding commas where needed. If a sentence does not need a comma, write *C* after the number.

1. Above a glider soared gracefully.
2. If ten inches of snow was melted it would yield about an inch of water.
3. Yes that is a wonderful idea.
4. Before the final exam I studied all my old tests.
5. Deciding the trail was too steep the hikers turned back.
6. After practice in the gym we will meet in Room 3B.
7. No announcement was made prior to the meeting.
8. In 1776 54 delegates signed the Declaration of Independence in Philadelphia.
9. After dinner I will meet you at the library.
10. Down the chimney of our house dropped a bird's nest.
11. From above the clouds the pilot could see the eye of the hurricane.
12. While cooking vegetables lose some of their vitamins.
13. After he had become completely deaf Beethoven wrote most of his best works.
14. Rising 986 feet into the air the Eiffel Tower is Europe's tallest structure.
15. Like many other writers Edgar Allan Poe never earned much money from his writing.
16. Well water often tastes better than tap water.
17. Waving to Mary Sue entered the bus.

18. Insulated by thick layers of blubber whales can dive deep into the icy depths of the ocean.
19. Into the pool jumped Randy and his friends.
20. Because a quorum was not present a vote could not be taken.

EXERCISE 10   Time-out for Review
Write the following paragraphs, adding commas where needed.

At Home in the Water

Pinnipeds are fin-footed mammals with limbs that are used as paddles or flippers. The three main kinds of pinnipeds are the walrus the sea lion and the seal. All pinnipeds are meat eaters and they all live in the water. Most pinnipeds live in the cold waters of the Arctic and the Antarctic oceans but several forms live in freshwater lakes. Since pinnipeds spend most of their lives in the water they have become well adapted to this kind of existence. Their tapered streamlined bodies make them excellent swimmers. Their thick layer of blubber gives them added buoyancy and helps keep them warm.

Searching for food pinnipeds can dive two or three hundred feet below the water's surface. When they are underwater their nostrils close. Most pinnipeds have sharp backward-pointing teeth. This feature makes it possible for a pinniped to seize prey and direct it down its throat. Since pinnipeds are sociable animals they live together much of the time in large herds.

Commas That Enclose

Some expressions interrupt the flow of a sentence. These expressions generally add information that is not needed to understand the main idea of the sentence. If one of these interrupters comes in the middle of a sentence, a comma is placed before and after the expression to set it off.

The movie**, to tell the truth,** was rather boring.

Sometimes an interrupting expression comes at the beginning or the end of a sentence. When an interrupter appears in one of these places, only one comma is needed to separate it from the rest of the sentence.

To tell the truth, the movie was rather boring.
The movie was rather boring, **to tell the truth.**

Direct Address. Names, titles, or words that are used to address someone are set off by commas. These expressions are called nouns of *direct address*.

17j Use commas to enclose nouns of direct address.

Norm, may I borrow your camera?
Your essay, **Marc,** was excellent.
Have you had dinner, **Pearl**?

EXERCISE 11 Using Commas with Direct Address
Write each sentence, adding commas where needed.

1. What's for dinner tonight Mom?
2. Ladies and gentlemen please be seated.
3. Yes Thomas you may work with Flora.
4. I had a wonderful time my friend.
5. Could you tell me Ms. Rann if Dr. Saltus is in?
6. Of course Margaret you can join us.
7. I'll give you the list Tim at Saturday's meeting.
8. Perhaps the next bus will be less crowded Mary.
9. Joan did I leave my books at your house?
10. In ten minutes class you should put your tests on my desk.

EXERCISE 12 Writing Sentences
Write three sentences that follow the directions below. Use commas where needed.

1. Include direct address at the beginning of the sentence.
2. Include direct address in the middle of the sentence.
3. Include direct address at the end of the sentence.

Parenthetical Expressions. A parenthetical expression provides additional information or related ideas. It is related only loosely to the rest of the sentence. The word or words that make up a parenthetical expression could be removed without changing the meaning of the sentence.

17k ▶ Use commas to enclose parenthetical expressions.

Common Parenthetical Expressions

after all	for instance	of course
at any rate	generally speaking	on the contrary
by the way	I believe (guess,	on the other hand
consequently	hope, know)	moreover
however	in fact	nevertheless
for example	in my opinion	to tell the truth

By the way, did you buy a newspaper?

The movie, **in my opinion,** was very realistic.

We'll attend the meeting, **I guess.**

José, **on the other hand,** can come with us.

Other expressions, as well, can be used as parenthetical expressions.

Benjamin Franklin, **we are told,** taught himself three different languages.

According to this article, only three percent of Norway is under cultivation.

Dolphins, **it is known,** communicate with each other.

Contrasting expressions, which usually begin with *not,* are also considered parenthetical expressions.

Nashville, **not Knoxville,** is the capital of Tennessee.

East St. Louis is in Illinois, **not in Missouri.**

Marie, **not Saul,** is president of our class.

EXERCISE 13   **Using Commas with Parenthetical**
                            Expressions

Number your paper 1 to 10. Then write each sentence, adding commas where needed.

1. A fly's taste buds surprisingly enough are located in its feet.
2. Ostriches for instance have wings but cannot fly.
3. Eighty degrees I suppose is too hot for you.
4. Banana oil is derived from potatoes or beets not from bananas.
5. The movie after all won an Academy Award.
6. Jefferson was the third president not the second.
7. The witch-hazel plant blooms only in cold months I believe.
8. Nina like her two brothers is good in math.
9. The book in my opinion was the best that I have ever read.
10. On the other hand palm trees live up to 100 years.

EXERCISE 14   **Writing Sentences**

Write five sentences that follow the directions below. Use commas where needed.

1. Include *in fact* at the beginning of the sentence.
2. Include *by the way* at the beginning of the sentence.
3. Include *however* in the middle of the sentence.
4. Include *I know* in the middle of the sentence.
5. Include *of course* at the end of the sentence.

Appositives. An appositive with its modifiers identifies or explains a noun or pronoun in the sentence. *(See pages 111–113.)*

> The old firehouse**, a town landmark,** is being restored.

17l ▶ Use commas to enclose most appositives and their modifiers.

316

Notice in the following examples that an appositive can come in the middle or at the end of a sentence. If an appositive comes in the middle of a sentence, two commas are needed to enclose it.

Aerobics**, a type of exercise,** is fun to do.
Hanna received a wonderful present**, a down vest.**

Commas are *not* used if an appositive identifies a person or thing by telling which one or ones. Usually these appositives are names and have no modifiers.

My sister **Barbara** will travel to Ohio with me.
The book ***Oliver Twist*** was written by Charles Dickens.
We **students** want more time on the computers.

EXERCISE 15 **Using Commas with Appositives**
Number your paper 1 to 10. Then write each sentence, adding commas where needed. If a sentence does not need any commas, write *C* after the number.

1. Antarctica a large mass of land wasn't really explored until the twentieth century.
2. The name *Caroline* means "strong."
3. Carmel one of the oldest towns in California was founded as a Spanish mission.
4. Have you ever visited Columbia the capital of South Carolina?
5. Zachary Taylor the twelfth president never voted in his life.
6. Francisco Coronado a Spanish explorer brought the first horse to America in 1540.
7. The novelist Rudyard Kipling wrote *Kim.*
8. Hindi the official language of India is spoken by only 35 percent of the population.
9. Alvin Parker once flew a glider a plane without a motor 644 miles.
10. I just bought a new thesaurus a most useful reference book.

EXERCISE 16 Writing Sentences

Write ten sentences that use each of the following groups of words as appositives. Use commas where needed.

EXAMPLE   my favorite author
POSSIBLE ANSWER   Isaac Asimov, my favorite author, writes
                   science fiction stories.

1. my favorite dessert   6. a good friend of mine
2. a food rich in protein   7. a book I have read
3. a recent movie   8. a new TV program
4. an exciting sport   9. a large city
5. an interesting hobby   10. my favorite course

EXERCISE 17 Time-out for Review

Number your paper 1 to 10. Then write each sentence, adding commas where needed. If a sentence does not need any commas, write *C* after the number.

1. Women not men are in the majority in the United States.
2. No the peak month for colds is not July.
3. The vanilla plant a member of the orchid family is cultivated in various tropical countries.
4. Everyone is afraid of my dog Twinkles.
5. Wait Loretta while I make a telephone call.
6. No one knows the origin of the story of Paul Bunyan the legendary lumberjack.
7. Many people you will find do not enjoy television quiz shows.
8. Book reports like compositions should be very well organized.
9. Let's have hamburgers for dinner tonight Mom.
10. Why that's a wonderful idea!

Nonessential Elements. Sometimes a participial phrase or a clause is not essential to the meaning of a sentence.

17m Use commas to set off nonessential participial phrases and nonessential clauses.

318

A participial phrase or a clause is nonessential if it provides extra, unnecessary information.

NONESSENTIAL   Homing pigeons**, used as messengers,** fly at a speed of 30 miles an hour. [participial phrase]

NONESSENTIAL   Three inches is the annual rainfall in Yuma, Arizona**, which is in the southwestern part of the state.** [clause]

If the nonessential phrase and clause in the preceding examples were dropped, the main idea of the sentences would not be changed in any way.

Homing pigeons fly at a speed of 30 miles an hour.
Three inches is the annual rainfall in Yuma, Arizona.

If a participial phrase or a clause is essential to the meaning of a sentence, no commas are used. Essential phrases and clauses usually identify a person or thing and answer the question *Which one?* Adjective clauses that begin with *that* are always essential.

ESSENTIAL   We enjoyed the film **playing at the Plaza.** [participial phrase]

ESSENTIAL   The runner **who crossed the finish line second** is my sister. [clause]

ESSENTIAL   The house **that has stood for years on the corner of Elm and Park** will be torn down. [clause]

If the essential clause and phrase in the preceding examples were dropped, necessary information would be missing. The main idea of the sentences would be incomplete.

The house will be torn down. [Which house?]
We enjoyed the film. [Which film?]
The runner is my sister. [Which runner?]

NOTE: Nonessential and essential elements are also called *nonrestrictive* and *restrictive.*

EXERCISE 18 **Using Commas with Nonessential Elements**
Number your paper 1 to 20. Then write each sentence,
adding commas where needed. If a sentence does not need
any commas, write *C* after the number.

1. Home-grown vegetables that are not properly canned
   can cause botulism.
2. We saw two bear cubs hiding in a hollow tree.
3. The pronghorn antelope living only in North America
   has no close relatives.
4. A sport that many Scots enjoy is curling.
5. Curling which resembles bowling is played on ice.
6. Huskies warmed by their thick coats can sleep in the
   snow.
7. Ogunquit which is on the ocean is a resort town in
   southern Maine.
8. Where is the watch that Dad gave you for your birthday?
9. Mount McKinley located near the Arctic Circle may
   well be the world's coldest mountain.
10. A book that I enjoyed reading is *David Copperfield*.
11. Samuel Houston for whom the city of Houston was
    named was a frontier hero.
12. Mozart gave a concert at an age when most children are
    just starting school.
13. The stag alarmed by the loud noise raised its head.
14. People who work on high bridges must have nerves of
    steel.
15. A flock of wild geese flying in a V-shaped formation
    passed high above us.
16. The man pictured on the $10,000 bill is Salmon P.
    Chase.
17. Buy the fishing pole that is made out of fiberglass.
18. The Sandwich Islands which are now called the Ha-
    waiian Islands were discovered by Captain Cook.
19. An inch of rain covering one city block weighs about
    160 tons.
20. This is the tulip that won first prize at the flower show
    yesterday.

EXERCISE 19 Time-out for Review

Write the following paragraph, adding commas where needed.

A man who lives in California constructed a musical robot. The amazing thing about his achievement however is that he made it in 1940! The robot named Isis looked like a woman. Sitting on a couch Isis would play the zither. The zither a musical instrument has 30 to 40 strings. Anyone who was within a 12-foot radius could ask Isis to play any of 3,000 tunes. A person's voice explained one computer expert touched off her controls. The machinery that was inside Isis included 1,187 wheels and 370 electromagnets. No one knows in spite of extensive research what happened to Isis the first robot musician.

Commonly Used Commas

When you tie your shoelaces, you no longer have to think how to do it. You do it automatically. There are some comma rules that you have been using for so many years now that they probably are also automatic. Following is a brief review of those rules.

Dates and Addresses. For clarity, commas are used to separate the elements in a date or an address from each other.

17n ▸ Use commas to separate the elements in dates and addresses.

Notice in the following examples that a comma is also used to separate a date or an address from the rest of the sentence.

DATE On Tuesday, March 3, 1985, my sister was born.
ADDRESS I have lived at 29 Bank Street, Long Beach, California, for ten years.

A comma is not used to separate the state and the ZIP code.

Send your letter to Art Supplies, 500 West 52nd Street, New York, New York 10019.

Titles and Degrees. Titles or degrees that follow a person's name should be set off by commas.

> **17o** Use commas to enclose titles or degrees after a name.

TITLE   Did Harry Chen, Jr., carry on his father's business?
DEGREE   Elizabeth Marshall, D. D. S., is my sister.

Letters. The salutations of some letters and the closings of all letters should be followed by a comma.

> **17p** Use a comma after the salutation of a friendly letter and after the closing of all letters.

SALUTATION   Dear Uncle Bert,   Dear Mom,
CLOSING   Sincerely yours,   Love,

EXERCISE 20   Using Commas

Write each sentence, adding commas where needed.

1. On July 4 1826 both John Adams and Thomas Jefferson died.
2. Send the check to R. Matthews Jr. 365 Jade Street Springfield Illinois 62702.
3. On May 30 1896 the first automobile accident in the United States occurred in New York New York.
4. On July 4 1956 1.23 inches of rain fell in one minute at Unionville Maryland.
5. *Ebony* is published by Johnson Publishing Company 820 South Michigan Avenue Chicago Illinois 60695.
6. Mail your requests to Ms. Lois Burbank 59 Chatham Street Greenville South Carolina 29609.
7. On December 6 1773 the American colonists staged the famous Boston Tea Party.

8. Address the envelope to Patricia Hartman Ph.D. and include extra postage.

9. On April 30 1812 Louisiana was admitted to the Union.

10. Write to Curtis Circulation Company 645 Madison Avenue New York New York 10014 for information.

EXERCISE 21 Writing Sentences

Write two sentences. The first should include the month, date, and year of your birth. The second should include all the elements of your current address. Remember to include commas where needed.

Application to Writing

After you write, edit your work to be sure you have used commas correctly.

EXERCISE 22 Editing for Commas

Write the following paragraphs, adding commas where needed.

The Eagle

The bald eagle of course is not bald. It was named at a time when *bald* meant "white." Because it has white feathers on its head the adult eagle has its present name. In contrast to its white head and tail the bald eagle's body and wings are brown. Its eyes beak and feet are yellow. An eagle can be more than three feet long and its wingspan may be more than seven feet. Its toes end in talons which are strong claws.

An eagle is a hunter. It feeds mainly on dead or dying fish but sometimes will eat small animals. It swoops down picks up its prey in its talons and flies off. An eagle which weighs eight to twelve pounds is able to carry an animal weighing as much as seven pounds!

Even though the bald eagle is the national emblem it has become an endangered species. Steps have been taken in recent years however to protect this magnificent bird.

323

CHAPTER REVIEW

A. Number your paper 1 to 10. Write an appropriate end mark for each sentence. Then label each sentence *declarative, imperative, interrogative,* or *exclamatory.*

1. The longest worm in recorded history measured 180 feet
2. Have you ever tasted homemade peanut butter
3. Will you please erase the board
4. Store the snow tires in the basement
5. The most common blood type in people throughout the world is type 0
6. Look out for that live wire
7. How tall is the Washington Monument
8. No birds have teeth
9. Mom asked if you want dessert
10. Is the tomato a fruit or a vegetable

B. Number your paper 1 to 20. Write each sentence, adding commas where needed. If a sentence does not need any commas, write *C* after the number.

1. Pablo is your birthday on Tuesday March 6?
2. Gazelles and prairie dogs seldom drink water.
3. The Mariana Trench in the Pacific the lowest point on Earth is 36,198 feet below sea level.
4. Jennifer is only one day older than her cousin.
5. An old farmhouse owned by Jordan Brown stands near a grassy meadow.
6. On Monday January 16 my brother will enter the Army at Fort Dix New Jersey.
7. After our long hike up Mount Washington we were very tired but we had big appetites.
8. In Switzerland official notices are printed in French German Italian and Romansch.
9. Generally speaking a worker bee may live for six months but a queen bee may live for six years.
10. No Leslie doesn't live in Louisville Kentucky anymore.

11. The pumpkin like other squashes was unknown in Europe before the discovery of America.
12. Why I hardly know how to answer your question.
13. Where in the world Alice did you find that old book?
14. The Mayo Clinic one of the world's largest medical centers treats patients from all over the world.
15. The first woman's rights convention met at Seneca Falls New York on July 19 1848.
16. A brilliant crescent moon shone above us.
17. During our trip to New Hampshire we saw the Presidential Range.
18. My cousin Cathy will be visiting us next summer.
19. Before locking up the custodian turned off the lights.
20. Using the computer for the first time Jill learned fast.

MASTERY TEST

Number your paper 1 to 10. Write each sentence, adding commas where needed. Then write an appropriate end mark.

1. The impala which can leap 30 feet is one of the most agile graceful antelopes
2. Yes the divers raised the submarine *Squalus*
3. William Henry Harrison died on April 4 1841 after being president for only one month
4. Anne don't forget to bring your bathing suit a towel and your sneakers
5. Mules according to my uncle are not stupid at all
6. Before you could enter the stadium how long did you have to stand in line
7. The pecan not the peanut is a true nut
8. Will you make a dress out of this soft silky material
9. After nearly sinking the boat was towed to shore
10. Order the tools from Ace Company 1790 State Street Chicago Illinois 65329 before Friday

18

Underlining and Quotation Marks

Number your paper 1 to 10. Then write each sentence, adding underlining, quotation marks, and other punctuation marks needed with direct quotations. Only a sentence with a speaker tag *(he said, she asked)* should be considered a direct quotation.

EXAMPLE   Sail the boat with care Sue cautioned.
ANSWER   "Sail the boat with care," Sue cautioned.

1. Which trail do you want to take the guide asked.
2. Jud requested Please don't disturb me.
3. Your assignment is to read the chapter Floods of Gold in Tom Sawyer.
4. There are two i's in my name.
5. Since we won't finish today replied Agnes let's quit early.
6. Please lend me your bicycle Nat pleaded.
7. I felt so good today Kathleen said The sun was out for the first time in three days.
8. The pep rally was very exciting Doreen exclaimed.
9. The phrase draggin' wagons referred to racing cars in the fifties.
10. Have you seen the most recent edition of TV Guide?

Try to imagine what it would be like if no one spoke for one whole hour during the school day. That probably would never happen. Most people are involved in conversations from the moment they get up in the morning to the moment they go to sleep. As a result, learning the rules for quotation marks is indispensable. Quoting someone's exact words adds realism to stories and letters. Direct quotations add support and interest to reports and compositions.

This chapter will cover the uses of quotation marks with direct quotations, as well as with titles. First, however, the uses of underlining will be reviewed.

UNDERLINING

Italics is a type of print that slants to the right. Since you cannot write or type in italics, you must use underlining instead.

ITALICS	George just read *Robinson Crusoe*.
UNDERLINING	George just read <u>Robinson</u> <u>Crusoe</u>.

Certain letters, numbers, words, and titles should be underlined.

18a ▶ Underline letters, numbers, and words when they are used to represent themselves. Also underline foreign words that are not generally used in English.

LETTERS, NUMBERS	My <u>2</u>'s look like <u>Q</u>'s.
WORDS, PHRASES	The word <u>bud</u> has several meanings.
FOREIGN WORDS	<u>E pluribus unum</u> is printed on several United States coins.

Notice in the first example above that only the *2* and the *Q* are underlined — not the apostrophe and the *s*.

Underlining is also used to set off certain titles.

18b Underline the titles of long written or musical works that are published as a single unit. Also underline titles of paintings and sculptures and the names of vehicles.

BOOKS	<u>Jane Eyre</u>, <u>White Fang</u>
NEWSPAPERS	<u>Washington Post</u>, <u>Chicago Tribune</u>
PERIODICALS	<u>Newsweek</u>, <u>Reader's Digest</u> [In general, do not underline *the* before newspaper or periodical titles.]
PLAYS, MOVIES	<u>Our Town</u>, <u>The Wizard of Oz</u>
BOOK-LENGTH POEMS	<u>Evangeline</u>, <u>Gareth and Lynette</u>
RADIO AND TV SERIES	<u>Mystery Theater</u>, <u>Nova</u>
LONG MUSICAL WORKS	<u>Faust</u>, <u>La Traviata</u>
WORKS OF ART	<u>Totem Head</u> [a sculpture]
SHIPS, PLANES, OTHER CRAFT	<u>Titanic</u>, <u>Spirit of St. Louis</u>, <u>Challenger</u>, <u>Columbia</u>

EXERCISE 1   Using Underlining

Write each sentence. Then underline each letter, number, word, or group of words that should be italicized.

1. The expression going full blast began in the steel mills.
2. Before preparing his speech, Peter bought a copy of the book 10,000 Jokes, Toasts, and Stories.
3. There are two m's, two t's, and two e's in the word committee.
4. Who sang the tenor's part in The Marriage of Figaro?
5. The Boston Globe recently ran an article on nutrition.
6. What does the expression vincit omnia veritas mean?
7. I hope to fly on the Concorde some day.
8. About 1500, Bosch painted The Ship of Fools.
9. Who is the hero in The Last of the Mohicans?
10. In the sixties the expression flake out meant "to sleep."
11. The Pirates of Penzance is a famous light opera.
12. Is the Daily Mirror London's largest newspaper?
13. Facetious contains the vowels a, e, i, o, and u.
14. The launching of Sputnik I began the Space Age.
15. The Mona Lisa hangs in the Louvre in Paris.

QUOTATION MARKS

When you use quotation marks, always remember that they come in pairs. They are placed at the beginning and at the end of uninterrupted quotations and certain titles.

Quotation Marks with Titles

You have just learned that titles of long works are underlined. Most of these long works are made up of smaller parts. The titles of these smaller parts should be enclosed in quotation marks.

18c ▶ Use quotation marks to enclose the titles of chapters, articles, stories, one-act plays, short poems, and songs.

CHAPTERS Read "I Am Born," the first chapter in David Copperfield.

ARTICLES Have you seen the article "Frozen Foods Get Hot Again" in Newsweek?

SHORT POEMS My favorite poem in Famous 20th Century Poetry is "Sea Lullaby."

EXERCISE 2 Using Quotation Marks with Titles
Write each sentence, adding quotation marks and underlining where needed.

1. Tourism Is Up is the lead story in the Miami Herald.
2. The familiar lullaby Rock-a-Bye Baby dates back to the Elizabethan Age.
3. Edgar Allan Poe wrote the short stories The Pit and the Pendulum and The Gold Bug.
4. I read Mending Wall in the book Selected Poems of Robert Frost.
5. Did you read the chapter Health and Nutrition in your science book?
6. The Old Lady Shows Her Medals is a short one-act play, but The Diary of Anne Frank has two acts.

7. Who sang the old song Bridge over Troubled Waters?
8. Glorious Jones or the Catnip Hangover is a very humorous chapter in the book The Fur Person.
9. The Sea and Sinbad's Ship is the first part of Rimsky-Korsakov's symphonic suite Scheherazade.
10. Two of Robert Frost's most famous poems are Birches and Stopping by Woods on a Snowy Evening.

Quotation Marks with Direct Quotations

The most important thing to remember when writing direct quotations is that quotation marks enclose only the *exact words* of a speaker. In other words, quotation marks are used only with a *direct quotation*.

18d ▶ Use quotation marks to enclose a person's exact words.

"I just finished my homework," Tammy said.
Roberta said, "I can't stay after school today."

Sometimes when you write, you may paraphrase what someone has said — without using his or her exact words. When you paraphrase, you are indirectly quoting a person. Do not use quotation marks with *indirect quotations*.

Tammy said that she had just finished her homework.
Roberta said she couldn't stay after school today.

In the first example above, the word *that* signals the indirect quotation. In the second example, *that* is understood.

A one-sentence direct quotation can be written in several ways. It can be placed before or after a speaker tag such as *she said* and *Bill asked*. In both cases, quotation marks enclose the person's exact words — from beginning to end.

"Yesterday we went skating," Beth added.
Beth added, "Yesterday we went skating."

For variety or emphasis, a quotation can also be interrupted by a speaker tag. When this interruption occurs, you need two pairs of quotation marks because quotation marks enclose *only* a person's exact words — not the speaker tag.

> "Yesterday," Beth added, "we went skating."

If you want to quote more than one sentence, put quotation marks at the beginning and at the end of the entire quotation. It is not necessary to put quotation marks around each sentence within a quotation — unless a speaker tag interrupts.

> Beth added, "Yesterday we went skating. We got to the lake early and left when the sun began to set. What a great day we had!"

EXERCISE 3   Using Quotation Marks with Direct Quotations

Write each sentence, adding quotation marks where needed. Place a comma or an end mark that follows a quotation *inside* the closing quotation marks.

1. Report to the field now, ordered the coach.
2. Elbert Hubbard once said, Don't make excuses — make good.
3. It is easy, said Aesop, to be brave from a safe distance.
4. I always forget my locker combination when I'm in a rush, announced Leslie.
5. Rain is forecast for tomorrow. Maybe we should cancel the picnic, Betty suggested.
6. Don't be nervous, the drama coach told everyone.
7. Of course, said Mom, I'm going to the open house.
8. The park attendant cautioned, Don't feed the bears.
9. I'm sorry, Ann apologized, that I forgot the tapes.
10. Margo stated, We all need to help. Our goal is to raise 50 dollars. A car wash could be our answer.

Commas with Direct Quotations.   When you are reading quoted material aloud, your voice naturally pauses between the speaker tag and the direct quotation. In written material these pauses are indicated by commas.

18e Use a comma to separate a direct quotation from a speaker tag. Place the comma inside the closing quotation marks.

"The apples aren't ripe yet," Lance cautioned.
Lance cautioned, "The apples aren't ripe yet."
"The apples," Lance cautioned, "aren't ripe yet."

Notice in the last example that two commas are needed.

EXERCISE 4   Using Commas with Direct Quotations
Write each sentence, adding quotation marks and commas where needed.   Place commas and end marks that follow a quotation *inside* the quotation marks.

1. Come with us to the baseball game Gene urged.
2. Hale said My Chihuahuas weigh only a pound.
3. There are two sides to every argument he said until you take a side.
4. The traffic was terrible Dad complained.
5. Moy reported Terns migrate halfway around the world twice a year.
6. Roy boasted I passed my driver's test today.
7. You're taking my coat Alice warned.
8. I just learned Kara stated that lightning often strikes the same spot more than once.
9. Ken announced The answer is quite simple.
10. Ocean waves Bryan said are sometimes 80 feet high.
11. Mrs. Lewis asked us Have you ever eaten oysters?
12. Did you know Elroy asked that George Washington left no direct descendants?
13. Mercury can be seen by the naked eye a few times a year the lecturer explained.
14. Basketball the coach told us is a matter of good sense and teamwork.
15. An angry man opens his mouth and shuts his eyes said Cato.
16. The mango explained Robert is a tropical fruit.
17. One should eat to live wrote Benjamin Franklin not live to eat.

18. The young of the opossum said the speaker are smaller at birth than a honeybee.
19. Jerry shouted Watch out for that car!
20. From one of the rooms in the deserted house a voice cried out Who's there?

End Marks with Direct Quotations. End marks come at the end of a quoted sentence—just as they do in a sentence that is not a quotation.

18f ▶ Place a period inside the closing quotation marks when the end of the quotation comes at the end of the sentence.

Carlos said, "Tonight I'll dry the dishes."
"Tonight," Carlos said, "I'll dry the dishes."

If a quotation comes at the beginning of a sentence, the period follows the speaker tag.

"Tonight I'll dry the dishes," Carlos said.

A period comes at the end of each sentence within a quotation that has more than one sentence.

"Tonight I'll dry the dishes," Carlos said. "I washed them last night. I also washed them the night before that."

Sometimes you may want to quote a question someone has asked or a sentence someone has said with strong feeling.

18g ▶ Place a question mark or an exclamation point inside the closing quotation marks when it is part of the quotation.

Martin asked, "Is that the telephone or the doorbell?"
"Is that the telephone," Martin asked, "or the doorbell?"
"Is that the telephone or the doorbell?" Martin asked.
Kim screamed, "Watch out for that hole!"
"Watch out for that hole!" Kim screamed.

A question mark and an exclamation point are placed *inside* the closing quotation marks when they are part of the

333

quotation. When these punctuation marks are part of the whole sentence, however, they are placed *outside* the closing quotation marks.

Did I hear Roger say, "I found your tennis shoes"**?**
[The whole sentence is the question, not the quotation.]

It was the happiest moment of my life when she said, "You won"**!** [The whole sentence is exclamatory, not the quotation.]

Notice that, in these cases, the end marks for the quotations are omitted.

EXERCISE 5   Using End Marks with Direct Quotations
Write each sentence, adding commas and end marks where needed.

1. "The ancient Egyptians first began to make glass in 3500 B.C." Karen explained
2. Quentin asked "Did you know that the Navahos are the largest Indian tribe in America"
3. "I just learned" Mary said "that a year on Jupiter is 12 times longer than a year on Earth"
4. Tim suggested "You can cook the hot dogs at the picnic I have other things to do"
5. Marvin exclaimed "That greyhound was clocked at 4.17 miles an hour"
6. I almost fell out of my chair when Mr. Banner announced "We'll skip the quiz today"
7. "You're picking poison ivy" Mavis screamed
8. "Did you know" Clyde asked "that blood is six times thicker than water"
9. Did you hear Betty say "I second the motion"
10. "When is the test in English" Cindy asked
11. From the rock they shouted to us "Have you found the trail yet"
12. "Look out for that rattlesnake" cried Muriel
13. "Why did you throw away the map" Lee asked "I thought you were saving it as a souvenir"

14. The guide shouted "Don't go so close to the edge"
15. "We have nothing to fear" said Franklin Roosevelt "but fear itself"
16. Hurry and tell everyone that the health inspector said "Don't drink the tap water"
17. "Watch this" Allison cried "I've learned to do a figure eight"
18. Dan boasted "I made ten baskets tonight"
19. "Will you help me put on this diving suit" Mark asked his brother
20. Who wrote "All the world's a stage"

Capital Letters with Direct Quotations. Each sentence of a quotation begins with a capital letter—just as a regular sentence does.

18h ▶ Begin each sentence of a direct quotation with a capital letter.

"**C**all Jean at six o'clock," my sister said.
My sister said, "**C**all Jean at six o'clock."

If a single-sentence quotation is interrupted by a speaker tag, use only one capital letter—at the beginning of the sentence.

"**C**all Jean," my sister said, "at six o'clock."

EXERCISE 6   Using Capital Letters with Direct Quotations
Write each sentence, adding capital letters and end marks where needed.

1. "is Finland or California larger" we asked
2. someone in the first row answered, "the state of California is larger"
3. "the end of reading is not more books," Holbrook Jackson said, "but more life"
4. my science teacher joked, "if it weren't for Edison, we'd be watching TV by candlelight"

5. "it doesn't matter where a man comes from," Henry Ford once said "we hire a man, not his history"
6. "there are at least 1,500 varieties of mosquitoes," reported Karen
7. "a baby is born every 8½ seconds in the United States," Alice stated "that's amazing"
8. "did you know," Lai asked, "that President Tyler was the father of 15 children"
9. my brother announced, "practice starts in ten minutes"
10. "the toast was burned," he complained "and the eggs were hard what's more, the orange juice had seeds in it"
11. "have you seen Mary this afternoon" Kevin asked
12. "come to the light," said mother "do you expect me to see your splinter in the dark"
13. the teacher asked, "can anyone describe an atom"
14. "look out" shouted Jonathan
15. did Mr. Dean say, "come here"
16. "that's outrageous" Jim exclaimed "a birdhouse costing $10,000 was built in Quebec in 1975"
17. "did you know," Carol asked, "that Eskimos have more than 20 words to describe snow"
18. "we should meet after school we need to discuss the freshman dance," Kenneth said
19. it was the most exciting moment of my life when the judge said, "you have won first prize"
20. "this is an interesting fact," Joe said "milk is heavier than cream"

EXERCISE 7 Time-out for Review

Write each sentence, adding capital letters, quotation marks, and other punctuation marks where needed. Then check your answers carefully.

About Beasts

1. a cat has absolute honesty Ernest Hemingway noted
2. someone once said it's nice for children to have pets — until the pets start having children
3. if things went by merit Mark Twain announced you would stay out and your dog would go in

4. young gorillas are friendly Will Cuppy said but they soon learn

5. Samuel Butler said the hen is an egg's way of producing another egg

6. if insects ever take over the world he mused I hope they remember that I invited them to all my picnics

7. all animals are equal George Orwell said but some are more equal than others

8. money will buy a pretty good dog commented Josh Billings but it won't buy the wag of its tail

9. what modest claim do kittens make David Irvine asked they claim the ownership of humans

10. animals are such agreeable friends George Eliot stated they ask no questions and pass no criticisms

Quotation Marks with Dialogue and Long Quotations

Writing stories and reports sometimes requires special treatment of direct quotations. Stories often contain dialogue between two or more persons. Reports sometimes include long quoted passages. Following are the rules that cover these special applications of direct quotations.

Writing Dialogue. *Dialogue* means "a conversation between two or more persons." Dialogue is treated in a special way so that a reader knows who is speaking.

18i When writing dialogue, begin a new paragraph each time the speaker changes.

In the following excerpt from *Dr. Jekyll and Mr. Hyde,* each sentence follows the rules for direct quotations that you have just studied. Notice, however, that a new paragraph begins each time Mr. Utterson or Poole speaks.

"I saw Mr. Hyde go in by the old dissecting door, Poole," he said. "Is that right, when Dr. Jekyll is from home?"

"Quite right, Mr. Utterson, sir," replied the servant. "Mr. Hyde has a key."

"Your master seems to repose a great deal of trust in that young man, Poole," resumed the other.

EXERCISE 8   Editing for Quotation Marks

Correctly rewrite the following dialogue between Sherlock Holmes and Sir Henry. Add any needed punctuation and indent each time there is a change of speaker.

The practical point which we now have to decide Sir Henry said Holmes is whether it is or is not advisable for you to go to Baskerville Hall. Why should I not go? There seems to be danger. Do you mean danger from this family fiend Sir Henry asked or do you mean danger from human beings? Well, that is what we have to find out.

——SIR ARTHUR CONAN DOYLE, *THE HOUND OF THE BASKERVILLES*

Quoting Long Passages.   When you write a report and want to support a point, you might want to quote more than one paragraph from a book.

18j   When quoting a passage of more than one paragraph, place quotation marks at the beginning of each paragraph — but at the end of only the last paragraph.

Closing quotation marks are omitted at the end of each paragraph, except the last one, to indicate to a reader that the quotation is continuing.

"Chicagoans were out in force on Thanksgiving Day, 1895. They came to see a new-fangled contraption called the automobile. A few of the gasoline-powered horseless carriages were going to race. [no quotation marks]

"The route lay from the heart of Chicago to a nearby suburb and back. The road measured exactly 54.36 miles. The winner would have to cover that terrific distance without breaking down. [no quotation marks]

"J. Frank Duryea busted the tape 7 hours and 17 minutes after the start of the race. He had covered the distance at an average speed of 7.5 miles an hour!" [closing quotation marks]

✒ *Application to Writing*

After you have written a dialogue, check to make sure that you have used quotation marks correctly.

EXERCISE 9 Writing Dialogue
Write a brief imaginary conversation in which you speak with a famous person. Punctuate the dialogue correctly.

EXERCISE 10 Writing Dialogue
Write a brief imaginary conversation between two visitors to your hometown twenty years from now. What changes, for example, might they see? Be sure to punctuate the dialogue correctly.

CHAPTER REVIEW

Write each sentence, adding underlining, capital letters, quotation marks, and other punctuation marks where needed.

1. where asked Ina did you find those earrings
2. a sign in one hairdresser's shop read we curl up and dye for you
3. I just read Oliver Twist Jan said it was better than any movie version I have ever seen
4. news Ben Bradlee once said is the first rough draft of history
5. have you ever read the Christian Science Monitor Dan asked
6. Cathleen asked is the ocean rough today
7. Ken declared I'm going to be the new class president

8. please don't break us apart the sign over the bananas read we grew up together
9. that was an incredible pass exclaimed Dave
10. work is the best escape from boredom Eleanor Dean once said
11. who said little things affect little minds
12. defeat is not the worst of failures said G. E. Woodberry not to have tried is the true failure
13. we saw a production of the Shakespearean play As You Like It at the Lyric Stage Cheryl announced
14. life shrinks or expands in proportion to one's courage Anaïs Nin commented
15. Voltaire once said common sense is not so common
16. it was an extremely exciting moment when he said we will win in spite of the odds
17. it is easier to fight for one's principles said Alfred Adler than to live up to them
18. life just is ex-governor Jerry Brown once said you have to flow with it let it happen
19. what is happiness Albert Schweitzer asked it is nothing more than health and a poor memory
20. the only way to have a friend said Ralph Waldo Emerson is to be one
21. Jamie exclaimed what a surprise this is
22. if you're too busy Pat stated please call me
23. why are you sitting there Julia asked
24. Thomas H. Bayly is famous for saying absence makes the heart grow fonder
25. have you ever seen the movie Casablanca Jennifer asked
26. don't eat now Mom said dinner is in ten minutes
27. your assignment for tonight Mr. Franklin said is to read the feature article in Newsweek
28. are we supposed to read the book Grapes of Wrath or the poem by Robert Frost Cynthia asked
29. I was amazed to hear the coach say no practice today
30. The concert Greg said is tomorrow night

MASTERY TEST

Number your paper 1 to 10. Then write each sentence, adding underlining, quotation marks, and other punctuation marks needed with direct quotations. Only a sentence with a speaker tag should be considered a direct quotation.

1. The lead article in Time was entitled Computers in the Classroom.
2. That Jeff proudly proclaimed is a soft sculpture of a tomato.
3. Does that word have one or two l's?
4. Stop that car the woman yelled.
5. Did anyone take the dog out Mom asked.
6. In the 40s moolah was a slang expression meaning money.
7. The special exhibit at the museum was great Pat said I learned so much.
8. Read the third chapter in your history book, We the People.
9. Mr. Henry explained This old chair is a valuable antique.
10. I want to hear the weather forecast Meg said.

19

Other Punctuation

The most costly punctuation error of all times occurred in 1962. A hyphen was omitted from a set of directions that was being sent to the *Venus* space probe rocket. As a result of the omission, the rocket self-destructed. Most errors that you make in punctuation will not have such disastrous results. Nevertheless, correct punctuation is necessary for clear communication — right here on Earth.

APOSTROPHES

Including apostrophes in certain words is as important as spelling those words correctly. Without an apostrophe, the first sentence in the following examples does not make any sense. With an apostrophe, however, the meaning of the sentence instantly becomes clear.

Well go with you to the game tonight.
We'll go with you to the game tonight.

In addition to being used in contractions, apostrophes are commonly used with nouns and some pronouns to show ownership or relationship.

Possessive Forms of Nouns and Pronouns

The possessive form of a noun shows ownership, possession, or relationship. The possessive form is used when an *of* phrase could be substituted for the noun.

Lani's guitar = the guitar of Lani
the Spensers' garage = the garage of the Spensers

As you can see from these examples, nouns have a special form to show possession. An apostrophe or an apostrophe and an *s* are added.

Possessive Forms of Singular Nouns. To form the possessive of a noun, first decide if the noun is singular or plural.

343

19a   Add *'s* to form the possessive of a singular noun.

Do not add or omit a letter. Just write the word and put *'s* at the end.

baby + 's = baby's   Give me the baby**'s** blanket.
Gary + 's = Gary's   That is Gary**'s** baseball glove.
week + 's = week's   What were your week**'s** wages?
boss + 's = boss's   Where is your boss**'s** office?

The *'s* goes on the last word of compound words and the names of most businesses and organizations.

The passerby**'s** report of the accident was accurate.
The jack-in-the-box**'s** spring was broken.
The Mahoney Oil Company**'s** service is dependable.
Lord & Taylor**'s** advertisements are very colorful.

NOTE: Occasionally a singular noun, such as the name *Prentiss,* will end in *s.* If the noun—especially a name—is two or three syllables long, it might be awkward to pronounce with *'s.* Add only an apostrophe *(Prentiss').*

EXERCISE 1   **Forming the Possessive of Singular Nouns**
Write the possessive form of each noun. Then use five of the forms in sentences of your own.

1. apple	6. mother-in-law	11. morning
2. Pep Club	7. brother	12. Bess
3. starfish	8. Mike	13. Hope College
4. Georgia	9. sailor	14. maid-of-honor
5. month	10. Reese Company	15. Mr. Clemens

Possessive Forms of Plural Nouns.   There are two rules to follow to form the possessive of plural nouns.

19b   Add only an apostrophe to form the possessive of a plural noun that ends in *s.*

19c   Add *'s* to form the possessive of a plural noun that does not end in *s.*

Deciding which rule to follow is very simple if you take two steps. First, write the plural of the noun—just as it is. Second, look at the ending of the word. If the word ends in *s*, add only an apostrophe. If it does not end in *s*, add an apostrophe and an *s*.

PLURAL	ENDING	ADD		POSSESSIVE
babies	s	'	=	babies'
foxes	s	'	=	foxes'
mice	no *s*	's	=	mice's
children	no *s*	's	=	children's

EXERCISE 2 Forming the Possessive of Plural Nouns

Write the possessive form of each noun. Then use five of the forms in sentences of your own.

1. friends
2. boxes
3. weeks
4. deer
5. boys
6. wolves
7. tomatoes
8. girls
9. Lutzes
10. cities
11. books
12. geese
13. stores
14. clouds
15. albums
16. men
17. Smiths
18. women
19. papers
20. Ryans

EXERCISE 3 Forming the Possessive of Nouns

Number your paper 1 to 20. Then write the possessive form—singular or plural—of each underlined word.

EXAMPLE It is <u>Fred</u> turn to do the dishes, not <u>Carol</u>.
ANSWER Fred's—Carol's

1. Are <u>men</u> shoe sizes different from <u>women</u>?
2. The <u>Drama Club</u> presentation this year was superb.
3. My <u>uncle</u> store is a few <u>minutes</u> walk from here.
4. A long article about my <u>brother</u> wedding appeared in <u>Madison</u> newspaper.
5. The <u>girls</u> and <u>boys</u> uniforms were passed out this morning.
6. <u>Sarah</u> sisters got jobs at a <u>children</u> day camp.
7. Jill won the <u>National Film Association</u> annual award.
8. A <u>secretary</u> job involves more duties than a <u>typist</u>.
9. After the <u>day</u> ride, the horses were put in <u>Carlos</u> barn.

10. My <u>sister-in-law</u> car is pale blue.
11. One of the performers in Buffalo <u>Bill</u> Wild West Show was Annie Oakley.
12. Mr. <u>Brown</u> new car was finally delivered after a <u>month</u> delay.
13. <u>Beth</u> hobby is collecting <u>actors</u> autographs.
14. After an <u>hour</u> search, Roger found <u>Trixie</u> leash under the couch.
15. That <u>pitcher</u> control has improved enough to earn the <u>coach</u> praise.
16. Was that story in <u>today</u> or <u>yesterday</u> newspaper?
17. From my <u>grandparents</u> porch, we could see an <u>oriole</u> nest in the maple tree.
18. <u>Mike</u> trumpet solo and the Johnson <u>sisters</u> duet were the hits of the show.
19. Linda <u>Kelly</u> prize-winning poster is on the bulletin board in the <u>teachers</u> room.
20. Mom found <u>Larry</u> basketball in <u>Ben</u> room.

Possessive Forms of Pronouns. Unlike nouns, personal pronouns do not use an apostrophe to show possession. Instead, they change form: *my, mine, your, yours, his, her, hers, its, our, ours, their,* and *theirs.*

19d Do not add an apostrophe to form the possessive of a personal pronoun.

The bicycle is **hers.**
A spider spun **its** web in the doorway.

Indefinite pronouns, however, form the possessive the same way singular nouns do — by adding 's. *(See page 33 for a list of common indefinite pronouns.)*

19e Add 's to form the possessive of an indefinite pronoun.

This seems to be everyone**'s** favorite song.
Someone**'s** purse was left under the seat.

EXERCISE 4   Using the Possessive of Pronouns
Write the correct form of the pronoun in parentheses.

1. Are these gloves (yours, your's)?
2. (Anyone's, Anyones') solution is better than none.
3. The mountain is beautiful with (its, it's) top covered with snow.
4. I gave my speech yesterday, but Jan hasn't given (hers, her's) yet.
5. (No one's, No ones') predictions came true.
6. I hope (everybody's, everybodys') time was well spent.
7. Those sandwiches are (ours, our's).
8. Has (everyones, everyone's) test been graded?
9. It was (nobody's, nobodys') fault but my own.
10. The blue towels are (their's, theirs).

Apostrophes to Show Joint and Separate Ownership. Sometimes it is necessary to show that something belongs to more than one person.

19f ▶ To show joint ownership, make only the last word possessive in form.

These are Nan and Joanne's records. [The records belong to both Nan and Joanne.]

The only exception to this rule applies when one word showing joint ownership is a possessive pronoun. In such cases, the noun must also show possession.

This is Karen's and **my** computer.

Separate ownership is shown in a different way from joint ownership.

19g ▶ To show separate ownership, make each word possessive in form.

These are Nan's and Joanne's records. [Each girl has her own records.]

EXERCISE 5   Using Joint and Separate Ownership
Number your paper 1 to 10. Then correctly write each word
that needs an apostrophe or an apostrophe and an *s*.

EXAMPLE   Don and Jan father is a Little League umpire.
 ANSWER   Jan's

1. I picked up Dad and Mike shirts from the cleaners.
2. Mrs. Hayden is Joyce and my history teacher.
3. Martha and Nick car was just painted red.
4. Donna and Ray poems were published in the paper.
5. My father hobbies include golfing and fishing.
6. Someone hat was found under the bleachers.
7. Eli Whitney inventions changed the course of history.
8. In Ambrose Bierce story, a snake eyes seemed to have a
   hypnotic effect.
9. Dad and Uncle Fred farm has 1,000 acres of corn.
10. Dan spent three weeks vacation on Mr. Murray farm.

EXERCISE 6   Using the Possessive of Nouns and Pronouns
Number your paper 1 to 10. Then correctly write each
incorrect word in the following sentences. Some words are
missing apostrophes. Other words include apostrophes that
are incorrectly placed.

EXAMPLE   After an hours rest the boys' were ready to go.
 ANSWER   hour's — boys

1. My uncles ranch is a days ride from Rock Springs.
2. In almost all cities', buses have replaced trolleys.
3. The winter coats in the mens' department are on sale.
4. Everyone's is coming to you're party.
5. Frank and Judy's suggestions' were unanimously accepted by the members of the club.
6. No ones' composition has been hung on Mrs. Ryans
   bulletin board.
7. Teds efforts were well rewarded, but her's were not.
8. The girls' auditioned for the plays director.
9. Eds cats' have a separate entrance to the house.
10. These tapes are our's, not their's.

Other Uses of an Apostrophe

Apostrophes have other uses besides showing the possessive of nouns and some pronouns.

Apostrophes with Contractions. A contraction is a shortcut. It usually combines two words into one. An apostrophe is added to take the place of one or more missing letters.

19h   Use an apostrophe in a contraction to show where one or more letters have been omitted.

The following examples show how some contractions are formed.

do + no̶t = don't   you + wou̶l̶d = you'd
has + no̶t = hasn't   let + u̶s = let's
we + a̶re = we're   there + i̶s = there's
I + wi̶ll = I'll   who + i̶s = who's
they + ha̶ve = they've   of + the̶ + clock = o'clock

In all these examples and in most contractions, no letters are added, and no letters are changed around. There is one common exception: *will + not = won't.*

NOTE: Do not confuse a contraction with a possessive pronoun. *It's, you're, they're, there's,* and *who's* are contractions. *Its, your, their, theirs,* and *whose* are possessive pronouns.

EXERCISE 7   Using Apostrophes with Contractions

Write the contraction for each pair of words. Then write a short conversation in which you use at least five of the contractions.

1. are not	6. do not	11. we will	16. were not
2. will not	7. is not	12. that is	17. they are
3. did not	8. let us	13. I would	18. there is
4. has not	9. I have	14. does not	19. I am
5. you are	10. we have	15. have not	20. who is

EXERCISE 8   Distinguishing between Contractions and Possessive Pronouns

Write the correct word in parentheses.

1. (Its, It's) now or never.
2. Tell me how you want (your, you're) eggs cooked.
3. I don't know if (their, they're) home or not.
4. If (theirs, there's) anything you need, let me know.
5. (Whose, Who's) taking care of your cats?
6. Do you know if (your, you're) invited?
7. These suitcases must be (theirs, there's).
8. (Whose, Who's) bicycle did you borrow?
9. (Its, It's) wingspread is seven feet.
10. Did you speak to (their, they're) teachers?

EXERCISE 9   Writing Sentences

Write ten sentences that use each of the following words correctly.

1. its
2. it's
3. their
4. they're
5. theirs

6. there's
7. whose
8. who's
9. your
10. you're

Apostrophes to Form Some Plurals.   Certain items form their plural by adding 's.

19i   Add 's to form the plural of numbers, letters, symbols, and words that are used to represent themselves.

You often write *g*'s for *q*'s.
Why did you put two *!*'s after that sentence?
You use too many *and*'s in your writing.

NOTE: The items in the examples above should be underlined (italicized). *(See page 327.)* However, the 's should not be underlined.

EXERCISE 10 Using Apostrophes
Number your paper 1 to 10. Then correctly write each word that needs an apostrophe or an apostrophe and an *s*. If a sentence is correct, write *C* after the number.

EXAMPLE   Isnt this blue notebook yours?
ANSWER   Isn't

1. If you take our spare tire, leave theirs.
2. Is that everyone decision?
3. Ina writes all her capital *P* with style.
4. That red-plaid suitcase is hers.
5. The winning number had five *3* and three *5* in it.
6. Someone jacket was left in the gym.
7. This windbreaker doesnt come in both boys and men sizes.
8. Couldnt that boat be theirs?
9. My brother bookkeeper is planning to take a month vacation in Puerto Rico.
10. Theres a surprise waiting for you in the bottom of the kitchen drawer.

EXERCISE 11 Time-out for Review
Number your paper 1 to 10. Then correctly write the words that need an apostrophe.

Is It a Moth?

Has a moth ever turned one of your sweaters into a tasty meal? If so, you might be able to prevent future feasts by knowing the difference between a moth and a butterfly. Listen carefully. Recognizing the difference wont be easy. First, look at the insects feelers. If theyre thin, they belong to a butterfly. A moths feelers are usually broad and feathery. Next, observe the insect when its resting. Butterflies wings are folded in an upright position, with the wings undersides facing you. A moth sits holding its wings horizontally, with only the upper sides of the wings showing. If this information doesnt help, youd better buy a winters supply of mothballs.

SEMICOLONS AND COLONS

A *semicolon* (;) is a combination of a comma and a period. It is used to indicate a pause greater than that of a comma, but not a full pause like that of a period. Semicolons are used mainly between the clauses of a compound sentence. A *colon* (:) is used mainly to introduce a list of items.

Semicolons

Independent clauses in a compound sentence can be joined by a conjunction and a comma. *(See page 309.)*

Ken's favorite sport is tennis, **but** mine is hockey.

Clauses in a compound sentence can also be joined by a semicolon.

Ken's favorite sport is tennis; mine is hockey.

19j ▶ Use a semicolon between the clauses of a compound sentence that are not joined by a conjunction.

Use a semicolon only if the clauses are closely related.

INCORRECT   A mosquito bite is not a bite; mosquito bites can be painful.

CORRECT   A mosquito bite is not a bite; it is a puncture.

Semicolons with Transitional Words. The following list contains transitional words that, with a semicolon, can be used to combine the clauses of a compound sentence.

Common Transitional Words		
accordingly	furthermore	moreover
consequently	hence	nevertheless
for example	however	otherwise
for instance	instead	therefore

19k ▶ Use a semicolon between clauses in a compound sentence that are joined by certain transitional words.

Notice in the following examples that the transitional words are preceded by a semicolon and followed by a comma.

> The weather was perfect**; nevertheless,** I stayed indoors and studied.
> The camping trip was fun**; for instance,** we swam each day in the lake.

NOTE: Some of the transitional words listed above can also be used as parenthetical expressions within a single clause. *(See page 315.)*

JOINING CLAUSES   The meeting started at eight o'clock**; however,** we were late.

WITHIN A CLAUSE   The meeting**, however,** won't start until eight o'clock.

EXERCISE 12 Using Semicolons with Compound Sentences

Number your paper 1 to 10. Then write each sentence, adding a semicolon where needed. If a sentence does not need a semicolon, write *C* after the number.

1. Panama hats are not made in Panama most are made in Ecuador.
2. Over 60,000 deaths a year result from high blood pressure nevertheless, most are avoidable.
3. The American jay is bright blue however, its Canadian cousin is gray.
4. Lee was elected president furthermore, she was elected by a unanimous vote.
5. Irrigation is used on many farms in fertile areas moreover, it is an absolute necessity in desert areas.
6. The first baseball catcher's mask was worn in 1875 the first chest protector was used in 1885.
7. The Kennedys, nevertheless, were able to join us for dessert.

8. The *knot* is not a measure of length it is a measure of speed.
9. Everyone is born farsighted nevertheless, most develop 20/20 vision at about five years of age.
10. Babe Ruth was elected to baseball's Hall of Fame in 1936 Lou Gehrig became a member in 1939.

EXERCISE 13   Using Semicolons with Compound Sentences

Number your paper 1 to 10. Then write each sentence, adding a semicolon and a *comma* where needed.

1. An ailurophile loves cats an ailurophobe hates cats.
2. George Washington chose the site of the White House however he never lived there.
3. The sweet potato and the yam are not the same moreover the yam is almost never seen in this country.
4. A male kangaroo is called a boomer a female kangaroo is called a flyer.
5. The emu is an unusual species of bird for example it is the male that mothers the young.
6. Type O is the most common blood type in the world type AB is the rarest.
7. A polecat is not a cat at all the term designates a skunk.
8. Post the announcements in the supermarkets otherwise no one will find out about the school fair.
9. A crocodile cannot move its tongue it is rooted to the base of its mouth.
10. The giant panda of western China resembles a bear however it is more closely related to the raccoon.

Semicolons to Avoid Confusion.   Sometimes a semicolon is used to take the place of a comma between the clauses of a compound sentence.

19l ▷ Use a semicolon instead of a comma between the clauses of a compound sentence if there are commas within a clause.

354

To get to Maine from New York, we travel through Connecticut, Massachusetts, and New Hampshire; but the trip takes us only four hours.

A semicolon takes the place of a comma in another situation as well.

19m ▶ Use a semicolon instead of a comma between the items in a series if the items contain commas.

I have relatives in Rochester, New York; in Boulder, Colorado; and in Tallahassee, Florida.

NOTE: See Chapter 17 for the rules for commas.

EXERCISE 14   Using Semicolons to Avoid Confusion
Number your paper 1 to 10. Then write each sentence, adding a semicolon and *commas* where needed.

1. In 1976, there were over 110 million TV sets in the United States over 375 million radios and over 125 million telephones and today there are even more.
2. The awards were presented at a special ceremony on Friday February 2 1985 and a press conference was held afterward.
3. This year I am taking math history English and Spanish but my favorite subject is science.
4. There are more Irish in New York City than in Dublin Ireland more Italians in New York than in Rome Italy and more Jews in New York than in Tel Aviv Israel.
5. Receiving awards were the pitcher the catcher and the second baseman but the third baseman won a college scholarship.
6. The bloodmobile will be at the school on Wednesday October 12 Friday October 14 and Friday October 21.
7. We had a choice of going bowling seeing a movie or visiting friends but we decided to stay at home.
8. They visited Jacksonville Miami and Tampa but they chose to live in Daytona Beach.

9. The students elected to the school board's special committee are Jenny Young a freshman Wayne Gray a sophomore and Kevin Seymour a senior.
10. Jennifer's address is 32 Beverly Drive Springfield Illinois but she will be moving soon to Indiana.

EXERCISE 15   Time-out for Review

Number your paper 1 to 20. Then write each sentence, adding a semicolon and commas where needed.

1. Plastics make ideal electrical parts they are nonconductors of electricity.
2. We have Mother's Day in the United States but the English have Mothering Sunday.
3. Computer chips were unknown a generation ago however they now play an important role in industry.
4. I spoke with our advisor the principal and the committee members and they are all in agreement.
5. The Arabian camel has one hump the Bactrian camel has two.
6. Viking ships had oars as well as sails consequently the vessels were not completely dependent upon the wind.
7. The tourist trap looked expensive but its wares were reasonable.
8. The movie however was much too long.
9. The porpoise is not a fish it is a mammal.
10. I didn't win the marathon nevertheless running in it was a good experience.
11. Yesterday the temperature was 32 degrees in Lima Ohio 58 degrees in Waycross Georgia and 80 degrees in Hollywood Florida.
12. The world is not round it is an oblate spheroid.
13. Will you get my homework assignments for I'll be out of town on Friday.
14. Some things are not what they seem to be for example "magic" is only a series of illusions.
15. Termites are not related to ants they are part of the cockroach family.

16. Everyone had a good time working on the car wash moreover it was a huge success.
17. I have packed the books the records and the tapes but I don't know what to do next.
18. Cicadas have their hearing organs in their stomachs crickets have theirs in their knees.
19. Take a lunch with you otherwise you may not get anything to eat.
20. *E* is the most frequently used letter in the English alphabet *q* is the least frequently used.

EXERCISE 16 Writing Sentences
Write a compound sentence that follows each of the directions below.

1. Use a comma and a conjunction to join two independent clauses.
2. Use a semicolon to join two independent clauses.
3. Use a semicolon and the transitional word *nevertheless* to join two independent clauses.
4. Use a semicolon and the transitional word *however* to join two independent clauses.
5. Use a conjunction and a semicolon to join one or two independent clauses that contain commas.

Colons

A colon is used most often to introduce a list of items.

19n ▶ Use a colon before most lists of items, especially when the list comes after an expression like *the following*.

All volunteers will need the following: a notebook, a pen, and a comfortable pair of walking shoes.
There are four methods of catching fish: hooking, netting, spearing, and trapping.

NOTE: Commas should separate the items in the series.

Never use a colon directly after a verb or a preposition.

INCORRECT My three favorite subjects are: math, science, and woodworking.

CORRECT My three favorite subjects are math, science, and woodworking.

CORRECT These are my favorite subjects: math, science, and woodworking.

Colons are also used in a few other situations.

19o Use a colon in certain special situations.

HOURS AND MINUTES	5:30 A.M.
BIBLICAL CHAPTERS AND VERSES	John 3:16
SALUTATIONS IN BUSINESS LETTERS	Dear Sir:

EXERCISE 17 Using Colons
Number your paper 1 to 10. Then write each sentence, adding a colon where needed. If a sentence does not need a colon, write *C* after the number.

1. Kathleen left the Boston airport at 10 40 A.M. and arrived in Bermuda at 1 10 P.M.
2. Cargo planes carry almost anything white mice, toupees, and even small private planes.
3. While you're at the drugstore, please buy aspirin, toothpaste, and cotton balls.
4. I made note of my favorite Bible verse, I Corinthians 13 13.
5. For the hike you should bring the following a snack, a canteen of water, and suntan lotion.
6. The ocean floor is divided into three main regions continental shelf, slope, and abyss.
7. At 11 15 A.M., the minister read Psalms 62 5, the text for his sermon.
8. I've been very busy taking care of two rabbits, one cat, three dogs, and a turtle.

9. In colonial times medicines included the following powdered frogs, crabs' eyes, and pine bark.
10. I have relatives in Kentucky, Utah, and Arizona.

HYPHENS

Although a hyphen is used mainly to divide a word at the end of a line, it has other uses as well.

Hyphens with Numbers and Words

Hyphens are used with certain numbers and fractions.

19p ▸ Use a hyphen when writing out the numbers *twenty-one* through *ninety-nine.* Also use a hyphen when writing out a fraction that is used as an adjective.

Thirty-two people entered the writing contest.
Jane owned a two-thirds share of the property.

When a fraction is used as a noun, no hyphen is needed.

The recipe calls for **two thirds** of a cup of flour.

Hyphens with Compound Nouns. The parts of some compound nouns should be separated by hyphens.

19q ▸ Use a hyphen to separate the parts of some compound nouns.

Mrs. Knight is my great-grandmother.
Ray was elected secretary-treasurer.

Hyphens with Certain Prefixes. Hyphens are used to separate certain prefixes and the suffix *-elect* from their root words.

19r ▸ Use a hyphen after certain prefixes and before the suffix *-elect.*

359

Hyphens Used with Prefixes and Suffixes

Use hyphens in the following situations.

1. Between a prefix and a proper noun or proper adjective (all-American, mid-Atlantic, pre-Columbian) [Notice that only the proper noun or the proper adjective begins with a capital letter — not the prefix.]
2. After the prefix *self-* (self-righteous, self-satisfied)
3. After the prefix *ex-* when it means "former" or "formerly" (ex-convict, ex-governor, ex-senator)
4. After a person's title when it is followed by the suffix *-elect* (president-elect)

EXERCISE 18   Using Hyphens

Number your paper 1 to 10. Then correctly write each word that should be hyphenated. If no word in the sentence needs a hyphen, write *C* after the number.

1. I will enjoy having a new sister in law.
2. Did the convention follow the two thirds rule?
3. Sixty eight freshmen attended the assembly.
4. Instead of depending upon her parents so much, Lynn should become more self reliant.
5. After being out of office for two terms, the ex mayor of Philadelphia ran again.
6. I have typed one half of my report.
7. The president elect will hold a news conference.
8. I'm giving Jamie a jack in the box for his second birthday.
9. Send a self addressed envelope with your inquiry.
10. My brother is the ex president of the Student Council.

Hyphens with Divided Words

Although you should avoid dividing words whenever possible, sometimes it is necessary.

19s ▸ Use a hyphen to divide a word at the end of a line.

The following six guidelines will help you divide words correctly.

Dividing Words

1. Divide words only between syllables.
   gym nas tics: gym-nastics or gymnas-tics

2. Never divide a one-syllable word.
   myth   rhyme   strength

3. Never separate a one-letter syllable from the rest of the word. For example, the following words should never be divided.
   DO NOT BREAK   e-vent   sleep-y   o-boe   i-tem

4. A two-letter word ending should not be carried over to the next line.
   DO NOT BREAK   cred-it   hang-er   part-ly

5. Divide hyphenated words only after the hyphens.
   mother-in-law   maid-of-honor   attorney-at-law

6. Do not divide a proper noun or a proper adjective.
   Beckerman   Memphis   Atlantic   Indian

EXERCISE 19   Using Hyphens to Divide Words

Number your paper 1 to 30. Add a hyphen or hyphens to show where each word can be correctly divided. If a word should not be divided, write *no* after the number.

1. event	11. galaxy	21. silent
2. amazement	12. through	22. phrase
3. satin	13. action	23. Timothy
4. hamster	14. jury	24. forgery
5. growth	15. drop-off	25. cracked
6. invoice	16. Cairo	26. icy
7. son-in-law	17. single	27. seven
8. busy	18. stretch	28. flip-flop
9. mention	19. obey	29. avoid
10. lather	20. empire	30. crater

EXERCISE 20   Time-out for Review

Number your paper 1 to 10. Then write each sentence, adding semicolons, colons, and hyphens where needed. If a sentence is correct, write *C* after the number.

1. There are four commonwealths in the United States Kentucky, Massachusetts, Pennsylvania, and Virginia.
2. The life span of a trout is four years a goldfish can live to be twenty five.
3. Thirty five species of coconuts are known.
4. Kevin White, an ex mayor of Boston, held that office for four terms.
5. The largest state in the union is Alaska it is more than twice the size of Texas.
6. After the name *Smith,* the most common names are *Jones, Johnson, Williams,* and *Brown.*
7. My great aunt is arriving on the 6 10 P.M. flight.
8. A cheetah can run about 70 miles an hour, an ostrich 30, and a jackrabbit 35 but the top speed for a human is only 27 miles an hour.
9. Most fish do not have a keen sense of hearing however, they have a keen sense of smell.
10. More than three fourths of all flowers have an unpleasant odor or no odor at all.

✒ *Application to Writing*

Always edit your writing for correct punctuation.

EXERCISE 21   Editing for Proper Punctuation

Write the following paragraphs, adding apostrophes, semicolons, colons, and hyphens where needed.

A Real Jumper

    Whos the worlds champion jumper? If youre thinking of a person, youre wrong. The kangaroo lays claim to this title. This curious-looking Australian mammal cannot walk however, it sure can jump. It can easily hop over a parked car. It can also travel over thirty nine miles an hour.

The kangaroo has some unusual physical characteristics a small head, large pointed ears, very short front limbs, and hind quarters the size of a mules. Its feet sometimes measure ten inches from the heel to the longest toe. The kangaroos thick tail is so strong that it can use the tail as a stool. The kangaroo is a vegetarian it will not eat another animal.

CHAPTER REVIEW

Number your paper 1 to 20. Then write each sentence, adding all needed punctuation.

1. Rattlesnakes do not lay eggs they give birth to living young.
2. The worlds largest gem is a topaz that weighs 596 pounds.
3. The soybean is a versatile vegetable for example 400 different products can be made from it.
4. Greg wont be satisfied until hes totally self sufficient.
5. The following famous people had red hair George Washington, Thomas Jefferson, and Mark Twain.
6. Out of the seventy two votes, Lenny Burns received a two thirds majority.
7. When Snuffys leash broke, he ran out of the Holahans yard.
8. The official name of India is not *India* it is *Bharat.*
9. My brother in law is the president elect of the Athletic Club.
10. Salt is found on Earth in three basic forms salt water, brine deposits, and rock salt crystal.
11. A snake has no ears however its tongue is extremely sensitive to sound vibrations.
12. Adolf Hitlers real name was Adolf Schicklgruber.
13. The people on the panel included Terry Hayden, an editorial writer Thelma Casey, a fashion consultant and Judith Howe, a high school teacher.

363

14. Today there are more than 7,000 varieties of apples nevertheless only 20 varieties are widely grown.
15. Twenty two people will arrive for dinner at 6 30 P.M.
16. The hot dog is not an American invention it was first produced in Germany.
17. No ones script was left in the auditorium.
18. Sources for his report included books, magazines, and filmstrips but he forgot to document them.
19. Dont leave the dog outside in its house if its going to rain.
20. Shuffleboard has had many names over the years shoveboard, shovel-penny, and shovelboard.

MASTERY TEST

Number your paper 1 to 10. Then write each sentence, adding apostrophes, semicolons, colons, and hyphens where needed.

1. A chameleons tongue is as long as its body.
2. Sometimes a camel does not drink water for days, weeks, or even months yet it can drink twenty five gallons of water in half an hour.
3. The ex mayors speech will be televised tonight.
4. To almost everyones surprise, elephants can swim.
5. Shouldnt we be at the theater by 8 15 P.M.?
6. In the laboratory all the mices and rats cages must be kept spotlessly clean.
7. In his later years George Frideric Handel was blind nevertheless, he continued to compose music.
8. Henrys story contains too many *and*s and *so*s.
9. The smallest antelope is the size of a rabbit the largest antelope can weigh up to 1,500 pounds.
10. Two beautiful countries will be visited on the tour Switzerland and Sweden.

STANDARDIZED TEST ▬▬▬

MECHANICS

Directions: Decide which numbered part in each sentence contains an error in capitalization or punctuation. In the appropriate row on your answer sheet, fill in the circle containing the same number as the incorrect part. If there is no error, fill in *4*.

SAMPLE   My high school | is on | Hudson avenue. | None
           1   **2**   **3**   **4**

ANSWER   ① ② ❸ ④

1. The world's | highest waterfall is in | Venezuela. | None
    1   **2**   **3**   **4**

2. Enrico caruso | was a famous | opera star. | None
    1   **2**   **3**   **4**

3. Can Ken, Rita, | and Laura | be here at 6:30. | None
    1   **2**   **3**   **4**

4. Before Dr. Bell | spoke, he took | a deep breath. | None
    1   **2**   **3**   **4**

5. The date however, | couldn't be | July 8, 1971. | None
    1   **2**   **3**   **4**

6. Is your mother | a Democrat | or a republican? | None
    1   **2**   **3**   **4**

7. Mr Kelly met | Jane's tiny but | fierce kitten. | None
    1   **2**   **3**   **4**

8. Harold H. Higgins | belongs to no | political party. | None
    1   **2**   **3**   **4**

9. Will the annual | Fall fair be held | on Labor Day? | None
    1   **2**   **3**   **4**

10. Art Forms, Inc., | has fifty six | Italian clocks. | None
    1   **2**   **3**   **4**

11. My sister's-in-law | car is old, but | it's reliable. | None
    1   **2**   **3**   **4**

12. Wasn't that | the ex governor of | the state of Maine? | None
    1   **2**   **3**   **4**

13. On Labor Day | twenty-one committee members attended |
    1   **2**

    the Browns party. | None
       3   **4**

14. Did I misspell | *vacuum* | on my physics test? | None
          1   **2**   **3**   **4**
15. That copy of *Oliver Twist* | isn't theirs; | it's ours. | None
              1   **2**   **3**   **4**

Directions: Choose the answer that shows the correct way to write the underlined part in each sentence. On your answer sheet, fill in the circle containing the same number as your answer.

SAMPLE She noticed the mysterious <u>stranger but</u> he did not.
            1. stranger, but
            2. stranger: but
            3. stranger but

ANSWER ① ② ③

16. The meeting was called for <u>8 15 P.M.</u>
    1. 8.15 P.M.
    2. 8:15 P.M.
    3. 8:15 PM

17. <u>dear sir or madam</u>
    1. Dear Sir or Madam
    2. Dear sir or madam:
    3. Dear Sir or Madam:

18. <u>sincerely yours</u>
    1. Sincerely yours,
    2. Sincerely Yours,
    3. Sincerely yours

19. Harry <u>said please</u> cross the street carefully.''
    1. said ''Please
    2. said, ''please
    3. said, ''Please

20. Paul said, ''I was sorry when <u>the party was over.</u>
    1. the party was over.''
    2. the party was over''.
    3. the party was over.''.

Unit 4

Vocabulary and Spelling

20
Vocabulary

"The saddest words of tongue or pen
Are those you didn't think of then."
— BETTY PILLIPP

Start now to enlarge your vocabulary. You may then have the words you need when the occasion arises.

WORD MEANING

Very often you will come across words that are new to you.

Mr. Forester spoke laconically.

Perhaps you know that *laconically* means "briefly," or "using a minimum of words," but more likely it is a new word to you. One way to learn its meaning is to look it up in a dictionary. In this chapter you will learn several other ways to unlock the meanings of words.

Context Clues

One of the best ways to learn the meaning of a word is through context clues. The *context* of a word is the sentence, the surrounding words, or the situation in which the word occurs. The following examples show the four most common kinds of context clues.

DEFINITION OR RESTATEMENT	During the storm, travelers were detoured because the **isthmus,** a narrow strip of land connecting two larger landmasses, was flooded. [The word *isthmus* is defined within the sentence.]
EXAMPLE	You may find a **fossil** here, perhaps like the one with an imprint of a leaf in our science lab. [The word *fossil* is followed by an example that is known to the readers or listeners.]
COMPARISON	The mayor said that tax **revenue,** like personal income, should be spent wisely. [The word *like* compares *revenue* to its synonym *income*.]
CONTRAST	**Contemporary** students learn more about computers than students did a few years ago. [A contrast is drawn between today's students (*contemporary* students) and students of the past.]

EXERCISE 1   Using Context Clues

Number your paper 1 to 20. Then write the letter of the word or phrase that is closest in meaning to the underlined word.

1. The team members gathered in a huddle but <u>dispersed</u> when the coach blew her whistle.
   (A) cheered   (B) scattered   (C) exercised
   (D) planned   (E) answered

2. Because ferns, orchids, and bromeliads are <u>indigenous</u> to the tropics, they must be grown in hothouse conditions in the north.
   (A) unknown   (B) exotic   (C) warlike
   (D) unemployed   (E) native

3. Louise Nevelson <u>salvages</u> useless scraps of metal and wood and transforms them into famous sculptures.
   (A) builds   (B) creates   (C) rescues
   (D) destroys   (E) judges

4. Ms. Ord thought that the impatient <u>patron</u> should wait her turn in line, like others in the store.
   (A) owner   (B) speaker   (C) prisoner
   (D) customer   (E) hypnotist

5. We were fascinated by the insect, but Carl seemed <u>oblivious</u> of it.
   (A) devious   (B) clear   (C) unaware
   (D) pale   (E) superior

6. We planted <u>perennial</u> flowers, those that will bloom all year, in our garden.
   (A) perfect   (B) timid   (C) slippery
   (D) victorious   (E) lasting

7. The politician accused his opponents of <u>contriving</u> to defeat his proposal.
   (A) scheming   (B) lying   (C) electing
   (D) grieving   (E) answering

8. The idea was <u>infamous,</u> a scheme no fair or honest person could accept.
   (A) disgraceful   (B) unknown   (C) childlike
   (D) diseased   (E) well-known

9. My <u>hypothesis,</u> the way I explain it, is that Shana made the phone call.
   (A) mistake   (B) theory   (C) dream
   (D) publicity   (E) thanks

10. The city's <u>fiscal</u> policy is to keep the sales tax as low as possible.
    (A) financial   (B) unpopular   (C) overall
    (D) military   (E) graceful

11. The use of <u>automation</u> in farming, such as mechanized cultivators and feeding troughs, has greatly increased the efficiency of agriculture.
    (A) tractors   (B) business   (C) resources
    (D) machinery   (E) computers

12. Have an expert <u>appraise,</u> or estimate the worth of, a major purchase before you buy it.
    (A) record   (B) buy   (C) evaluate
    (D) announce   (E) glorify

13. Winning the blue ribbon is her <u>incentive</u> to practice daily for the race.
    (A) excuse   (B) reward   (C) payment
    (D) idea   (E) motivation

14. The program features Julia Child, a <u>connoisseur</u> of fine food.
    (A) scientist   (B) expert   (C) actor
    (D) reporter   (E) artist

15. Although city streets are <u>congested</u> during the rush hour, traffic decreases between 6 P.M. and 7 A.M.
    (A) clogged   (B) deserted   (C) paved
    (D) wide   (E) narrow

16. Heavy rain fell continuously for four days, ending the drought and <u>saturating</u> the soil.
    (A) dissolving   (B) soaking   (C) drying
    (D) planting   (E) mixing

17. Her <u>graphic</u> description enabled her readers to picture each object in the room in detail.
    (A) musical   (B) vague   (C) geometric
    (D) vivid   (E) exaggerated

18. National park land cannot be <u>exploited</u> for resorts, industries, or other money-making projects.
    (A) explored   (B) defended   (C) used for profit
    (D) increased in value   (E) observed

19. The <u>benefactor</u> who contributed money to build a new workshop remains anonymous.
    (A) builder   (B) donator   (C) mayor
    (D) worker   (E) writer

20. The detective <u>deduced</u> that the crime had been committed by his long-time business associate.
    (A) subtracted (B) defended (C) reduced
    (D) concluded (E) investigated

Prefixes and Suffixes

Words in English often have Latin or Greek roots, prefixes, and suffixes. These word parts offer clues to help you unlock the meanings of words. A *root* is the part of a word that carries the basic meaning. A *prefix* is one or more syllables placed in front of the root to modify the meaning of the root or to form a new word. A *suffix* is one or more syllables placed after the root to change its part of speech. In the following examples, notice how the meaning of each word part is related to the meaning of the word as a whole.

WORD	PREFIX	ROOT	SUFFIX
dissimilarity (state of being unlike)	dis- (not)	-similar- (alike)	-ity (state of)
independence (state of not relying)	in- (not)	-depend- (to rely)	-ence (state of)
intergalactic (relating to area between galaxies)	inter- (between)	-galaxy- (star system)	-ic (relating to)
transporter (one who carries across)	trans- (across)	-port- (to carry)	-er (one who)

Since the meanings of words in our language often change over years of use, you will not always find a perfect match between their meanings and the meanings of their Latin and Greek word parts. Even so, a knowledge of prefixes, roots, and suffixes can help you figure out the meanings of thousands of words.

COMMON PREFIXES AND SUFFIXES

Prefix	Meaning	Example
com-, con-	with, together	con + form = to become the same shape
dis-	not, lack of	dis + harmony = a lack of agreement
extra-	outside, beyond	extra + curricular = outside the regular school courses
in-, il-, im-	in, into, not	im + migrate = to come into a country, il + legal = not lawful
inter-	between, among	inter + state = among or between states
post-	after	post + date = to give a later date
re-	again	re + occur = to happen again
sub-	under	sub + standard = under the standard
trans-	across	trans + atlantic = across the Atlantic

Suffix	Meaning	Example
-ance, -ence	state of	import + ance = state of being important
-er	one who or that	foreign + er = one who is foreign
-ful	full of	hope + ful = full of hope
-ic	relating to	atom + ic = relating to atoms
-ite	resident of	Milford + ite = resident of Milford
-ity	state of	active + ity = state of being active
-less	without, lack of	pain + less = without pain

EXERCISE 2   Using Prefixes and Suffixes

Number your paper 1 to 20. Write the prefix or the suffix that has the same meaning as the underlined word or words. Then write the complete word defined after the equal sign.

EXAMPLE   <u>under</u> + marine = beneath the water
ANSWER   sub — submarine

1. <u>among</u> + stellar = taking place among the stars
2. <u>together</u> + press = to squeeze together
3. depend + <u>state of</u> = the state of relying on someone or something for support
4. patriot + <u>relating to</u> = relating to love of country
5. <u>across</u> + plant = to lift from one place across and to reset in another
6. <u>not</u> + similar = not like
7. actual + <u>state of</u> = state of being real
8. speech + <u>without</u> = without conversation
9. <u>after</u> + game = following a game
10. <u>not</u> + frequent = not habitual
11. <u>again</u> + examine = to inspect again
12. <u>between</u> + cede = to go between; to act as mediator in a dispute
13. Brooklyn + <u>resident</u> = one who lives in Brooklyn
14. contend + <u>one who</u> = one who strives in a competition or debate
15. <u>not</u> + mortal = not subject to death
16. <u>with</u> + verse = to talk with
17. meaning + <u>full</u> = full of meaning or purpose
18. solid + <u>condition</u> = state of being solid
19. <u>after</u> + graduate = student continuing his or her education after high school or college graduation
20. <u>across</u> + marine = extending across the sea

EXERCISE 3   Using Prefixes

Number your paper 1 to 10. Then write the letter of the phrase that is closest in meaning to the word in capital letters. The prefixes you have learned in this chapter will help you determine the meanings of the capitalized words.

1. DISUNITY   (A) agreement with (B) agreement between (C) lack of agreement
2. INTERVENE   (A) come into (B) come together (C) come between
3. TRANSPOLAR   (A) extending across a polar region (B) moving out of a polar region (C) extending under a polar region
4. SUBMERGE   (A) put underwater (B) place together (C) float across
5. EXTRAORDINARY   (A) after what is usual (B) beyond what is usual (C) among what is usual
6. CONJUNCTION   (A) joining together (B) not joining (C) joining across
7. POSTPONE   (A) delay to a future time (B) move across a barrier (C) place under
8. IMPLODE   (A) collapse inward (B) burst out of (C) fly across at a high speed
9. REACTIVATE   (A) give energy again (B) be energetic with (C) take away energy
10. IMPARTIAL   (A) lacking parts (B) not favoring one side (C) after each part

Synonyms and Antonyms

A *synonym* is a word that has nearly the same meaning as another word. An *antonym* is a word that means the opposite of another word.

SYNONYMS affable : friendly   terminate : finish
ANTONYMS affable : hostile   terminate : begin

Your dictionary contains information on synonyms. Often a dictionary entry will also explain the slight differences between them. *(See pages 405–406.)*

A kind of specialized dictionary for synonyms is called a *thesaurus*. A thesaurus lists words and their synonyms and usually includes a thorough index to make words easy to find. *(See page 421.)*

EXERCISE 4 Recognizing Synonyms

Number your paper 1 to 20. Write the letter of the word that is closest in meaning to the word in capital letters. Then check your answers in a dictionary.

1. ACUTE   (A) lovely (B) mountainous (C) sharp
   (D) prior (E) hasty
2. COMPREHEND   (A) write (B) bother (C) lose
   (D) collect (E) understand
3. COURIER   (A) spy (B) gentleman (C) pilot
   (D) employer (E) messenger
4. DEBRIS   (A) ruins (B) corruption (C) debt
   (D) poverty (E) confidence
5. EXASPERATE   (A) depart (B) irritate
   (C) increase (D) reduce (E) evaporate
6. EXEMPT   (A) perfect (B) empty (C) required
   (D) excused (E) important
7. GENTEEL   (A) real (B) selfish (C) polite
   (D) nonspecific (E) lifeless
8. INTEGRITY   (A) honesty (B) cleverness
   (C) wealth (D) annoyance (E) fame
9. KNOLL   (A) holiday (B) noise (C) mound
   (D) forest (E) merrymaker
10. LUDICROUS   (A) fortunate (B) questionable
    (C) laughable (D) happy (E) shy
11. MUTUAL   (A) active (B) changed (C) deep
    (D) shared (E) solitary
12. NARRATE   (A) tell (B) judge (C) notch
    (D) separate (E) believe
13. OBSOLETE   (A) outdated (B) lost (C) hidden
    (D) wrecked (E) reversed
14. OBSTRUCT   (A) teach (B) disagree (C) build
    (D) hinder (E) watch
15. PHENOMENAL   (A) lucky (B) remarkable
    (C) hasty (D) musical (E) unemotional
16. RANDOM   (A) unlikely (B) spoiled (C) chance
    (D) organized (E) conservative
17. RESTRAINT   (A) quiet (B) echo (C) review
    (D) army (E) control

18. SKEPTICAL (A) visual (B) fragile (C) doubting
    (D) incomplete (E) timid
19. SOLITUDE (A) sleeplessness (B) isolation
    (C) sorrow (D) strength (E) concern
20. VALIANT (A) boastful (B) timid (C) precious
    (D) careless (E) brave

EXERCISE 5 **Recognizing Antonyms**
Number your paper 1 to 20. Write the letter of the word that
is most nearly opposite in meaning to the word in capital
letters. Then check your answers in a dictionary.

1. ABSTRACT (A) hazy (B) total (C) honest
    (D) concrete (E) theoretical
2. ADJACENT (A) distant (B) acceptable
    (C) vague (D) accidental (E) near
3. ADVERSE (A) unreliable (B) favorable
    (C) clever (D) hostile (E) risky
4. BIZARRE (A) crowded (B) familiar (C) odd
    (D) commercial (E) unreasonable
5. BREVITY (A) briefness (B) wittiness
    (C) dullness (D) wordiness (E) slowness
6. COMPRESS (A) expand (B) point (C) accuse
    (D) squeeze (E) impress
7. CRUCIAL (A) unimportant (B) required
    (C) stern (D) unbelievable (E) refined
8. DISSIMILAR (A) truthful (B) different
    (C) prompt (D) genuine (E) alike
9. ESSENTIAL (A) unnecessary (B) secret
    (C) incorrect (D) tall (E) easy
10. EXEMPT (A) taxed (B) dependent
    (C) excused (D) perfect (E) obligated
11. HACKNEYED (A) thoughtful (B) overused
    (C) skilled (D) original (E) wide
12. IMPROVISE (A) disprove (B) react
    (C) increase (D) plan (E) stop
13. INFAMOUS (A) pleasant (B) untrustworthy
    (C) honorable (D) huge (E) shady

14. OBSTRUCT   (A) refuse (B) assist (C) improve
   (D) suggest (E) obtain
15. PHENOMENAL   (A) poisonous (B) brilliant
   (C) ordinary (D) pitiful (E) generous
16. REPEL   (A) attract (B) unfasten (C) struggle
   (D) reject (E) forget
17. SKEPTICAL   (A) uncertain (B) trusting
   (C) reckless (D) false (E) truthful
18. SUPERFLUOUS   (A) inferior (B) extra
   (C) normal (D) heavy (E) necessary
19. SYNTHETIC   (A) inefficient (B) artificial
   (C) rhythmic (D) lasting (E) natural
20. VERSATILE   (A) variable (B) unnecessary
   (C) skilled (D) turning (E) specialized

EXERCISE 6   Recognizing Analogies

Number your paper 1 to 15. First decide how the two words in capital letters are related. Then indicate your answer by writing *synonyms* or *antonyms* after the proper number. Next decide which pair of words — A, B, or C — is related in the same way. Then write the letter of your answer.

EXAMPLE   WILD:TAME :: (A) sleepy:tired
          (B) empty:full (C) loud:noisy
ANSWER   antonyms — B

1. COLD:HOT :: (A) high:low (B) kind:gentle
   (C) fast:quick
2. SLIM:THIN :: (A) young:old (B) open:closed
   (C) careful:cautious
3. LATE:EARLY :: (A) round:circular
   (B) right:wrong (C) distant:far
4. SOAR:GLIDE :: (A) raise:lower
   (B) watch:observe (C) arrive:depart
5. REASON:LOGIC :: (A) courage:bravery
   (B) fantasy:reality (C) joy:sorrow
6. VALID:LEGAL :: (A) certain:sure
   (B) tall:short (C) rough:smooth

7. QUALIFIED:ELIGIBLE :: (A) hopeful:discouraged
   (B) fair:just   (C) tidy:messy
8. FOREIGN:ALIEN :: (A) peaceful:calm
   (B) wet:dry   (C) soft:hard
9. GENUINE:AUTHENTIC :: (A) real:imaginary
   (B) hungry:full   (C) fortunate:lucky
10. WEAKNESS:STAMINA :: (A) box:carton
    (B) car:automobile   (C) beginning:conclusion
11. COMPETITION:RIVALRY :: (A) safety:danger
    (B) cooperation:teamwork   (C) top:bottom
12. CURE:REMEDY :: (A) cause:effect
    (B) guilt:innocence   (C) value:worth
13. USEFUL:FUTILE :: (A) wicked:evil
    (B) true:false   (C) prompt:punctual
14. THOUGHTFUL:PENSIVE :: (A) hazy:bright
    (B) necessary:essential   (C) wide:narrow
15. DOUBTFUL:DUBIOUS :: (A) tart:sweet
    (B) alert:watchful   (C) shiny:dull

INCREASING YOUR VOCABULARY

One good way to build your vocabulary is to use your dictionary regularly. When you come across a word you do not know, look it up. Read the definitions. Then check the etymology, or history, of the word. *(See page 406.)* You may discover a prefix, suffix, or root that will help you unlock the meaning of many other words.

Another useful technique for increasing your vocabulary is to keep a notebook. Jot down new words and their meanings. Look back at these words from time to time. As your list grows, so will your vocabulary.

Vocabulary List

The following list contains words that you are likely to find in your reading. Since all of them appeared earlier in this chapter, you should already be familiar with their meanings. Review the list and see how many words you can define. Look up those you are unsure of in a dictionary and include them in your vocabulary notebook.

Vocabulary List

abstract	converse	impartial	random
actuality	courier	improvise	remedy
acute	crucial	incentive	reoccur
adjacent	debris	indigenous	repel
adverse	deduce	infamous	restraint
affable	disperse	integrity	revenue
alien	dissimilar	intercede	rivalry
appraise	dubious	interstellar	salvage
authentic	eligible	isthmus	saturate
automation	essential	knoll	skeptical
benefactor	exasperate	laconic	solitude
bizarre	exempt	ludicrous	stamina
brevity	exploit	mutual	submerge
comprehend	fiscal	narrate	substandard
compress	fossil	oblivious	superfluous
conform	futile	obsolete	synthetic
congestion	genteel	obstruct	transplant
connoisseur	graphic	patron	valiant
contemporary	hackneyed	pensive	valid
contrive	hypothesis	perennial	versatile

CHAPTER REVIEW

Number your paper 1 to 20. Then write the letter of the word or phrase that is closest in meaning to the word in capital letters.

1. EXASPERATE   (A) annoy (B) fizzle (C) excite
   (D) transfer (E) surpass
2. INDIGENOUS   (A) native (B) furious
   (C) roundabout (D) introductory (E) specific
3. DUBIOUS   (A) rough (B) doubtful (C) clear
   (D) repeated (E) confident

4. CONTEMPORARY   (A) modern (B) pleasant
   (C) brief (D) plain (E) thoughtful
5. DISPERSE   (A) travel (B) decide (C) gather
   (D) scatter (E) believe
6. CONTRIVE   (A) avoid (B) twist (C) scheme
   (D) forget (E) choose
7. VALIANT   (A) curious (B) convincing
   (C) weak (D) amusing (E) courageous
8. AUTHENTIC   (A) copied (B) peaceful
   (C) angry (D) genuine (E) changed
9. STAMINA   (A) deadlock (B) endurance
   (C) success (D) wisdom (E) defeat
10. SYNTHETIC   (A) cheap (B) gaudy (C) artificial
    (D) cone-shaped (E) cooperative
11. REVENUE   (A) income (B) debt (C) injury
    (D) echo (E) retreat
12. BREVITY   (A) humor (B) fright (C) brightness
    (D) honesty (E) briefness
13. INTEGRITY   (A) freedom (B) honesty
    (C) disloyalty (D) disappointment (E) confusion
14. OBSOLETE   (A) outdated (B) new (C) costly
    (D) powerful (E) round
15. REPEL   (A) answer (B) reject (C) argue
    (D) lift (E) decide
16. CRUCIAL   (A) expensive (B) forgotten
    (C) important (D) smart (E) coded
17. SUPERFLUOUS   (A) extra (B) flowing
    (C) large (D) bold (E) conceited
18. LUDICROUS   (A) clear (B) fortunate
    (C) clumsy (D) laughable (E) hidden
19. FUTILE   (A) hopeful (B) important (C) lazy
    (D) thrifty (E) useless
20. ADVERSE   (A) positive (B) unfavorable
    (C) talkative (D) twisted (E) hopeful

21
Spelling

While spelling is easier for some people than for others, everyone can learn to become an accurate speller. This chapter will show you ways to improve your spelling skills.

SPELLING IMPROVEMENT

The following suggestions will help you improve your spelling.

Methods for Improving Your Spelling

1. Begin a spelling notebook. List the words you find difficult to spell in compositions, letters, and tests. By reviewing your list regularly, you will master each word.
2. When writing, use a dictionary to check the spelling of words you are unsure of. Guessing is unreliable.
3. Proofread your writing carefully. In the rush of getting your thoughts down on paper, you may put an extra letter in a word or leave a letter out. Careful proofreading will eliminate these kinds of errors.
4. Sound out each syllable to avoid dropping letters.

   math **e** matics   Feb **ru** ary   tem **per a** ture
5. Use memory tricks for words you frequently misspell. The most useful memory tricks are ones you devise yourself. The following are some examples.

bargain	You **gain** by a bar**gain**.
criticize	A **critic critici**zes.
committee	2 *m*'s, 2 *t*'s, 2 *e*'s
together	We went **together to get her** ticket.

EXERCISE 1 Using the Dictionary for Problem Words
Write the word that you think is spelled correctly in each pair. Then check your answer in a dictionary. Enter in your notebook any words you misspelled.

The
Tiny
Fiddler

1. The lowly cricket is no (ordinary, ordinery) insect.
2. (All though, Although) most insects are disliked, the cricket has many friends.
3. For (censuries, centuries) the Chinese and Japanese have kept crickets as pets.
4. The crickets are kept in (elaborate, elabrate) cages.
5. Some of the most expensive cages are (quiet, quite) luxurious.
6. Supporters of the cricket admire its (fiddling, fiddeling), the pleasant music of a summer evening.
7. This admiration is not (unanimous, unanymous), however.
8. Isaac Stern, a (famouse, famous) violinist, was once momentarily defeated by a tiny competitor.
9. He delayed a concert five minutes while (attendents, attendants) feverishly tried to find the tiny fiddler.
10. The cricket was (finally, finely) found, happily nestled in a potted palm.

EXERCISE 2 Recognizing Misspelled Words
Write the letter preceding the misspelled word in each group. Then write the word correctly. Check your answers in a dictionary and enter in your notebook any words you misspelled.

EXAMPLE   (A) illegal (B) vegetable (C) missile
          (D) definit (E) forty
ANSWER   (D) definite

1. (A) abbreviation (B) boulevard (C) extream
   (D) incident (E) insistence
2. (A) bureau (B) confer (C) forgery
   (D) honorary (E) literture
3. (A) fasinating (B) guarantee (C) illustrate
   (D) limousine (E) manipulate

4. (A) irritate (B) luxury (C) mischeif
   (D) organic (E) presence
5. (A) authentic (B) brillance (C) disguise
   (D) interview (E) miniature
6. (A) mysterious (B) ocasionally (C) prestige
   (D) prosperous (E) reasonable
7. (A) legislasure (B) merchandise (C) notch
   (D) rebel (E) referee
8. (A) punctual (B) resign (C) resteurant
   (D) similarity (E) speculate
9. (A) ridicilous (B) sizable (C) thesaurus
   (D) unanimous (E) veteran
10. (A) coupon (B) chrystal (C) dissatisfied
    (D) melancholy (E) orchestra

SPELLING RULES

Many words in English are easier to spell if you know a few common rules. Some of these rules concern spelling patterns—the choice between *ie* or *ei*, for example. Others concern forming plurals and adding prefixes and suffixes. Knowing these rules can help you spell hundreds of words correctly.

Spelling Patterns

The following rhyme can help you spell words with the *ie* or *ei* pattern.

> Put *i* before *e*
> Except after *c*
> Or when sounded like *a*
> As in *neighbor* and *weigh*.

This simple rhyme contains three rules.

i before *e*		except after *c*		sounded like *a*	
believe	field	ceiling	receipt	freight	sleigh
brief	piece	conceit	receive	reign	veil

Although these rules apply in most cases, the following words are exceptions.

ancient	efficient	either	leisure
conscience	species	neither	seize
sufficient	foreign	height	weird

NOTE: The rules for spelling the *ie/ei* pattern apply only when these letters appear in the same syllable. Notice in the following examples that the *i* and *e* appear in separate syllables.

be ing	re imburse	sci ence	soci ety

Other words that often cause confusion are those ending with a "seed" sound. Keep in mind that only one word in English, *supersede,* is spelled with a *-sede* ending. Three words — *exceed, proceed,* and *succeed* — are spelled with a *-ceed* ending. All other words that end in the same sound are spelled with a *-cede* ending, including *concede, precede, recede,* and *secede.*

EXERCISE 3   Using Spelling Patterns
Write each word, adding either *ie* or *ei*.

1. th__f	6. bel__f	11. p__ce	16. br__f
2. n__ce	7. c__ling	12. r__ns	17. rec__ve
3. y__ld	8. rec__pt	13. n__ther	18. retr__ve
4. w__gh	9. gr__ve	14. dec__ve	19. n__ghbor
5. h__ght	10. __ght	15. rel__ve	20. l__sure

EXERCISE 4   Using Spelling Patterns
Write each word, adding *-sede, -ceed,* or *-cede*.

1. re__	3. ac__	5. suc__	7. pre__	9. super__
2. ex__	4. se__	6. con__	8. pro__	10. inter__

Plurals

Forming the plural of a noun is no mystery when you have the following guidelines to help you.

Regular Nouns. To form the plural of most nouns, simply add *s*. If a noun ends in *s*, *ch*, *sh*, *x*, or *z*, add *es* to form the plural.

SINGULAR	artist	symbol	maze	sardine
PLURAL	artists	symbols	mazes	sardines
SINGULAR	loss	church	dish	fox
PLURAL	losses	churches	dishes	foxes

Nouns Ending in y. Add *s* to form the plural of a noun ending in a vowel and *y*.

SINGULAR	day	display	journey	toy
PLURAL	days	displays	journeys	toys

Change the *y* to *i* and add *es* to a noun ending in a consonant and *y*.

SINGULAR	memory	trophy	lady	society
PLURAL	memories	trophies	ladies	societies

EXERCISE 5   Forming Plurals
Write the plural of each of the following nouns.

1. theme
2. valley
3. crash
4. comedy
5. virus
6. reflex
7. theory
8. tomboy
9. waltz
10. image
11. ability
12. stitch
13. holiday
14. apology
15. trapeze
16. galaxy
17. effect
18. trolley
19. issue
20. vacancy

Nouns Ending in o. Add *s* to form the plural of a noun ending in a vowel and *o*.

SINGULAR	ratio	studio	rodeo	igloo
PLURAL	ratios	studios	rodeos	igloos

The plurals of nouns ending in a consonant and *o* do not follow a regular pattern.

SINGULAR	echo	veto	silo	ego
PLURAL	echoes	vetoes	silos	egos

Add *s* to form the plural of a musical term ending in *o*.

SINGULAR	alt**o**	du**o**	pian**o**	cell**o**
PLURAL	altos	duos	pianos	cellos

When in doubt about a plural, consult a dictionary. *(See pages 399–400.)* If the dictionary does not give a plural form, the plural usually ends in *s*.

Nouns Ending in *f* or *fe*. To form the plural of some nouns ending in *f* or *fe*, simply add *s*.

SINGULAR	belief	gulf	chef	fife
PLURAL	beliefs	gulfs	chefs	fifes

To form the plural of other nouns ending in *f* or *fe*, change the *f* to *v* and add *es*.

SINGULAR	half	shelf	leaf	knife
PLURAL	hal**ves**	shel**ves**	lea**ves**	kni**ves**

There is no sure way to tell which method should be used to form the plural of nouns ending in *f* or *fe*. Use a dictionary to check the plural forms of these words when you write them.

EXERCISE 6   Forming Plurals
Write the plural of each noun, using the rules just covered. Then check your answers in a dictionary.

1. radio	6. soprano	11. roof	16. elf
2. stereo	7. hero	12. chief	17. calf
3. shampoo	8. potato	13. gulf	18. self
4. solo	9. taco	14. giraffe	19. thief
5. trio	10. yo-yo	15. tariff	20. wife

Other Plural Forms. The following box lists examples of nouns that do not form the plural by adding *s* or *es*. Study these words so that you will remember them when you write them.

Irregular Plurals

tooth, teeth	child, children	ox, oxen
foot, feet	woman, women	mouse, mice
goose, geese	man, men	die, dice

Same Form for Singular and Plural

Chinese	sheep	scissors
Japanese	moose	headquarters
Swiss	salmon	series
Sioux	surf	politics

Compound Nouns. Most compound nouns are made plural the way other nouns are.

ways	men	offices	boxes
hallways	snowmen	post offices	music boxes

In some compound nouns, however, the main word appears in the first part of the compound. Notice in the following examples that the first part is made plural.

SINGULAR	son-in-law	attorney-at-law	passerby
PLURAL	sons-in-law	attorneys-at-law	passersby

EXERCISE 7   Forming Plurals
Write the plural of each of the following words.

1. bedroom
2. eyeglass
3. runner-up
4. fire fighter
5. mother-in-law
6. mouse
7. louse
8. foot
9. tooth
10. child
11. deer
12. salmon
13. Swiss
14. pliers
15. corps
16. pen pal
17. trout
18. woman
19. Chinese
20. passerby

Prefixes and Suffixes

A *prefix* is one or more syllables placed in front of a root to form a new word. When you add a prefix to a root, do not change the spelling of the root.

in + accurate = inaccurate
pre + arrange = prearrange
dis + satisfy = dissatisfy
re + evaluate = reevaluate
ir + regular = irregular

re + set = reset
over + load = overload
mis + spell = misspell
over + rate = overrate
il + legal = illegal

A *suffix* is one or more syllables placed after a root to change its part of speech. The suffixes *-ness* and *-ly* are simply added to the root.

open + ness = openness
plain + ness = plainness

cruel + ly = cruelly
real + ly = really

When you add other suffixes, you sometimes change the spelling of the root. The following are some rules for adding suffixes.

Words Ending in e. Drop the final *e* before a suffix that begins with a vowel.

drive + ing = driving
sane + ity = sanity

isolate + ion = isolation
tone + al = tonal

Keep the final *e* before a suffix that begins with a consonant.

care + ful = careful
like + ness = likeness

price + less = priceless
state + ment = statement

The following examples are exceptions to these rules.

courage — courageous
pronounce — pronounceable

argue — argument
true — truly

EXERCISE 8 Adding Suffixes
Write each word, adding the suffix shown. Remember to make any necessary spelling changes.

1. lone + some
2. move + ment
3. like + ness
4. note + able
5. true + est

6. slide + ing
7. create + ed
8. sure + ly
9. one + ness
10. wire + ed

11. love + ly
12. close + est
13. peace + ful
14. stare + ing
15. hope + ful

389

Words Ending in y. To add a suffix to most words ending in a vowel and *y*, keep the *y*.

enjoy + able = enjoyable   stay + ing = staying
convey + ed = conveyed   joy + ful = joyful

To add a suffix to most words ending in a consonant and *y*, change the *y* to *i* before adding the suffix.

easy + ly = easily   happy + ness = happiness
rely + ance = reliance   worry + ed = worried

The following examples are exceptions to these rules.

SUFFIX BEGINNING WITH *i*   studying   denying

SOME ONE-SYLLABLE WORDS   daily   shyness

EXERCISE 9   Adding Suffixes
Write each word, adding the suffix shown. Remember to make any necessary spelling changes.

1. fly + ing
2. try + ed
3. deny + al
4. dense + ity
5. glory + ous
6. busy + ness
7. worry + ed
8. play + ful
9. ply + able
10. defy + ant
11. shy + est
12. pay + ing
13. dry + ly
14. rely + ed
15. boy + ish

Doubling the Final Consonant. Sometimes the final consonant in a word is doubled before a suffix is added. This happens when the suffix begins with a vowel and the word satisfies *both* of the following rules.

• The word has only one syllable or is stressed on the final syllable.

• The word ends in one consonant preceded by one vowel.

ONE-SYLLABLE WORD	stop + ing sto**pp**ing	grin + ed gri**nn**ed	red + est re**dd**est
FINAL SYLLABLE STRESSED	re**fer** + al refe**rr**al	be**gin** + er begi**nn**er	pre**fer** + ing prefe**rr**ing

390

EXERCISE 10   Adding Suffixes

Write each word, adding the suffix shown. Remember to make any necessary spelling changes.

1. hot + est
2. sad + en
3. drop + ed
4. trim + ing
5. swim + er

6. flip + ant
7. regret + ed
8. spoil + age
9. clear + ing
10. smart + est

11. design + er
12. grim + est
13. step + ing
14. pain + ed
15. flat + en

Commonly Misspelled Words

The words in the following list are frequently used and commonly misspelled. Study them carefully, following the suggestions on page 382.

Spelling Demons

absence	defendant	license	prejudice
accidentally	disappear	literature	privilege
achieve	discipline	loneliness	probably
acquaintance	eighth	maintenance	pronunciation
already	embarrass	marriage	psychology
always	emphasize	mathematics	recommend
analyze	exaggerate	mileage	restaurant
anonymous	familiar	misspell	rhythm
appearance	fascinating	mortgage	scissors
attendance	foreign	muscle	secretary
beginning	fourth	necessary	separate
benefited	government	neighbor	sergeant
bureau	grammar	nickel	sincerely
calendar	guarantee	ninety	souvenir
cemetery	handkerchief	occasionally	succeed
column	height	occurrence	syllable
committee	immediately	omitted	thorough
conscience	interesting	parallel	tomorrow
courageous	interfere	particularly	truly
courteous	irrelevant	permanent	unnecessary
criticize	knowledge	persuade	villain
curiosity	laboratory	possess	weird

CHAPTER REVIEW

Number your paper 1 to 30. Write the letter preceding the misspelled word in each group. Then write the word, spelling it correctly.

1. (A) niece (B) ratios (C) happyness
2. (A) intercede (B) foriegn (C) innumerable
3. (A) embarass (B) seize (C) engagement
4. (A) offered (B) criticize (C) atheletics
5. (A) conceit (B) branches (C) niether
6. (A) accidentally (B) thinness (C) payed
7. (A) peaceful (B) immediatly (C) misstep
8. (A) twentieth (B) rideing (C) argument
9. (A) journies (B) rained (C) proceed
10. (A) trapped (B) knives (C) permited
11. (A) mispell (B) relieve (C) patios
12. (A) immobile (B) occuring (C) betrayal
13. (A) forcible (B) spying (C) mathmatics
14. (A) surprised (B) reign (C) ridiculeous
15. (A) realy (B) stepping (C) valleys
16. (A) passersby (B) leafs (C) holidays
17. (A) caring (B) decieve (C) studying
18. (A) receipt (B) beliefs (C) easyly
19. (A) echos (B) misguided (C) geese
20. (A) joyful (B) seperate (C) interfere
21. (A) biggest (B) delaying (C) liesure
22. (A) generaly (B) boxes (C) roofs
23. (A) pettiness (B) disatisfied (C) writer
24. (A) anonymous (B) likeness (C) dayly
25. (A) editors in chief (B) grammer (C) eighth
26. (A) bushes (B) sadness (C) nieghbor
27. (A) pianoes (B) worrying (C) succeed
28. (A) waltzes (B) babys (C) diaries
29. (A) inaccurate (B) secede (C) hopful
30. (A) insincere (B) peachs (C) deceit

STANDARDIZED TEST

VOCABULARY AND SPELLING

Directions: Decide which underlined word in each sentence is misspelled. On your answer sheet, fill in the circle containing the same letter as your answer. If no word is misspelled, fill in *e*.

SAMPLE   The <u>scientist</u> <u>analyzed</u> the <u>chemicals</u> in the
                     a   **b**   **c**

        <u>labratory</u>.   <u>None</u>
         d   **e**

ANSWER   ⓐ ⓑ ⓒ ⓓ ⓔ

1. In <u>eighth</u> grade Maria studied <u>grammer</u>, composition,
     a   **b**
   <u>literature</u>, and <u>mathematics</u>.   <u>None</u>
   c   **d**   **e**

2. In our <u>thorough</u> search of the attic, we found an old
         a
   <u>calender</u>, a <u>handkerchief</u>, and a <u>nickel</u> dated 1898. <u>None</u>
   b   **c**   **d**   **e**

3. If you are <u>uncertain</u> about the <u>pronunciation</u> of a word,
         a   **b**
   <u>refer</u> to a <u>dictionery</u>.   <u>None</u>
   c   **d**   **e**

4. My <u>neighbor</u> took a <u>fascinating</u> trip to a <u>foreign</u> country
      a   **b**   **c**
   for <u>ninety</u> days.   <u>None</u>
      d   **e**

5. In order to <u>achieve</u> your goals, it is <u>necessary</u> to practice
         a   **b**
   <u>discipline</u>, to work hard, and to gain <u>knowledge</u>.   <u>None</u>
   c   **d**   **e**

6. Our family <u>ocasionally</u> goes to that <u>restaurant</u> for a <u>truly</u>
        a   **b**   **c**
   <u>delicious</u> meal.   <u>None</u>
   d   **e**

7. Because the famous rock star will <u>appear</u> <u>tomorrow</u>, the
                   a   **b**
   <u>attendence</u> at the <u>concert</u> will be large.   <u>None</u>
   c   **d**   **e**

8. We all <u>benifited</u> from the <u>committee's</u> <u>decision</u> to appoint

           a   **b**   **c**

a new <u>secretary.</u> <u>None</u>

          d   **e**

9. It is <u>particularly</u> <u>interesting</u> that our cat <u>always</u> <u>disappears</u>

       a   **b**   **c**   **d**

after dinner. <u>None</u>

             e

10. When spelling the words <u>irrelevant</u>, <u>hastily</u>, and <u>sincerely</u>,

                               a   **b**   **c**

I <u>omitted</u> important letters. <u>None</u>

  d   **e**

Directions: Choose the word that is most nearly *opposite* in meaning to the word in capital letters. In the appropriate row on your answer sheet, fill in the circle containing the same letter as your answer.

SAMPLE REVEAL (a) show (b) explode (c) conceal
                         (d) tell

ANSWER ⓐ ⓑ ⓒ ⓓ

11. VALIANT (a) cowardly (b) unveiled (c) false
                  (d) brave

12. DUBIOUS (a) real (b) huge (c) detailed (d) certain

13. REPEL (a) attract (b) detest (c) release (d) punish

14. FUTILE (a) ineffective (b) useful (c) expected
             (d) medieval

15. ADVERSE (a) allied (b) opposite (c) favorable
                 (d) unfavorable

16. AFFABLE (a) reserved (b) comical (c) unusual
               (d) friendly

17. RANDOM (a) haphazard (b) planned (c) rare
                (d) accidental

18. CRUCIAL (a) unimportant (b) primary (c) painful
               (d) essential

19. BREVITY (a) speed (b) courage (c) wordiness
               (d) shortness

20. GENTEEL (a) final (b) rude (c) patient (d) smart

Reference Skills

22

The Dictionary

In 1828, Noah Webster published his famous *American Dictionary of the English Language.* From that time on, students have used the dictionary more often than any other reference book.

Today's dictionaries vary in size and length. Every library has a thick, heavy dictionary that usually lies open on a pedestal. These large dictionaries are called *unabridged,* or unshortened, dictionaries. *Abridged,* or student, dictionaries are a shortened form for easy reference at home or school. Listed below are several popular dictionaries.

UNABRIDGED DICTIONARIES
The Random House Dictionary
Webster's Third New International Dictionary

STUDENT DICTIONARIES
Webster's New World Dictionary
Webster's Ninth New Collegiate Dictionary
The American Heritage Dictionary
Scott, Foresman Advanced Dictionary

In this chapter, you will discover the variety of information available in a dictionary and learn how to use this valuable resource efficiently.

WORD LOCATION

Dictionaries are organized to help you find the information you need quickly. Once you become familiar with the arrangement, you will be able to find words more easily.

Alphabetical Order

From beginning to end, the dictionary is a single, alphabetical list. Words beginning with the same letters are alphabetized by the first letter that is different.

squash	squint
squawk	squirm
squeak	squirt

Compound words, abbreviations, prefixes, suffixes, and proper nouns are also listed in alphabetical order.

SINGLE WORD — **ac ro nym** (ak′rə nim), *n.* word formed from the first letters or syllables of other words, such as UNESCO (United Nations Educational, Scientific, and Cultural Organization). [<Greek *akros* tip + *onyma* name] —**ac′ro nym′ic,** *adj.*

HYPHENATED COMPOUND — **a cross-the-board** (ə krôs′ᴛʜə bôrd′), *adj.* applying to all members of a group, industry, etc.; general.

TWO-WORD COMPOUND — **acute angle,** angle less than a right angle; any angle less than 90 degrees.

PREFIX — **ad-,** *prefix.* **1** to; toward, as in *admit, administer, adverb, advert.* See also **a-, ab-, ac-, af-, ag-, al-, an-, ap-, ar-, as-,** and **at-.** **2** at; near, as in *adjacent, adrenal.* [<Latin]

ABBREVIATIONS — **AF,** Air Force.
A.F. or a.f., audio frequency.
AFL or A.F.L., American Football League.

PROPER NOUN — **Alaska Standard Time,** the standard time in central Alaska and all of Hawaii, two hours behind Pacific Standard Time; Hawaii Standard Time.

SUFFIX — **-ally,** *suffix forming adverbs.* in a ——ic manner: *Basically* = *in a basic manner.* [<*-al¹* + *-ly¹*]

From SCOTT, FORESMAN ADVANCED DICTIONARY by E. L. Thorndike and Clarence L. Barnhart. Copyright © 1983 Scott, Foresman and Company. Reprinted by permission.

Compound words are alphabetized as if there were no space or hyphen between each part. Abbreviations are alphabetized letter by letter, not by the words they stand for.

EXERCISE 1   Alphabetizing Words

Make three columns on your paper and number them 1 to 3.
Then list each group of words to show how they would be
alphabetized in a dictionary.

1. glaze	2. hiccup	3. beehive
glow	hi-fi	bee tree
glimpse	hike	bee
glimmer	hgt.	beeline
glossy	hickory	beetle-browed
gloomy	hilarious	bd.
glacier	high-pitched	beech
glance	hibernate	beetle
glisten	hide	beet
glamour	high jump	bazaar

Guide Words

Guide words tell you at a glance which words can be
found on each page of a dictionary. They are printed at the
top of each page in heavy type. Each pair of guide words
shows the first and last words defined on the page. The
guide words *attain/auction,* for example, show you that
attorney and *auburn* appear on that page.

EXERCISE 2   Using Guide Words

Make four columns on your paper. At the top of the columns, write the following page numbers and guide words.
Then write each word in the proper column.

761 screen/seafood	763 seasonal/secret
762 seal/season	764 secretary/see

section	secure	sculpture	secrecy
seasoning	script	search	sediment
scribble	second	sedan	seasick
seaweed	security	scurry	scythe
seam	seaport	seashore	secret

INFORMATION IN AN ENTRY

All of the information given for a word is called an *entry*. Each entry contains four main parts.

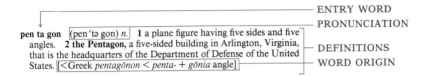

From SCOTT, FORESMAN ADVANCED DICTIONARY by E. L. Thorndike and Clarence L. Barnhart. Copyright © 1983 Scott, Foresman and Company. Reprinted by permission.

Entry Word

The entry word in heavy type tells you (1) how to spell a word, (2) whether to capitalize it, and (3) where it may be divided at the end of a line.

Spelling. The entry word shows the correct spelling of a word. Alternate spellings are also given after some entry words. If one spelling is more common than the other, most dictionaries list the preferred spelling first. If the two spellings of a word do not fall near each other alphabetically, the alternate spelling is listed separately.

> coun·sel·or *or* coun·sel·lor \'kaún(t)-s(ə-)lər\ *n* **1** : ADVISER **2** : LAWYER; *specif* : one that gives advice in law and manages cases for clients in court **3** : one who has supervisory duties at a summer camp — coun·sel·or·ship\-,ship\ *n*
>
> **grey** *var of* GRAY

By permission. From Webster's Ninth New Collegiate Dictionary © 1983 by Merriam-Webster Inc., publishers of the Merriam-Webster® Dictionaries.

Plural nouns, comparatives and superlatives of adjectives, and principal parts of verbs are also given if their spelling is irregular.

chime (chīm), *n.,* *v.,* **chimed, chim ing.** —*n.* **1** set of bells tuned to a musical scale and played by hammers or simple machinery. **2** the musical sound made by a set of tuned bells. —*v.i.* **1** ring out musically: *The bells chimed at midnight.* **2** agree; be in harmony.

chi na ber ry (chī′nə ber′ē), *n., pl.* **-ries.** **1** tree native to Asia and widely cultivated in warm regions for its purplish flowers and yellow, berrylike fruits.

choose (chüz), *v.,* **chose, cho sen, choos ing.** —*v.t.* **1** pick out; select from a number. **2** prefer and decide; think fit. —*v.i.* make a choice. [Old English *cēosan*]

chop py (chop′ē), *adj.,* **-pi er, -pi est.** **1** making quick, sharp movements; jerky. **2** moving in short, irregular, broken waves: *The sea is choppy today.*

From SCOTT, FORESMAN ADVANCED DICTIONARY by E. L. Thorndike and Clarence L. Barnhart. Copyright © 1983 Scott, Foresman and Company. Reprinted by permission.

Words formed by adding a prefix or suffix to the entry word are often shown at the end of an entry. These words are called *derived words.*

self less (self′lis), *adj.* having no regard or thought for self; unselfish.
—**self′less ly,** *adv.* —**self′less ness,** *n.*

From SCOTT, FORESMAN ADVANCED DICTIONARY by E. L. Thorndike and Clarence L. Barnhart. Copyright © 1983 Scott, Foresman and Company. Reprinted by permission.

EXERCISE 3   Editing for Spelling Errors

The following paragraph contains 20 commonly misspelled words. Number your paper 1 to 20. Using a dictionary, write the correct spelling of each word.

Sharks

Sharks are some of the most fasinating cretures in the ocean. These fish posess a highly developed brain and a sharp sense of sight and smell. They have no bones. Insted, thier skeletins are made of a tough, elastik substence called cartillage. In order to obtain oxagen, they remane in constent motion, even while sleeping. Their need for food, however, is not so demanding. They can last for weeks or even months without eatting. Though sientists have learned much in recent years, these complex and captivateing swimers continu to inspire curiousity.

Capitalization.   The entry word will be printed with a capital letter if a word should be capitalized. If a word should be capitalized only in certain uses, the word will be shown with a capital letter near the appropriate definition.

400

Milky Way, **1** a broad band of faint light that stretches across the sky at night. It is made up of countless stars too far away to be seen separately without a telescope. **2** the galaxy in which these countless stars are found; Galaxy. The sun, earth, and the other planets around the sun are part of the Milky Way.

mar a thon (mar′ə thon), *n.* **1** a footrace of 26 miles, 385 yards (42.2 kilometers). **2** any race over a long distance. **3** any activity that calls for endurance. **4 Marathon,** plain in Greece about 25 miles (40 kilometers) northeast of Athens. After the Athenians defeated the Persians there in 490 B.C., a runner ran all the way to Athens with the news of the victory.

From SCOTT, FORESMAN ADVANCED DICTIONARY by E. L. Thorndike and Clarence L. Barnhart. Copyright © 1983 Scott, Foresman and Company. Reprinted by permission.

Syllables. When writing, you sometimes need to divide a word at the end of a line. Since a word may be divided only between syllables, use a dictionary to check where each syllable ends. *(See the rules on pages 360–361 for dividing words at the end of a line.)*

sus·pense·ful   char·ac·ter   per·fec·tion

EXERCISE 4   Using a Dictionary for Editing

Copy the following paragraph, correcting the errors in spelling, capitalization, and hyphenation. Underline each correction.

Starlit
Skies

At night thosands of stars appear accross the sky. Over the centurys, stargazers have observed that some stars form particuler shapes. These star clusters are called constellations. Two of the most familar are ursa major, great bear, and ursa minor, little bear. Within these constellations are the big dipper, the little dipper, and the bright north star. Some constellations can be observed only durring certain seasons. Leo, the Lion, appears in Spring. During the winter, orion, the Hunter, is visable. At present, over eigthy constellations have been identifyed in the night sky.

Pronunciation

To learn how to pronounce a word correctly, you can look it up in the dictionary. A phonetic spelling is shown in parentheses after each entry word.

clang (klang)   **knack** (nak)

401

A *pronunciation key* at the front of the dictionary shows what sound each phonetic symbol stands for. Most dictionaries also place a partial key on every other page.

PARTIAL PRONUNCIATION KEY

a hat	i it	oi oil	ch child	a in about
ā age	ī ice	ou out	ng long	e in taken
ä far	o hot	u cup	sh she	ə = i in pencil
e let	ō open	ù put	th thin	o in lemon
ē equal	ô order	ü rule	ŦH then	u in circus
ėr term			zh measure	< = derived from

From SCOTT, FORESMAN ADVANCED DICTIONARY by E. L. Thorndike and Clarence L. Barnhart. Copyright © 1983 Scott, Foresman and Company. Reprinted by permission.

By comparing the phonetic spelling to the symbols in the key, you can tell how to pronounce the word. For example, the key shows that *zh* stands for the *s* sound in *measure*. Notice that *zh* is used to show the pronunciation of *s* in the following words.

pleas·ure (plezh′ər)   **treas·ure** (trezh′ər)

Diacritical Marks. In the key above, marks are shown over some of the vowels to indicate different vowel sounds. For example, the different sounds of *o* are represented in the following ways.

hot   ōpen   ôrder

The marks over *open* and *order* are called diacritical marks. To find out how a vowel with a diacritical mark is pronounced, you simply refer to the key.

odd (od)   [*o* as in *hot*]
ode (ōd)   [*o* as in *open*]
off (ôf)   [*o* as in *order*]

The Schwa. In some words, the vowels *a, e, i, o,* and *u* are pronounced *uh*. Most dictionaries use the phonetic symbol ə to represent this sound if it comes in an unaccented syllable. This symbol is called a schwa.

a·bout (ə bout′)   **lem·on** (lem′ən)   **li·bel** (lī′bəl)

Accent Marks. In some words, one syllable receives more emphasis than any other. An accent mark is used to indicate a syllable that should be stressed.

lob·ster (lob′stər)   **de·sign** (di zīn′)

If two syllables should be stressed, the syllable receiving the most stress is marked with a *primary accent*. The syllable receiving slightly less emphasis is marked with a *secondary accent*.

PRIMARY ACCENT

en·er·get·ic (en′ər jet′ik)

SECONDARY ACCENT

EXERCISE 5 Marking Pronunciation
Using a dictionary, write the phonetic spelling of each word.

EXAMPLE   reputation
ANSWER   (rep′yə tā′shən)

1. mocha
2. discus
3. nova
4. hedge
5. kiwi
6. alpaca
7. incisor
8. geyser
9. chinchilla
10. quiver
11. kayak
12. hydrophobia
13. equestrian
14. jerboa
15. catamaran
16. salamander
17. generation
18. armadillo
19. apogee
20. perigee

Definitions

A dictionary is a handy reference for finding the meanings of a word. The following entry for *train* shows the kind of information provided to make each meaning clear.

PART OF SPEECH

NUMBERED DEFINITION

EXAMPLE

train (trān), *n.* **1** a connected line of railroad cars. **2** a line of people, animals, wagons, trucks, etc., moving along together; caravan. **3** part that hangs down and drags along behind: *the train of a gown.* **4** sequence: *lose one's train of thought.* **5** succession of conditions following some event: *The flood brought starvation and disease in its train.* —*v.t.* **1** bring up; rear; teach: *train a child.* **2** make skillful by teaching and practice: *train an apprentice.* **3** discipline and instruct (an animal) to be useful, obedient, perform tricks, race, etc. **4** make fit for a sport, etc., as by proper exercise and diet; *train a swimmer.* **5** bring into a particular position: *Train the vine around this post.* —*v.i.* make oneself fit, as by proper exercise and diet: *train for a race.*

PART OF SPEECH

PART OF SPEECH

From SCOTT, FORESMAN ADVANCED DICTIONARY by E. L. Thorndike and Clarence L. Barnhart. Copyright © 1983 Scott, Foresman and Company. Reprinted by permission.

In the entry for *train,* the abbreviations *n.* and *v.* show that *train* can be used as a noun or a verb. Dictionaries use the following abbreviations for the eight parts of speech.

n. noun	*pron.* pronoun	*prep.* preposition
v. verb	*adj.* adjective	*conj.* conjunction
	adv. adverb	*interj.* interjection

When you look up a word, consider which meaning applies in the sentence you are reading or writing.

EXERCISE 6 Choosing the Appropriate Definition
Write the definition of *train* in the entry above that matches its use in each sentence.

1. Julie had *trained* her frog Lilypad to jump two feet.
2. I lost my *train* of thought during my speech!
3. Peter *trained* for two years to be an electrician.
4. Sara *trained* the horse's mane to curl.
5. The court jester tripped over the *train* of the king's robe.

EXERCISE 7 Finding the Meaning of a Word
The underlined words in the following sentences have several meanings. Using a dictionary, write the definition that fits the use of the word in each sentence.

1. The plane <u>gathered</u> speed as it raced down the runway.
2. He <u>gathered</u> from the evidence that they were guilty.
3. I want to <u>review</u> my notes before the final exam.

4. The new movie received a disappointing <u>review</u>.
5. The sign on the fence warned us not to <u>poach</u>.
6. While I pour the milk, you <u>poach</u> the eggs.
7. The joggers began the final lap around the <u>track</u>.
8. NASA officials will <u>track</u> the orbit of the shuttle.
9. Jessie carried his <u>pocket</u> camera everywhere.
10. Before long the miners discovered a <u>pocket</u> of gold.

Usage Labels. A dictionary indicates the present standing of words by such labels as *obsolete, informal,* and *slang.*

dress er (dres′ər), *n.* **1** piece of furniture with drawers for clothes and usually a mirror; bureau. **2** piece of furniture with shelves for dishes. **3** OBS. table on which to get food ready for serving. —— OBSOLETE

choos y or **choos ey** (chü′zē), *adj.* INF. particular or fussy. —— INFORMAL

hu mong ous (hyü mung′gəs), *adj.* SLANG. extraordinarily large; huge. [perhaps blend of *huge, monstrous,* and *enormous*] —— SLANG

From SCOTT, FORESMAN ADVANCED DICTIONARY by E. L. Thorndike and Clarence L. Barnhart. Copyright © 1983 Scott, Foresman and Company. Reprinted by permission.

Obsolete means that this definition of *dresser* is found in writing of an earlier period but is no longer in use. *Informal* and *slang* indicate words that are currently used in informal situations but are not acceptable in formal speaking and writing.

Synonyms. Synonyms are words that have similar meanings. Many dictionaries provide synonyms at the end of an entry.

care ful (ker′fəl, kar′fəl), *adj.* **1** thinking what one says; watching what one does. **2** showing care; done with thought or effort. **3** full of care or concern: *She was careful of the feelings of others.*
Syn. 1 Careful, cautious, wary mean watchful in speaking and acting. **Careful** means being observant and giving serious attention and thought to what one is doing, especially to details: *He is a careful driver.* **Cautious** means very careful, looking ahead for possible risks or dangers, and guarding against them by taking no chances: *She is cautious about making promises.* **Wary** emphasizes the idea of being mistrustful and on the alert for danger or trouble: *He is wary of overly friendly people.* —— SYNONYMS

From SCOTT, FORESMAN ADVANCED DICTIONARY by E. L. Thorndike and Clarence L. Barnhart. Copyright © 1983 Scott, Foresman and Company. Reprinted by permission.

Notice that *careful, cautious,* and *wary* are all related to being watchful, but the meaning of each is slightly different. When writing, use a dictionary to help you find a synonym that expresses your exact meaning.

Word Origins

Modern English words are derived from many languages, old and new. The history, or *etymology,* of a word is shown in brackets at the beginning or end of an entry.

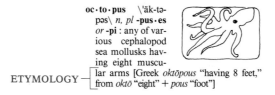

oc·to·pus \'äk-tə-pəs\ *n, pl* **-pus·es** *or* **-pi** : any of various cephalopod sea mollusks having eight muscular arms [Greek *oktōpous* "having 8 feet," from *oktō* "eight" + *pous* "foot"]

ETYMOLOGY —

By permission. From Webster's School Dictionary © 1980 by Merriam-Webster® Inc., publishers of the Merriam-Webster Dictionaries.

The following abbreviations are used by many dictionaries to indicate the language of origin. A complete list of abbreviations is given at the front of most dictionaries.

L	Latin	OE	Old English	Sp	Spanish
Gk	Greek	ME	Middle English	It	Italian
Ar	Arabic	OF	Old French	G	German
Skt	Sanskrit	F	French	D	Dutch

EXERCISE 8   Discovering Word Origins

Using a dictionary, write the language or languages each word came from.

EXAMPLE   pretzel
ANSWER   German, Latin

1. noodle
2. macaroni
3. waffle
4. apple
5. asparagus
6. crouton
7. pickle
8. macaroon
9. spinach
10. olive

CHAPTER REVIEW

Number your paper 1 to 15. Then use the following dictionary entries to answer each question.

can ta loupe or **can ta loup** (kan′tl ōp), *n.* kind of muskmelon with a hard, rough rind and sweet, juicy, orange flesh. [<French *cantaloup* < Italian *Cantalupo* papal estate near Rome where first cultivated]

can tan ker ous (kan tang′kər əs), *adj.* hard to get along with because of a nature that is ready to make trouble and oppose anything suggested; ill-natured; quarrelsome. [Middle English *contecker* contentious person < *conteck* strife, quarreling < Anglo-French] —**can tan′ker ous ly,** *adv.*

can ter (kan′tər), *v.t., v.i.* gallop gently. —*n.* a gentle gallop. [short for *Canterbury (gallop)*]

can to (kan′tō), *n., pl.* **-tos.** one of the main divisions of a long poem. [< Italian < Latin *cantus* song]

cap., 1 capacity. **2** capital. **3** capitalize. **4** *pl.* **caps.** capital letter.

cap il lar y (kap′ə ler′ē), *n., pl.* **-lar ies,** *adj.* —*n.* a blood vessel with a very slender, hairlike opening. Capillaries join the end of an artery to the beginning of a vein. —*adj.* **1** of or in the capillaries. **2** like a hair; very slender. [< Latin *capillaris* of hair, hairlike < *capillus* hair]

Cap ri corn (kap′rə kôrn), *n.* **1** tropic of Capricorn. **2** a southern constellation seen by ancient astronomers as having the rough outline of a goat. **3** the 10th sign of the zodiac. [< Latin *capricornus* < *caper* goat + *cornu* horn]

cap ti vate (kap′tə vāt), *v.t.,* **-vat ed, -vat ing.** hold captive by beauty, talent, or interest; charm; fascinate: *The children were captivated by the story.*

From SCOTT, FORESMAN ADVANCED DICTIONARY by E. L. Thorndike and Clarence L. Barnhart. Copyright © 1983 Scott, Foresman and Company. Reprinted by permission.

1. Which entry word has two accepted spellings?
2. Which entry word should be capitalized?
3. Which entry words have four syllables?
4. Show where *canter* should be divided at the end of a line.
5. Which syllable in *capillary* should be loudest? Which syllable should be stressed slightly?
6. What does *cantankerous* mean?
7. How many meanings are given for *Capricorn*?
8. Which entry contains an example sentence?
9. Which entry word can be used as a noun or a verb?
10. Which entry word can be a noun or an adjective?
11. How do you spell the plural of *canto*? Of *capillary*?
12. How do you spell the principal parts of *captivate*?
13. What part of speech is *cantankerously*?
14. Which three entry words are derived from Latin?
15. Which entry word is derived from French and Italian?

23

The Library

A library is a storehouse of knowledge. It is the best place to start when gathering information for a report in English, social studies, science, or any other subject. Libraries contain both printed materials (books and magazines) and nonprinted materials (tapes and films). Many school libraries and media centers also have audiovisual and electronic equipment. This chapter will discuss the kinds of resources available in a library and will show you how to find what you need quickly.

LIBRARY ARRANGEMENT

A library is organized in a way that helps you find information easily. There is one section for fiction, one for nonfiction, one for reference books, and one for magazines and newspapers. In some sections the books are arranged on the shelves in alphabetical order. In others they are arranged in numerical order.

Fiction

In the fiction section, books are shelved alphabetically by the author's last name. Following are some special rules that will help you locate a book of fiction.

- Two-part names are alphabetized by the first part of the name.

  LaRosa   **Mac**Donald   **O**'Connor   **Van** Dyke

- Names beginning with *Mc* and *St.* are alphabetized as if they began with *Mac* and *Saint.*
- Books by authors with the same last name are alphabetized by their first names.
- Books by the same author are alphabetized by title, skipping *a, an,* and *the* at the beginning.

EXERCISE 1   Finding Fiction
Number your paper 1 to 10. List the following fiction books in the order in which you would find them on the shelves.

Is That You, Miss Blue? by M. E. Kerr
To Kill a Mockingbird by Harper Lee
Gentlehands by M. E. Kerr
Never Cry Wolf by Farley Mowat
The Member of the Wedding by Carson McCullers
Rebecca by Daphne DuMaurier
Child of Fire by Scott O'Dell
Cherokee Trail by Louis L'Amour
Onions in the Stew by Betty MacDonald
The Skating Rink by Mildred Lee

Nonfiction

Most libraries use the Dewey decimal system to arrange books in the nonfiction section. Under this system, each book is assigned a number according to its subject and is shelved in numerical order. The following chart shows which numbers are assigned to each general subject.

Dewey Decimal System

000–099 General Works (reference books)
100–199 Philosophy
200–299 Religion
300–399 Social Science (law, education, economics)
400–499 Language
500–599 Science (mathematics, biology, chemistry)
600–699 Technology (medicine, inventions)
700–799 Fine Arts (painting, music, theater)
800–899 Literature
900–999 History (biography, geography, travel)

This arrangement makes finding books about a particular subject easy. If you want to find nonfiction books about science, go to the rows marked 500–599. If you are looking for nonfiction books about literature, you know they will be in the rows marked 800–899.

Because there are so many books about each general subject, the Dewey decimal system divides each of the ten main subjects into smaller categories.

800–899 Literature

800–809	General	850–859	Italian
810–819	American	860–869	Spanish
820–829	English	870–879	Latin
830–839	German	880–889	Greek
840–849	French	890–899	Other

Nonfiction books related to American literature are assigned numbers between 810–819. Since ten numbers are not enough to cover the many books about American literature, decimal numbers are used too.

One category of nonfiction books includes biographies and autobiographies. In most libraries these books are kept in a separate section. They are shelved in alphabetical

American Literature: 810–819

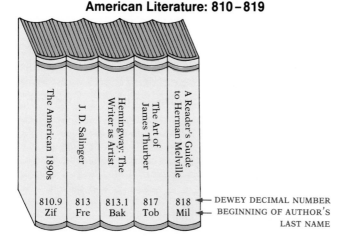

The American 1890s	J. D. Salinger	Hemingway: The Writer as Artist	The Art of James Thurber	A Reader's Guide to Herman Melville
810.9 Zif	813 Fre	813.1 Bak	817 Tob	818 Mil

— DEWEY DECIMAL NUMBER
— BEGINNING OF AUTHOR'S LAST NAME

order by the subject's last name instead of the author's last name. Each book is labeled either *B* for *biography* or *92* (a shortened form of *920*). For example, a biography of George Washington is labeled in one of the following ways.

BIOGRAPHY ⟶ **B**   92
or
BEGINNING OF ⟶ WAS   WAS
SUBJECT'S LAST NAME

EXERCISE 2   Understanding the Dewey Decimal System

Using the chart on page 410, write the range of numbers and the general category for each book.

EXAMPLE   *Math and After Math*
ANSWER   500s — Science

1. *The Joy of Music*
2. *All About Language*
3. *Basic Biology*
4. *The Making of a Surgeon*
5. *You and the Law*
6. *The Enjoyment of Chemistry*
7. *Trial by Jury*
8. *The Oxford Anthology of English Literature*
9. *To a Young Dancer*
10. *The Heroic Age of American Invention*

THE CARD CATALOG

The card catalog is a cabinet of small file drawers. It contains cards for all books, record albums, tapes, and filmstrips in the library. The cards are arranged alphabetically. The front of each drawer is labeled to show what part of the alphabet it contains.

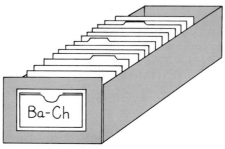

Card Catalog File Drawer

The card catalog contains three cards for every book. To find a book, you may look under (1) the author's name, (2) the title, or (3) the subject.

Author Cards

When you want to find books by a particular author, look for the author's last name in the card catalog. To find books by Melvin Berger, for example, find *Berger* in the drawer marked *B*. Following is the author card for *Computers in Your Life* by Melvin Berger.

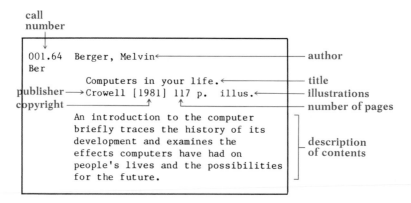

Title Cards

When you know the title but not the author, you can see if the library has the book by looking up the title card. Title cards are alphabetized by the first word in the title (except *a, an,* and *the*). If you want the book *Computers in Your Life,* look for the title card in the drawer that holds the *C*'s.

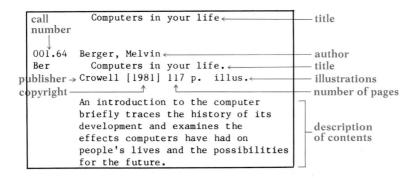

Subject Cards

When you are writing a report or doing a project, you will use subject cards more often than title or author cards. If you want information about computers, for example, look up *computers* in the drawer that holds the *C*'s. There you will find subject cards for all the books about computers that the library has. On a subject card, the subject is listed at the top in capital letters.

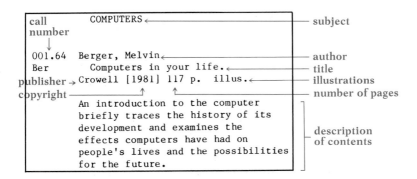

Notice that all three cards for *Computers in Your Life* provide the same information. Any one of these cards can tell you what the book is about and how to find it on the shelves.

Steps for Finding Books

1. Find out if the library has the book you want by finding the author card, the title card, or the subject card in the card catalog.
2. Read the card to see if the book is likely to contain the information you need. Check the copyright date to see how current the information is.
3. On a slip of paper, copy the call number, the title, and the name of the author for each book you want to find.
4. Use the call number to find each book. The first line of the call number tells which section of the library to look in.

F or FIC	fiction section
B or 92	biography section
Dewey number	nonfiction section

Then find each book on the shelves by looking for its call number, located on the spine.

Cross-Reference Cards

In addition to three cards for each book, a card catalog contains "see" and "see also" cards. A "see" card tells you that the subject you have looked up is under another heading. A "see also" card lists other subjects you could look up for more information on your topic.

CARS see AUTOMOBILES	AUTOMOBILES see also SPORTS CARS TRUCKS

EXERCISE 3   Using the Card Catalog

Write the letter or letters of the drawer in which you would find each of the following in the card catalog.

EXAMPLE   Mary O'Hara
ANSWER   N – Ph

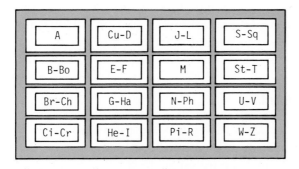

1. tigers
2. *Africa in History*
3. Mark Twain
4. *The Chocolate War*
5. Emily Post
6. *The Edge of Space*
7. oceans
8. Jean Craighead George
9. *A Circle of Children*
10. Madeleine L'Engle

EXERCISE 4   Alphabetizing Catalog Cards

Write the first three letters that you would look under to find each of the following in the card catalog.

1. popular music
2. Scott O'Dell
3. *A Single Light*
4. moons of Jupiter
5. John LeCarre
6. *A Tree Grows in Brooklyn*
7. forms of transportation
8. *The Double Planet*
9. nineteenth-century inventions
10. *The Milky Way Galaxy*

EXERCISE 5   Writing Catalog Cards

Write an author card, a title card, and a subject card using the following information.

Getting into Pro Baseball, by Mike Dyer, published by Franklin Watts, Inc., ©1979, 81 pages, Dewey decimal number 796.35

REFERENCE MATERIALS

Most libraries have a separate area called a reference room. This room contains encyclopedias, dictionaries, atlases, almanacs, and reference books on specific subjects. Since reference books may not be taken out of the library, reference rooms have study areas where people can use these materials. The following sections discuss the kinds of reference works available in most libraries.

Encyclopedias

Encyclopedias provide basic information on many subjects. When you are gathering information for a report, an encyclopedia is a good place to start. Subjects are arranged in alphabetical order in each volume. Letters on the spine show what part of the alphabet each volume covers. A volume labeled Nel-O, for example, would contain information on the North Pole, the octopus, and the Olympic Games. Within each volume, *guide words* tell you at a glance which entries are on each page.

Many encyclopedias provide an index in a separate volume or at the end of the last volume. The index can tell you if your subject is discussed in more than one place. Cross-references to other entries may also be provided at the end of an article. After the article on *sky*, for example, one encyclopedia says, *"See also:* Astronomy, Horizon, and Light."

The yearbooks that accompany an encyclopedia may provide additional information. Published annually, yearbooks contain up-to-date information on recent developments and events.

General Encyclopedias

Collier's Encyclopedia	*Encyclopaedia Britannica*
Encyclopedia Americana	*The New Columbia Encyclopedia*
Compton's Encyclopedia	*World Book Encyclopedia*

Specialized References

Specialized references are devoted to specific kinds of information. They include specialized encyclopedias, biographical references, literary references, atlases, almanacs, and specialized dictionaries.

Specialized Encyclopedias. Hundreds of specialized encyclopedias are available on every subject from auto racing to weaving. Because they concentrate on a specific subject, specialized encyclopedias provide more information on a subject than general encyclopedias do.

Specialized Encyclopedias

The Mammals of America	*Encyclopedia of World Art*
Encyclopedia of Physics	*The Baseball Encyclopedia*
Peoples of the Earth	*Encyclopedia of Chemistry*

International Wildlife Encyclopedia
The Illustrated Encyclopedia of World Coins
McGraw-Hill Encyclopedia of Science and Technology

Biographical References. To find information about famous people, past and present, use biographical references. Some biographical references contain only a paragraph of facts. Others contain long articles about each person in the volume.

Current Biography is one of the best sources of information about well-known people. Since 1940 it has provided biographies of world leaders in politics, entertainment, the arts, education, and sports. *Current Biography* is published monthly in pamphlet form and then collected into a yearly volume. A combined index covers the years from 1940 to 1970. A ten-year index covers 1971 to 1980. An index is also included at the back of every yearly volume.

Who's Who in America is a different kind of biographical reference. The entries are short and contain only the facts of birth, education, occupation, awards, family, and so on, about living Americans. A list of abbreviations used in the entries is provided at the front of each volume.

> SPIELBERG, STEVEN, motion picture dir.; b. Cin., Dec. 18, 1947; B.A., Calif. State Coll., Long Beach, 1970. Won film contest with 40-minute war movie, Escape to Nowhere, at age 13; made film Firelight at age 16, and made 5 films while in coll.; became TV dir. at Universal Pictures at age 20, directed segments of TV series including Night Gallery, Marcus Welby, M.D., Columbo, also TV movies Duel, 1971, Something Evil, 1972; dir. motion pictures: The Sugarland Express, 1974, Jaws, 1975, Close Encounters of the Third Kind, 1977, 1941, 1979, Raiders of the Lost Ark, 1981; producer film I Wanna Hold Your Hand, 1978. Recipient several Acad. awards. Author: (with Patrick Mann) Close Encounters of the Third Kind.

Who's Who in America is published every other year. Another biographical reference, *Who's Who*, is published every year. It contains similar information about people from all over the world.

BIOGRAPHICAL REFERENCE BOOKS	*Current Biography*
	Who's Who
	Who's Who in America
	Dictionary of American Biography
	Dictionary of National Biography
	Webster's Biographical Dictionary
	American Authors 1600–1900
	British Authors of the Nineteenth Century
	American Men and Women of Science
	Dictionary of Scientific Biography

EXERCISE 6   Using Biographical References

Using a biographical reference, briefly explain how each of the following Americans achieved fame.

EXAMPLE   Levi Strauss

ANSWER   manufacturer of Levi jeans

1. Emmett Kelly
2. Margaret Rudkin
3. Charles Lindbergh
4. Jessi Shambaugh
5. Abner Doubleday
6. Laura Ingalls Wilder
7. Samuel Wilson
8. Francis Scott Key
9. Jeannette Rankin
10. Grandma Moses

References about Literature. Have you ever wondered where a quotation is from and who said it? A *book of quotations* can provide the answers. It can also give you the complete quotation and other quotations on the same subject. Books of quotations are arranged either by subject or by author. An index of first lines or key words leads you to the correct page. Following are some well-known books of quotations.

BOOKS OF   *Bartlett's Familiar Quotations*
QUOTATIONS   *Home Book of Quotations*
                          The Oxford Dictionary of Quotations

Another kind of literary reference is the *index*. Indexes are useful for finding a particular poem, short story, or play. An index will tell you the names of books that contain the work. You can then use the card catalog to see if the library has one of those books. Three especially useful indexes by Granger are the following.

INDEXES   *Index to Poetry*
                    Short Story Index
                    Play Index

A third kind of literary reference is the *handbook,* or companion. Some handbooks give plot summaries or describe characters. Others explain literary terms like *imagery* or *plot* or give information about authors.

HANDBOOKS   *The Oxford Companion to American Literature*
                          The Oxford Companion to English Literature
                          The Reader's Encyclopedia

Atlases. An atlas, or book of maps, provides information about cities, countries, continents, mountains, lakes, and other geographical features. Some atlases also give information about population, climate, natural resources, and industries. Historical atlases show you maps of the world during different times in history.

ATLASES *Atlas of World History*
Goode's World Atlas
Hammond's Medallion World Atlas
National Geographic Atlas of the World
Rand McNally International World Atlas

Almanacs. Almanacs contain up-to-date facts and statistics about such subjects as population, weather, government, business, and sports. Here you find which countries have had earthquakes, what movies were most successful, and who won the most-valuable-player awards. They also contain historical facts and geographic information. Most almanacs are published yearly.

ALMANACS *Information Please Almanac*
World Almanac and Book of Facts
Hammond's Almanac

EXERCISE 7 Using an Almanac
Answer the following questions using an almanac.

1. What is the state song of Kansas?
2. What is Alaska's state motto?
3. What is the nickname for Ohio?
4. Who is the only player to receive the Heisman Trophy two consecutive years?
5. Who was awarded the Nobel Peace Prize in 1964?
6. Who was the first American to receive the Nobel Prize in Literature?
7. Which president's portrait is on the $5,000 bill?
8. What is pictured on the back of the $50 bill?
9. Which city in the United States was the first to host the Olympic Games? In what year?
10. What is the wind-chill factor if the temperature is 20°F and the wind is blowing 25 miles per hour?

Specialized Dictionaries. Besides abridged and unabridged dictionaries, a library has many specialized dictionaries. One kind is the foreign language dictionary, which shows the translation of English words into a foreign language. Other dictionaries provide information in specialized fields like medicine, music, and computer science.

SPECIALIZED
DICTIONARIES
Harvard Dictionary of Music
Concise Dictionary of American History
McGraw-Hill Dictionary of the Life Sciences
Dictionary of Word and Phrase Origins

Another kind of specialized dictionary lists synonyms. A *dictionary of synonyms* or a *thesaurus* can help you make exact word choices.

Webster's New Dictionary of Synonyms
Roget's Thesaurus in Dictionary Form

The following entries from *Roget's* show several synonyms for *news, nibble,* and *niche.*

news, *n.* information, intelligence, tidings.
nibble, *v.* bite, crop, graze.
niche, *n.* compartment, nook, hole, corner; recess, recession, indentation.

When choosing a synonym, keep in mind that no two words have exactly the same meaning. Be sure to select the word that has the precise meaning you want.

EXERCISE 8   Using Specialized References
List one kind of reference book other than a general encyclopedia that would contain information about each of the following.

EXAMPLE   U.S. population
POSSIBLE ANSWER   almanac

1. famous Americans
2. records in sports
3. countries in Asia
4. Spanish phrases
5. synonyms for *run*
6. the source of a quotation
7. the location of the Alps
8. the life of Thomas Edison
9. dates of past hurricanes
10. twentieth-century art

The Vertical File. Pamphlets, catalogs, and newspaper clippings are also available in most libraries. These materials are stored in a filing cabinet called the vertical file. Items are kept in folders and arranged alphabetically by subject.

Readers' Guide to Periodical Literature. Magazines and journals are among the best sources of current information. An index called the *Readers' Guide to Periodical Literature* can help you find articles on almost any subject. The complete *Readers' Guide* is an index to articles, stories, and poems published in over 175 magazines. Many schools subscribe to the abridged *Readers' Guide,* which indexes about 60 magazines.

The complete *Readers' Guide* is issued in paperback form twice a month during most months and once a month in February, July, and August. A quarterly issue comes out every three months and a hardbound volume at the end of each year.

Articles are listed alphabetically by subject and by author.

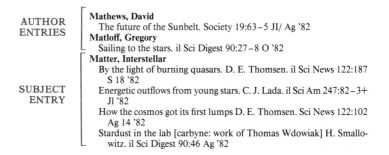

AUTHOR ENTRIES

Mathews, David
   The future of the Sunbelt. Society 19:63–5 Jl/ Ag '82
Matloff, Gregory
   Sailing to the stars. il Sci Digest 90:27–8 O '82

SUBJECT ENTRY

Matter, Interstellar
   By the light of burning quasars. D. E. Thomsen. il Sci News 122:187
      S 18 '82
   Energetic outflows from young stars. C. J. Lada. il Sci Am 247:82–3+
      Jl '82
   How the cosmos got its first lumps D. E. Thomsen. Sci News 122:102
      Ag 14 '82
   Stardust in the lab [carbyne: work of Thomas Wdowiak] H. Smallo-
      witz. il Sci Digest 90:46 Ag '82

Each entry in the *Readers' Guide* provides all the information you need to locate articles on a particular subject. Notice how the information is listed in the entry below.

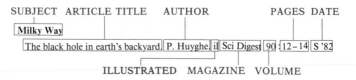

SUBJECT   ARTICLE TITLE   AUTHOR   PAGES DATE

Milky Way

The black hole in earth's backyard. P. Huyghe. il Sci Digest 90 :12–14 S '82

ILLUSTRATED   MAGAZINE   VOLUME

To save space, abbreviations are used. For example, in the entry on page 422, *Sci Digest* stands for *Science Digest* and *il* stands for *illustrated*. A list of abbreviations is provided at the front of every volume.

When you want to find articles on a particular subject, begin with the latest copy of the *Readers' Guide* and work backward. This way you will find the most recent articles first. A list of magazines available in the library is often posted near the *Readers' Guide*.

EXERCISE 9   Using the *Readers' Guide*
Using the *Readers' Guide*, list two recent magazine articles on four of the following subjects. List the title of the article, the name of the magazine, the date of publication, and the pages on which the article may be found.

astronomy	law	music
gymnastics	youth	nuclear power
journalism	pollution	marine biology

CHAPTER REVIEW

A. Following is a list of library resources. After the proper number on your paper, write the best resource for answering each question.

card catalog	book of quotations
general encyclopedia	index to poetry
specialized encyclopedia	atlas
specialized dictionary	almanac
biographical reference	*Readers' Guide*

EXAMPLE   What is the size of Iceland?
ANSWER   atlas

1. What are the names of three books about horses?
2. Explain the meaning of the Olympic symbol.
3. What are four synonyms for *laugh*?

4. What is Louis Fabian Bachrach, Jr., famous for?
5. What is a Tasmanian wolf?
6. Who wrote the poem "Miniver Cheevy"?
7. Why is Vladimir Horowitz famous?
8. What are the names of five coastal towns in the Canadian province of Newfoundland?
9. How does calligraphy differ from handwriting?
10. Who wrote the line, "The world is too much with us"?
11. What is the history of candles?
12. What magazine articles were written about recreation vehicles last year?
13. How many miles is it from Los Angeles to Tokyo?
14. Who wrote the line, "I ought; therefore I can"?
15. What was going on last month in soccer?
16. What is the longitude and latitude of Dallas?
17. What is the meaning of *closure* in math?
18. Why was Jack Dempsey famous?
19. Have articles on helicopters been published recently?
20. What was the lowest temperature ever recorded in Michigan?

B. Find the answers to the first ten questions using the reference section of your library.

Unit 6

Composition

24

Words and Sentences

Good writing sparkles like jewelry. Well-chosen words are the gems that catch the eye, and varied, uncluttered sentences are the golden chains that link them. Writing that sparkles leaves an impression in the reader's imagination.

The following paragraph describes what summer might be like on Mars. Notice how the vivid words and smooth, varied sentences help the picture sparkle with life.

> Summer burned the canals dry. Summer moved like a flame upon the meadows. In the empty Earth settlement, the painted houses flaked and peeled. Rubber tires upon which children had swung in back yards hung suspended like stopped clock pendulums in the blazing air.
> —RAY BRADBURY, "DARK THEY WERE AND GOLDEN EYED"

This chapter will show you how to choose vivid words and use them in smooth, varied sentences.

WORD CHOICE

Words that convey exactly what you mean guarantee that a reader will understand your message.

24a Use **specific words** to express your meaning exactly. Use **figurative language** to appeal to your reader's imagination.

Specific Words

Both of the following examples describe the same item on a restaurant menu. The first example uses general words that leave only a vague impression. The second uses specific words that whet the appetite.

GENERAL   Cooked meat covered with a good sauce, served with cooked potatoes and good cooked vegetables

SPECIFIC   Barbecued spareribs smothered in a tangy sauce, served with french-fried potatoes and crisp steamed broccoli

General words can mean different things to different people. Specific words leave an exact picture in the reader's mind.

The following examples show a range of general to specific words for different parts of speech.

	GENERAL	MORE SPECIFIC	SPECIFIC
NOUNS	meat	pork	spareribs
	clothes	pants	blue jeans
ADJECTIVES	uneasy	nervous	jittery
	thin	delicate	fragile
VERBS	went	walked	strolled
	saw	watched	examined
ADVERBS	happily	gleefully	exuberantly
	soon	promptly	now

EXERCISE 1   Writing Specific Words

Number your paper 1 to 20. Then write two specific words for each general word.

1. bad	6. cute	11. boat	16. funny
2. saw	7. good	12. loud	17. exciting
3. got	8. went	13. sadly	18. slowly
4. nice	9. said	14. kind	19. building
5. old	10. room	15. flew	20. pretty

EXERCISE 2   **Replacing General Words with**
                 Specific Words

Write a specific word to replace the underlined word or
words in each sentence.

EXAMPLE   The movie was <u>great</u>.
POSSIBLE ANSWER   hilarious

1. Kathy's dad took us out for <u>dessert</u> after the movie.
2. While we were eating, we <u>talked about</u> the movie.
3. Kathy thought the acting was convincing, but the story
   was <u>weak</u>.
4. I thought the scenes with the Martians were <u>good</u>.
5. The chase scenes were comical because the four-legged
   Martians <u>walked oddly</u>.
6. Kathy's dad thought the special effects were <u>poor</u>.
7. He <u>laughed</u> during one scene when you could see the
   strings attached to the spaceship.
8. Before leaving the <u>place where we were having dessert</u>,
   each of us gave the movie a grade.
9. I gave it an <u>excellent grade</u>, but Kathy and her dad gave
   it a D+.
10. Later that night I dreamed that green <u>creatures</u> were
    chasing me with report cards.

Denotation and Connotation

All words convey a literal meaning, the meaning found in
a dictionary. This meaning is called *denotation*. Many
words, however, also stir up emotions. This extra level of
meaning is called *connotation*.

We went on a **trip** in July.
We went on **vacation** in July.

The denotations of *trip* and *vacation* are similar, but
vacation has an extra level of meaning. It brings many
feelings immediately to mind: freedom from your usual
routine, fun, relaxation, new scenery. All these connotations give a reader extra pleasure.

Some words have similar denotations but opposite connotations. The words *determined* and *pigheaded*, for example, both mean *strong-willed*. *Pigheaded*, however, creates a negative mental image, while *determined* is associated with positive qualities.

EXERCISE 3 Choosing Connotations

Write the word with the connotation given in brackets.

EXAMPLE   Ellen is very (frank, blunt). [negative]
ANSWER   blunt

1. Every October the old maple (paints, litters) the lawn with its falling leaves. [positive]
2. The mare ran (courageously, recklessly) into the flaming barn to save her colt. [positive]
3. We did our chores (leisurely, lazily). [negative]
4. The rabbit (scrambled, scampered) across the lawn. [positive]
5. My sister showed her report card (boastfully, proudly). [positive]
6. She woke up suddenly to escape from the (nightmare, dream). [negative]
7. The express train was (filled, crammed) with passengers. [negative]
8. Earl was known for his (booming, powerful) voice. [positive]
9. The (loud, jarring) ring of the telephone startled the baby. [negative]
10. The (glaring, bright) sun made driving difficult in the afternoon. [negative]

Figurative Language

Specific words with rich connotations help readers understand your message. Another way to convey your message is to appeal to your reader's imagination by using figurative language.

429

Similes and Metaphors. The two most common figures of speech are similes and metaphors. Both stimulate the reader's imagination by expressing a similarity between two things that are essentially different.

> SIMILE Summer moved **like a flame** upon the meadows. — RAY BRADBURY
>
> METAPHOR The road was **a ribbon of moonlight.**
> — ALFRED NOYES

Summer and flame are two different things, but they share the quality of intense heat. Roads and ribbons are not alike, but on a moonlit night a road can share the shiny, winding appearance of a ribbon. Notice that similes state the comparison with the words *like* or *as*. Metaphors imply a comparison, or simply say that one thing is another.

EXERCISE 4   Distinguishing between Similes and Metaphors

Write *simile* or *metaphor* to identify each figure of speech.

1. My brother's room is a federal disaster area.
2. With crashing cymbals and booming drums, the symphony was like a thunderstorm.
3. Good friends revolve around Sandra as the planets revolve around the sun.
4. Hope went through me like a faint breeze over a lake. — ANTOINE DE SAINT-EXUPERY
5. The coach growled when his players quit too soon.
6. Her secret was as dark as her eyes.
7. Hermit crabs, like frantic children, scamper on the bottom sand. — JOHN STEINBECK
8. All the strength went out of me, and I toppled forward like an undermined tower. — MARK TWAIN
9. Memories poured from every corner of the old house.
10. The black bat, night, has flown. — TENNYSON

Clichés. Some comparisons that were once clever and striking have become dull with overuse. Worn-out expressions are called *clichés*.

CLICHÉ   I changed my mind **on the spur of the moment.**

Few people reading that sentence would actually picture a rider's boot spur. The phrase *spur of the moment* is so commonplace that it has lost its power to stimulate the imagination.

If you find yourself using a simile or metaphor that you have heard before, replace it with a fresh comparison. Following are just a few of the clichés that now deaden our language.

CLICHÉS   knock me over with a feather
make a mountain out of a molehill
as cool as a cucumber
as easy as pie
turn over a new leaf

EXERCISE 5 Revising to Eliminate Clichés

Replace each cliché in sentences 1 to 5 with a fresh simile or metaphor. Then replace the remaining five clichés with specific language. Underline your changes.

EXAMPLE   He was <u>hot under the collar</u>.
POSSIBLE ANSWER   He was <u>ignited with anger</u>.

Tryouts

1. Everyone told me the tryouts for the school play would be <u>as easy as *A, B, C*</u>.
2. When I was called to read my lines, however, I was <u>shaking like a leaf</u>.
3. There were so many juniors and seniors trying out that I felt <u>like a black sheep</u>.
4. My throat was <u>as dry as a bone</u>.
5. I <u>spit out</u> the first few lines with difficulty.
6. I felt <u>like a rat in a maze</u> trying to read my lines.
7. Then the director stopped me and told me to <u>start from scratch</u>.
8. This time I was <u>as cool as a cucumber</u>.
9. I was <u>sharp as a tack</u> as I read my lines with feeling.
10. When the cast list was announced the next day, <u>it was music to my ears</u>.

EXERCISE 6 On Your Own

Think of a character you have read about or make one up. Write one sentence using specific language to describe the character's special qualities. Then write three sentences that express those qualities in similes and three sentences that express them in metaphors.

Writing Extra

Metaphors are especially useful in describing abstract qualities, such as freedom, happiness, love, and honesty. By combining a metaphor with specific verbs, you can describe an abstract quality in a poem. Read the following examples. Then try one or two of your own.

Youth	**Friendship**
Youth is a fire,	Friendship is a sun,
Crackling on a dance floor,	Beaming radiant life,
Sparking on the streets,	Drying floods of tears,
Smoldering in lonely rooms,	Burning off damp despair,
Extinguished by the rains	Eclipsed by jealousy.
of age.	

SENTENCE VARIETY

Good writing flows with the natural and varied rhythms of speech. Notice the variety of sentence length and structure in the following passage.

> Before it was really light, he had his baits out and was drifting with the current. One bait was down forty fathoms. The second was at seventy-five, and the third and fourth were down in the blue water at one hundred and twenty-five fathoms.
>
> — ERNEST HEMINGWAY, *THE OLD MAN AND THE SEA*

24b ▶ Vary the beginning, length, and structure of your sentences.

Sentence Beginnings

The most natural way to begin a sentence is with the subject. If too many sentences begin in the same way, however, even a gripping story will sound dull. The following examples show how Hal Borland varied his sentence beginnings in his novel *When the Legends Die*.

SUBJECT **The boy** caught trout in the pool and watched for his friend, the bear.

ADVERB **Reluctantly,** the boy fastened the collar on the bear cub.

PHRASE **For days** he watched them. [prepositional phrase]

Driving with one hand, he headed for home. [participial phrase]

CLAUSE **If he rode the horse with its own rhythm,** he could ride every horse in the herd. [adverb clause]

NOTE: For a review of phrases and clauses, *see Chapters 8–10.* You may also wish to review the rules for punctuating introductory elements, *pages 311–312.*

EXERCISE 7   Varying Sentence Beginnings

Vary the beginnings of each of the following sentences by using the openers suggested in parentheses.

EXAMPLE   We can see about 3,000 stars on a clear night. (prepositional phrase)

ANSWER   On a clear night, we can see about 3,000 stars.

The
Stars

1. Only the nearest and brightest stars are visible in the vast sea of stars. (prepositional phrase)
2. Fainter and invisible stars stretch endlessly beyond the reaches of our imagination. (adverb)
3. There are 100 billion stars in just our own galaxy, the Milky Way. (prepositional phrase)
4. The Milky Way would look like a giant fried egg if we could look down on it. (adverb clause)

433

5. Our sun is actually just one star in the galaxy. (adverb)
6. The Milky Way, bulging in the middle, spans 10,000 light-years at the center. (participial phrase)
7. Our solar system travels 250 miles per second, although we do not feel the motion. (adverb clause)
8. One complete orbit around the galaxy nevertheless takes 250 million years. (adverb)
9. Orbiting stars form graceful spiral arms in the outer part of the galaxy. (prepositional phrases)
10. One spiral arm, extending through the constellations Perseus and Cassiopeia, reaches out 7,000 light-years from the sun. (participial phrase)

Sentence Combining

Too many short sentences in a row force readers to limp through a passage. To help readers, combine short sentences into longer, varied ones. Study the examples below.

Combining Short Sentences into Simple Sentences

A. Handlers can usually train dogs. Training is in basic obedience. Training takes about eight weeks.

Handlers can usually train dogs **in basic obedience in about eight weeks.** [prepositional phrases]

B. Handlers and dogs work together. This strengthens the bond between pet and master.

Handlers and dogs work together, **strengthening the bond between pet and master.** [participial phrase]

C. A training collar helps the handler correct the dog. It is the handler's most important tool.

A training collar, **the handler's most important tool,** helps correct the dog. [appositive phrase]

D. Kindness is also important. Praise is important too.

Kindness and **praise** are also important. [compound subject]

E. Soon your dog will heel on command. Soon your dog will sit on command.

Soon your dog **will heel** and **sit** on command. [compound verb]

Combining Short Sentences into Compound Sentences

F. The dog should be confined before each session. The place of confinement should be comfortable.

The dog should be confined before each session, but **the place of confinement should be comfortable.** [compound sentence: use coordinating conjunctions *and, but, or, for, yet, so*]

Combining Short Sentences into Complex Sentences

G. Mother dogs use a barking sound to get their pups to obey. The barking sound resembles the word *out.*

Mother dogs use a barking sound, **which resembles the word *out*,** to get their pups to obey. [adjective clause: use relative pronouns *who, whom, whose, which, that*]

H. Handlers can also use this sound. Dogs have a long memory of their mothers' stern corrections.

Handlers can also use this sound **because dogs have a long memory of their mothers' stern corrections.** [adverb clause: use subordinating conjunctions such as *after, although, because, unless, until*]

EXERCISE 8 Combining Pairs of Sentences

Combine each pair of sentences using the models on pages 434–435. Use commas where needed.

EXAMPLE We wanted to do something different on our vacation. We chose backpacking in the wilderness. (compound: F)

ANSWER We wanted to do something different on our vacation, so we chose backpacking in the wilderness.

1. We walked the entire distance. We had packs on our backs. (simple: A)
2. I could carry my own pack. It weighed fifty pounds. (complex: H)
3. The trail was steep and hazardous. It had been a logging road. (complex: G)
4. We came to a lookout tower. It was in good condition. (simple: A)
5. I climbed the tower. I strapped my camera around my neck. (simple: B)
6. Fog had covered the valley. I couldn't see a thing. (compound: F)
7. A river came down from the mountains. It flowed east. (simple: E)
8. A footpath followed the river. An old railroad track followed the river. (simple: D)
9. I didn't write any letters home. We were away from mailboxes for two weeks. (complex: H)
10. The vacation was a real learning experience. It was a high point in my life. (simple: C)

Rambling Sentences

A sentence that rambles on too long is as hard to follow as a series of short, limping sentences.

RAMBLING   The buzz saw screams as you watch the tree come up the conveyor belt and as it hits the saw, the chips fly to the right and left, and when the log reaches the end of the saw, the log folds over into two slabs and goes through the saw again.

REVISED   The buzz saw screams as you watch the tree come up the conveyor belt. As it hits the saw, chips fly to the right and left. Once through the saw, the log folds over into two slabs and goes through the saw again.

Untangle sentences that string too many ideas together. Separate the ideas into a mixture of short and long sentences and avoid long strings of phrases and clauses.

EXERCISE 9   Revising Rambling Sentences
Revise the following rambling sentences. Use capital letters and punctuation where needed.

1. Our cat is an old, orange tiger who has become quite blind, but he doesn't like to admit it, and instead he has memorized the inside of the house and much of the yard, and he pats the places where he is going to step, and he uses his senses of touch, smell, and hearing in place of his eyesight.

2. Owls can watch an object with both eyes, as people do, but they cannot move their eyes, so they have to turn their heads to watch anything that moves, and their big, round eyes make them look wise although they are no smarter than other birds and not even as smart as crows and ravens.

3. Winchester House is the name of a huge, rambling mansion in San Jose, California, that was built by Sarah Winchester who was heir to the Winchester fortune, and who believed that she would go on living as long as she was adding to the house which has 160 rooms, 200 doors, and 47 fireplaces.

EXERCISE 10   On Your Own
Clip a paragraph from a magazine or newspaper. Then answer the following questions.

1. How many words are in each sentence?
2. How does each sentence begin?
3. How many simple sentences, compound sentences, and complex sentences does it contain?

CONCISE SENTENCES

Compact cars go farther on a gallon of gasoline than do huge gas guzzlers. In the same way, concise sentences deliver more meaning from each word than do repetitive and wordy ramblings.

24c Express your meaning in as few words as possible.

Redundancy

Unnecessary repetition is called *redundancy*. In a redundant sentence, the same idea is expressed more than once with no new shades of meaning.

REDUNDANT The **hungry** wolf ate **ravenously.**
CONCISE The wolf ate **ravenously.**

REDUNDANT The **hot, steamy** asphalt shimmered.
CONCISE The **steamy** asphalt shimmered.

EXERCISE 11 Eliminating Redundancy
Revise each sentence by eliminating the redundancy.

1. Do you have a spare pencil that you are not using?
2. Friday is the final deadline for the report.
3. Each and every member of the class must help.
4. Can you keep this secret confidential?
5. I can begin to get started on the project now.
6. Blood donors are constantly needed all of the time.
7. Jill and Al agreed mutually to drop the argument.
8. Everyone laughed throughout the entire movie.
9. The lawyer explained the rights of young juveniles.
10. The descending waterfall was graceful.

Wordiness

Like redundancy, wordiness adds nothing to the meaning of a sentence and distracts your reader.

438

Empty Expressions. One way to avoid wordiness is to rid your sentences of empty expressions. Notice how the revisions improve the following sentences.

WORDY   I can't go to the movies **due to the fact that** I have my guitar lesson tonight.

CONCISE   I can't go to the movies **because** I have my guitar lesson tonight.

WORDY   **There are** dozens of games that resemble checkers.

CONCISE   Dozens of games resemble checkers.

Empty Expressions

the thing that	due to the fact that
on account of	the reason that
what I want is	the thing/fact is that
in my opinion	there is/are/was/were
It is/was	what I mean is that
It seems as if	I believe/feel/think that

EXERCISE 12   Eliminating Empty Expressions
Revise each sentence, eliminating the empty expressions or replacing them with more precise language.

EXAMPLE   The thing that I enjoy is skiing.
POSSIBLE ANSWER   I enjoy skiing.

1. We canceled the game due to the fact that it rained.
2. The reason that I called was to ask if you need help.
3. Because of the fact that he was sick, his report is late.
4. One thing I really hate is getting up early.
5. There are some places in the river that are dangerous.
6. I believe that drivers should wear seat belts.
7. What the rebellious child wanted was attention.
8. We can't ride our bikes on account of the traffic.
9. What I want is a crisp spinach and mushroom salad.
10. The thing that interests me is astronomy.

Wordy Phrases and Clauses. Another way to avoid wordiness is to shorten wordy phrases and clauses. In many cases a single word can take the place of a phrase.

WORDY   Archaeologists found ancient tools **made of stone.** [participial phrase]

CONCISE   Archaeologists found ancient **stone** tools. [adjective]

WORDY   Elana spoke to the shy horse **in a gentle tone.** [prepositional phrase]

CONCISE   Elana spoke **gently** to the shy horse. [adverb]

Similarly, a wordy adjective clause can be replaced with a shorter phrase—or even a single word.

WORDY   People **who are in show business** lead a hectic life of rehearsals and performances.

CONCISE   People **in show business** . . . [prepositional phrase]

WORDY   In Yosemite, **which is a national park in California,** cars are forbidden past a certain point.

CONCISE   In Yosemite, **a national park in California,** cars . . . [appositive phrase]

WORDY   Climates **that are dry** are good for people with allergy problems.

CONCISE   **Dry** climates . . . [adjective]

EXERCISE 13   Shortening Wordy Phrases and Clauses
Revise each sentence by shortening the wordy phrase or clause.

1. Beverly likes chicken <u>cooked with barbecue sauce</u>.
2. Students <u>who are trying out for band</u> should come to school on Saturday morning.

440

3. An exchange student <u>who came to our neighborhood from France</u> lives with our neighbors.
4. Roger, <u>who is a polio victim</u>, competed in the marathon in a wheelchair.
5. Games <u>that are in good condition</u> will be accepted for the charity drive.
6. Luis organized his bookshelf <u>in a neat way</u>.
7. The motel had a pool <u>that was heated</u>.
8. The storm <u>that came in from the west</u> left ten inches of snow.
9. Buildings <u>along the riverfront</u> are being torn down to make room for a park.
10. I love to read the novels <u>written by the author Mark Twain</u>.

EXERCISE 14 On Your Own
For comic effect, the poet Ogden Nash purposely breaks the rules for writing concise sentences. Read the following example. Then find other humorous poems by Nash that contain rambling, wordy sentences.

One thing I like less than most things is
   sitting in a dentist chair with my
   mouth wide open,
And that I will never have to do it again
   is a hope that I am against hope hopen.
                     —OGDEN NASH, FROM "THIS IS GOING
                        TO HURT JUST A LITTLE BIT"

CHAPTER REVIEW

Revise each sentence to eliminate the problem indicated in parentheses.

Up in the Air

1. Some people do not like going into tall skyscrapers. (redundancy)
2. Fear of heights makes some people feel sick as a dog in skyscrapers. (cliché)

3. Acrophobiacs sometimes lose their balance and fall down. Acrophobiacs are people afraid of heights. (needs combining)

4. The tallest skyscrapers move as much as three feet in the wind. (general verb)

5. People who are riding in the elevator can hear it hit the sides of the shaft when the top of the building sways. (wordy clause)

6. Because of the fact that skyscrapers sometimes sway in the wind, some people feel airsick when they are on the upper floors. (empty expression)

7. Some people have phobias about fire and are afraid that fire will break out while they are in a skyscraper, but most skyscrapers, however, have extensive sprinkling systems to put fires out, and firefighters are specially trained in handling high-rise fires. (rambling)

8. Teamwork and expert training are both necessary to put out the flicker in these huge structures. (wrong connotation)

9. People who work in skyscrapers usually adjust to the height. They usually enjoy all the advantages. (needs combining)

10. One of the chief advantages is the bird's-eye view. (cliché)

11. Due to the fact that they provide an excellent view, some skyscrapers have an observatory on the top floor. (empty expression)

12. These observatories are open to the public, and anyone can visit them. (redundancy)

13. A city viewed from this height looks neat. (general adjective)

14. Restaurants are also often placed at the top of skyscrapers, and they can offer both a great meal and a fantastic view, which will draw a lot of customers, although the meals can be expensive. (rambling)

15. Visiting a skyscraper observatory is a fun family outing. Visiting a skyscraper restaurant is also fun for the family. (needs combining)

Chapter Summary

Words and Sentences

Word Choice
1. Use specific words to express your meaning exactly.
2. Choose words with connotations that match the feelings you wish to convey.
3. Create fresh similes and metaphors to appeal to your reader's imagination. Avoid clichés.

Sentence Variety
4. Vary your sentences by using different sentence beginnings.
5. Vary the length of your sentences by combining short, choppy sentences and untangling long, rambling ones.

Concise Sentences
6. Express your meaning in as few words as possible. Eliminate redundancy, empty expressions, and wordy phrases and clauses.

25

Paragraphs

A sentence simply *expresses* a thought, but a paragraph *develops* a thought, expanding on it and making it clear to readers. The indented line at the beginning of a paragraph signals readers that a new thought is going to be developed. Well-constructed paragraphs, aided by these visual signals, make your thoughts easy to follow.

25a A **paragraph** is a group of related sentences that present and develop one main idea.

Look for the main idea and its development in the following paragraph.

Childhood Treasures

Aunt Sally's cabinet of art supplies was like a toy chest to me. The top shelf, beyond my reach, had an endless supply of paper. There was stiff, brilliant-white paper for water-colors, blank newsprint for charcoals, glossy paper, dull paper, tracing paper. On the second shelf sat oozing tubes of bright-colored oils, bottles of the blackest ink, and cartons of chalk in sunrise shades of pastels. The third shelf, my favorite, held the damp lumps of gray clay, waiting to be shaped into creatures only my aunt and I would recognize. On the bottom shelves were brushes, rags, and turpentine. Despite the thorough clean-ups Aunt Sally insisted on, that cabinet was a paradise of play for me on countless Sunday afternoons.

The main idea of this paragraph is presented in the first sentence. The other sentences expand the main idea with specific details. The last sentence, by returning to the main idea, makes the paragraph complete. In this chapter you will learn how to recognize the qualities that make a well-structured, well-developed paragraph.

PARAGRAPH STRUCTURE

In a good paragraph, every sentence serves a purpose. Notice the purpose of each sentence in the paragraph that follows.

Eskimo Customs

TOPIC SENTENCE: STATES THE MAIN IDEA

The activities of the Eskimo are determined by the seasons and, of course, by the weather. During the dark stormy winter months, when the sun hardly shows itself above the arctic horizon before it disappears again, hunters are confined to their homes for days at a time. In

SUPPORTING SENTENCES: DEVELOP THE MAIN IDEA

the summer, during the weeks when the sun does not set at all, the Eskimo lose all sense of time, and hunters often paddle about in their canoes until they are exhausted. People are up at all hours, and there is always noise and laughter outside. Visitors barge in at all hours, too, expecting to be fed and entertained. This constant activity exhausts even the sturdiest and hardiest Eskimo.

CONCLUDING SENTENCE: PROVIDES A STRONG ENDING

Many of them confess that although they look forward to the sun and warmth during the severe winter, they feel relieved when the weather begins to turn colder, the sun begins to set, and their lives resume a regular day-and-night routine.

— SONIA BLEEKER, *THE ESKIMO*

Paragraphs are as varied as the people who write them. Some, for example, state the main idea in two sentences rather than one. Some do not have concluding sentences.

To make certain that your message will be understood, learn to write paragraphs with a clear topic sentence, a body of supporting sentences, and an effective concluding sentence.

Topic Sentence

A topic sentence can be the first sentence in a paragraph, the last sentence, or any one of the middle sentences. Wherever it occurs, it serves the same purpose.

25b ▶ A **topic sentence** states the main idea of the paragraph.

Because it states the main idea, the topic sentence is usually more general than the other sentences in the paragraph. Notice how the following topic sentence is more general than the sentences that develop it.

The Heavy Task of Fighting Fires

TOPIC
SENTENCE

Fighting a major fire takes tremendous strength and endurance. The protective clothing that a fire fighter wears into a burning building will weigh more than 20 pounds. To protect himself from the smoke, the fire fighter will usually wear an oxygen tank and mask. These self-contained breathing units may weigh as much as 50 pounds. The weight of the hose and other tools that the fire fighter carries will raise the total weight to more than 100 pounds.

—WALTER BROWN/NORMAN ANDERSON, *FIRES*

Although a topic sentence is more general than other sentences in the paragraph, it is still specific enough to be covered adequately in one paragraph.

TOO GENERAL	Fire fighting is an interesting job.
TOO GENERAL	Fire fighting is hard work.
GENERAL BUT LIMITED	Fighting a major fire takes tremendous strength and endurance.

The following guidelines summarize the purpose of a topic sentence.

Topic Sentences

1. A topic sentence states the main idea.
2. A topic sentence limits the main idea to one aspect of the subject that can be adequately covered in the paragraph.
3. A topic sentence is more general than the sentences that develop it.

EXERCISE 1   Identifying Topic Sentences

Write the topic sentence from each paragraph.

1. The Lovesick Sunflower

In one Greek myth, a nymph called Clytie fell in love with the glorious sun god Apollo. Apollo, however, did not even notice her. He was too busy riding his golden chariot through the sky, beginning and ending the day. Morning to night, Clytie stared up at the sky, watching Apollo's sun chariot move from east to west. She soon stopped eating and drank only dew. The other gods, pitying her, decided to change her into the sunflower. With the legend of Clytie and Apollo, the Greeks explained why sunflowers always keep their faces turned to the sun.

2. The Red River

The Red River Valley, its 110,000 square miles shared by Minnesota, North Dakota, and Manitoba, is a magnificence, producing about the highest farm income of any place on Earth. The river itself is ridiculous, an insult to human reason and all expectations. It is narrow; it is mud-lined; it barely flows at times; it floods most frightfully about once every generation, turning the flatlands into a vast lake. It goes east, west, and south in order to go north. The river, according to one roustabout quoted by historian Vera Kelsey, resembles "a reluctant and homesick pig being driven on a straight road to market."

— ERIC SEVAREID

3. The Olympic Miracle

At the 1960 Olympics in Rome, spectators witnessed something of a miracle when Wilma Rudolph won three gold medals. Sixteen years earlier, Wilma had been stricken with scarlet fever and pneumonia. For several years after that, she could not use her left leg at all. Through patience and hard-driving will, she gradually regained the use of her leg. Wilma began running nonstop and soon was in training to become a world-class runner. In front of cheering crowds in Rome, she came in first in the 100– and 200–meter runs, and she saved the day for her teammates in the 400–meter relay.

4. Robert E. Peary at the North Pole

Since the North Pole is actually a mathematical pinpoint, it was impossible to determine its precise location. Peary, however, had striven too long and too hard for this moment not to wish to realize it to the full. For his own personal satisfaction he had to be able to feel that he had actually stood exactly on the North Pole itself, at 90°. Peary had the Eskimo Ootah hitch a double team of dogs to a light sledge, and in this triumphal chariot he went back and forth across an area of about eight or ten miles. At some moment during these marches and counter-marches he passed over "the point where north and south and east and west blend into one."

—MARIE PEARY STAFFORD, *DISCOVERER OF THE NORTH POLE*

EXERCISE 2 Choosing the Better Topic Sentence

Write the letter of the topic sentence that most closely follows the guidelines on page 447.

1. a. Life can be difficult at times.
   b. Being a good friend can be difficult at times.
2. a. Dolphins are always friendly to humans.
   b. Dolphins are amazing creatures.
3. a. Many people like camping.
   b. Pitching a tent is easy if you follow directions.
4. a. A healthy person exercises both body and mind.
   b. Good health is the most important thing.

5. a. Holidays are nice.
   b. Holidays provide relief from everyday routines.
6. a. Today's movies use computers for special effects.
   b. Movies today are very exciting.
7. a. Folk songs are part of life.
   b. Folk songs reveal a country's values.
8. a. Dinner should be eaten in peace.
   b. A dinnertime quarrel can upset digestion.
9. a. Many medical discoveries were made by accident.
   b. There have been some interesting discoveries.
10. a. Bats use sonar to locate prey.
    b. Bats are complex animals.

Supporting Sentences

Readers are natural question-askers. Supporting sentences answer the reader's questions and form the main body of the paragraph.

25c ▶ **Supporting sentences** explain or prove the topic sentence with specific details, facts, examples, or reasons.

Following is the topic sentence of a paragraph about Robert Peary's successful return from the North Pole.

On the sixth of September, 1909, the gallant little *Roosevelt* steamed into Indian Harbor, Labrador, and from the wireless tower on top of a cliff two messages flashed out.

Readers will naturally wonder, "What were the two messages?" The supporting sentences answer that question.

The first was to Peary's anxiously waiting wife, more eager, if the truth were known, to hear of her husband's safety than of the discovery of the Pole. This message read: "Have made good at last. I have the Pole. Am well. Love." The second one was to his country, for which he had sacrificed so much. It read: "Stars and Stripes nailed to the North Pole. Peary."
—MARIE PEARY STAFFORD, *DISCOVERER OF THE NORTH POLE*

When you write supporting sentences, try to anticipate your readers' questions and answer them.

EXERCISE 3   Identifying Supporting Sentences
Write the two topic sentences. Then after each one, write the numbers of the sentences that support it.

Topic Sentences
A. Spices come from different parts of plants.
B. Peppertrees are unrelated to the pepper plant.

Supporting Sentences
1. Peppertrees are ornamental.
2. Mustard is a yellow powder or paste made from seeds.
3. Cinnamon is the dried inner bark of a small tree.
4. They belong to the family of sumac trees.
5. Ginger comes from the root of a tropical plant.
6. Flowers of the peppertree are white.
7. Saffron is from the pistil of the saffron plant.
8. The blossoming trees give off a delicate fragrance.
9. Garlic is a bulb from an herb in the lily family.
10. These fragrant trees are grown mainly for shade.

EXERCISE 4   Writing Supporting Sentences
Write each topic sentence. Then write three sentences that could support each one.

1. What a person wears reveals much about his or her personality.
2. There are three good reasons why everyone should take a vacation once a year.
3. It's hard to imagine life without a telephone.
4. Old photographs can help you understand history.
5. Before you can drive a car, you have to meet certain requirements.
6. Having friends of different ages helps make you a well-rounded person.
7. Saturdays are usually less fun than Sundays.

8. Gifts are as much for the giver as for the receiver.
9. Everyone has a unique way of expressing friendship.
10. Winter in a cold climate can be enjoyable.

Concluding Sentence

A paragraph that stands alone often needs a concluding sentence to wrap up the ideas presented in the paragraph.

25d ▶ A **concluding sentence** adds a strong ending to a paragraph.

Following are several good ways to end a paragraph.

Concluding Sentences

A concluding sentence may
1. restate the main idea using different words.
2. summarize the paragraph.
3. add an insight about the main idea.
4. show how you feel about the subject.

Although some repetition in the concluding sentence is useful, an exact repetition or an over-simplified summary adds no real meaning. The following paragraph has a weak concluding sentence.

An All-Around Player

Although Babe Ruth is best remembered for his home runs, he was also a great pitcher. In 1916, he led the American League in earned-run percentage. He won 23 games that year, including nine shutouts. The next year he won 24. Until 1961, Ruth held the record for pitching scoreless innings in the World Series. As you can see, Ruth was a great pitcher as well as a home-run king.

Any of the following sentences would add a stronger ending. They have less repetition and more meaning.

Ruth's home runs are remembered in the Hall of Fame, but the pitching of this all-around star should not be forgotten. [restates main idea]

Ruth's impressive pitching statistics show that he was more than a great hitter. [summarizes]

Rare indeed are the athletes who, like Ruth, excel in more than one position. [adds an insight]

What a remarkable, all-around champion Ruth was! [shows feeling]

EXERCISE 5 Writing Concluding Sentences
The concluding sentences in the following paragraphs are weak. After the proper number on your paper, write two different concluding sentences for each paragraph.

1. Chasing Rainbows

Whenever you are standing with a light source behind you and misty water in front of you, you can see a rainbow. The biggest, most complete rainbows are created when the sun is close to the horizon. You can also sometimes see a rainbow in the mist from a waterfall or the spray from a garden hose. Now and then even a full moon on a rainy night will create a faint rainbow. I have just told you about the ways you can see rainbows.

2. Hailstones

Hailstones consist of many onion-like layers of ice. In certain weather conditions, small ice crystals drop into a band of very cold moisture. Some of this moisture freezes onto the crystal, forming the first layer. Updrafts then carry the hailstone back up, and when it drops again another layer is formed. The process continues until the hailstone is too heavy to be lifted by updrafts, and then it drops to the earth. That is how hailstones are formed.

3. Jane Austen's Novels

By writing only about what she knew, Jane Austen set a good example for other writers. She did not know or write about wars, disasters, mob scenes, or great adventures.

She lived the quiet life of a small-town girl. Yet 170 years later, her novels are still widely read and enjoyed. Her word pictures about people of all types, wise and foolish, continue to delight readers. She certainly set a good example for other writers.

EXERCISE 6　On Your Own
Skim through the magazines at home or in a library, looking for a well-written paragraph with a topic sentence, a body of supporting sentences, and a concluding sentence. Copy it (or clip it out if the magazine is your own) and save it for Exercise 10.

PARAGRAPH DEVELOPMENT

A topic sentence is like a baseball score. It gives the general idea without the specifics of how the game developed. Readers, like sports fans, want to know the details. They want to see the idea in the topic sentence developed play by play. A well-developed paragraph gives readers the full account.

Methods of Development

A good topic sentence will usually give you a clue about how to develop the main idea of your paragraph. Consider the questions raised by the following topic sentences and think about the kind of supporting information that would best answer them.

DESCRIPTIVE DETAILS	Everything about the house was eerie. [What *specific details* about the house made it seem eerie?]
FACTS/ EXAMPLES	In the past fifty years, the gorilla population has declined drastically. [What *facts* or *examples* show the decline in population?]

REASONS   People living alone should adopt a pet.
[What are your *reasons* for this opinion?]

INCIDENT   I learned early in life that temper tantrums
don't pay off. [What *incident* led you to this
conclusion?]

COMPARISON/   Despite their similarities, guitars and
CONTRAST   banjos are two very different instruments.
[What are the *similarities?* What are the
differences?]

STEPS IN   Even an inexperienced gardener can grow
A PROCESS   healthy, tangy radishes. [What *steps* should
be followed?]

25e   Use the **method of development** most appropriate for your
topic sentence.

EXERCISE 7   **Recognizing Methods of Development**
Use the examples on pages 453–454 to help you decide how
each paragraph is developed. Indicate your answer by writing *descriptive details, facts/examples, reasons, incident, comparison and/or contrast,* or *steps in a process.*

1. Home Site

Mama had picked the spot for our log house. It nestled at the edge of the foothills in the mouth of a small canyon and was surrounded by a grove of huge red oaks. Beyond our house we could see miles and miles of the mighty Ozarks. In the spring the aromatic scent of wildflowers, redbuds, pawpaws, and dogwoods, drifting on the wind currents, spread over the valley and around our home.

— WILSON RAWLS

2. Taking the Plunge

Most experts agree that swimming is the healthiest form of vigorous exercise. Because water offers so little resistance, swimmers are unlikely to experience the muscle strain associated with land sports such as jogging and tennis. Yet, swimming strengthens many areas of the body—arms, legs, torso, and neck. Most importantly, if done regularly, it is strenuous enough to condition the heart and lungs. See your doctor before starting any new exercise program, but don't be surprised if he tells you to go jump in a lake!

3. Two Great Men

There are many similarities between Mahatma Ghandi and Martin Luther King, Jr. Both believed in nonviolent resistance to laws they felt were unfair. Both were men whose powers of leadership rallied millions behind their cause. Both leaders struggled for equal rights for oppressed peoples, and both met a tragic end.

4. Upside-Down Painting

Even a museum employee may wonder how to hang an abstract painting. Which edge is the top? Which is the bottom? Henri Matisse's abstract painting <u>The Boat</u> hung upside down at the Museum of Modern Art in New York from October 18 to December 11, 1961. More than 100,000 people looked at <u>The Boat</u>, and not one of them noticed that it was upside down. Finally, after 47 days, an art expert discovered the mistake, and at least one museum employee had a bad case of embarrassment.

5. Space Junk

If you think roadside litter is a problem, consider some of the junk that is floating around space. About 3,400 pieces of trackable debris are orbiting Earth, according to the North American Defense Command in Colorado, which uses radar to keep tabs on space junk. Everything from spent rocket boosters to broken solar panels is on the list. As long as the debris stays in space or burns up on reentry, it gets little attention from the public. When space junk litters the planet, problems start.

—ADAPTED FROM *NATIONAL WILDLIFE*

6. Be Prepared

Following a recipe is easy if you are properly prepared. First clear a work area in the kitchen. Then read the recipe from start to finish to make sure you understand the general idea. When you have finished, go back to the beginning of the recipe. One by one, collect the ingredients and place them in your work area. Also bring out measuring spoons, sifters, and any other equipment the recipe requires. When all of your ingredients and utensils are in place, you are properly prepared and can make your favorite recipe easily.

Writing Extra

Descriptive details bring an object into sharp focus. Test your ability to develop descriptive details by writing puzzle poems. Think of an object and four or five details that describe it. Without naming the object, use the details in a poem ending with the line "What is it?" See if your classmates can guess what you are describing. Following are two examples.

Too small to hold,
Big enough to flood a heart,
Salty, hot, sprung from sadness,
Bringing relief.
What is it?

Solid and round,
More like gray than white,
Stitched in orange,
Echoing with cheering crowds and
   the crack of good wood.
What is it?

Answers: teardrop, old baseball

Unity

In an effort to develop a paragraph fully, a writer sometimes strays from the main idea and ends up confusing the reader. A well-developed paragraph has several supporting sentences, but they all relate directly to the topic sentence. This quality of good paragraphs is called *unity*.

25f ▶ Achieve **unity** by making sure all the supporting sentences relate to the topic sentence.

In the following paragraph, two sentences that destroy the unity are crossed out. Read the paragraph twice — once with the sentences that stray and once without. Notice that the revised paragraph is easier to understand.

Candlelight

Candles, which go back to prehistoric times, were a chief source of light for 2,000 years. The first candle may have been discovered by accident when a piece of wood or cord fell into a pool of lighted fat. In ancient times, crude candles were made from fats wrapped in husks or moss. ~~Early people also used torches.~~ Later, a wick was placed inside a candle mold and melted wax was poured into the mold. ~~The first lamps used a dish of oil and a wick.~~ Candles could be used to carry light from place to place and could be stored indefinitely.

EXERCISE 8 Recognizing Sentences That Destroy Unity
Read the paragraph and decide which two sentences stray from the subject. Write these sentences.

The First Cheap Car

Henry Ford was not the first person to build a car, but he was the first to figure out how to make cars cheaply. His assembly-line methods resulted in huge savings and changed the car from a luxury to a necessity. The mass-produced Model T sold for about $400, a price the average wage earner could afford. Ford sold over 15 million cars from 1908 to 1927. Ford reduced the workday for his employees from 9 to 8 hours. He set the minimum wage at five dollars a day. By building a cheap, easy-to-operate car, Ford changed the nation.

Coherence

A paragraph with *coherence* is well organized and tightly knit.

25g ▶ Achieve **coherence** by presenting ideas in logical order and by using transitional expressions.

The following chart shows some common methods of organization and some transitional expressions.

Methods of Organization		
Chronological Order		
This method is used with events or stories to tell what happened first, second, third, etc. It is also used with steps in a process.		
TRANSITIONS		
first	later	after
second	then	finally
third	next	by evening
before	while	at noon
Spatial Order		
This method is used in descriptions to show how objects are related in location.		
TRANSITIONS		
beside	left	farther
behind	right	at the top
above	across	in front of
below	north	in the center
beyond	south	at the bottom
Order of Importance, Interest, or Degree		
This method is often used in paragraphs that persuade or explain. It presents ideas in order of least to most (or most to least) important, interesting, or sizable.		
TRANSITIONS		
also	furthermore	to begin with
first	moreover	more important
finally	in addition	most important

EXERCISE 9 Identifying Elements of Coherence
After the proper number on your paper, write the method of
organization used in each paragraph.

1. A House in the Woods

The house was on the left side of the lane, a hundred
yards back from the gate. It was a wooden house, like most
of them in that country, and the paint had mostly disappeared from it. The barn was on the right. The well was a
little in front of the house, boxed in with lumber and
having a wheel above it for the rope which held the bucket
to run through. There were three big oaks around the
house; the whole group of buildings, weathered and gray,
looked rather desolate and bleak against the dark pine
woods that grew behind them. — ROBERT MURPHY

2. Gold Rush

James Marshall started a race for gold. The story begins
in 1848 when Marshall was helping Captain John Sutter
build a sawmill in California. The mill wheel was not
working properly, so Marshall stood in the river that
turned the wheel to study the flow of water. Suddenly he
noticed gleaming colors in the water. The colors turned
out to be nuggets of gold. Soon word of Marshall's discovery had reached far and wide, and the gold rush of 1849
had begun.

3. Endless Speeches

Sometimes to delay an important vote, a U.S. senator
will deliver an endless speech called a *filibuster*. William
V. Allen spoke for 14 hours and 45 minutes in 1893.
Senator Huey Long filibustered for 15 hours and 30 minutes in 1925. Robert LaFollette spoke for 18 hours and 23
minutes against a currency bill in 1908. Senator Strom
Thurmond filibustered for 24 hours and 18 minutes in
1957. Since 1959, a two-thirds vote of the Senate can limit
the big talkers to one hour.

EXERCISE 10   On Your Own

Paste the paragraph you chose for Exercise 6 on a piece of white paper. In the upper left-hand corner of the paper, identify the method of development used in the paragraph. Underline the topic sentence and contribute your paragraph to a class folder for writing ideas.

CHAPTER REVIEW

Read the following paragraph. Then answer each question.

Curious Manners

The manners of seventeenth-century French society may strike modern Americans as curious. For example, wearing a hat inside the home was considered the height of good manners. A gentleman was even supposed to keep his hat on during dinner. Meals often had four courses with forty plates in each course. Offering a sneezing person the use of your handkerchief was considered a great offense. Most curious of all, it was considered highly impolite to say "God bless you!" outloud, but it was most proper to say it to yourself silently. However curious they may seem, these manners, like all rules of etiquette, allowed people to treat one another with respect.

1. What is the topic sentence?
2. What are the supporting sentences?
3. What question do the supporting sentences answer?
4. Which of the ways to end a paragraph on page 451 has this author chosen?
5. What method of development is used in this paragraph?
6. What phrase in sentence 2 gives you a clue about the method of development?
7. What other method of development might be used?
8. Which sentence strays from the topic?
9. What method of organization is used?
10. What phrase in sentence 6 gives you a clue about the method of organization?

Chapter Summary

Paragraphs

1. A paragraph is a group of related sentences that present and develop one main idea.

Paragraph Structure

2. A topic sentence states the main idea.
3. Supporting sentences explain or prove the topic sentence with specific details, facts, examples, or reasons.
4. A concluding sentence adds a strong ending to a paragraph.

Paragraph Development

5. Use the method of development most appropriate for your topic sentence.
6. Achieve unity by making sure all the supporting sentences relate to the topic sentence.
7. Achieve coherence by presenting ideas in logical order and by using transitions.

26

Expository Paragraphs

Paragraphs that explain are called *expository*. You have probably written many expository paragraphs—in a letter to a friend, a report for a club newsletter, or an answer to an essay test. The subjects of expository paragraphs range widely from simple, everyday things to the great puzzles of nature—from blue jeans to black holes in space. Whatever their subject, you can recognize expository paragraphs by remembering their purpose.

26a The purpose of an **expository paragraph** is to explain, to give directions, or to inform.

In the following expository paragraph, the writer's purpose is to explain a process.

The Birth of an Island

Millions of years ago, a volcano built a mountain on the floor of the Atlantic. In eruption after eruption it pushed up a great pile of volcanic rock, until it had accumulated a mass a hundred miles across at its base. Finally its cone emerged as an island with an area of about 200 square miles. Thousands of years passed, and thousands of thousands. Eventually the waves of the Atlantic reduced the cone to a shoal—all of it, that is, but a small fragment which remained above the water. This fragment we know as Bermuda. —RACHEL CARSON, *THE SEA AROUND US*

The purpose of the next expository paragraph is to give directions for handling orphaned baby mammals.

Orphans from the Wild

A very small baby that has no hair or whose eyes are not yet open may be picked up in your bare hands. Gently slide your fingers under the baby, scoop it up, and cradle it in your palms. Most babies, particularly very small ones, will enjoy the warmth of your hands. Adjust your fingers to fit snugly around the baby, so it can absorb the maximum warmth from your fingers, but not so snugly that it can't shift its position. The tiny, hairless baby will become quiet almost at once and will soon drop off to sleep.

—WILLIAM J. WEBER, *WILD ORPHAN BABIES*

The writer's purpose in the following paragraph is to provide the reader with information about the reasoning power of chimpanzees.

Food for Thought

Dr. Wolfgang Koehler did a great many experiments with chimpanzees in which he found that they were able to solve very difficult problems. In one experiment he hung some bananas from the ceiling of a cage. He then placed some boxes around the cage. The chimps stacked the boxes like blocks and got their bananas. Next he placed the bananas outside the cage and gave the chimps two sticks that were not long enough to reach. The chimps fitted the two sticks together and got their bananas. One animal, who could not reach a banana hanging from the ceiling of his cage, took the scientist by the hand, placed him just under the banana and climbed up on his shoulders. Apparently the animal was quite capable of reasoning a solution. It did not need to learn through trial and error.

—GLORIA KIRSHNER, *FROM INSTINCT TO INTELLIGENCE*

In this chapter you will learn the process of writing expository paragraphs.

PREWRITING

The first stage in the writing process is called *prewriting*. During this stage you generate ideas, allow your thoughts to take shape, and arrive at an organized plan for writing.

Your first goal during prewriting is to think of possible subjects. As you explore your interests and experiences, jot down all ideas that come to mind. Make lists or just write freely for a few minutes, letting your mind lead from one thought to the next. Your scattered thoughts will soon take the shape of clear ideas.

EXERCISE 1   Thinking of Subjects

Write each partial sentence and complete it with as many items as you can. Save your paper for Exercise 3.

1. Outside of school, I've learned how to . . .
2. My hobbies are . . .
3. The sports and games I most enjoy are . . .
4. The careers that interest me the most are . . .
5. My jobs around the house include . . .
6. The TV shows I like the most are about . . .
7. The people I admire most are . . .
8. Places I would like to visit are . . .
9. The things I've done to earn money are . . .
10. I've always wondered why . . .

Choosing a Subject

Once you have thought of several possible subjects, the next step is to choose one.

26b

> **Choosing an Expository Subject**
>
> 1. Choose a subject that interests you.
> 2. Choose a subject that will interest your audience.
> 3. Choose a subject you know enough about now or can learn enough about later to explain accurately.

Many explanations come from firsthand experience and observation. Others require research — reading books and magazines and talking with experts. Before choosing a subject, measure what you know about it. The following questions may help you decide if you know enough about your subject to write a complete paragraph.

- What do I already know about the subject?
- Do I know enough to explain it thoroughly to others?
- If not, what else do I need to know?
- Where can I find that information?

EXERCISE 2 Identifying Subjects That Need Research
Number your paper 1 to 10. Then decide which subjects you could write about from firsthand experience and which would need more research. Indicate your answer by writing *experience* or *research* after the proper number.

1. adjusting to high school
2. high schools in Europe
3. celebrating Independence Day
4. the rings of Saturn
5. ways to make friends

6. TV comedies
7. sharks
8. pets
9. favorite cousins
10. piloting a 747

EXERCISE 3 Choosing a Subject
Number your paper 1 to 5, leaving ten blank spaces between each number.

a. After each number, write a possible subject for an expository paragraph. You may want to use the ideas you wrote in Exercise 1.
b. On the lines after each subject, list what you know about each one.
c. Review the guidelines for choosing a subject on page 464. Then circle the subject that comes closest to following all three guidelines.

Limiting a Subject

Once you have chosen a subject, the next step is to limit it.

26c ▸ Limit your subject so that it can be adequately covered in one paragraph.

The following chart shows examples of general subjects that have been gradually limited.

GENERAL SUBJECT	MORE LIMITED	LIMITED SUBJECT
games	board games	chess
football	backs	running backs
sports	basketball	fouls
novels	*Great Expectations*	the character Pip
trees	sequoias	age of sequoias

After you have arrived at a limited subject, focus your thoughts by expressing the main idea in a phrase.

LIMITED SUBJECT	basketball fouls
FOCUS	why players sometimes commit fouls on purpose

EXERCISE 4 Limiting Subjects

Make three columns on your paper and label them <u>General Subject</u>, <u>More Limited</u>, and <u>Limited Subject</u>. Number the first column 1 to 10 and list the general subjects given. Then limit each subject by completing the other two columns.

EXAMPLE	Cars		
POSSIBLE ANSWER	<u>General Subject</u>	<u>More Limited</u>	<u>Limited Subject</u>
	cars	old cars	Ford Model T

1. music
2. bicycles
3. races
4. water sports
5. caves

6. airplanes
7. actors and actresses
8. the Olympics
9. fire fighting
10. electronic equipment

EXERCISE 5   Focusing Limited Subjects

Number your paper 1 to 5. Write five of your limited subjects from Exercise 4. Then write a phrase that focuses your
thoughts for each one.

EXAMPLE   Ford Model T
POSSIBLE ANSWER   why the Ford Model T was so popular

Listing Details

Once you have limited your subject, the next step is to list
details that will help you explain it. There are many kinds of
details that may be used to develop a paragraph. *(See pages
453–454.)* Expository paragraphs often contain facts, examples, incidents, definitions, comparisons and contrasts, or
steps. The choice depends on the purpose of the paragraph
and the kinds of questions a reader may have about the
subject.

26d   List **details** that suit the purpose of your paragraph and that
explain the subject clearly to the reader.

The focus of your subject often offers a clue to the kinds of
details you should use. In the following example, the focus
calls for facts.

LIMITED SUBJECT   the heart

FOCUS   how hard the human heart works

FACTS   • beats between 60 and 80 times per
minute
• pumps a little more than 5 quarts of
blood each minute
• in an average lifetime, beats 3 billion
times
• work done by heart over lifetime is
equivalent to lifting 70 pounds every
minute of your life

The focus of the following subject calls for examples.

LIMITED SUBJECT   UFO's

FOCUS   possible explanations of UFO's

EXAMPLES   • aircraft and weather balloons
• orbiting space satellites
• sunlight glowing on ice crystals in clouds
• hoaxes

Brainstorming.   One way to generate a list of details for an expository paragraph is to brainstorm. *Brainstorming* means writing down every idea that comes to mind when you think about your subject. The best way to begin is to make a list of questions your readers may have about your subject. Then brainstorm for details that answer those questions. Your list may include a combination of different kinds of details, such as facts and examples. List as many details as you can. You may not use all of them in your final paragraph, but make sure you have three to five good ones to use.

EXERCISE 6   Listing Details
Write each focused subject after the proper number on your paper. Then under each one, write a list of details that would help you explain the subject. Use the questions to help you brainstorm.

1. **FOCUSED SUBJECT**   school spirit at our school
   • How is school spirit shown at games?
   • How is school spirit shown by club members?
   • How do students show school spirit in the halls and in classes?
2. **FOCUSED SUBJECT**   the importance of self-confidence
   • How do you know a person has it?
   • How does a person without it behave?
   • How important is it?

3. **FOCUSED SUBJECT**   classes that tenth graders take
   - How many classes do they take?
   - Which ones are required?
   - What classes can they choose?
4. **FOCUSED SUBJECT**   the benefits of owning a pet
   - How is a pet a great friend?
   - How can a pet be a useful member of your family?
   - How can owning a pet teach you responsibility?
5. **FOCUSED SUBJECT**   how to get ready to study
   - Where do you go to study?
   - What furniture and atmosphere should your study area have?
   - What do you do first to prepare to study? second? third?
   - Why are the study areas and the steps of preparation important?

Writing Extra

Listing examples can also help you write a four-line poem. Start by thinking of a general subject. Make it the title of your poem. Next, think of three examples that illustrate that subject. Finally, think of one surprise example — one that does not quite follow the pattern. Read the following "example poems." Then try one or two poems of your own.

GENERAL SUBJECT	**Homes**
EXAMPLE	Eagles live in lofty nests,
EXAMPLE	Bats in lonely caves,
EXAMPLE	Salmon in cold northern streams,
SURPRISE EXAMPLE	People in memories.

GENERAL SUBJECT	**Musical Instruments**
EXAMPLE	Fluttering flutes,
EXAMPLE	Booming basses,
EXAMPLE	Clear-voiced clarinets,
SURPRISE EXAMPLE	A laughing child.

Arranging Details in Logical Order

For an explanation to be clear to a reader, ideas need to be organized in a logical, understandable way. When organizing your ideas for an expository paragraph, keep the following guidelines in mind.

26e

Organizing Details

1. Group related items together.
2. Arrange details in order of importance, interest, or degree.
3. For appropriate subjects, arrange details in chronological order or spatial order.

In following the second guideline, you may arrange your details in the order of *least to most* or *most to least*. In the following paragraph, the details are organized in order of importance.

Training a Seeing-Eye Dog

MAIN IDEA

Dogs who will aid the blind must be trained to overcome some basic fears. To learn how to keep calm in a crowd, the dogs are taken to school playgrounds when students are leaving school. The dogs are sharply corrected if they get excited in all the bustle. To overcome fear of loud noises, they must hold still while blanks are fired above their heads. Sometimes they are even trained on an airport runway. Especially important is overcoming fear of heights, for the day may come when a dog will have to lead its master down a fire-escape. A well-trained dog is more than a pair of eyes; it can also be a life-saver.

DETAILS IN ORDER OF LEAST TO MOST IMPORTANT

CONCLUDING SENTENCE

Some special subjects call for chronological or spatial order. *Chronological order* is time order. It places items in the order they happened. *Spatial order* arranges items according to where they are located. Examples of spatial

470

order are near to far, top to bottom, east to west, or the reverse of these. The following model paragraphs demonstrate the use of chronological and spatial order.

Cracking an Ancient Code

MAIN IDEA

Although the Rosetta Stone was discovered in 1799, the ancient Egyptian hieroglyphics written on it remained a mystery for twenty more years. The first to try cracking the code was Silvestre de Sacy. He managed to figure out that some signs referred to proper names, but the rest stumped him. He turned his work over to a Swedish expert, David Akerblad, who made

DETAILS IN TIME ORDER

a little more progress. Then Sir Thomas Young, an Englishman, set to work on the code. He discovered that some of the signs stood for sounds as well as ideas. The real honor of cracking the Rosetta code belongs to Jean François Champollion. After years of careful study, he had his first breakthrough in 1821. The puzzle pieces then began to fall swiftly into place. Others may have paved the way, but

CONCLUDING SENTENCE

Champollion deserves the credit for discovering a 1500-year-old secret.

A Formidable Mountain Barrier

MAIN IDEA

The Sierra Nevada is a chain of peaks 400 miles long, longer than any one range of the American Rockies. The range stretches from Tehachapi Pass in the south nearly to Lassen Peak in the north where the Sierra block disappears beneath sheets of younger volcanic

DETAILS IN SPATIAL ORDER

rocks. The Sierra's western flank rises gradually from one of the world's richest agricultural areas, the great Central Valley, while to the east the mountains rise in a magnificent abrupt escarpment to soar 7,000 to 10,000 feet above the arid basin of the Owens Valley. With not a

CONCLUDING SENTENCE

single river passing through the range, the Sierra forms a formidable mountain barrier.

— FRED BECKEY, *MOUNTAINS OF NORTH AMERICA*

471

After you have listed details that explain your subject, organize your list by putting the details in order of importance, chronological order, or spatial order. You will then be ready to begin writing your paragraph.

EXERCISE 7   Arranging Details in Logical Order
Write each subject. Then list the details in a logical order. Underneath each list, write the method you used to organize the details: *chronological order, spatial order,* or *order of importance, interest, or degree.*

1. **FOCUSED SUBJECT**   calories burned per hour
   DETAILS • roller skating — 330 per hour
      • cleaning your room — 70 per hour
      • running (10 mph) — 900 per hour
      • bicycling (5 mph) — 200 per hour
      • sitting and thinking — 5 per hour
      • touch football — 400 per hour
      • walking — 110 per hour
2. **FOCUSED SUBJECT**   fall holidays
   DETAILS • Veteran's Day, November 11
      • Thanksgiving, fourth Thursday of November
      • Halloween, October 31
3. **FOCUSED SUBJECT**   muscles helped by swimming front crawl
   DETAILS • leg muscles in kicking
      • arm and chest muscles in reaching
      • waist and lower back in side-to-side motion
      • neck in breathing motion
4. **FOCUSED SUBJECT**   places to see buffalo
   DETAILS • ranches — 100 to 300
      • zoos — 15 to 20 in fenced-off areas
      • Yellowstone National Park — thousands in wild
      • Wichita Mountains Wildlife Refuge — 650
      • National Bison Range — 350 buffalo in wild

5. **FOCUSED SUBJECT**   famous volcanic eruptions this century

   DETAILS   • Mt. Pelee—1902
   • Mt. St. Helens—1980
   • Mt. Agung—1963
   • Mt. Katmai—1912

EXERCISE 8   On Your Own

Write a plan for an expository paragraph using what you have learned about prewriting on pages 464–472. Follow the steps below. Then save your paper for later use.

a. Choose and limit a subject.
b. Write a phrase that indicates the focus.
c. List details that explain your focused subject.
d. Arrange the details in a logical order.

WRITING

After prewriting, you are ready for the next stage of the writing process: *writing the first draft.* Although the first draft does not need to be polished, it should contain all the elements of a paragraph. You learned in Chapter 25 that these elements are a topic sentence, supporting sentences, and a concluding sentence.

Writing a Topic Sentence

By the time you are ready to write a topic sentence, you already have some prewriting notes that include your focused subject and organized list of details. You can now use those notes to write a clear topic sentence. A topic sentence should express the main idea of your paragraph and bind together all the supporting details.

Suppose you had decided to write about whales. Your prewriting notes might look like this.

FOCUSED SUBJECT   spouts of the great whales
DETAILS   • different spouts for different whales
          • blue whale — tall and slender spout
          • gray whale — low and bushy
          • right whale — V-shaped, like a heart
          • sperm whale — spout blown forward at an angle

If you next try to express the main idea in one sentence, you might write the following.

Some whale spouts are low, while others are tall.

If you examine this sentence, however, you can see that it does not bind together all the details. It does not cover the V-shaped spout of the right whale or the angled spout of the sperm whale. A revised sentence does the job better.

Whalewatchers can tell one kind of great whale from another by the shape of its spout.

Use the following steps when writing a topic sentence.

26f

Steps for Writing a Topic Sentence

1. Look over your prewriting notes.
2. Express your main idea in one sentence.
3. Rewrite the topic sentence until it binds together all the supporting details.

EXERCISE 9   Writing a Topic Sentence
Number your paper 1 to 5. Read the following examples of prewriting notes for expository paragraphs. Then write a topic sentence for each example.

1. **FOCUSED SUBJECT**   people whose names became words
   DETAILS   • Earl of Sandwich   • George Ferris
                 • Samuel A. Maverick   • Levi Strauss

474

2. **FOCUSED SUBJECT**   danger of storm tides
   DETAILS   • occur with storms in low-lying areas
   • rise in water level is very sudden
   • no chance for escape
   • claim ¾ of lives lost in hurricanes
3. **FOCUSED SUBJECT**   things to do in national parks
   DETAILS   • camping   • hiking
   • canoeing   • observing wildlife
4. **FOCUSED SUBJECT**   agility of wild cats
   DETAILS   • can walk long distances and run very fast
   • cheetah can run at 70 mph; lion sometimes 60 mph
   • can jump high and far—as much as 30 feet
   • can swim very well
5. **FOCUSED SUBJECT**   equipment needed to pan for gold
   DETAILS   • garden spade for digging in stream bed
   • sturdy metal pan for stirring away dirt
   • tweezers to pick out gold pieces
   • pill bottle to store your findings

Writing the Body of an Expository Paragraph

When you are satisfied with your topic sentence, you can move on to the body of the paragraph. The *body* is made up of supporting sentences. You will use your list of supporting details to write the body of your paragraph. To change your organized list into the body, follow these steps.

26g ▶

Steps for Writing the Body

1. Write a complete sentence for each item on your list.
2. Combine sentences that seem to go together.
3. When necessary, add transitional words and phrases to help one sentence lead smoothly into the next. *(See page 480.)*

475

Notice how the notes below can be turned into complete sentences to form the body of a paragraph.

FOCUSED SUBJECT   human-powered flight
DETAILS   • centuries-long dream of humans to fly
           • failure of early attempts to attach wings to arms
           • twentieth century: sailplanes and gliders, carried by updrafts, launched by machines (catapults, motor vehicles, airplanes)
           • hang glider; people can launch themselves; like coasting of birds

Human-Powered Flight

TOPIC SENTENCE

For centuries men and women dreamed of being able to soar like birds. Many hopeful but impractical inventors tried to adapt human arms to flap like wings, often with tragic results. True soaring became possible in this century with sailplanes or gliders. These are carried by updrafts but are mechanically launched by catapults, motor vehicles, or airplanes. A later design, the hang glider, enabled people to glide and soar by launching themselves from hills. This is the nearest approach to the "coasting" flight of birds that human beings have achieved.

BODY

CONCLUDING SENTENCE

— DAVID WILSON, "HUMAN-POWERED FLIGHT"

EXERCISE 10   Writing the Body of an Expository Paragraph

Write the body of an expository paragraph using the following notes. Include the topic and concluding sentences on your paper.

TOPIC SENTENCE   Although dinosaurs were large in bulk, they were small in intelligence.

NOTES   • Brontosaurus — 70 feet long, 40 tons, brain the size of an apricot

- Tyrannosaurus—50 feet long, 10 tons, smaller brain than Brontosaurus
- Stegosaurus—10 tons, brain smallest of all (size of walnut); first to become extinct

CONCLUDING SENTENCE The limited brainpower of dinosaurs may partly explain why all these bulky creatures eventually became extinct.

Writing a Concluding Sentence

Many paragraphs within a longer piece of writing do not need a *concluding sentence.* Each paragraph moves smoothly into the next one. A paragraph that stands alone, however, often does not seem complete without a concluding sentence. *(See page 451.)*

To write a concluding sentence, read over the topic sentence and body of your paragraph. Then think of a sentence that will serve one or more of the following functions.

26h

Writing a Concluding Sentence

A concluding sentence may
- restate the main idea in different words.
- summarize the paragraph, picking up key ideas or terms.
- evaluate the details.
- add an insight that shows new understanding of the main idea.

The concluding sentence of "Human-Powered Flight" on page 476 evaluates the details of the paragraph. The writer might have concluded with any of the following concluding sentences.

Humans have long dreamed of flight and doubtless will seek new ways to make their dream come true. [restates main idea]

After the failures of the early inventors, gliders and hang gliders have allowed humans to mimic the flight of birds. [summarizes]

When you consider the obstacles to human flight, the persistent attempts of men and women to fly are really remarkable. [adds an insight]

EXERCISE 11 Writing Concluding Sentences
Write two possible concluding sentences for the following expository paragraph.

A Blast Felt 'Round the World

When the Volcano Krakatoa erupted in Indonesia more than a century ago, its effects were felt around the world. People thousands of miles away heard the noise. Within a short time, dust from the explosion was in both northern and southern skies, giving the sun and moon a blue-green color and creating spectacular sunsets. The dust encircling the earth blocked about ten percent of the sun's rays, so temperatures around the world were lower than average for the next three years.

EXERCISE 12 On Your Own
Look over your notes from Exercise 8. Then using what you have learned in this chapter about writing, turn them into the first draft of an expository paragraph. Save your draft for later use.

REVISING

The third stage of the writing process is *revising*. During this stage, writers improve their first drafts. As you revise, look at your paragraph with a fresh eye, as if you were a reader seeing it for the first time.

Checking for Unity

A paragraph has *unity* when all the other sentences in the paragraph support the topic sentence. *(See page 456.)* Because a paragraph with unity keeps the reader's attention on the main idea, it is easy to follow.

The following paragraph lacks unity. The sentences that stray off the subject are crossed out.

The Real McCoy

Elijah McCoy became famous as the inventor of an oiling system for machines. ~~Granville T. Woods was another black inventor.~~ In the 1870s, factory owners had to turn off all their machines before oiling them. McCoy's system, developed in 1872, allowed the machines to be oiled while they were still running, saving time and money for the factory owners. ~~McCoy also held patents for an "Ironing Table" and a "Lawn Sprinkler."~~ McCoy applied his system to steam engines, including those on locomotives, and to the air brakes on trains. His system was so much better than others that when people bought new machinery, they always asked, "Is this the real McCoy?" To this day, we use that expression to mean "the real thing."

26i ▶ Achieve **unity** in a paragraph by eliminating any sentences that stray from the main idea.

EXERCISE 13   Checking for Unity

Decide which three sentences in the following paragraph stray from the subject. Then write the three sentences on your paper.

Busy Nights

Sleeping is for rest, but parts of our body are very active when we dream. For centuries people have wondered about the meaning of dreams. In the dream state, our closed eyes dart around rapidly, following the action of our dream. Sleep expert Dr. Dement did many experiments to learn about our dreams. Our brain waves are also as active as when we are awake. Our breathing is sometimes faster, and our heart rate increases. If people are awakened each time they enter the dream state, they will make up for lost dream time the next night. Although our large muscles are limp and relaxed, our eyes, brains, and breathing systems get little rest when we dream.

Checking for Coherence

Coherence is the glue of the paragraph, the quality that makes each sentence seem connected to the one before and after it. *(See page 458.)* Following are several techniques for achieving coherence.

Transitions.   One of the steps in writing and revising the body of a paragraph is to add words and phrases that make one sentence lead smoothly into the next. These words and phrases are called *transitions*.

26j ▶   A **transition** is a word or phrase that shows how ideas, events, or descriptive details are related.

The following chart shows some common transitions and the types of relationships they point out.

Common Transitions			
Order of Importance	Chronological Order	Spatial Order	General
even more	after	above	also
finally	as soon as	ahead	besides
first	at first	behind	despite
more important	at last	below	for example
most	first, second	higher	however
one reason	later	inside	in addition
to begin with	meanwhile	outside	while

EXERCISE 14 **Recognizing Transitions**

List the transitions used in the following paragraph.

Days of Our Lives

Although the calendar we use today is the most accurate one yet devised, it has many irregularities. First of all, we have two different types of years: common years and leap years. Second, the number of days in each month varies. April and June, for example, have 30 days, while May and July have 31 and February 28 or 29. Finally, many holidays fall on a different day each year and cause considerable confusion. Despite its problems, however, the calendar we use today has been keeping time successfully for more than 400 years.

Other Techniques for Achieving Coherence. You learned in this chapter how to organize the details of your paragraph in a logical order. *(See page 470.)* Using a logical order helps your readers follow your thoughts. You can also give your paragraph coherence by occasionally repeating a key word or by replacing it with a pronoun, a synonym, or other alternative expression. As you read the following paragraph, notice the nouns and pronouns that refer to the key word *tree*.

Death of a Tree

For a great **tree** death comes as a gradual transformation. **Its** vitality ebbs slowly. Even when life has abandoned **it** entirely **it** remains a **majestic thing.** On some hilltop a dead **tree** may dominate the landscape for miles around. Alone among living things **it** retains **its** character and dignity after death. Plants wither; animals disintegrate. But a dead **tree** may be as arresting, as filled with personality, in death as **it** is in life. Even in **its** final moments, when the **massive trunk** lies prone and **it** has moldered into a ridge covered with mosses and fungi, **it** arrives at a fitting and noble end. **It** enriches and refreshes the earth. Later, as part of other green and growing things, **it** rises again. —EDWIN WAY TEALE, *DUNE BOY*

Following is a summary of the five techniques for achieving coherence.

26k ▶

Techniques for Achieving Coherence

1. Use transitional words and phrases.
2. Organize your ideas logically.
3. Occasionally repeat key words.
4. Use synonyms or alternative expressions in place of key words.
5. Use pronouns in place of key words.

EXERCISE 15   Checking for Coherence

The following paragraph is logically organized and uses transitions, but it still lacks coherence. Using techniques 3 through 5 above, revise the paragraph so the sentences are more tightly linked. Write the revised paragraph on your paper.

A Brilliant Wanderer

Of all the planets, Venus is the most noticeable. Venus shines so brightly that Venus sometimes casts a shadow. Venus has even been mistaken for an unidentified flying object. Venus also attracts attention because of the wandering path it follows. At times, Venus blazes high in the sky long after the sun has set. At other times, Venus appears to move closer to the sun and to set soon after the sun. For a short time, Venus is invisible to skywatchers. Later, however, Venus reappears as a morning star, rising before the sun. Venus's brightness and wandering behavior make Venus one of the most interesting planets to observe.

Using a Revision Checklist

In addition to checking your paragraph as a whole, always check your sentence structure and word choice. Use the following checklist to help you revise every expository paragraph you write.

> **Revision Checklist**
>
> **Checking Your Paragraph**
>   1. Do you have a clear topic sentence?
>   2. Does your paragraph have unity?
>   3. Does your paragraph have coherence? Did you use transitional words and phrases?
>   4. Do you have a strong concluding sentence?
>
> **Checking Your Sentences**
>   5. Do your sentences have variety?
>   6. Did you combine sentences that go together?
>   7. Did you avoid rambling sentences?
>   8. Did you trim away any unnecessary repetition?
>
> **Checking Your Words**
>   9. Did you choose specific words that have appropriate connotations?
>   10. Did you use descriptive words that bring your subject to life?

EXERCISE 16   On Your Own

Using the checklist above, revise the paragraph you wrote for Exercise 12. Ask a classmate to read your paragraph to be sure you have expressed your ideas clearly and logically. Save your paper for later use.

EDITING

The final stage in the writing process is *editing*. The purpose of editing is to polish your paper for readers. The following checklist will help you edit your work. You may want to use the proofreading symbols on page 617 to make corrections.

26m ▶

Editing Checklist

1. Are your sentences free of errors in grammar and usage?
2. Did you spell each word correctly?
3. Did you use capital letters where needed?
4. Did you punctuate sentences correctly?
5. Did you indent your paragraph?
6. Did you recopy your paragraph as needed?
7. Is your handwriting clear?
8. Are your margins even?

EXERCISE 17　On Your Own

Use the checklist above to edit the paragraph you revised in Exercise 16. Ask a classmate to look it over to see if you missed any error.

CHAPTER REVIEW

Using what you have learned about prewriting, writing, revising, and editing, write an expository paragraph on one of the following subjects or on one of your own. Use the Steps for Writing an Expository Paragraph on page 485 to guide you.

1. signs of the season
2. playing on a team
3. why you joined a club
4. the meaning of your name
5. equipment for gymnastics
6. robots
7. air traffic control
8. your favorite commercial on television
9. the mystery of the Bermuda Triangle
10. movies made from books

Steps for Writing

Expository Paragraphs

✓ **Prewriting**

1. Make a list of subjects and measure what you know about the ones that interest you the most. Then choose one subject. *(See pages 464–465.)*
2. Limit and focus your subject. *(See page 466.)*
3. Make a list of details. *(See pages 467–468.)*
4. Arrange your details in a logical order. *(See pages 470–472.)*

✓ **Writing**

5. Write a topic sentence. *(See pages 473–474.)*
6. Turn your list into the body of the paragraph. *(See pages 475–476.)*
7. Add a concluding sentence. *(See pages 477–478.)*

✓ **Revising**

8. Using the Revision Checklist, check paragraph structure, unity, coherence, sentences, and words. *(See page 483.)*

✓ **Editing**

9. Using the Editing Checklist, check your grammar, usage, spelling, mechanics, and neatness. *(See page 484.)*

27

Other Kinds
of Paragraphs

There are four main types of paragraphs, each with a special purpose. An *expository* paragraph explains, informs, or gives a set of directions. A *narrative* paragraph tells a real or imaginary story. A *descriptive* paragraph paints a vivid picture of a person, object, or scene. A *persuasive* paragraph expresses an opinion and tries to convince with reasons, facts, and examples. In Chapter 26 you learned how to write expository paragraphs. This chapter will show you how to write other kinds of paragraphs.

NARRATIVE PARAGRAPHS

Any time your purpose in writing is to tell what happened, you will be writing a narrative. You may write a story for the school newspaper about what happened at a state tournament. You may answer a test question by telling what happened at the Boston Tea Party. You may record in a diary the events of the day. All these are examples of narration.

486

A **narrative paragraph** tells a real or an imaginary story.

Structure of a Narrative Paragraph

Every good paragraph that stands alone has a topic sentence, supporting sentences, and a concluding sentence. *(See pages 445–452.)* In a narrative paragraph, each element performs a special purpose in the telling of a story.

Topic Sentence. The topic sentence in a narrative paragraph serves one of three purposes. It can make a general statement that tells what the story will be about, capture the reader's attention, or set the scene for the story.

GENERAL STATEMENT
On July 17, 1972, thirteen-year-old Karen Edwards became a hero.

CAPTURES ATTENTION
"They're drowning!" shouted an onlooker, frozen in fear.

SETS THE SCENE
It was a warm, sunny day, perfect for splashing around in the motel pool.

Supporting Sentences. The supporting sentences in a narrative paragraph tell the story event by event. Notice how the supporting sentences in the following paragraph, based on a true story, tell all the events in the order they happened.

Rescue!

TOPIC SENTENCE
For thirteen-year-old Karen Edwards, July 17, 1972, became a day to remember. She was resting on the side of a motel pool in Duncansville, Pennsylvania, when she saw a young boy struggling in the deep end. Then she saw the boy's father dive in after him and not come up.

SUPPORTING SENTENCES
While others stood by, Karen jumped in and towed the drowning boy to the side. Tired but not waiting to rest, she went back for the father, who was floating face down. As she dragged

CONCLUDING
SENTENCE

him to the side, he began struggling, his waving arms splashing water in Karen's eyes. Her chest heaving, she finally made it to the side of the pool, and in a few minutes father, son, and Karen were all well. Karen's quick thinking and heroic effort had saved two lives.

—L.B. TAYLOR, JR., *RESCUE!*

Like the rescue story, most stories are about some conflict or problem. The supporting sentences tell how the problem developed, what happened at its height, and how it was resolved. In the course of telling the story, the supporting sentences answer the questions *Who? What? Where? Why? When?* and *How?*

Concluding Sentence. The concluding sentence in a narrative paragraph is especially important if the topic sentence is an attention-getter or a scene-setter. A good concluding sentence either summarizes the story or makes a point about its meaning.

SUMMARIZES   Karen's quick thinking and heroic effort had saved two lives.

MAKES A
POINT   The onlookers who did nothing may have saved themselves from danger, but they will never know the feeling of a hero's pride.

The following chart summarizes the structure of a narrative paragraph.

27b

Structure of a Narrative Paragraph

1. The **topic sentence** makes a general statement about the story, captures attention, or sets the scene.
2. The **supporting sentences** tell the story, event by event, of how the problem developed, what happened at its height, and how it was resolved.
3. The **concluding sentence** summarizes the story or makes a point about its meaning.

EXERCISE 1   Writing Topic Sentences

Write a topic sentence for each of the following narrative subjects. The events that would make up the story could be real or imaginary.

1. going to the dentist and having a cavity drilled
2. witnessing the launching of a space shuttle
3. riding in an airplane for the first time
4. being lost
5. an argument with a friend that was later patched up
6. the proudest day of your life
7. a day something happened you never dreamed would happen
8. winning an athletic contest
9. a narrow escape from danger
10. a time you helped someone in need

Chronological Order and Transitions

Usually the most logical organization for a narrative paragraph is chronological order. In a paragraph organized chronologically, transitions show how events are related in time.

27c ▶ In **chronological order** (time order), events are arranged in the order in which they happened. **Transitions** show how the events are related in time.

The following narrative paragraph is organized chronologically. The transitions are in heavy type.

Thirst

TOPIC
SENTENCE

I never thought I would prefer a glass of water to birthday cake, but that's what happened when I had my tonsils out. It was **the morning before** my fourteenth birthday. I

MORNING

woke up in the recovery room thinking only of WATER. **Then** a nurse wheeled me to my room where my mother was waiting. She told us that

AFTERNOON

DINNERTIME

NEXT
MORNING

CONCLUDING
SENTENCE

all I could have was chipped ice, and definitely no water. **Immediately** I asked my mother for a cup of ice, but it melted so slowly that my thirst wasn't quenched. **Throughout the long afternoon** I dozed in thirsty misery, waking only to get more ice and see my mother patiently reading a book. **At dinnertime** my mother left for fifteen minutes, and I **finally** saw my chance to get a good gulp of water. The ice in the pitcher had melted, and **just as** I was pouring a glass of cold, wonderful water, a nurse came in and whisked it away. I was still miserable **the next morning until** I heard some voices singing "Happy Birthday" and saw my mom and the nurse enter my room. They had a big pitcher of water with a bright red ribbon around it. That water tasted better than any birthday cake before or since.

The following chart lists transitions commonly used in chronological writing.

Transitions for Chronological Order			
after	during	afterwards	immediately
before	at last	finally	after a while
later	at noon	just as	in December
next	first	meanwhile	last night
when	second	suddenly	the next day
while	until	on Monday	by evening
then	early	as soon as	throughout the day

EXERCISE 2   Using Chronological Order and Transitions
Make the following list of events into a narrative paragraph that uses chronological order and transitions. First, write the sentences in chronological order. Then go back and add transitions that show how the events are related. Underline each transition.

- teacher told me I should try for all-state choir
- wanted to wear my good-luck pin to tryouts but couldn't find it
- teacher rehearsed with me for two weeks to help get me ready
- got a letter in the mail a few days later saying I had made it
- ran downstairs to show my father
- heard something crack under my running feet
- looked down and saw my pin — smashed
- sang "The Star-Spangled Banner" at audition, wishing I had my pin
- miss the pin but glad to learn success doesn't depend on good-luck charm

Point of View

In a narrative paragraph, the person telling the story is called the *narrator*. The narrator can tell the story from one of two *points of view*. If the narrator participates in the story and uses such personal pronouns as *I, we, our,* and *us,* the story is called a *first person narrative*. If, however, the narrator stands back from the action and tells what happened to others, the story is called a *third person narrative*.

FIRST PERSON
In **my** younger and more vulnerable years, **my** father gave **me** some advice that **I**'ve been turning over in **my** mind ever since. — F. SCOTT FITZGERALD, *THE GREAT GATSBY*

THIRD PERSON
Just then the hyena stopped whimpering in the night and started to make a strange, human, almost crying sound. **The woman** heard it and stirred uneasily. **She** did not wake. — ERNEST HEMINGWAY, "THE SNOWS OF KILIMANJARO"

As you plan your narrative paragraph, decide which point of view would be better for your story.

27d ▶ If you are a character in the story, use a **first person point of view.** If your story is about what happened to others, use a **third person point of view.**

EXERCISE 3 Recognizing Point of View

Determine the point of view of each of the following excerpts. Indicate your answer by writing *first person* or *third person* next to the proper number on your paper.

1. The sled started with a bound, and they flew on through the dusk, gathering smoothness and speed as they went, with the hollow night opening out below them and the air singing by like an organ. — EDITH WHARTON, *ETHAN FROME*

2. Before Roger Chillingworth could answer, they heard the clear, wild laughter of a young child's voice, proceeding from the adjacent burial-ground. — NATHANIEL HAWTHORNE, *THE SCARLET LETTER*

3. There was no shame in his face. He ran like a rabbit. — STEPHEN CRANE, *THE RED BADGE OF COURAGE*

4. If that staid old house near the green at Richmond should ever come to be haunted when I am dead, it will be haunted, surely, by my ghost. — CHARLES DICKENS, *GREAT EXPECTATIONS*

5. I looked at him steadfastly. His face was leanly composed; his eyes dimly calm. — HERMAN MELVILLE, "BARTLEBY THE SCRIVENER"

6. She was shown into the breakfast-parlour, where all but Jane were assembled, and where her appearance created a great deal of surprise. — JANE AUSTEN, *PRIDE AND PREJUDICE*

7. I went back to the Devon School not long ago, and found it looking oddly newer than when I was a student there fifteen years before. — JOHN KNOWLES, *A SEPARATE PEACE*

8. In this manner we journeyed for about two hours, and the sun was setting when we entered a region infinitely more dreary than any yet seen. — EDGAR ALLAN POE, "HOP-FROG"

9. Happily the sunshine fell more warmly than usual on the lilac tufts the morning Eppie was married, for her dress was a very light one. — GEORGE ELIOT, *SILAS MARNER*

10. I dragged myself heavily through the warm, blue spring morning toward school, dressed like a carnival cowboy. — JAMES ALAN MCPHERSON, "WHY I LIKE COUNTRY MUSIC"

EXERCISE 4   On Your Own
To help you think of a good subject for a narrative paragraph, keep a journal for one week. Every evening, start your journal entry with the day, date, and following question: "What happened today that could make a good story?" Then list the events in chronological order. Save your entries for later use.

DESCRIPTIVE PARAGRAPHS

When your purpose in writing is to help a reader visualize an object, a scene, or a person, you are writing description. You might lose your gym bag and have to write a letter to the lost-and-found department describing it. On a literature test you might be asked to describe the appearance of a character in a book. You might want to describe the sights, sounds, and smells of a school fair in a letter to a friend. Using colorful words and careful organization can make your reader see, hear, smell, taste, and feel what you are describing.

27e A **descriptive paragraph** creates a vivid picture in words of a person, an object, or a scene.

Structure of a Descriptive Paragraph

In the following descriptive paragraph, the writer's purpose is to paint the picture of strangely-shaped desert trees.

Twisted Shapes

TOPIC SENTENCE: INTRODUCES SUBJECT

Beside the river was a grove of tall, naked cottonwoods . . . so large that they seemed to belong to a bygone age. They grew far apart, and their strange twisted shapes must have come about from the ceaseless winds that bent them to the east and scoured them with sand,

SUPPORTING SENTENCES: PAINT THE SCENE WITH SPECIFIC DETAILS

and from the fact that they lived with very little water, — the river was nearly dry here for most of the year. The trees rose out of the ground at a slant, and forty or fifty feet above the earth all these white, dry trunks changed their direction, grew back over their base line. . . . High up in the forks, or at the end of a preposterous length of twisted bough, would burst a faint bouquet of delicate green leaves. . . . The

CONCLUDING SENTENCE: SUMMARIZES IMPRESSION

grove looked like a winter wood of giant trees, with clusters of mistletoe growing among the bare boughs.

—WILLA CATHER, *DEATH COMES FOR THE ARCHBISHOP*

Notice that Cather's topic sentence suggests an overall impression of the grove, hinting that the cottonwoods make a strange sight. The supporting sentences call on the reader's imagination and senses to picture these trees, detail by detail. Adding up all the specific details, the reader can recreate a complete picture of the grove. The concluding sentence frames that picture, in this case by summarizing it in a simile that compares the grove to a wintertime forest with mistletoe.

The following chart summarizes the structure of a descriptive paragraph.

Structure of a Descriptive Paragraph

1. The **topic sentence** introduces the subject, often suggesting an overall impression of the subject.
2. The **supporting sentences** supply details that bring the picture to life.
3. The **concluding sentence** summarizes the overall impression of the subject.

EXERCISE 5   Writing Topic Sentences

For each of the following descriptive subjects, write two topic sentences. The first sentence should suggest a positive overall feeling about the subject. The second should suggest a negative overall impression.

EXAMPLE   an old house in the woods
POSITIVE   Nestled deep in the woods, with smoke
IMPRESSION   curling gracefully from the chimney, the old house was a welcome shelter for woodland travelers.
NEGATIVE   Hidden, as if abandoned, in a remote
IMPRESSION   part of the woods, the old house was as peculiar as its sole inhabitant.

1. a stray dog
2. nightfall on the beach
3. a city park on a summer afternoon
4. a person you meet for the first time
5. a car

Specific Details and Sensory Words

At the core of every good descriptive paragraph is one main impression. It can be scary, peaceful, barren, lush, frigid, warm, forbidding, or inviting. Whatever the overall impression is, it will come to life for readers only if the supporting details *show* rather than *tell*. You can show readers — make them see, hear, smell, and feel your impression of a subject — by using specific details and sensory words. Notice the details that appeal to the senses in the following paragraph.

Harbored for the Night

In the breeze-cooled cabin of the *Jodi-Lee,* daylight seems ages ago. Outside, the dark, cool waters splash in whispers against the hull in an ageless rhythm. Creaking ropes and mellow clangs of other boats blend in a harbor hush. The musty smell of wet wood is carried by the breeze. All around the harbor, the damp night air cools away the sunburns from the day. In the *Jodi-Lee,* the moon is a comforting nightlight.

The writer used the following specific details and sensory words to create an overall impression of the harbor.

SPECIFIC DETAILS	SENSORY WORDS
cabin of boat	breeze-cooled
water against hull	dark, cool, splash, whispers, rhythm
other boats	creaking, clangs, hush
wet wood	musty
night air, sunburns	damp, cools
moon	nightlight

The last sentence of the paragraph is a metaphor, comparing the moon to a nightlight. Metaphors and similes add richness to a descriptive paragraph by creating striking comparisons. *(See page 430.)*

27g ▸ Use **specific details, sensory words,** and **striking comparisons** to bring your description to life.

EXERCISE 6   Recognizing Specific Details and Sensory Words

Read the following paragraph. Then make two columns on your paper, labeling one *Specific Details* and the other *Sensory Words.* Use words from the paragraph to fill in both columns with at least five items.

By the time the fire had been reduced to smoldering ashes, it was already beginning to get light. The crowd of curious onlookers had mostly dispersed, and the remaining homeless had been swept away by local charity groups. The shrunken, black skeleton of the building looked defeated as it loomed over the awakening city and contrasted with the brightening sky. The dirty firemen collected near the still shiny engine and, after wiping the soot off their faces and hands, drove away. Finally all was silent, and the orange arms of the sun reached greedily, grabbing and pulling at invisible handholds in the pinkish sky.

—CYNTHIA GREEN, STUDENT WRITER

EXERCISE 7   Writing Sentences with Sensory Words
Reread the paragraph in Exercise 6. Then use your imagination to add to the description by doing the following.

1. Write two sentences describing the sounds you might hear in this scene. Underline the sensory words you use.
2. Write two sentences describing the smells that might go with this scene. Underline the sensory words.
3. Write two sentences for this scene that appeal to the sense of touch. Underline the sensory words.
4. Write a sentence in the paragraph that contains a metaphor.
5. Write two more comparisons, similes or metaphors, that could be added to this description.

Writing Extra————————————————

To discover the power of sensory words, try to describe an emotion in a poem that uses only sensory details. The following examples may give you some ideas.

Sympathy	Fear!
A firm clasp of hands,	Screeching brakes,
Voices in harmony,	Quickening footsteps,
Crackling logs glowing red,	Breaking glass,
Hot cocoa in mugs.	A siren before dawn.

Spatial Order and Transitions

Often the most natural way to organize a descriptive paragraph is to use spatial order. Transitions tell how details are related in space.

27h ▶ In **spatial order** details are arranged according to their location. **Transitions** make clear the spatial relationships of details.

The chart below shows several ways to organize details in spatial order and the transitions used with each.

Spatial Order	Transitions
near to far (or reverse)	north, south, east, west, beyond, around, in the distance, close by, farther, across, behind
top to bottom (or reverse)	higher, lower, above, below, at the top (bottom)
side to side	at the left (right), in the middle, next to, beside, at one end, at the other end, to the East (West, North, South)
inside to outside (or reverse)	within, in the center, on the outside

In the following paragraph, the details are arranged in the order of side to side. The transitions in heavy type show the location of each item in the scene.

The Dooryard

Depending on how you look at it, we live in a wildflower garden or a weed patch. Our dooryard extends **from** the big old barn **on one side to** the vegetable garden **on the other, from** the home pasture **in the back to** the country road and the riverbank **in front.** I keep the grass **around** the house mowed, in season, for a lawn. The garden has a fence only theoretically rabbit- and woodchuck-proof;

that fence is thickly twined with vines, and catbirds and cardinals nest there. Half a dozen old apple trees are huge bouquets, loud with bees, **in the backyard** each May.

— HAL BORLAND, *THE COUNTRYMAN'S FLOWERS*

EXERCISE 8 Identifying Types of Spatial Order
Identify the type of spatial order used in each paragraph.

1. A Writer's Study
The study was a catastrophe. The floor consisted of a neat layer of partially typed-on pages and, near the desk chair, books and journals opened flat. On the seat of the chair, in place of the writer, was an empty glass, resting in a bowl which had perhaps held strawberry ice cream. The desk lamp was on and lit the countless pages of the writer's work and assorted writing and erasing tools. The shelves above the desk held books positioned at every imaginable angle. The crown of the mess was the stack of old newspapers on top of the bookcase. The scene lacked only the cap of the writer who clearly had gone out for air.

2. New Bicycle
Luis's new bike was a beauty, so beautiful in fact that I forgot for a moment to envy him. The gracefully thin, white-walled front wheel was attached to the frame with two sparkling chrome wheel locks. The handlebar turned downward in the racing style and was wrapped in red tape that matched the fire red of the frame. The gear levers were chrome and were not far from the soft, leather seat. In the center of the rear wheel was the source of speed— the five black gears and the chrome derailleur. Proud and smug, Luis watched my long gaze, but I was too filled with awe to care.

3. London at Night
The view from the balcony of the Royal Festival Hall could have been photographed for a travel guide. The navy blue tinge of the night sky made a luminous backdrop for the stars. On the far side of the Thames River, seemingly just below the deep blue sky, several old buildings stood

like huge guards, positioned shoulder to shoulder to protect the river. An orangish light, which must have come from lights placed on the buildings' lawns, illuminated them. The river itself was black and untraveled. Tourist boats all were docked. Along the near riverbank, a lamp-lit, concrete walk was filled with people in fancy evening dress and a few teenagers in blue jeans. Further from the river on the near bank stood the modern performing arts complex from which others like myself enjoyed the view of London.

4. The Big Game

The most important game of the year was almost under way. José Magarolas of our team crouched at center court, waiting to jump against Tech's big man. Positioned so that the tips of their sneakers nearly touched the white arc of the jump circle, our forwards, Jimmy Jones and Don Fox, stood against Tech's forwards. All four pairs of eyes already looked up into the space where the ball would soon be tossed. Further outside the jump circle, behind one pair of forwards, Blake Roberts and a Tech guard of equal height readied themselves. Ken Wan, our captain, and Tech's other guard jogged to their positions at opposite ends of the court, still further outside the center circle. The lights of the scoreboard showed only "Home," "Visitor," "00 to 00." Leaping and shouting along the edges of the court, cheerleaders for both teams stirred the crowd. From every seat around the court, in a multitude of red and green hues, Central and Tech fans screamed their delight that the championship game was about to begin.

EXERCISE 9   On Your Own

Choose five subjects. Then list at least five sensory words that describe each one. Save your paper for later use.

1. a lemon
2. a fish
3. a beach
4. your bedroom
5. the school gym
6. your family's kitchen
7. your best friend
8. a freshly-baked loaf of bread
9. a subway station
10. a mountain view

PERSUASIVE PARAGRAPHS

The skills of persuasion are powerful. You can use them to write a letter demanding a refund if you have bought a faulty product. You can use them in school to defend or disagree with a viewpoint or an action reported in the news. You can use them to convince the student council to start a new club. Any time your purpose is to sway your readers to share your opinion, you are writing persuasion.

27i > A **persuasive paragraph** states an opinion and uses facts, examples, and reasons to convince readers.

Structure of a Persuasive Paragraph

Notice how each sentence functions in the following persuasive paragraph.

Save the Shuttle

TOPIC SENTENCE: OPINION
Despite the general shortage of government money, the benefits of the space shuttle are so great that the program should be expanded.

SUPPORTING SENTENCES: FACTS AND EXAMPLES
First, each shuttle craft can be reused many times to carry satellites into and out of orbit. These satellites can perform a wide range of services that help people on Earth. They can predict weather on land and sea and forecast crop production around the globe. They can also relay power and communication beams. Second, the shuttle can carry materials for important construction projects in space, such as a space station. Most important, the shuttle allows science and industry a convenient laboratory for testing new ideas in technology and

CONCLUDING SENTENCE: FINAL APPEAL
medicine. Although the development costs are high, money on the space shuttle is well-spent.

The following chart shows the function of each part of a persuasive paragraph.

501

27j

> ### Structure of a Persuasive Paragraph
>
> 1. The **topic sentence** states an opinion on a topic of interest.
> 2. The **supporting sentences** use facts, examples, and reasons to back up the opinion.
> 3. The **concluding sentence** makes a final appeal to readers.

EXERCISE 10 **Writing Topic Sentences**
Write a topic sentence for each subject for a persuasive paragraph. Each sentence should clearly state an opinion.

1. commercials on television
2. the quality of public transportation
3. the age when one can legally drive
4. the use of computers in schools
5. having or not having an awards ceremony
6. keeping animals in zoos
7. allowing students involved in athletics, music, or other activities to miss classes
8. field trips
9. working part-time after school
10. the procedure for electing class officers

Facts and Opinions

Often the opinion stated in a persuasive paragraph will be at odds with the reader's opinion. To win the reader over to your side, you must present a convincing argument. Facts and real-life examples are your most important tools. Since facts are statements that can be proved true, the reader cannot argue with them. If you try to back up your opinion with more opinions, however, your reader will probably go right on disagreeing with you.

Use **facts** and **examples** to convince your reader. Do not use **opinions** to support your argument.

502

EXERCISE 11   Recognizing Facts and Opinions
Number your paper 1 to 10. For each statement write *F* if it is a fact or *O* if it is an opinion.

1. Towns have had fire engines for more than 2,000 years.
2. The school paper should include an advice column.
3. Not all students want to go on to college.
4. Any American citizen who is at least 18 years old can vote.
5. People should limit TV viewing to six hours a week.
6. The legal age for driving should be raised to 18.
7. Schools need a computer terminal for each student.
8. Animals cannot live without sleep.
9. Touring bikes are better than racing bikes.
10. Solar power will be the main power source of the future.

EXERCISE 12   Revising a Persuasive Paragraph
The writer of the following paragraph has not supported his or her opinion as persuasively as possible. Revise the paragraph by eliminating the four supporting sentences that are opinions rather than statements of fact.

A Better, Later Day

There are many good reasons why school should start later in the morning. Most high schools begin the day some time between 7:30 A.M. and 8:30 A.M. Nobody, student or teacher, is fully awake at that hour. I know many students who say they have difficulty with the homework for their first-period class because they are never very alert at such an hour. A student I interviewed said he got a "D" in his first period class but a "C-plus" or better in all his other subjects. We will all get low grades in our first-period class if we are forced to come to school so early! Another drawback of beginning school early is that in winter students have to get out of bed and some days even travel to school when it is still dark. Also, some students who work after school do not get proper sleep because they have to do their homework late at night. Whether they work or not, high school students stay up late and then have to get up too early. Most adults arrive at work at 9:00 A.M. If students were allowed to arrive at school at that hour, student health, attention in class, and grades might improve.

Order of Importance and Transitions

The most common way to organize facts, examples, and reasons in a persuasive paragraph is in order of importance. Transitions are used to make the order clear.

271 ▶ In **order of importance,** supporting evidence is arranged in the order of least to most (or most to least) important. **Transitions** show the relationships between ideas.

Transitions for Order of Importance		
also	for this reason	moreover
another	furthermore	more important
besides	in addition	most important
finally	in the first place	similarly
first	likewise	to begin with

In the following persuasive paragraph, the opinion is supported with three reasons presented in order of least to most important. The transitions are in heavy type.

Saving Our History

Instead of tearing down old buildings, cities should restore them. **In the first place,** cities gain a sense of pride when neglected buildings are restored by skillful workers. **Even more important,** the value of property goes up. Seeing the rebuilt homes, other people want to buy and rebuild. **Most important,** restored buildings save a city's history and give people a sense of their roots. A salvaged city is a salvaged history.

EXERCISE 13   Using Transitions

In the following paragraph, the ideas are arranged in order of importance, but the transitions are missing. Using the chart on page 504, rewrite this paragraph to include transitions where needed.

Buckling Up

Drivers should always wear their seat belts. Buckling up is a reminder to drive carefully. With seat belts fastened, drivers are more aware of the potential danger of accidents. Drivers wearing seat belts set a good example for other passengers. Like ship captains, drivers are the authority figures and passengers will follow their lead. Wearing seat belts saves lives and reduces the chances of serious injury. The National Safety Council estimates that more than 14,000 lives in the United States could be saved each year if riders wore seat belts. A five-second buckle-up could mean the difference between life and death.

Persuasive Language

If your ideas are expressed in polite and reasonable language, they will probably be well received. If your language is emotional or insulting, on the other hand, readers will not take you or your evidence seriously. You want readers to feel that your opinion is based on reason, not bias.

27m ▶ Avoid words that are **loaded** with bias and emotion.

LOADED WORDS	People who walk their mutts unleashed are fools and bad neighbors.
	Driving a car in the city is really stupid.
POLITE REASONABLE WORDS	People who walk their dogs unleashed risk danger to their pets and damage to their neighbor's property.
	There are many good reasons for using public transportation rather than driving your car in the city.

EXERCISE 14 Using Reasonable Language

Rewrite each of the following sentences, replacing loaded words with polite and reasonable language.

1. People who ride bicycles without wearing a helmet should have their heads examined.
2. Powerboat operators in their stinkpots make life miserable for the true sailors who use only nature's own power to move their boats.
3. There are few things more noble, virtuous, and patriotic than exercising your right to vote.
4. The space program is a lousy rip-off of the poor people of this country who have to foot the bill.
5. Boxing rules and regulations should be updated to the twentieth century to prevent barbaric bloodshed.
6. Network television is altogether an incredible bore.
7. Slow country living is superior in every way to tense, busy city living.
8. Study hall classes are zoos and a pain which teachers and students shouldn't have to tolerate.
9. Running is far superior to any other sport.
10. Hockey is a horror show for sick spectators.

EXERCISE 15 On Your Own

Find ideas for a persuasive paragraph by completing the following sentence. Save your work for later use.

If I could change three things in my school, I would . . .

CHAPTER REVIEW

A. Write a narrative paragraph on one of the following subjects or one of your own. (You may want to use your work from Exercise 4 for ideas.) Follow the Steps for Writing a Paragraph on page 508 as a guide.

1. your first dance
2. trying a new sport for the first time

3. losing something important
4. winning a contest
5. an accident
6. taking care of your baby brother or sister
7. your first day in a new school
8. attending a concert
9. helping a friend
10. going on a field trip

B. Write a descriptive paragraph on one of the following subjects or one of your own. (You may want to use your work from Exercise 9.) Follow the Steps for Writing a Paragraph on page 508.

1. a friend (features and clothing on a specific day)
2. a specific car
3. a piece of sports equipment
4. your lunch (dinner or breakfast) on a particular day
5. a natural sight (mountain, waterfall, forest clearing)
6. a photograph or painting
7. a specific animal or insect
8. a hat
9. an interesting building
10. a specific chair or sofa

C. Write a persuasive paragraph on one of the following subjects or one of your own. (You may want to use your work from Exercise 15 for ideas.) Follow the Steps for Writing a Paragraph on page 508.

1. school dress code
2. a dangerous intersection
3. changes in the cafeteria menu
4. changes in the school bus schedule
5. physical education as a required subject
6. bicycle lanes
7. television news versus newspaper
8. student council
9. keeping cars out of certain areas in cities
10. vocational schools or training

Steps for Writing

Paragraphs

✓ **Prewriting**
1. Determine the purpose of your paragraph and consider your readers.
2. Make a list of subjects and choose one that interests you the most.
3. Limit your subject so that it can be covered in one paragraph.
4. Write down everything that comes to mind when you think about your subject.
5. Arrange your notes in a logical order, crossing out details you do not plan to use in the paragraph.

✓ **Writing**
6. Write a topic sentence suited to your purpose.
7. Use your prewriting notes to write the supporting sentences.
8. Add a concluding sentence.

✓ **Revising**
9. Does your paragraph have all the elements shown in the appropriate Checklist on page 509?
10. Does your paragraph have unity?
11. Does your paragraph have coherence?
12. Do your sentences have variety?
13. Did you avoid rambling sentences?
14. Did you use vivid words?

✓ **Editing**
15. Check for errors in grammar or usage.
16. Check spelling, capitalization, and punctuation.
17. Did you indent correctly? Are your margins even?
18. Is your handwriting clear?

Checklists for Revising

Paragraphs

✓ **Narrative Paragraphs**
1. Does your topic sentence make a general statement about the story, capture attention, or set the scene?
2. Do the supporting sentences tell the story event by event?
3. Did you use chronological order with appropriate transitions?
4. Is your point of view consistent and appropriate to the story?
5. Does your concluding sentence summarize the story or make a point about its meaning?

✓ **Descriptive Paragraphs**
1. Does your topic sentence make a general statement, suggesting an overall impression of the subject?
2. Do the supporting sentences supply details that bring the picture to life?
3. Did you use striking comparisons?
4. Did you use spatial order with transitions?
5. Does your concluding sentence summarize the overall impression?

✓ **Persuasive Paragraphs**
1. Does your topic sentence state an opinion about a topic of interest?
2. Do your supporting sentences use facts, examples, and reasons to back up the opinion?
3. Did you use order of importance with appropriate transitions?
4. Did you avoid loaded words?
5. Does your concluding sentence make a final appeal to your readers?

28

Essays

Every person sees the world through a unique pair of eyes. Writing an essay is one way to share your special vision — to show others what you see and think.

28a An **essay** is a composition of three or more paragraphs that presents and develops one main idea.

You will have many occasions to write essays in school. In a literature class you may write an essay about what a certain poem means to you. In a history class you may write an essay about the freedoms you enjoy because of the Bill of Rights. You may keep a nature notebook for biology class and write essays about the beauty and mysteries of the natural world. You can use the essay form to explain, describe, or persuade.

ESSAY STRUCTURE

In a simple paragraph, the basic elements are a topic sentence, supporting sentences, and a concluding sentence. In an essay, the basic elements are paragraphs, but they share the same functions as the sentences in a paragraph. Study the comparisons in the following chart.

Elements in a Paragraph	Elements in an Essay
topic sentence expresses the main idea	introductory paragraph includes a thesis statement expressing the main idea
body of supporting sentences	body of supporting paragraph(s)
concluding sentence	concluding paragraph

Notice the three main elements of an essay in the following example.

Cat Lovers, Dog Lovers

INTRODUCTION   One controversy in this highly controversial era is that between those who love only cats and those who love only dogs. "I love dogs, but I can't stand cats" is a statement I often hear; or

THESIS STATEMENT   "I hate dogs, but I adore cats." I stand firmly on my belief that both dogs and cats give richness to life, and both have been invaluable to humankind down the ages.

BODY   Historians agree that dogs moved into humans' orbit in primitive days when they helped hunt, warned of the approach of enemies, and fought off marauding wildlife. In return, bones and scraps were tossed to them, and they shared the warmth of the first fires. Gradually they became part of the family clan.

As for cats, it was cats who saved Egypt from starvation during a period when rats demolished the grain supplies. Cats were imported from Abyssinia and became so valuable that they moved into the palaces. At one time a man who injured a cat had his eyebrows shaved off. When the cats died, they were embalmed and were put in the tombs of the Pharaohs along with jewels, garments, and stores of food to help masters in their journey to the land of the gods. There was even a cat goddess, and a good

511

CONCLUSION

many bas-reliefs picture her.

So as far as service to humankind goes, I do not see why we should discriminate between dogs and cats. Both have walked the long roads of history with humankind. As for me, I do not feel a house is well-furnished without both dogs and cats, preferably at least two of each. I am sorry for people who limit their lives by excluding either. I was fortunate to grow up with kittens and puppies and wish every child could have that experience.

— GLADYS TABER, *COUNTRY CHRONICLE*

Introduction

Like the topic sentence in a paragraph, the *introduction* in an essay prepares the reader for what is to follow. In a short essay, the introduction can usually be handled in one paragraph. The introductory paragraph has three purposes.

28b

Introductory Paragraph

1. It captures the reader's interest.
2. It reveals the writer's personality.
3. It contains the thesis statement, the controlling idea of the essay.

The thesis statement can appear anywhere in the first paragraph. It usually has the strongest effect, however, when it is the first or last sentence of the introduction. Wherever it occurs, its purpose is the same.

28c

The **thesis statement** states the main idea and purpose of the essay.

EXERCISE 1 Recognizing Thesis Statements
Write the thesis statement from each of the following introductory paragraphs.

1.

The difference between "a place in the country" and a farm is chiefly a matter of livestock. It is in New England, anyway. You can own 200 acres, you can pick your own apples, you can buy a small tractor—and you're still just a suburbanite with an unusually large lot. But put one cow in your pasture, raise a couple of sheep, even buy a pig, and instantly your place becomes a farm.

—NOEL PERRIN, "RAISING SHEEP"

2.

Merely as an observer of natural phenomena, I am fascinated by my own personal appearance. This does not mean that I am *pleased* with it, mind you, or that I can even tolerate it. I simply have a morbid interest in it.

—ROBERT BENCHLEY, "MY FACE"

3.

Analysts have had their go at humor, and I have read some of this interpretive literature, but without being greatly instructed. Humor can be dissected, as a frog can, but the thing dies in the process and the innards are discouraging to any but the pure scientific mind.

—E.B. WHITE, "SOME REMARKS ON HUMOR"

4.

The name "Indian Summer" has no valid relationship to the Indians that I can discover. There was no such season on the Indian calendar, which reckoned time by the moon and not the weather. The moons were named for the weather or for the seasonal occupation, but I can find no Indian Summer moon.

—HAL BORLAND, *AN AMERICAN YEAR*

5.

Running is the sport of the people. If it is not the largest participant sport already in terms of numbers, it no doubt is in terms of time devoted to it. It requires little in the way of skills or money, and no particular body type or age or location. It doesn't discriminate. Even at competitive levels it thrives on friendship. Where has it been all this time?

—ROBERT E. BURGER, *JOGGER'S CATALOG*

EXERCISE 2 Identifying Purpose in Thesis Statements
Identify the purpose implied in each of the following thesis statements. Indicate your answer by writing *descriptive*, *expository*, or *persuasive*.

1. Everything about my grandfather shows how full of life he is.
2. Great athletes have been the subjects of many fine movies.
3. People should adopt pets from a shelter rather than go to an expensive breeder.
4. Even as a sapling, the tree in my backyard had a majestic quality.
5. All cars should be equipped with inflatable air bags to prevent injury.

Body

The paragraphs that make up the body of an essay elaborate on the main idea presented in the thesis statement. Although all of the paragraphs relate to the main idea, each is a complete paragraph with a topic sentence, supporting sentences, and a concluding sentence if necessary. Notice how each paragraph in the body of the following essay develops a different aspect of the main idea.

My Guitar and I

INTRODUCTORY PARAGRAPH   Life in a big family can be hectic. Someone is always playing with the dog, usually riling him up to a fever pitch of barking and jumping. Someone else is always watching television, and in the same room two people might be listening to two different radio stations. When I need an escape, I go into my room and play my guitar.

THESIS STATEMENT   I lose the rest of the world when I play the guitar, but I find myself.

TOPIC SENTENCE   One reason the escape always works for me is that for a change I am listening only to *my* sounds. However weak my voice might be as I

514

sing along, at least it is *my* voice. If I hit the wrong string with my right hand, at least it is *my* mistake. Despite the shaky singing and missed notes, the music sounds good to me, and the rest of the world seems far away.

TOPIC
SENTENCE
The escape also works because playing the guitar takes concentration. I have been playing for only six months, so I still need to think about where my fingers should go to make the chords and pluck the right strings. As I concentrate on the guitar, I am not even aware of the hubbub in other parts of the house.

TOPIC
SENTENCE
Maybe the most valuable part of the escape is the chance it gives me to express my feelings. The songs I play depend on my mood. Sometimes I play quiet love songs. At other times I play sad, lonely songs or loud and angry ones. After each one, I feel as if I have had a good long talk with an understanding friend.

CONCLUDING
PARAGRAPH
By the time I leave my room, the television does not seem so loud anymore, and the dog seems like the best dog in the world. When I rejoin the world I bring more of myself with me, but I am glad to know the guitar will be there for the next time.

In this essay, the subject is developed by examining three topics contained within it. Each topic has a paragraph of its own.

28d ▶ Each paragraph in the **body** of an essay supports the thesis statement by developing a topic contained within it.

EXERCISE 3 Listing Supporting Topics
Choose five of the following thesis statements. Then list three topics that could serve as the basis for supporting paragraphs in the body. Save your work for Exercise 4.

EXAMPLE Hobbies can lead to money-making ventures.
POSSIBLE Gardeners can sell their goods.
ANSWER Photographers can take pictures at weddings.
Musicians can perform at dances.

1. Going to the beach is my idea of a perfect outing.
2. Being a student is a full-time job.
3. There are three spots in my hometown that I love.
4. Each holiday has an important meaning.
5. Every part of the weekend has its own special feeling.
6. The older you get, the harder it is to break bad habits.
7. I want to be remembered for three accomplishments.
8. Three movies stand out from all others I have seen.
9. If I could be some other creature, I would like to be a wild mustang.
10. My birthday always means a day of delights.

Conclusion

The *concluding paragraph*, as the final word on a subject, should be as strong as the introduction.

28e ▶ The **concluding paragraph** completes the essay and reinforces the main idea.

The final sentence of the conclusion should make an especially strong statement. Sometimes this sentence is called a *clincher* because it securely fastens the meaning of the essay in a reader's mind.

In the following concluding paragraph, notice how the author brings a graceful end to his essay on why we can never conquer space. In the clincher he emphasizes how the great distances of space make travel impossible in one human lifespan.

When you are next outdoors on a summer night, turn your head toward the zenith. Almost vertically above you will be shining the brightest star of the northern skies — Vega of the Lyre. It is twenty-six years away at the speed of light, near enough the point of no return for us short-lived creatures. Past this blue-white beacon, fifty times as brilliant as our sun, we may send our minds and bodies, but never our hearts. For no people will ever turn homewards from beyond Vega, to greet again those they knew and loved. —ARTHUR C. CLARKE, "WE'LL NEVER CONQUER SPACE"

EXERCISE 4   Writing Clincher Sentences
Write a clincher that could be used with each of the five subjects you chose in Exercise 3.

EXERCISE 5   On Your Own
Many well-known writers use the essay to write humor. Use the library to find comic essays by James Thurber, Robert Benchley, or Jean Kerr.

PREWRITING

During the *prewriting* stage of the writing process, your mind should be free to roam your beliefs, interests, and experiences. Remember that an essay is your special view of a subject.

Choosing a Subject

As your mind ranges freely over your interests, knowledge, and experiences, jot down any ideas that could be developed in an essay. Thinking about the purposes of essays — to describe, explain, or persuade — may also bring ideas to mind. The following guide questions may help you.

Questions for Thinking of Subjects

• What object, scene, or person could I describe vividly?

• What special knowledge or interests do I have that I could explain to others?

• What opinions do I have about school or home life, or about people's lives in general?

517

After listing as many possible subjects as you can, the next step is to choose one. Use the following guidelines to help you make your choice.

28f ▶

Choosing an Essay Subject

1. Choose a subject that interests you.
2. Choose a subject that will interest your readers.
3. Choose a subject that you can develop adequately in three to six paragraphs.

EXERCISE 6   Thinking of Subjects for Essays
Write the following headings on your paper. Then list at least five ideas under each one. When you are finished, you will have at least 20 possible subjects for an essay. Save your work for later use.

1. Places I Have Visited
2. Likes and Dislikes
3. Prized Possessions
4. My Idols

EXERCISE 7   Choosing a Subject
Write one subject from each list in Exercise 6. Then put a check next to the one that comes closest to following the guidelines above. Save your work for later use.

Limiting a Subject

When you limit your subject, you make sure that it can be covered in the length of an essay. Even more important, you bring your subject into focus.

To begin the process of limiting your subject, decide whether your purpose will be to describe, explain, or persuade. Then think about your audience. Who are your readers and what do they know about your subject?

The final step in limiting a subject is to list possible *focus points* that would suit your purpose and audience. Suppose you had decided to describe the Anza-Borrego Desert which you visited last year. You might draw up the following list.

SUBJECT	Anza-Borrego Desert
PURPOSE	Description
AUDIENCE	People who have never been there
FOCUS POINTS	• location and size
	• plant life
	• animal life
	• desolation

Any one of the focus points would be a suitably limited subject for an essay. Use the following steps when limiting a subject.

28g

Steps for Limiting an Essay Subject

1. Determine the purpose of your essay.
2. Determine your audience.
3. List focus points that suit your purpose and audience.
4. Choose one focus point as your limited subject.

EXERCISE 8 Limiting a Subject

List four possible focus points for each subject.

1. **SUBJECT**   kites
   PURPOSE   expository
   AUDIENCE   people with little experience with kites

2. **SUBJECT**   field trips
   PURPOSE   persuasive
   AUDIENCE   teachers

3. **SUBJECT**   monster movies
   PURPOSE   persuasive
   AUDIENCE   enthusiastic fans of monster movies

4. **SUBJECT**   the neighborhood swimming pool
   PURPOSE   descriptive
   AUDIENCE   people who have never seen it

5. **SUBJECT**   the oldest person you know
   PURPOSE   descriptive
   AUDIENCE   people who do not know him or her

Writing Extra

You can write a poem by limiting a subject. Use a general subject for your title. Then for each line of the poem, write a more limited version of the subject—a more sharply focused point. Use the following examples to help you think of ideas of your own. Try one poem with sound effects.

Holidays (Yay!)
Patriotic holidays (sis-boom-bah!)
The day our country was born (waa!)
Things to do and things to see and things to
barbecue (mmm!)
The fireworks' final shower (ah!)

My World
All living things in the sea, sky, and land,
The animal kingdom proud,
Mammals, with warm blood and love for their young,
My dog Roland and me.

Listing Supporting Ideas

After limiting your subject, you next need to list ideas that will help you develop it. Use brainstorming to help you list supporting ideas.

28h **Brainstorming** means writing down everything that comes to mind when you think of your limited subject.

If you had decided to write on the desolation of the Anza-Borrego Desert, your brainstorming notes might look like this.

FOCUS POINT Desolation of Anza-Borrego Desert
- barren, sandy land
- no hum of life
- no cars passed by on road through desert

- twisted cacti
- imagination runs wild in such desolation — thinking the fizz of my soft drink was hiss of snake
- low, bushy, almost dead-looking desert grasses
- only bright colors were blue sky and green cacti
- stillness — we all talked very softly
- on other side of mountains, all was green and lush
- sandy, craggy hills
- sand was white and beige
- sun burning down on you

As you brainstorm for ideas, put them down in the order you think of them. Keep the flow of your ideas going; do not stop to evaluate each one. Write until you feel you have exhausted your subject.

EXERCISE 9 **Listing Supporting Ideas**
Brainstorm for ideas about each of the following limited subjects. List at least five supporting ideas for each one.

1. how to prepare yourself for going before an audience
2. the warmth of Thanksgiving
3. how to ruin a perfectly good day
4. why people should relax and have fun on weekends

Outlining

The final step before writing the first draft is to organize your ideas. A good way to do this is to outline them.

28i **Outline** your supporting ideas to show where each idea fits into the overall plan.

Grouping Supporting Ideas. Start the process of outlining by looking over your list of supporting ideas. Decide which ideas are related. Then group your ideas into two or more categories. For example, if you look for categories in the list of ideas about the desert on pages 520–521, you might come up with the following groupings.

DESOLATE SIGHTS	LACK OF SOUND
barren, sandy land	stillness
twisted cacti	no hum of life
lack of color except for sky and cacti	no whir of passing cars
sandy, craggy hills	whispered speech
desert grasses	
beige and white sand	

Each category will serve as a topic to be developed in the body of your essay. Notice that some of the ideas on pages 520–521 did not fit in either category. Those ideas should be saved for possible use in the introduction or conclusion of your essay.

EXERCISE 10   Finding Categories

Following each subject is a partial list of supporting ideas. Four of them can be grouped in one category. A fifth does not belong. Write a category that contains four of the items in each group. Then write the appropriate items below it.

1. SUBJECT   Places to visit in Chicago
   * Museum of Science and Industry
   * Art Institute
   * Museum of Natural History
   * Sears Tower, world's tallest building
   * DuSable Museum of African-American History
2. SUBJECT   Favorite pastimes
   * backgammon
   * Scrabble
   * watching old movies
   * Chinese checkers
   * Monopoly
3. SUBJECT   Observing the sky
   * Saturn
   * Venus
   * Mars
   * Jupiter
   * The Big Dipper

4. **SUBJECT**   The movie *The Wizard of Oz*
   - main character is Dorothy
   - Tin Man wants a heart
   - Lion wants courage
   - begins and ends in Kansas
   - Scarecrow wants a brain
5. **SUBJECT**   Places I'd like to see
   - China
   - Maine
   - Japan
   - Mexico
   - France

Organizing Your Ideas.   Once you have grouped your ideas the next step is to decide the order in which you will present them. The following chart shows some common ways to order items.

Types of Order	
SPATIAL ORDER	Items arranged in order of location (near to far, front to back, top to bottom, or the reverse of these)
CHRONOLOGICAL ORDER	Items arranged in order of time
ORDER OF IMPORTANCE	Items arranged in order of importance, interest, or degree (least to most, most to least, smallest to biggest, etc.)
DEVELOPMENTAL ORDER	Items of equal importance arranged in an order that will be logical to the reader

If you were to choose developmental order for the desert topics, you could begin your outline by assigning each main topic a Roman numeral.

   I. Desolate sights
   II. Lack of sound

Next list the supporting ideas in each category under the appropriate topic. If you have a fairly long list of points in a category, think of *subtopics* and organize your supporting points under them.

MAIN TOPIC	I. Desolate sights
SUBTOPIC	A. Features of landscape
SUPPORTING POINTS	1. Barren sandy land

I. Desolate sights
   A. Features of landscape
      1. Barren sandy land
      2. Sandy, craggy hills
      3. Twisted cacti
      4. Desert grasses
   B. Lack of color
      1. Beige and white sand
      2. Only bright colors in cacti and sky
II. Lack of sound
   A. No sound of natural life
   B. No sound of other human life
      1. No whir of cars
      2. Own voices in whispers

After you have finished your outline, use the following guidelines to check its form.

28j

Checking an Outline

1. Did you use Roman numerals for main topics?
2. Did you use capital letters for subtopics?
3. Did you use Arabic numerals for supporting points under subtopics?
4. If you include subtopics under main topics, do you have at least two?
5. If you include supporting points under subtopics, do you have at least two?
6. Did you indent as shown in the model above?
7. Did you capitalize the first word of each entry?

EXERCISE 11 Outlining

Copy the outline on page 525. Then complete it using the following unsorted entries.

CPR stands for Cardio-Pulmonary Resuscitation
when to use
all swimming strokes
four blows on the back first to try to remove caught item
how to hold and tow a person
for drowning victims
technique for reviving heart beat
YMCA pools
no air going in or out of victim's mouth
American Heart Association — 8-hour course

SUBJECT   Lifesaving Techniques

I.
   A. Required skills for aquatic lifesaving
     1.
     2.
     3. How to give mouth-to-mouth resuscitation
   B. Where to get certified
     1. Red Cross
     2. Boy Scouts
     3.
II. For choking victims
   A.
     1.
     2. If victim gives universal sign of choking — hand grasping throat
   B. What to do
     1.
     2. Then a tight squeezing thrust from behind around chest or abdomen
III. For victims of heart failure
   A. What CPR is
     1.
     2.
   B. Where to learn CPR
     1. Red Cross — 6-hour course
     2.

EXERCISE 12   On Your Own

Choose and limit a subject for an essay. (You may want to use a subject from Exercise 7.) Then brainstorm a list of supporting ideas and organize them into an outline. Review pages 517–524 to help you. Save your work for later use.

WRITING

The second stage of the writing process is *writing the first draft*. With a completed outline before you, writing the first draft is a matter of transforming the information in your outline into the sentences and paragraphs of your essay.

Writing the Thesis Statement

The outline you have completed is for the body of your essay. It does not include the introduction and conclusion. Begin your first draft by working on the thesis statement.

28k ▶

> **Steps for Writing A Thesis Statement**
>
> 1. Look over your outline.
> 2. Express your main idea in one sentence.
> 3. Revise your sentence until it covers all your supporting ideas and makes your purpose clear.

Study the problems in the following thesis statements about the Anza-Borrego Desert.

I am going to write about the desolation of the desert. [You want your reader to picture the desert, not you *writing* about the desert. Avoid such openings as *This paper will be about* or *In this paper I will.*]

The Anza-Borrego Desert is the hottest place I have ever visited. [The statement does not cover ideas about desolate sights and lack of sounds.]

Everyone should visit the Anza-Borrego Desert. [Your purpose is to describe, not to persuade.]

The following sentence meets all the requirements of a strong thesis statement.

In the Anza-Borrego Desert, every detail for miles around adds to the sense of desolation.

EXERCISE 13 Writing Thesis Statements
Each of the following items includes the main topics and subtopics from an outline. For each item write a thesis statement that would state the main idea of the essay and cover all the ideas listed as subtopics.

1. I. Uses of computers
       A. Can perform many tasks that save people time
       B. Can be used as teaching tools
   II. Limitations of computers
       A. Cannot think creatively
       B. Dependent on human programming and maintenance

2. I. Physical advantages of exercise
       A. Means of controlling weight
       B. Way to tone and condition muscles
   II. Psychological advantages of exercise
       A. Relieves tension and stress
       B. Provides a feeling of accomplishment

3. I. The city on Saturday morning
       A. Absence of people and cars hurrying to work
       B. Beauty of vacant streets
   II. The city at midday Saturday
       A. Shoppers
       B. Traffic jams and noise
  III. The city on Saturday night
       A. People elegantly dressed
       B. Popular spots: cinemas, music halls
       C. Glittering city lights

4.   I. Short Stories
         A. Are to the point and have punch
         B. Take less time to read
     II. Novels
         A. Get reader more involved with characters
         B. Create a world that reader enters for a while

5.   I. Movies based on novels
         A. *The Outsiders*
         B. *Ordinary People*
         C. *The Hobbit*
     II. Movies based on plays
         A. *Romeo and Juliet*
         B. *The Miracle Worker*
         C. *West Side Story*

Writing the Introduction

Besides containing the thesis statement, the introductory paragraph should also capture the reader's attention and reveal the writer's personality. To find ideas for the introductory paragraph, look over your prewriting notes. You may find that you did not include in your outline all the details you listed. Some of these might be suitable for the introduction. Notice how an idea that was left out of the outline about the desert can be worked into the introductory paragraph.

We approach the Anza-Borrego Desert in southern California from the west, driving through lush, velvety green mountains, forested and thriving with life. Suddenly, as we leave the mountains behind, the landscape takes on the character of a planet long ago deserted of all life. In the Anza-Borrego Desert, every detail for miles around adds to the sense of desolation.

The following suggestions may help you write an introductory paragraph.

281 ▶

Suggestions for Beginning an Essay

1. Begin with an incident that shows how you became interested in your subject.
2. Begin by giving some background information.
3. Begin with an example that catches the reader's attention.

EXERCISE 14   Analyzing Essay Beginnings

Read each introductory paragraph. Write the thesis statement. Then write *incident, background information,* or *example* to indicate which technique for beginning an essay was used.

1.

Last summer I was riding my bike down a deserted street that had old railroad tracks running down the middle. To make a left turn, I had to cross those tracks. I had done it a hundred times before, but that day in June my front tire caught in the groove of the track and down I went. I was lucky. Although I was badly bruised and in pain for a week afterward, I had broken no bones. Most important, I hadn't hit my head. As soon as I was well, I began doing some research on bicycle safety. I now firmly believe that no one should ride a bike without wearing a safety helmet.

2.

Tiger is fourteen years old. Although he is not as playful as when he was a pup, he still looks forward eagerly to his walks outside. He has been the pet of caring owners all his life, owners who feed him properly, protect him from disease with shots, and give him a loving home. With proper care, all dogs should be able to live a long life.

3.

The game of chess has three main stages, with obvious names. The first stage is called the *opening.* Then comes the *middle game,* and finally the *end game.* The middle game depends on the careful thought of each player, but the opening and end game often follow a set strategy. The best way to learn openings and end games is to study the strategies of the great masters.

Writing the Body

To write the first draft of the body of your essay, you need to accomplish two main goals.

28m Use the phrases in your outline to write complete, varied sentences with vivid words. Use transitions to connect your thoughts smoothly.

Using Your Outline. A good outline will do most of the work of writing the body for you. Follow the order of your outline and include all the points you have listed. Each Roman numeral represents one paragraph in the essay body. Use the phrase next to the Roman numeral as the basis for a topic sentence. Then use the subtopics and supporting points to develop the paragraph.

Connecting Your Thoughts. Whether you are linking sentences in a paragraph or paragraphs in an essay, you can use the following techniques for connecting your thoughts.

Ways to Connect Sentences and Paragraphs

1. Repeat a key word from an earlier sentence.
2. Use a synonym or alternative expression to refer to a key word or phrase used earlier.
3. Use a pronoun in place of a word used earlier.
4. Use transitional words and phrases such as *first, most important, however, next, for example,* and *similarly. (See pages 480, 490, 498, and 504 for lists of other transitions.)*

Notice how the ideas from the outline on page 524 can be shaped into the body of an essay. Words and phrases that make the essay flow smoothly are in heavy type.

INTRODUCTION

We approach the Anza-Borrego Desert in southern California **from the west,** driving through lush, velvety green mountains, forested and thriving with life. **Suddenly, as we leave the mountains behind,** the landscape takes on the character of a planet long ago deserted of all life.

THESIS STATEMENT

In the Anza-Borrego Desert, every detail for miles around adds to the sense of desolation.

FIRST PARAGRAPH IN BODY: ROMAN NUMERAL I IN OUTLINE

In such a setting, our eyes search in vain for a sign of the thriving life **on the other side of the mountains.** The barren, sandy land is mostly flat, **but** craggy hills, worn into strange shapes by the wind-driven sand, lurch **up from the desert floor** in scattered patterns. Cacti contorted into menacing human shapes cast gray shadows **over the sand and scraggly desert grasses.** Colors are faded; the sand is a dull beige or a bleached-out white. Only the leathery green of the cacti and the blue of the cloudless sky serve as reminders that the bright colors of life even exist.

SECOND PARAGRAPH IN BODY: ROMAN NUMERAL II IN OUTLINE

Not only is the sight of the desert desolate, **but also** sounds seem to exist only in some distant memory. There are no sounds of natural life, no calling birds or rustling leaves. There are **also** no sounds of human life, no whir of cars down the hot asphalt road that seems forgotten. So complete is the silence of the desolate area that we speak in the whispers of an unbelieving awe.

EXERCISE 15 Writing from an Outline

Using the following outline, write two paragraphs that could form the body of a short essay on Tips for Curing Insomnia. Use the guidelines on page 530 to be sure you have connected your sentences and paragraphs smoothly. Save your work for later use.

SUBJECT   Tips for Curing Insomnia

THESIS   By practicing a few simple habits, people who
STATEMENT   suffer from insomnia can get more sleep.

I. Things to do before going to bed
  A. Eating and drinking
    1. No big meals before bed
    2. If hungry, cheese or a hard-boiled egg
    3. Warm milk
  B. Clearing your mind
    1. Allowing no more than fifteen minutes to worry about a problem
    2. Setting the problem aside and reading
II. Things to do once you are in bed
  A. Counting, backwards or forwards
  B. Relaxing techniques
    1. Imagining each section of your body weighs ten tons
    2. Imagining yourself doing a tiring job

Writing the Conclusion

To think of ideas for a conclusion, refer once again to your prewriting list for ideas that you decided not to use in other parts of your essay. Remember that the final sentence, the clincher, should be especially strong. The following chart shows ways to end your essay.

28n

Ways to End an Essay

1. Summarize the essay or restate the thesis statement in new words.
2. Add an insight that shows a new or deeper understanding of the thesis statement.
3. Refer to ideas in the introduction to bring the essay full circle.
4. Appeal to the reader's emotions.

Notice how an idea left out of other parts of the essay about the desert has been used in the conclusion.

> As if to make up for the emptiness all around, the imagination fills with fears and threats. What seems to be the hiss of some venomous snake turns out to be the gentle fizz of a just-opened soft drink. What we thought was a permanently ruined car that would leave us stranded forever has cooled down and starts up easily. Not until we cross the mountains once again do our thoughts turn from snakes and sunstrokes to the everyday worries of ordinary life.

The final step in writing the first draft is to think of a title for your essay. Read over your whole composition. Look for phrases that suggest ideas for a title. Then make up a title that captures in a word or phrase the spirit of your essay.

28o A **title** should make your readers curious enough to want to read on.

EXERCISE 16   Writing an Introduction and a Conclusion
Write an introductory paragraph for the essay on Tips for Curing Insomnia in Exercise 15. Then write a short concluding paragraph that could complete the essay. Save your paper for Exercise 17.

EXERCISE 17   Writing Titles
Make a list of four possible titles for the essay about the desert. Then make a list of four possible titles for the essay you completed in Exercise 16.

EXERCISE 18   On Your Own
Using your outline from Exercise 12, write the first draft of a short essay. Think of a good title for your essay and write it at the top of your paper. Save your paper for later use.

REVISING

The third stage of the writing process is *revising*. In this stage, you check and improve your first draft. You may also add new thoughts or insights that would further develop your subject.

Checking for Unity and Coherence

Your main purpose in revising is to make your message as easy as possible for readers to understand.

28p ▶ Check your essay for **unity** and **coherence.**

If your essay has unity, your readers will not be distracted by paragraphs or sentences that wander off the point. If your essay has coherence, readers will understand your message because it is presented in a logical order.

Unity. As you revise your essay, check for unity on both the essay level and the paragraph level. On the essay level, check to make sure that every paragraph develops or supports the thesis statement. On the paragraph level, check to make sure that every sentence in a paragraph supports the topic sentence. Cross out any that stray from the point. *(See page 479.)*

Coherence. An essay has coherence if it is logically organized and if ideas are smoothly linked with transitions and other connecting techniques. Check the order of your ideas and determine if your transitions between paragraphs are clear. *(See page 530.)* Also examine each paragraph within the essay for well-ordered supporting sentences with clear transitions. *(See pages 480–482.)*

534

Revision Checklist

The following checklist will guide you step-by-step through the process of revising an essay.

Revision Checklist

Checking Your Essay
1. Do you have a strong introduction?
2. Does your thesis statement make your subject and purpose clear?
3. Does your essay have unity?
4. Does your essay have coherence?
5. Do you have a strong conclusion with a clincher?

Checking Your Paragraphs
6. Does each paragraph have a topic sentence?
7. Is each paragraph unified?
8. Is each paragraph coherent?

Checking Your Sentences and Words
9. Are your sentences varied?
10. Did you avoid rambling sentences and redundancy?
11. Did you use specific words?
12. Did you use figurative language and sensory words?

EXERCISE 19   On Your Own
Use the checklist above to revise the essay you wrote in Exercise 18. Save your paper for later use.

EDITING

The final stage of the writing process is *editing*. When you edit an essay, you groom it neatly for inspection by readers. Use the following checklist as a guide. You may use the proofreading symbols on page 617.

28r ▶

> **Editing Checklist**
> 1. Are your sentences free of errors in grammar and usage?
> 2. Did you spell each word correctly?
> 3. Did you use capital letters where needed?
> 4. Did you punctuate sentences correctly?
> 5. Did you indent each paragraph?
> 6. Did you use correct manuscript form? *(See pages 614– 616.)*
> 7. Is your handwriting clear?

EXERCISE 20   On Your Own
Use the checklist above to edit your essay from Exercise 19.

CHAPTER REVIEW

Write an essay on one of the following subjects or on one of your own. Use the steps on page 537 to guide you.

Subjects for a Descriptive Essay
1. a hospital
2. a baseball park
3. the school cafeteria
4. a creature from a science-fiction movie
5. your dog or cat

Subjects for an Expository Essay
6. high-school football rules
7. how household work is divided among your family
8. your favorite day of the week
9. the best (or worst) purchase you ever made
10. how to make a costume for a costume party

Subjects for a Persuasive Essay
11. males and females should take home economics
12. advice to a younger person on how to avoid a mistake
13. suggested changes for television programming
14. your opinions about freedom vs. rules
15. assembly programs at school

Steps for Writing

✓ **Prewriting**
1. Make a list of possible subjects and choose one. *(See pages 517–518.)*
2. Limit your subject by determining your purpose, audience, and focus point. *(See pages 518–519.)*
3. Brainstorm a list of supporting ideas. *(See pages 520–521.)*
4. Organize your list of ideas into an outline. *(See pages 521–524.)*

✓ **Writing**
5. Write a thesis statement. *(See pages 526–527.)*
6. Write an introduction that includes your thesis statement. *(See pages 528–529.)*
7. Use your outline to write the paragraphs in the body. *(See pages 530–531.)*
8. Use connecting devices to link your thoughts. *(See page 530.)*
9. Add a concluding paragraph. *(See pages 532–533.)*
10. Add a title. *(See page 533.)*

✓ **Revising**
11. Using the Revision Checklist, check your essay for structure, unity, coherence, well-developed paragraphs, and varied and lively sentences and words. *(See page 535.)*

✓ **Editing**
12. Using the Editing Checklist, check your grammar, spelling, mechanics, and manuscript form. *(See page 536.)*

29

Narratives

For centuries upon centuries, people have been held spellbound by a good story. They have listened or read intently, waiting eagerly to find out what happens next. Storytellers know that vivid characters facing and resolving a conflict are sure to create suspense.

29a A **narrative** is a well-developed story about characters resolving a conflict or problem.

If you have written a letter to your parents telling what happened your first day of camp, you have written a narrative account. If you have written a history paper telling the events that led to the Declaration of Independence, you have written a narrative. Any event out of the ordinary is a good source for a narrative.

FRAMEWORK OF A NARRATIVE

Stories generally proceed in a set rhythm. The beginning of a story is usually more slowly paced than the end. A slower pace gives readers a chance to get to know the narrator, setting, and characters. These elements form the framework of a story.

Narrator

The person who tells a story is called the *narrator*. Readers see the events of a story through the eyes, or *point of view,* of the narrator. The following chart describes some different points of view from which a story can be told.

Point of View	Type of Narrator
FIRST PERSON	Participant in the action; relates the events as he or she sees them; uses *I, we, us,* and *our*
THIRD PERSON OBJECTIVE	Does not participate in the action; relates the words and actions of the characters but not their thoughts or feelings
THIRD PERSON OMNISCIENT (ALL-KNOWING)	Does not participate in the action; relates the words and actions of the characters as well as their thoughts and feelings

Following are examples of different points of view.

FIRST PERSON **I** dove in after him, hoping to beat him to the island. **I** felt the splash of his huge arms striking the tepid blue water with machine-like precision.

THIRD PERSON OBJECTIVE **Jimmy** dove in after **Sonny,** trying to beat **him** to the island. **He** glanced at Sonny's huge arms striking the tepid blue water with machine-like precision. **Back at the cottage, Ted** prepared for the clam bake.

THIRD PERSON OMNISCIENT **Jimmy** dove in after **Sonny, hoping** to beat **him** to the island. **He thought** how Sonny's huge arms were like a machine striking the tepid blue water. **Back at the cottage, Ted** prepared for the clam bake, **checking off in his mind** the tasks **he** needed to accomplish by seven o'clock.

Notice that the third person objective narrator can relate two events happening simultaneously in two different places. The omniscient narrator can relate not only simultaneous events but also the characters' thoughts and feelings.

If you are writing a story about yourself, first person is probably the most natural point of view to use. If you are writing about a set of characters that does not include yourself, use third person objective or omniscient. Once you choose a point of view for your story, use it consistently throughout.

EXERCISE 1   Writing from Different Points of View
The following list contains the bare bones of a story that could be told in one paragraph. Write three versions of the story using a different point of view in each version.

Points of View
1. First person as Sherry
2. Third person objective
3. Third person omniscient

Events
- 14-year-old Sherry Marks home alone one evening
- falls asleep listening to radio
- her dog Silver's barking wakes her up at 10:30 P.M.
- Sherry tells him to hush; tries to go back to sleep
- Silver keeps barking; runs to back door
- Sherry puts on her shoes; Silver leads her to garage
- As they get closer, Sherry smells smoke and runs back to the house to call the fire department
- Parents arrive home at 11:00; fire already out
- Silver gets new rawhide bone as reward

EXERCISE 2   Writing from an Unusual Point of View
Some of the most imaginative narratives have been written from the point of view of an animal in the story. Experiment with this unusual point of view yourself by writing a fourth

version of the story in Exercise 1. For this version, imagine you are Silver and write a first person narrative from your canine point of view.

Setting

The setting of a story is the environment in which the action takes place. It is like the backdrop of scenery on a stage. A setting with carefully planned sensory details sets a mood. The mood of the setting often matches the thoughts and feelings of the main character. For example, if a character is confused or troubled, the setting might include a dense fog or a storm. When the character's problem is resolved, the sun might shine clearly or the night sky may be brilliant with stars.

29c ▶ Match the **setting** of your story to the characters' thoughts and feelings and to the mood you wish to create.

EXERCISE 3 Choosing Settings
Number your paper 1 to 5. Then write the letter of the setting best suited to each character.

Characters	Settings
1. a teenage girl who feels insignificant	a. a room with curtains drawn; drizzling rain outside
2. a boy who is sick	b. a bright, sunny day in June
3. an older woman who is looking back over her life with satisfaction	c. a busy downtown street corner
4. a boy who has just learned that he was voted most valuable baseball player	d. a night with dense fog
5. a detective who is trying to solve a confusing case	e. a porch facing a golden, summer sunset

Characters

In most stories, the focus is on one central character who has a problem or conflict. The other characters either help or hinder the main character in resolving the problem. The most interesting characters are those who seem lifelike and understandable. Use the following guidelines to create life-like characters.

29d

Ways to Reveal Character

1. Use sensory details to describe a character's appearance.
2. Reveal a character's thoughts and feelings through actions, dialogue, and description.
3. With an omniscient narrator, use narration to record thoughts and feelings.
4. Make dialogue sound as natural as real-life conversation.

In the following excerpt, notice how description is used to make the character seem true to life.

> He wore no hat, and his thick, iron-gray hair was brushed straight back from his forehead. It was so long that it bushed out behind his ears, and made him look like the old portraits I remembered in Virginia. He was tall and slender, and his thin shoulders stooped. . . . His eyes were melancholy, and were set back deep under his brow.
>
> —WILLA CATHER, *MY ANTONIA*

A character's thoughts and feelings may be revealed in a number of ways. A third person omniscient narrator relates the inner life of the characters along with the outer actions, as in the following excerpt.

> Aloo hastened her steps. She felt nervous and panicky.
>
> —GRACE OGOT, "THE EMPTY BASKET"

A first person or third person objective narrator can show a character's thoughts and feelings through actions, dialogue, and description.

ACTIONS	Ben rushed up the sidewalk like a scared cat.
DIALOGUE	Maria blurted out, "I won't wait any longer. I'm going to search for her myself!"
DESCRIPTION	When the officer was told the news, his face momentarily was blank as a chalkboard. Then the corners of his mouth and his chin became set. His eyes fixed on a spot over the soldier's shoulder.

EXERCISE 4 Writing Description

Choose one of the following characters and write a paragraph describing the character's appearance. Use sensory details, similes, and metaphors. *(See pages 495 and 430.)*

1. a miserly young man
2. a boy who lacks self-confidence
3. the neighborhood bully
4. a wise and loving grandmother

EXERCISE 5 Writing Dialogue

Write a dialogue of about ten lines between Cara Pham, a bossy girl, and Thang, her timid older brother. Cara wants Thang to see a movie with her, but Thang has already seen the movie Cara has chosen. The first two lines are provided for you. You may wish to review the rules for writing dialogue on pages 337–338.

"Thang, how 'bout seeing a movie tonight?" Cara asked in the sweet tone of voice Thang had come to dread.

"Uh, well, ah, I don't know. What did you have in mind?"

EXERCISE 6 Writing Narration

Write a paragraph for a narrative about Mike, a high school student. Reveal his thoughts and feelings as he combs the neighborhood looking for his lost house key. Use an omniscient third person narrator. A first sentence is provided.

Mike began to imagine all the horrible things that would happen if he didn't find his key.

EXERCISE 7　On Your Own

To help you think of ideas for stories, make a chart with the following headings. Then list as many ideas in each column as you can. Save your notes for later use.

Events in My Life   Unusual Settings   Interesting People

PLOT

The *plot* is the core of a story. It tells what happens to the characters in the given setting. The pace of the story quickens as the plot unfolds. The following chart shows the steps for developing a plot.

29e

Developing a Plot

1. Introduce the event or circumstance that triggers the action.

FROM WITHIN A CHARACTER	• decision to try something new • desire to change circumstances
FROM THE OUTSIDE WORLD	• receipt of letter or phone call • accident

2. Develop the conflict facing the main character.

CONFLICT WITH SELF	• struggle with conscience • struggle against old ways
CONFLICT WITH OTHERS	• family • friends • enemies
CONFLICT WITH NATURE	• storms • disease • fire

3. Conclude with the resolution of the conflict and the outcome.

OVERCOMING OBSTACLES	• gaining new wisdom • feeling at peace
FAILING TO OVERCOME	• accepting shortcomings • resolving to try again

Writing Extra

The limerick, a nonsense poem, contains many of the elements of a narrative. Study the following example and try to write a few of your own. Starter lines are provided.

CHARACTER	There once was a boy named Drew
TRIGGERING EVENT	who woke up one night in a zoo.
CONFLICT	"I'm a boy, not a ram,
RESOLUTION	so I'm going to scram!"
OUTCOME	And he fled without further ado.
	—ANONYMOUS
STARTER LINES	There once was a boy from Rangoon
	Who wanted to go to the moon . . .

A SAMPLE NARRATIVE

As you read the following narrative, look for all the elements you have learned about: narrator, setting, characters, and the steps in the unfolding of a plot.

A Day's Wait

SETTING, CHARACTERS, TRIGGERING EVENT

He came into the room to shut the windows while we were still in bed and I saw he looked ill. He was shivering, his face was white, and he walked slowly as though it ached to move.

"What's the matter, Schatz?"

"I've got a headache."

"You better go back to bed."

"No. I'm all right."

"You go to bed. I'll see you when I'm dressed."

FIRST PERSON POINT OF VIEW

But when I came downstairs he was dressed, sitting by the fire, looking a very sick and miserable boy of nine years. When I put my hand on his forehead I knew he had a fever.

"You go up to bed," I said, "you're sick."

"I'm all right," he said.

When the doctor came he took the boy's temperature.

CONFLICT

"What is it?" I asked him.

"One hundred and two."

Downstairs, the doctor left three different medicines in different colored capsules with instructions for giving them. One was to bring down the fever, another a purgative, the third to overcome an acid condition. The germs of influenza can only exist in an acid condition, he explained. He seemed to know all about influenza and said there was nothing to worry about if the fever did not go above one hundred and four degrees. This was a light epidemic of flu and there was no danger if you avoided pneumonia.

Back in the room I wrote the boy's temperature down and made a note of the time to give the various capsules.

"Do you want me to read to you?"

THOUGHT SHOWN THROUGH DESCRIPTION

"All right. If you want to," said the boy. His face was very white and there were dark areas under his eyes. He lay very still in the bed and seemed very detached from what was going on.

I read aloud from Howard Pyle's *Book of Pirates;* but I could see he was not following what I was reading.

"How do you feel, Schatz?" I asked him.

"Just the same, so far," he said.

THOUGHT SHOWN THROUGH ACTION

I sat at the foot of the bed and read to myself while I waited for it to be time to give another capsule. It would have been natural for him to go to sleep, but when I looked up he was looking at the foot of the bed, looking very strangely.

"Why don't you try to go to sleep? I'll wake you up for the medicine."

"I'd rather stay awake."

THOUGHT
SHOWN
THROUGH
DIALOGUE

After a while he said to me, "You don't have to stay in here with me Papa, if it bothers you."

"It doesn't bother me."

"No, I mean you don't have to stay if it's going to bother you."

I thought perhaps he was a little light-headed and giving him prescribed capsules at eleven o'clock I went out for a while.

It was a bright, cold day, the ground covered with a sleet that had frozen so that it seemed as if all the bare trees, the bushes, the cut brush and all the grass and the bare ground had been varnished with ice. I took the young Irish setter for a little walk up the road and along a frozen creek, but it was difficult to stand or walk on the glassy surface and the red dog slipped and slithered and I fell twice, hard, once dropping my gun and having it slide away over the ice.

We flushed a covey of quail under a high clay bank with overhanging brush and I killed two as they went out of sight over the top of the bank. Some of the covey lit in trees, but most of them scattered into brush piles and it was necessary to jump on the ice-coated mounds of brush several times before they would flush. Coming out while you were poised unsteadily on the icy, springy brush they made difficult shooting and I killed two, missed five, and started back pleased to have found a covey close to the house and happy there were so many left to find on another day.

At the house they said the boy had refused to let anyone come into the room.

"You can't come in," he said. "You mustn't get what I have."

SENSORY
DESCRIPTION

I went up to him and found him in exactly the position I had left him, white-faced, but with the tops of his cheeks flushed by the fever, staring still, as he had stared, at the foot of the bed.

I took his temperature.

"What is it?"

"Something like a hundred," I said. It was one hundred and two and four tenths.

"It was a hundred and two," he said.

"Who said so?"

"The doctor."

"Your temperature is all right," I said. "It's nothing to worry about."

"I don't worry," he said, "but I can't keep from thinking."

"Don't think," I said. "Just take it easy."

"I'm taking it easy," he said and looked straight ahead. He was evidently holding tight onto himself about something.

"Take this with water."

"Do you think it will do any good?"

"Of course it will."

I sat down and opened the *Pirate* book and commenced to read, but I could see he was not following, so I stopped.

HIGH POINT OF CONFLICT

"About what time do you think I'm going to die?" he asked.

"What?"

"About how long will it be before I die?"

"You aren't going to die. What's the matter with you?"

"Oh, yes, I am. I heard him say a hundred and two."

"People don't die with a fever of one hundred and two. That's a silly way to talk."

"I know they do. At school in France the boys told me you can't live with forty-four degrees. I've got a hundred and two."

He had been waiting to die all day, ever since nine o'clock in the morning.

"You poor Schatz," I said. "Poor old Schatz. It's like miles and kilometers. You

548

RESOLUTION   aren't going to die. That's a different thermometer. On that thermometer thirty-seven
is normal. On this kind it's ninety-eight."
  "Are you sure?"
  "Absolutely," I said. "It's like miles and
kilometers. You know, like how many kilometers we make when we do seventy miles in
the car?"
  "Oh," he said.

OUTCOME   But his gaze at the foot of the bed relaxed
slowly. The hold over himself relaxed too,
finally, and the next day it was very slack and
he cried very easily at little things that were
of no importance.   — ERNEST HEMINGWAY

EXERCISE 8 Thinking of Plots

Each of the following sentences can serve as an event that
triggers the action of a narrative. Write each one on your
paper. Then write one sentence describing a possible conflict, another sentence describing how the character might
try to resolve the conflict, and a final sentence that tells the
outcome.

1. A boy loses his wallet which contains money he had
   saved to buy his father a birthday present.
2. Some students have climbed a mountain but realize
   that it will be dark before they can get down it.
3. Someone you dislike shows up uninvited at your party.
4. An adopted child decides to find her natural parents.
5. Someone in your club insults you and you leave angrily.
6. A friend borrows money from you every day during
   lunch but never pays you back.
7. Your family wins the state lottery.
8. A girl takes the family car without permission and
   drives to a concert.
9. Even when your team is leading by a wide margin, your
   coach never puts you in the game.
10. A friend asks to copy your answers during a test.

EXERCISE 9   On Your Own

Using your notes from Exercise 7, sketch a plan for a story by filling in the following chart.

Narrator/point of view:
Setting:
Characters and brief descriptions:
Event triggering action:
Conflict:
Struggle to resolve conflict:
Outcome:

CHAPTER REVIEW

Write a short narrative of your own. You may use your notes from Exercise 9, the suggested subjects below, or any other idea you may have. Use the Steps for Writing a Narrative on page 551 to help you.

1. the day your pet ran away
2. how someone you met changed your life
3. the championship game
4. witnessing a pickpocket in action
5. being tricked
6. a difficult decision
7. trapped in a storm with no electrical power
8. overcoming fears (heights, snakes, close spaces)
9. overcoming a handicap with strength of will
10. crash landing on the planet Zarton
11. how you saved someone's life
12. a terrible babysitting experience
13. living on the moon
14. having a famous person for a brother or sister
15. camping in the woods

Steps for Writing

Narratives

✓ **Prewriting**
1. Drawing on your own experiences, make a list of interesting events, settings, and characters that could form the basis of a story.
2. Choose a subject from your list and determine the point of view best suited to it. *(See page 539.)*
3. Make a sketch that shows the basic elements of your story, like the one on *page 550.*

✓ **Writing**
4. Use the setting to create a mood appropriate for your story. *(See page 541.)*
5. Reveal characters through action, dialogue, description, and narration. *(See pages 542–543.)*
6. Unfold the plot in steps. *(See page 544.)*

✓ **Revising**
7. Is your point of view consistent? *(See page 539.)*
8. Does the setting match the characters' thoughts and feelings? *(See page 541.)* Did you use sensory descriptions?
9. Did you use natural-sounding dialogue?
10. Does your plot have an event that triggers the action, a conflict, a resolution, and an outcome? *(See page 544.)*
11. Did you add a title?

✓ **Editing**
12. Is your story free of errors in grammar and usage?
13. Did you punctuate and indent quotations correctly? *(See pages 330–338.)*
14. Did you spell and capitalize words correctly?
15. Is your handwriting clear? Are your margins even?

30

Reports

One good source of material for compositions is your own storehouse of experiences and knowledge. Another good source is the experience and knowledge of others, which you can learn about by doing research. When you write your research findings in a composition, you are writing a report. While an essay or a narrative can be based on personal experience, a report is based on facts taken from several sources.

30a   A **report** is a composition based on research drawn from books, periodicals, and interviews with experts.

Throughout high school you will be writing reports in many different classes. Outside of school, many jobs require the ability to do research and state your findings in a written report. Since the main purpose of reports is to convey information, you will be using the skills and techniques of expository writing. You will also be using your library skills to find the information for your report. Review Chapter 23 to help you find your way around the library easily.

EXERCISE 1 Identifying Subjects for Reports
Some of the following subjects are suitable for an essay or a narrative, while others are suitable for a report. Write only those subjects suitable for a report.

1. my trip to the west coast
2. the invention of the bicycle
3. how women won the right to vote
4. the day Mom came home with a new baby
5. the education and training necessary for becoming an astronaut
6. immigrants to the United States in the last five years
7. the inventions of Granville T. Woods
8. favorite places to go in the city
9. the time I tried out for the basketball team
10. the possibility of life on other planets

PREWRITING

Part of the challenge of writing a report is keeping track of bits and pieces of information from several different sources. Before doing anything else, gather the supplies you will need to organize your work. These include a folder with pockets, index cards, paper clips, and rubber bands. As your work proceeds, you will have a ready-made filing system for your research.

Choosing and Limiting a Subject

You can gather ideas for reports in a number of different ways. The following suggestions may help you start your search for a good subject.

Finding Ideas for Reports

1. Using the Dewey decimal system *(see pages 409–411)*, find your favorite section of the library. Then walk up and down the aisles, looking for titles that catch your eye.
2. Skim through a variety of magazines.
3. Skim through any volume of an encyclopedia.
4. Ask other people — family and friends — what they would like to know more about.

Keep a list of ideas for reports. When you have five to ten good possibilities, use the guidelines below to choose one.

30b

Choosing a Subject

1. Choose a subject you would like to know more about.
2. Choose a subject your readers might like to know more about.
3. Choose a subject that can be covered adequately in a short report.
4. Choose a subject on which there is likely to be sufficient information in the library.

Once you have chosen a subject, the next step is to limit it. One way to limit a subject is to break it down into its different parts or aspects. Suppose you had decided to write a report on the movie *The Wizard of Oz*. You might list the following aspects.

SUBJECT The Wizard of Oz

ASPECTS the story
the cast
the music
special effects

Once you have listed the various aspects of your subject you will be able to determine whether or not your subject is limited enough to be covered in a short report. To cover all the aspects listed for *The Wizard of Oz* subject would require a very long report. Any *one* of the four aspects would be a suitably limited subject for a short report.

30c Limit a subject for a report by listing aspects of the subject and selecting one aspect on which to report.

EXERCISE 2 Identifying Limited Subjects

Decide which of the following subjects are suitable for a short report and which are too large. Indicate your answer by writing *limited* or *too large* next to the proper number.

1. the history of Mexico
2. celebrations of Mexican Independence Day
3. horses
4. television
5. Superman: from comic strip to movie
6. World War II
7. how airplane wings bring about lift
8. the Apollo space mission
9. dancing
10. basic steps in square dancing

EXERCISE 3   Limiting a Subject

Beside the proper number on your paper, list at least three aspects of each of the following subjects. Then in each list underline one aspect that is suitably limited for a short report and that interests you.

EXAMPLE   football
POSSIBLE   history of the game
ANSWER   rules of the game
                popularity of the game
                great players
                economics of the game

1. robots
2. pop music
3. automobiles
4. fashion
5. earthquakes
6. water sports
7. musical instruments
8. national parks
9. movies
10. careers

Gathering Information

Before starting your library work, make a list of questions to focus your research. If you had decided to write on the limited subject of special effects in *The Wizard of Oz,* your pre-research questions might include the following.

- When was the movie made?
- Who did the special effects?
- What scenes used special effects?
- How were those effects achieved?
- How much did the effects cost?

Follow the steps listed below to gather the information needed to answer your questions.

30d

Steps for Gathering Information

1. Begin by consulting a general reference work such as an encyclopedia to get an overview of your subject and, often, a list of books with more information.
2. Use the subject cards in the card catalog to find more books on your subject. *(See page 413.)*
3. Consult *The Readers' Guide to Periodical Literature* to find magazine articles on your subject. *(See page 422.)*
4. Make a list of all your sources. For each source, record the author, title, copyright year, publisher's name and location, and call number.
5. Assign each source on your list a number that will identify it easily in your notes.

Following is how a list of sources on special effects in *The Wizard of Oz* might look. Each source has been assigned a number.

Books

Down the Yellow Brick Road, by Doug McClelland, 1976, Pyramid Books, New York 791.437 W792M ①

The Making of The Wizard of Oz, by Aljean Harmetz, 1977, Alfred A. Knopf, New York 791.437 W792H ②

Magazines

Newsweek, August 21, 1939, pp. 23–24 ③

Senior Scholastic, September 18, 1939, p. 32 ④

Good Housekeeping, August 1939, pp. 40+ ⑤

Newspapers

<u>New York Times</u>, February 5, 1939, Section IX, page 5,
   column 6   ⑥
<u>New York Times</u>, July 11, 1939, page 28, column 4   ⑦

EXERCISE 4   **Gathering Information**

Use the library to list four sources on each of the following subjects. At least one of the sources should be a magazine article. Follow all the Steps for Gathering Information on page 556, including steps 4 and 5.

1. pollution in Lake Erie
2. hot-air balloon races
3. Sally Ride, America's first woman in space
4. hang gliding
5. how the National Football League was formed

Taking Notes and Summarizing

As you begin to study your sources, refer often to your list of questions about your subject. The questions will help keep your thoughts and notes focused on your subject. Before writing any notes, skim your sources with the following question in mind: "Where in this source is the information I need for my report?"

Once you have located the relevant portion of a source, you are ready to take notes. Prepare your note cards by writing the identifying number of your source in the upper right-hand corner. Keep the following goals in mind as you read the source again and begin taking notes.

30e   The goals of **notetaking** are to summarize the main points in your own words and to record quotations that you might use in your report.

For any direct quotation you record, be certain that you copy the words exactly and enclose them in quotation marks. Also be sure to record the name of the person who made the statement and the page on which it appears.

The following information is from *The Making of The Wizard of Oz*, the second source on the list on page 556. The note card below shows how this information can be summarized and recorded.

> Basically, what Gillespie [the special effects director] knew about tornados in 1938 was that "we couldn't go to Kansas and wait for a tornado to come down and pick up a house." Everything beyond that was an experiment. "You don't quite know how to go about it, so you begin to think and wonder. I was a pilot for many years and had an airplane of my own. The wind sock they used in airports in the old days to show the direction of the wind has a shape a little bit like a tornado and the wind blows through it. I started from that. We cast a cone out of thin rubber. We were going to whirl the rubber cone and rotate it. But tornados are called twisters and the rubber cone didn't twist. So that was rather an expensive thing down the drain. We finally wound up by building a sort of giant wind sock out of muslin." The giant thirty-five-foot muslin tornado was — technically — a miniature.

Sample Note Card

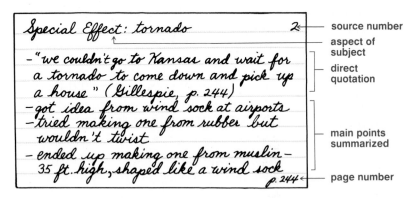

EXERCISE 5 Taking Notes and Summarizing

The following excerpt is from page 165 of the book *The Making of Star Trek — The Motion Picture*. It tells how Alex Weldon, special-effects supervisor, created one memorable effect. Assume that this source has been assigned the identifying number 3 and make a note card for it. Summarize the main points in your own words and record any quotation that might be used in a report. Use the card on page 558 as an example.

> Alex's most spectacular effects were prepared in connection with [the movie's] only exterior set built at Paramount—the planet Vulcan. Location scenes had already been shot at Yellowstone [National Park], and it was up to Alex to find a way of duplicating the swirling pools of milky steam with a look of authenticity. Both dry ice and steam machines were used. The steam given off by the combination of these two came bubbling to the surface by means of hidden tubing. To match the appearance of the swirling pools of water in the real Yellowstone, Alex used evaporated milk and white poster paint, mixed with water and poured into the set's pools. The pressure of the steam caused just the proper amount of movement in the pale white whirlpools and eddies duplicated in this enormous outdoor set.

Organizing Your Notes

When you finish taking notes from each source, sort your note cards into categories. For example, notes on the special effects in *The Wizard of Oz* might be sorted into the following categories, each containing cards from a number of different sources.

CATEGORY 1   general information: cost, year of release, quotation from reviews, name of special effects director
CATEGORY 2   the tornado
CATEGORY 3   the melting witch
CATEGORY 4   Glinda's arrival in the glass bubble
CATEGORY 5   the flying monkeys
CATEGORY 6   the horse-of-a-different-color
CATEGORY 7   the crystal ball

Since you have probably learned much about your subject from your research, your new knowledge should help you find even broader categories in which to group your notes. Study the following regroupings.

CATEGORY 1 general information
CATEGORY 2 hardest effect to achieve — tornado
CATEGORY 3 simple tricks — house being picked up, crystal ball, glass bubble, melting witch
CATEGORY 4 tricks that should have been simple but proved difficult — flying monkeys, horse-of-a-different-color

30f Group your notes into three or four main categories of information.

When you have narrowed your categories down to three or four main ones, clip all the note cards in each new category together and wrap the whole bundle with a rubber band. If some of your notes do not fit into any of the categories, clip them separately. You may be able to use them later for the introduction or conclusion.

EXERCISE 6 Making Categories

Number your paper 1 to 3. Think of three main categories into which the following tourist attractions in San Diego could be grouped. Write the categories next to the numbers. Then after each category, write the letters of the items that fit into the category.

Tourist Attractions in San Diego

a. Point Loma, historic lighthouse
b. Wild Animal Park
c. Old Town, historic mission
d. ocean
e. San Diego Zoo
f. nearby mountains

g. Sea World Aquarium
h. palm trees
i. nearby desert
j. *Star of India,* historic ship

Outlining

As a final step before writing the first draft, use the categories you created for your notes to form a rough outline. Each main category, or *main topic,* that you plan to cover in the body of the report will be assigned a Roman numeral. If you have a category of general information, you may wish to save that for the introduction.

Before assigning Roman numerals to your main topics, decide what type of order best suits your subject. *(See page 523.)* In longer papers such as reports, many writers use a variation of *order of importance,* putting the most interesting or dramatic information at the beginning *and* end of the paper where it will be best remembered by readers. Following is a rough outline, organized in this variation of order of importance.

OUTLINE FOR BODY

Special Effects in <u>The Wizard of Oz</u>
  I. Hardest effect: tornado
  II. Simple tricks
  III. Simple tricks made difficult by unexpected problems

When you are satisfied with the organization of your main topics, look over your note cards again and begin adding *subtopics* under the Roman numerals. Then add *supporting points* under the subtopics.

30g Convert your note-card categories into the main topics of an **outline.** Use your note cards to add subtopics, supporting points, and additional details to the outline.

Use the following example as a model for outlining your report.

Expanded Outline for Body of Report

MAIN TOPIC
SUBTOPIC
SUPPORTING POINTS

I. Hardest special effect: tornado
   A. First attempt
      1. Cost and materials
      2. Why it failed
   B. Attempt that succeeded
      1. Cost and materials
      2. How it moved
      3. Related effects

DETAILS FOR SUPPORTING POINT 3

         a. Storm clouds
         b. Dark sky
II. Simple tricks
   A. House being lifted by cyclone
   B. Crystal ball
   C. Glinda's glass bubble
III. Simple tricks made difficult by unexpected problems
   A. Flying monkeys
      1. Technique
      2. Problems
   B. Horse-of-a-different-color
      1. Technique
      2. Problems
         a. Objection of ASPCA
         b. Horses licking off Jell-O

EXERCISE 7 Outlining

Using the information about tourist attractions in San Diego in Exercise 6, write a simple outline. Show three main topics with at least three subtopics under each.

EXERCISE 8 On Your Own

Review what you have learned about prewriting on pages 553–562. Then choose and limit a subject for a report. Use the library to gather information, and take notes from each source on cards. Organize your information into categories and use those categories to write an outline of the body of your report. Save your notes for later use.

WRITING

Your main goal in writing the first draft is to use your outline and your notes to write a well-structured report. A strong thesis statement and clear organization will help your readers understand the information you gathered from your research.

Writing the Thesis Statement

The *thesis statement* in a report controls all the other parts of the composition. *(See page 512.)* Since it will serve as a guidepost for writing the rest of the report, it should be written first. Rework your thesis statement until it meets the following guidelines.

Writing a Thesis Statement

1. A thesis statement should make the main point of your report clear to the reader.
2. A thesis statement should be broad enough to include all the main topics listed in your outline.

The following thesis statement about *The Wizard of Oz* does not include all the main topics listed in the outline.

The hardest effect to achieve was the tornado.

A broader statement does the job better.

Although the effects in *The Wizard of Oz* looked magical, they were the result of hard work and creative problem-solving by the special effects director.

EXERCISE 9 Rewriting Thesis Statements
Rewrite each thesis statement to include all the main topics in the outline.

1. Some lifesaving techniques are simple enough for anyone to learn.
   I. Choking Maneuver
   II. Cardio-Pulmonary Resuscitation (CPR)
   III. Techniques only doctors should use
2. Dogs are beneficial to their masters' lives.
   I. Lower blood pressure in master
   II. Feeling of being needed
   III. Experiments letting jail prisoners have birds and hamsters
3. The Constitution of the United States grew out of the Articles of Confederation.
   I. Summary of Articles of Confederation
   II. Changes from Articles to Constitution
   III. Constitution as model for other countries
4. The DC-10 and the Boeing 747 jetliners are similar in many ways.
   I. Size and design
   II. Fuel economy
   III. Differences
5. Several American poets have expressed the true character of the country in their works.
   I. Mark Twain in the novel *Huckleberry Finn*
   II. Walt Whitman in the poem "I Hear America Singing"
   III. Carl Sandburg in the poem "Chicago"

Writing the First Draft

Like an essay, the report has three main parts: the introduction, the body, and the conclusion. In addition, a report often contains footnotes and a bibliography. The following chart shows the function of each part of a report.

Structure of a Report

TITLE	Suggests the subject of the report
INTRODUCTION	Captures reader's attention Provides necessary background information Contains thesis statement, usually at end
BODY	Supports thesis statement Each paragraph focuses on one main topic
CONCLUSION	Brings the report to a close, often by restating thesis in different words
FOOTNOTES	Give credit to other authors for words and ideas Appear at bottom of page
BIBLIOGRAPHY	Lists your sources of information Appears at end of paper

---

Notice how all the elements work together in the following sample report on special effects in *The Wizard of Oz.*

TITLE   The Wizardry of Oz

INTRODUCTION   The reviews were mixed when *The Wizard of Oz* was released in 1939 after two years and three million dollars were spent making it. Even the more negative reviews, however, had to admit that "the wizards of Hollywood have turned on their magic full force in the making of this film."[1] *Newsweek* cited the "realistically contrived cyclone."[2] Many others raved about the arrival of the Good Witch in a golden bubble, the skywriting of the Wicked Witch and her melting disappearance, the flying monkeys, talking trees, and

FOOTNOTES   [1] Rev. of <u>The Wizard of Oz,</u> dir. Victor Fleming, <u>Senior Scholastic,</u> 18 Sept. 1939, p. 32.
[2] "The Fabulous Land of Oz: Dream World Via Cyclonic Ride Re-created in Technicolor," <u>Newsweek,</u> 21 Aug. 1939, p. 23.

565

THESIS
STATEMENT

the horse-of-a-different-color. The creative special effects won the movie an Oscar in 1939 and left many people believing in the magic of Oz. Although the effects looked magical, they were the result of hard work and creative problem-solving by special effects director A. Arnold (Buddy) Gillespie.

FIRST
PARAGRAPH IN
BODY: ROMAN
NUMERAL I IN
OUTLINE

By far the most challenging effect was the twister. Gillespie knew he "couldn't go to Kansas and wait for a tornado to come down and pick up a house."[3] Instead he took his idea from the cone-shaped wind sock used at airports to indicate wind direction. First he made a similar cone out of rubber at a cost of $8,000, but the rubber did not twist properly and he had to start over. He finally built a 35-foot "miniature" cyclone out of muslin. He attached it to a machine that moved it along a track and forced a dusty substance through it to create the effect of a dust cloud. The $12,000 machine moved the muslin in a convincing twist. Meanwhile, a man perched above the machine made huge clouds of yellowish-black smoke from carbon and sulfur. In front of the cameras, glass panels covered with gray cotton lent a dark quality to the final film and hid the machinery making the effect.[4]

SECOND
PARAGRAPH IN
BODY: ROMAN
NUMERAL II IN
OUTLINE

A much simpler effect was the illusion that the cyclone lifted the house off the ground. A three-foot-high model of the house was first filmed falling onto a floor painted like the sky; later the film was simply reversed. The crystal ball in the witch's castle was simple too. It was made from a big empty bowl surrounding a screen. Film shot earlier was projected onto the screen, giving the illusion of a

FOOTNOTES

[3] Aljean Harmetz, The Making of The Wizard of Oz (New York: Alfred A. Knopf, 1977), p. 244.
[4] Harmetz, pp. 247–48.

face appearing inside the "crystal ball." Another simple effect was the glass bubble that appears to transport Glinda into Munchkinland. Gillespie's crew first filmed a silver ball, "just like a Christmas tree ornament, only bigger,"[5] by moving the camera closer and closer so the ball appeared to grow larger. Then, by layering one film on top of another, they added the scene of Munchkinland and finally Billie Burke, the actress playing Glinda.

THIRD PARAGRAPH IN BODY: ROMAN NUMERAL III IN OUTLINE

Some effects that should have been simple became complicated because of unexpected problems. The flying monkeys, for example, were suspended from a trolley with a total of 2,200 piano wires that moved them and their wings.[6] The wires, however, kept breaking, forcing the crew to repeat the scene time and again. Another problem was the horse-of-a-different-color, the creature that keeps changing hues. Six different white horses were used for the trick photography—each colored a different shade. The crew at first wanted to paint the horses, but the American Society for the Prevention of Cruelty to Animals protested. Finally the horses were "painted" with Jell-O, but the crew had to work fast because the horses kept licking it off![7]

CONCLUSION REFERS TO IDEA IN INTRODUCTION

The simplest trick of all was the melting disappearance of the Wicked Witch. "As for how I melted," said Margaret Hamilton, the actress playing the witch, "I went down through the floor on an elevator . . . leaving some fizzling dry ice and my floor length

FOOTNOTES

[5] Harmetz, pp. 254–55.

[6] Doug McClelland, <u>Down the Yellow Brick Road: The Making of The Wizard of Oz</u> (New York: Pyramid Books, 1976), p. 92.

[7] McClelland, pp. 92–3.

costume."[8] For nearly half a century that scene has brought cheers from believing audiences. Every detail of the movie, from the cyclonic ride to the electric tail wagger in the Cowardly Lion's costume,[9] was carefully planned by the creative and resourceful special effects team to make adoring audiences believe in the "magic" of Oz.

FOOTNOTES

[8] McClelland, pp. 96–7.
[9] Jane Hall, "The Wizard of Oz," <u>Good Housekeeping,</u> Aug. 1939, p. 137.

Bibliography

"The Fabulous Land of Oz: Dream World Via Cyclonic Ride Re-created in Technicolor." <u>Newsweek,</u> 21 Aug. 1939, p. 23, cols. 2–3; p. 24, col. 1.

Hall, Jane. "The Wizard of Oz." <u>Good Housekeeping,</u> Aug. 1939, pp. 40–1+.

Harmetz, Aljean. <u>The Making of The Wizard of Oz.</u> New York: Alfred A. Knopf, 1977.

Hoffmann, Frederick J. "L. Frank Baum." <u>World Book Encyclopedia.</u> 1983 ed.

McClelland, Doug. <u>Down the Yellow Brick Road: The Making of The Wizard of Oz.</u> New York: Pyramid Books, 1976.

Rev. of <u>The Wizard of Oz,</u> dir. Victor Fleming, <u>Senior Scholastic,</u> 18 Sept. 1939, p. 32.

Notice that when a first draft is written from an outline, transitions, such as *first, meanwhile,* and *another,* are used to link ideas and show how they are related. *(See pages 480, 490, 498, and 504.)*

EXERCISE 10   Recognizing Transitions
Make a list of all the transitional words and phrases used in the second paragraph of the body in the report on The Wizardry of Oz.

Using and Citing Sources

The law protects authors and publishers whose materials have been copyrighted. Using another person's words or ideas without proper credit is called *plagiarism,* a serious offense. You have already taken steps to avoid plagiarism by taking notes in your own words and recording the author, page, and exact words of any quotations you might use. Besides avoiding plagiarism, you should also work the source materials smoothly into your own writing.

Using Sources. The following tips may help you work quotations and borrowed ideas into your report.

30j

Tips for Using Sources

1. Use a quotation to finish a sentence you have started.

    Even the more negative reviews, however, had to admit that "the wizards of Hollywood have turned on their magic full force in the making of this film."

2. Quote a whole sentence. If you omit words from a quoted sentence, indicate the omission with ellipsis (. . .).

    "As for how I melted," said Margaret Hamilton, "I went down through the floor on an elevator . . . leaving some fizzling dry ice and my floor length costume."

3. Quote just a few words.

    Newsweek cited the "realistically contrived cyclone."

4. Paraphrase information from a source.

ORIGINAL SOURCE	"After a number of tests and experiments, they gave up the idea of animation, and we did it with miniature monkeys we cast and supported with 2,200 piano wires! The wires supported them on an overhead trolley and moved their wings up and down."
PARAPHRASE	The flying monkeys were suspended from a trolley with a total of 2,200 piano wires that moved them and their wings.

EXERCISE 11   Using Sources

Following is an explanation of how fires are classified. Read the paragraph. Then use it as a source for completing the assignments that follow it.

Classifying Fires

Fire fighters classify fires into four groups. Class A fires are those in which such things as wood or paper are burning. These fires can usually be put out with water. Class B fires are caused by burning liquids, such as gasoline, oil, or alcohol. Putting water on fires of this type usually results in spreading the fire, since the fuel will float on the water. Only carbon dioxide or dry chemical extinguishers can be safely used on these fires. The same type of chemicals can be used on Class C fires. These are caused by electrical wires or equipment that becomes overheated. If the current is still on, the person trying to put out the fire might be electrocuted if he put water onto the blaze. Class D fires are those rare ones in which certain metals burn. These special chemical fires require specific types of chemicals to put out the fires.

— WALTER R. BROWN, BILLYE W. CUTCHEN, AND NORMAN D. ANDERSON, *CATASTROPHES*

1. Write a sentence about Class B fires that ends with a quotation.
2. Write three sentences about Class C fires. One sentence should be a direct quotation from the source.
3. Write a sentence about fires that quotes just a few words from the source.
4. Write a sentence paraphrasing a part of the source.

Citing Sources.   Whenever you use source materials, such as in the chart on page 569, you must give credit to the authors. Notes that show the location of words or ideas in the original source are called *citations*. Footnotes are one type of citation. A very similar type is endnotes. Instead of identifying sources at the bottom, or foot, of the page, endnotes come at the end of the report, after the conclusion but before the bibliography. A third type of citation is parenthetical. These citations are contained in the report itself in parentheses following the borrowed material.

30k ▶ Cite the sources of information you include in your report by using **footnotes, endnotes,** or **parenthetical citations.**

Your teacher will tell you what type of citation to use.

If you use parenthetical citations, include enough information for a reader to find the original source.

PARENTHETICAL CITATION	<u>Newsweek</u> cited the "realistically contrived cyclone" (August 21, 1939, p. 23).

The form for footnotes and endnotes is the same. In the report itself, following the borrowed material, a number refers readers to the footnote or endnote with the same number. *(See the model report on pages 565–568.)* In the footnote or endnote, the reader will find three important pieces of information about the source: the author and title, publication information, and page number.

The following examples show the correct form for footnotes and endnotes.

Form for Footnotes

GENERAL REFERENCE WORKS	[1] Frederick J. Hoffman, "L. Frank Baum," <u>World Book Encyclopedia</u>, 1983 ed.
BOOKS WITH SINGLE AUTHOR	[2] Aljean Harmetz, <u>The Making of The Wizard of Oz</u> (New York: Alfred A. Knopf, 1977), p. 244.
BOOKS WITH MORE THAN ONE AUTHOR	[3] Joe Morella and Edward Epstein, <u>Judy: The Films and Career of Judy Garland</u> (New York: Citadel Press, 1969), p. 34.

ARTICLES IN
MAGAZINES

[4] Jane Hall, "The Wizard of Oz," <u>Good Housekeeping</u>, Aug. 1939, p. 137.

ARTICLES IN
NEWSPAPERS

[5] Frank S. Nugent, "A Critic's Adventure in Wonderland," <u>New York Times</u>, 5 Feb. 1939, Sec. 9, p. 5, col. 6.

For repeated references to a work already cited, you can use a shortened form of footnote.

REPEATED
REFERENCES

[8] Harmetz, p. 244.
[9] McClelland, p. 84.

Sources that have been cited in notes or mentioned in the report must also be listed in a bibliography.

30l ▶ A **bibliography** is an alphabetical list of sources used in a report, appearing at the end of the report.

The following examples show the correct form for bibliography entries. Notice that page numbers are given only for articles, not books.

Correct Form for Bibliography Entries

GENERAL
REFERENCE
WORKS

Hoffmann, Frederick J. "L. Frank Baum." <u>World Book Encyclopedia</u>, 1983 ed.

BOOKS WITH
SINGLE AUTHOR

Harmetz, Aljean. <u>The Making of The Wizard of Oz</u>. New York: Alfred A. Knopf, 1977.

BOOKS WITH
MORE THAN
ONE AUTHOR

Morella, Joe, and Edward Epstein. <u>Judy: The Films and Career of Judy Garland</u>. New York: Citadel Press, 1969.

ARTICLES IN
MAGAZINES

Hall, Jane. "The Wizard of Oz." <u>Good Housekeeping</u>, Aug. 1939, pp. 40–1+.

ARTICLES IN
NEWSPAPERS

Nugent, Frank S. "A Critic's Adventure in Wonderland." <u>New York Times</u>, 5 Feb. 1939, Sec. 9, p. 5, col. 1.

Always list sources alphabetically by the author's last name. Refer often to these examples and follow the order of information, the indentation, and the punctuation.

EXERCISE 12   Preparing Footnotes

The following footnotes for a report on Titan (Saturn's largest moon) do not have the correct form. Following the examples on pages 571–572, rewrite each note correctly.

¹ Randall Black. <u>Science Digest</u>, "Blimp on Titan," Aug. 1983, pp. 14–15.

² Ridpath, Ian, "The Living Void," <u>The Encyclopedia of Space Travel and Astronomy</u>, London: Octopus Books, 1979, p. 112.

³ Isaac Asimov, <u>The Universe: From Flat Earth to Quasar</u> Avon Books, New York, 1966, p. 38.

⁴ "Titan's Sea," <u>Omni</u>, by Patrick Moore Jul. 1983, p. 28.

⁵ New York Times: The Gases of Titan, June 21, 1983, Sec. 4, p. 2, col. 5

EXERCISE 13   Preparing a Bibliography

Following the examples on page 572, write a bibliography that includes all the sources in the notes in Exercise 12.

EXERCISE 14   On Your Own

Review what you have learned about writing the first draft of a report on pages 563–573. Use your outline from Exercise 8 to write a thesis statement, and the introduction, body, and conclusion of your report. Use and cite sources correctly. Save your work for later use.

Writing Extra

You can use your report-writing skills to write a poem. Try writing a short poem in which you report a fact or two that you learned from research. You may also include a quotation. The following poem about the completion of the first transcontinental rail line in 1869 may give you ideas.

The Golden Spike

For six years workers in two companies bent their backs,
Laying down the rails of the first transcontinental track.
When the race to the joining place in Utah was won,
Officials drove a golden spike to show all was done.

REVISING

Use the following checklist to revise the first draft of your report.

30m

Revision Checklist

Checking Your Report

1. Does your introduction contain a well-worded thesis statement?
2. Does the body support the thesis statement?
3. Did you use and cite sources correctly?
4. Did you use transitions?
5. Does your report have unity? *(See page 534.)*
6. Does your report have coherence? *(See page 534.)*
7. Does your conclusion add a strong ending?
8. Does your report have footnotes and a bibliography?
9. Does your report have a title?

Checking Your Paragraphs

10. Does each paragraph have a topic sentence?
11. Is each paragraph unified and coherent?
12. Does one paragraph lead smoothly into the next?

Checking Your Words and Sentences

13. Do your sentences have varied beginnings and varied lengths?
14. Did you avoid rambling sentences and fragments?
15. Did you avoid redundancy?
16. Did you use specific words?

EXERCISE 15 On Your Own

Using the Checklist on page 574, revise the report you wrote for Exercise 14. Save your paper for editing later.

EDITING

Editing is especially important when your composition is a report. Using and citing sources correctly requires special care. Make sure you can answer "yes" to all of the following questions. You may use the proofreading symbols on page 617 to edit.

30n

Editing Checklist

1. Did you check each sentence for errors in grammar and usage?
2. Did you spell each word correctly?
3. Did you capitalize correctly?
4. Did you punctuate correctly?
5. If you quoted a source, did you use the exact words, just as the author wrote them?
6. Did you place quoted material in quotation marks?
7. Did you give credit in footnotes to all sources from which you borrowed material?
8. Does your footnote form match that in the models on pages 571–572?
9. Are your footnotes numbered consecutively?
10. Does your bibliography form match the models on page 572?
11. Did you indent each paragraph?
12. Did you use correct manuscript form? *(See pages 614–616.)*
13. Is your handwriting clear?

EXERCISE 16 On Your Own

Edit your report from Exercise 15 by using the Checklist above.

CHAPTER REVIEW

Using what you have learned about prewriting, writing, revising, and editing, write a report on one of the following subjects or on one of your own. Use the Steps for Writing a Report on page 577 as a guide.

1. rodeos
2. mummies
3. the asteroid belt
4. the poetry of Lewis Carroll
5. the ocean floor
6. how fireflies are used in science
7. navigating by the stars
8. the air cushion vehicle (Hovercraft)
9. cars of the future
10. misconceptions about gorillas
11. behind the scenes at a broadway show
12. the underground railroad
13. the history of television
14. the history of the piano (or other instrument)
15. kabuki theater
16. country and western music
17. nutrition
18. soccer
19. solar energy
20. whale migration
21. the films of Walt Disney
22. the history of Williamsburg, Virginia
23. uses of laser
24. calligraphy
25. the history of jazz
26. white-water rafting
27. the paintings of Georgia O'Keeffe
28. noise pollution
29. weight training
30. deep-sea fishing

Steps for Writing

Reports

✓ **Prewriting**
1. Make a list of possible subjects and choose one to report on. *(See pages 553–554.)*
2. Limit your subject. *(See page 554.)*
3. Gather information from general reference books and other books, magazines, and newspapers. *(See pages 555–557.)*
4. Take notes on notecards. *(See pages 557–558.)*
5. Organize your notes into categories. *(See pages 559–560.)*
6. Use your categories and notes to help you outline the body of your report. *(See pages 561–562.)*

✓ **Writing**
7. Write a thesis statement. *(See page 563.)*
8. Write an introduction, body, and conclusion. *(See pages 564–565.)*
9. Avoid plagiarism by using and citing sources carefully. *(See pages 569–573.)*
10. Prepare footnotes and a bibliography. *(See pages 571–573.)*
11. Add a title.

✓ **Revising**
12. Using the Revision Checklist, check your report for structure, well-developed paragraphs, unity, coherence, emphasis, and varied and lively sentences and words. *(See page 574.)*

✓ **Editing**
13. Using the Editing Checklist, check your grammar, spelling, mechanics, manuscript form, and footnote and bibliography form. *(See page 575.)*

31

Letters

When you write a letter, you have a special purpose in mind. You know why you are writing and who will be reading your letter. Whether you are inviting a friend to a party, ordering something from a catalog, or registering a complaint to a company, you can shape your letter to suit your purpose and the receiver. In this chapter, you will learn the correct form for different types of letters.

FRIENDLY LETTERS

Some friendly letters are written as part of a regular correspondence between friends and relatives to share news and keep in touch. Other friendly letters serve such special purposes as accepting or declining invitations, expressing congratulations or sorrow, or thanking someone for a thoughtful gift. Whatever their purpose, friendly letters have five main parts.

31a ▶ The parts of a friendly letter are a **heading, salutation, body, closing,** and **signature.**

HEADING	The heading includes your full address with ZIP code. Write out the name of your state or use the abbreviation. *(See page 584 for a full listing of state abbreviations.)* Always include the date after your address.
SALUTATION	The salutation is your friendly greeting and is followed by a comma. Capitalize the first word and any proper nouns.
BODY	In the body of the letter, include your conversational message. Indent the first word in each paragraph.
CLOSING	End your letter with a brief, personal closing, followed by a comma. Capitalize the first word of the closing.
SIGNATURE	Your signature should be handwritten below the closing.

Correct Form for a Friendly Letter

> heading 2403 Marshall Road
> Leander, KY 41228
> November 16, 1986
> salutation
> Dear Aunt Florence,
> Thank you for the beautiful ski sweater – it's exactly what I wanted. I know how much effort went into making it, and I appreciate your thoughtfulness.   body
> When we go visiting next month, I'll be sure to wear it and show it off to all my friends. Thank you again for the lovely gift.
>
> closing Love,
> signature Andrea

NOTE: The envelope for a friendly letter may be handwritten. It should contain the same information as that on the envelope for a business letter. *(See pages 583–584.)* Be sure both addresses are clear and complete.

EXERCISE 1   Writing a Friendly Letter
Choose one of the following purposes for writing a friendly letter. Write the letter to a friend or relative. Make sure that your completed letter uses the correct form.

1. inviting someone to a surprise party
2. congratulating someone on becoming a cheerleader
3. thanking someone for a weekend visit
4. expressing sympathy for someone who broke a leg
5. declining an invitation to a Halloween party

EXERCISE 2   On Your Own
Write a letter to a friend or relative telling about the things that are going on in your life. To encourage an answer, end with questions to the person who will receive the letter.

Writing Extra

In friendly letters you have many choices of salutations and closings. To discover how expressive these parts of a letter can be, try writing a poem using only salutations and closings. In the following poems, the first stanza is made up of salutations; the second uses closings.

Coming and Going	**A Friend in Need**
Dear friend,	Dear down-in-the-mouth,
Darling girl,	Dear who-can-I-trust,
Dearest love,	Dear lost-in-a-fog,
HI!	Dear friend.
Lovingly yours,	Smilingly yours,
Eternally yours,	Reliably yours,
Fondly and warmly,	Sunnily yours,
BYE!	Your friend.

BUSINESS LETTERS

Most of the business letters you will write will call for some action on the part of the receiver. You may write to request information, to order merchandise, or to ask for a refund or exchange on faulty merchandise. To make sure busy companies understand your point, keep your letters simple and direct.

You may wish to sketch out a rough draft of your main message to make sure you have included all necessary information. Then you can prepare a neat, final version that uses the correct form.

Business Letter Form

Because a business letter is more formal than a friendly letter, it requires a more precise form. One of the most popular forms is called *modified-block form*. The examples in this chapter follow this form.

When writing a business letter, use white stationery, preferably 8 ½″ × 11″ in size. Whenever possible, type the letter, leaving margins at least one inch wide.

31b ▶ The parts of a business letter are a **heading, inside address, salutation, body, closing,** and **signature.**

HEADING   The heading of a business letter is the same as the heading of a friendly letter. Include your full address, followed by the date.

INSIDE ADDRESS   A business letter has a second address, called the *inside address*. Start the inside address two to four lines below the heading. Write the name of the person who will receive the letter, if you know it. Use *Mr., Ms., Mrs., Dr.,* etc. before the name. If the person has a title, such as *Personnel Director,* or *Manager,* write it on the next line. Write the receiver's address, using the same way of

581

identifying the state as you used in the heading. *(See page 584 for a listing of state abbreviations.)*

SALUTATION
Start the salutation, or greeting, two lines below the inside address. Use "Dear Sir or Madam" if you do not know the name. Otherwise, use the person's last name preceded by *Mr., Ms., Mrs.,* etc. Follow the salutation with a colon.

BODY
Two lines below the salutation begin the body or message of the letter. Single-space each paragraph, skip a line between paragraphs, and indent each new one.

CLOSING
In a business letter, use a formal closing, such as *Sincerely, Sincerely yours, Very truly yours,* or *Yours truly.* Start the closing two or three lines below the body. Line up the closing with the left-hand edge of the heading. Capitalize only the first letter, and place a comma after the closing, as you did in the friendly letter.

SIGNATURE
In the signature of a business letter, your name is written twice. First type (or print if your letter is handwritten) your name four or five lines below the closing. Then sign your name in the space between the closing and your typed name. Do not refer to yourself as *Mr.* or *Ms.* in the signature.

Keep a copy of the business letter in case you do not receive a reply in a reasonable amount of time and need to write a second letter. You can make copies with carbon paper or use the copying machines that are available in most libraries.

When you are writing a business letter, always make sure it is clearly written, has a neat appearance, and follows the correct form. A sample business letter is provided on the following page.

Correct Form for a Business Letter

heading   1411 Vista Drive
Oakland, CA 94611
July 16, 1986

inside address

Customer Service Department
Silvertone Tapes, Inc.
352 Rosemont Avenue
Olympia, WA 98502

salutation

Dear Sir or Madam:

    Recently I bought four Silvertone blank
tapes. Three of them work fine. The fourth
one, however, is defective. When I played   body
back a recording I made, the sound was garbled,
and I could not make out the voices.

    I have enclosed the defective tape, which
I would like you to replace. I would
appreciate it if you would send a new tape as
soon as possible.

closing   Yours truly,

signature   *Robert Tessler*

                  Robert Tessler

The Envelope

If you type the letter, also type the envelope. Place your name and address in the upper left-hand corner. The receiver's address, which is the same as the inside address in the letter, is centered on the envelope. Use the postal abbreviations for the state and include the ZIP code.

583

Correct Form for Business Envelopes

Robert Tessler
1411 Vista Drive   your name
Oakland, CA 94611   and address

            Customer Service Department
            Silvertone Tapes, Inc.   receiver's
            352 Rosemont Avenue   address
            Olympia, WA 98502

State Abbreviations

State	Abbr.	State	Abbr.
Alabama	AL	Montana	MT
Alaska	AK	Nebraska	NE
Arizona	AZ	Nevada	NV
Arkansas	AR	New Hampshire	NH
California	CA	New Jersey	NJ
Colorado	CO	New Mexico	NM
Connecticut	CT	New York	NY
Delaware	DE	North Carolina	NC
District of Columbia	DC	North Dakota	ND
Florida	FL	Ohio	OH
Georgia	GA	Oklahoma	OK
Hawaii	HI	Oregon	OR
Idaho	ID	Pennsylvania	PA
Illinois	IL	Puerto Rico	PR
Indiana	IN	Rhode Island	RI
Iowa	IA	South Carolina	SC
Kansas	KS	South Dakota	SD
Kentucky	KY	Tennessee	TN
Louisiana	LA	Texas	TX
Maine	ME	Utah	UT
Maryland	MD	Vermont	VT
Massachusetts	MA	Virginia	VA
Michigan	MI	Washington	WA
Minnesota	MN	West Virginia	WV
Mississippi	MS	Wisconsin	WI
Missouri	MO	Wyoming	WY

Letters of Request

Notice how the business form of the letter is used to request information.

Letter of Request

```
                                  3412 Falcon Road
                                  Mobile, Alabama   36619
                                  May 29, 1986


Dr. Alan Morley
Membership Director
National Science Club
8880 Wilton Drive
Cooperstown, New York 13326


Dear Dr. Morley:

    I learned about the National Science Club
in a magazine and am eager to know more about
it.  Please send me information on activities
the club sponsors, rules for membership, and
annual dues.  If a membership application is
required, please send me the necessary form.

    I would also be interested in learning
if there is a local chapter somewhere in the
Mobile area.  Thank you for your assistance.

                          Sincerely,

                          Carla Rodriquez

                          Carla Rodriquez
```

When writing a letter of request, be as specific as possible in naming the information you want. State your request politely. Then re-read your letter and check it for mistakes in grammar, usage, spelling, and punctuation.

EXERCISE 3   Correcting Errors in a Letter of Request

In the following letter, each line preceded by a number contains an error. Rewrite the letter, correcting each mistake. Then underline the ten corrections you made.

1 Arna Silverstein
2 364 Willow street
  Hainesburg, NJ 07832
3

Ms. Sandra Hanson
Consumer Services
Quality Computing, Inc.
4 1167 Sequoia Bulavard
5 Belmont, California 94002

6 Dear Ms. Hanson,

    I am thinking of buying a small home computer and have heard that your model #453-A has all the features I need. Would you please
7 send me a brochure describing this compueter
8 and information about it's current price.

9 I would also appreciate your sending a catalog of games and other software that can be used on this computer. Thank you very much.

10 Sincerely

Arna Silverstein

Arna Silverstein

Order Letters

The business form of the letter is also used to order merchandise from catalogs and advertisements. An order letter should give complete information, including the description, size, order number, price, and quantity of the item or items you want. If you enclose payment for your order, the letter should state the amount enclosed. The total amount should include the cost of each item and any shipping or handling charges required. Always recheck your addition before sending payment.

Order Letter

```
                              142 Harper Drive
                              Buffalo Gap, TX  79508
                              November 11, 1986


Capital Music Store
6554 Northwest Highway
Austin, TX  78756


Dear Sir or Madam:

     Please send me the following items from
your 1985 catalog.

     1 Starlite music notebook, size

        8 1/2" x 11", Order #267-C        $ 1.35

     1 music stand, Olympia model,

        Order #383-F                      $24.95

                          TOTAL       $26.30

     I have enclosed a money order for $30 to
cover the cost of merchandise plus $3.70 for
shipping and handling.

                    Sincerely yours,

                    Raymond Stevenson
                    Raymond Stevenson
```

EXERCISE 4 Writing an Order Letter

Use the following information to write an order letter.

ADDRESS   Order Department, The Cycle City,
          4212 Emerson Street, Emporia, Kansas 66801

ORDER   2 rolls of Ace handlebar tape, ½ inch, Order
          #33, $1 each; 4 Nite-glow reflectors, Order #48,
          $2.49 each; $1 for shipping and handling

Letters of Complaint

Following is an example of a letter of complaint.

Letter of Complaint

```
                              313 Lavender Way
                              Millville, PA  17846
                              September 7, 1986


Subscription Department
Sky and Stars Magazine
36 Parkway Drive
Evanston, IL   60201


Dear Sir or Madam:

    On August 4, I mailed an order form and
a check for $12.50 to cover the cost of
receiving your magazine for one year.  Two
weeks later I received a card indicating that
my first issue would arrive by September 1.
So far, I have not received a magazine.

    Please check into this problem and
notify me as soon as possible about your
findings.  Thank you for your cooperation.

                              Very truly yours,

                              Michael Fung

                              Michael Fung
```

Most companies with whom you do business want you to be satisfied with their products and services. If you have a complaint or need to notify them of an error, express yourself courteously. Give sufficient background information and recommend a reasonable solution to the problem. The letter on page 588 uses an appropriate tone for a letter of complaint.

EXERCISE 5 Revising a Letter of Complaint
The following paragraph uses an inappropriate tone for a letter of complaint. Rewrite the body, revising the tone so that it is polite but firm.

I can't understand how anyone can be so careless! I ordered a kit for building a model of a bird feeder (kit #34-SS) from your fall catalog, and you sent me a kit that does not include instructions. How do you expect a person to know how to put it together? I demand my money back.

EXERCISE 6 On Your Own
Imagine you are living in the twenty-third century. Write a business letter to a company or other organization requesting information, ordering merchandise, or making a complaint. Use your imagination to create the company name and address and the kind of information or merchandise that might be available in the future. Use the correct form for a business letter.

CHAPTER REVIEW

Imagine that you have lost your wallet. Write three letters: one to the store in which you lost it, one to a person who found it and mailed it to you, and one to a friend telling about your experience. Use the Steps for Writing a Letter on page 590 to help you.

Steps for Writing

✓ **Friendly Letter**
1. Use the proper form for a friendly letter. *(See page 579.)*
2. Check your letter for errors in grammar, usage, mechanics, and spelling.
3. Recopy your letter if necessary for neatness.
4. Include a return address on the envelope.

✓ **Business Letter**
1. Gather the information you will need to explain your request, order, or complaint accurately and completely.
2. Use the proper form for a business letter. *(See pages 581–583.)*
3. Use a salutation and closing appropriate for a business letter. *(See page 582.)*
4. Express your message briefly and politely in the body of the letter.
5. Use the correct form for the signature. *(See page 582.)*
6. Check your letter for errors in grammar, usage, spelling, and mechanics.
7. If possible, type the letter on white 8½″ × 11″ stationery, leaving margins at least one inch wide.
8. Keep a copy of your letter.
9. Address the envelope correctly. *(See pages 583–584.)*

STANDARDIZED TEST ▬▬▬

COMPOSITION

Directions: Decide which order is best for the sentences in each group. In the appropriate row on your answer sheet, fill in the circle containing the letter that indicates the best order.

SAMPLE   (1) Do you spend time sitting in buses, cars, and trains?
          (2) Try walking, biking, or running to your destination.
          (3) Furthermore, don't take that elevator; use the stairs.
          (4) Here are some easy ways to fit exercise into your daily routine.

        A 4 - 1 - 3 - 2   **C** 3 - 2 - 1 - 4
        B 2 - 1 - 4 - 3   **D** 1 - 4 - 2 - 3

ANSWER   Ⓐ Ⓑ Ⓒ Ⓓ

1. (1) Later they turn shiny green and in the fall, orange.
   (2) The leaflets are red only in the early spring.
   (3) This is not always true, however.
   (4) Many people believe that poison ivy is a reddish plant.

        A 4 - 3 - 2 - 1   **C** 1 - 3 - 4 - 2
        B 3 - 2 - 1 - 4   **D** 2 - 4 - 1 - 3

2. (1) A group of 120 Pilgrims sailed from England in 1620.
   (2) The settlement survived, however, to become Plymouth.
   (3) After 66 days the small group landed in New England.
   (4) Half of the group perished during the first winter.

        A 4 - 1 - 3 - 2   **C** 3 - 2 - 1 - 4
        B 1 - 3 - 4 - 2   **D** 2 - 1 - 3 - 4

3. (1) Then a huge red circle rose over the tall shapes.
   (2) From the bridge I watched the sun come up.
   (3) It began as a reddish glow behind the buildings.
   (4) As it rose, it made the gray buildings glow.

        A 2 - 4 - 1 - 3   **C** 4 - 2 - 1 - 3
        B 3 - 1 - 2 - 4   **D** 2 - 3 - 1 - 4

Directions: Decide which sentence best supports the topic sentence. Fill in the appropriate circle on your answer sheet.

SAMPLE Venus is close to Earth but is hard to see in detail.

    A Venus is sometimes called the Morning Star.

    B Its surface temperature can melt lead.

    C The planet is always covered by thick clouds.

ANSWER Ⓐ Ⓑ ©

4. The world's largest stadium is in Prague.

    A Prague is a city in Czechoslovakia.

    B The stadium can easily hold 240,000 spectators.

    C It was completed in 1934.

5. F. D. Roosevelt served the longest term of any president of the United States, and W. H. Harrison served the shortest.

    A Roosevelt served 12 years, and Harrison served 1 month.

    B Both men died of natural causes while in office.

    C Roosevelt was elected in 1932; Harrison in 1841.

6. The state of Arizona has some extraordinary scenery.

    A Arizona is in the Southwest, directly above Mexico.

    B Arizona did not become a state until 1912.

    C The Grand Canyon and the Painted Desert are in Arizona.

7. Through books I can do anything or be anyone.

    A I read two or three books every week.

    B I can be an astronaut or a baseball superstar.

    C One of my favorite books is about trains.

8. Elsie's suitcase becomes shabbier with each trip.

    A She just returned from a trip to Hong Kong.

    B The handle is wobbly; the sides are patched with tape.

    C Why won't she buy a new one?

9. Before setting up a tent, you must select a good site.

    A Be sure you have all the equipment you need.

    B Tents come in various shapes, materials, and sizes.

    C Don't camp on a slope or directly under trees.

10. Mrs. Lee felt sure her tailor shop would be successful.

    A She had thought about opening a shop for a long time.

    B There was no other place in town to have clothes altered.

    C She was very excited about starting her own business.

Unit 7

Test Taking

32

Classroom and Standardized Tests

Getting a high score on a test is much like playing a game well. To do either one, you have to know the rules, and you have to be prepared. If you know how to take various kinds of tests, you will have a great advantage over students who have not mastered this important skill.

CLASSROOM TESTS

There are two main kinds of classroom tests — objective tests and essay tests. An objective test calls for short answers. Some common types of objective tests are true-false, matching, fill-in-the-blank, and multiple choice.

An essay test requires an answer of a paragraph or more. This kind of test measures your understanding of important ideas and your ability to organize material and write clearly. The following steps will help you prepare a well-organized essay for a classroom test.

Steps for Writing an Essay Answer

1. Plan your time and strategy. Allow enough time for your answer, but plan to spend more time on the questions that are worth the most points. Begin with the questions you find easiest to answer. If you have a choice of questions, read each one carefully before you make your selection.

2. Read and interpret the directions. Be sure you understand what the question requires before you write your essay answer. Look for key words such as the following.

Analyze	Separate into parts and examine each part.
Compare	Point out similarities.
Contrast	Point out differences.
Define	Clarify the meaning.
Discuss	Examine in detail.
Evaluate	Give your opinion.
Explain	Tell how, what, or why.
Summarize	Briefly review the main points.

3. Organize your answer. Because your time will be limited, write a simple outline. Jot down your main points and number them in logical order.

4. Write your essay. Be sure to use the following procedures as you construct your essay. *(See page 537.)*

   - Write an introductory paragraph that states the main idea of your essay.

   - Follow the order of your outline. Write one paragraph for each main point and include a topic sentence in each paragraph.

   - Be specific. Back up each main point with facts, examples, and other supporting details.

   - Write a concluding paragraph that summarizes the main idea of your essay.

   - Proofread your essay, correcting any grammar, usage, punctuation, or spelling errors.

EXERCISE 1 **Interpreting Essay Test Questions**
Number your paper 1 to 10. Write the key word in each question. Then write one sentence that explains what the question requires you to do.

EXAMPLE   Explain the eruptions of Old Faithful in Yellowstone National Park.

ANSWER   Explain—Tell what Old Faithful is, and how and why it erupts.

1. How do the Andes Mountains of South America contrast with the Appalachian Mountains of the Eastern United States?
2. In three paragraphs summarize the plot of Jack London's novel *The Call of the Wild*.
3. Explain the process of photosynthesis.
4. Compare the personality of Tom Sawyer with that of Huckleberry Finn. Base your answer on your reading of *Tom Sawyer*.
5. In your own words, define *tropical rain forest*.
6. Contrast Amaroq with Jello in *Julie of the Wolves*.
7. Analyze Carl Sandburg's poem "Limited."
8. In a brief essay, evaluate the contributions of Benjamin Franklin to science.
9. James Thurber wrote, "You might as well fall flat on your face as lean over too far backward." Discuss his meaning.
10. Summarize the causes of the rise of civilization in the Nile Valley.

EXERCISE 2 **Answering an Essay Test Question**
Choose one of the questions in Exercise 1 and write an answer for it. Follow the steps listed on page 595.

EXERCISE 3 **Writing and Answering Your Own Question**
Write an essay question based on a subject you have studied in one of your courses this year. Then answer the question, following the steps on page 595.

596

STANDARDIZED TESTS

Standardized tests measure your progress, skills, and achievement. Their results can be compared with those of other students in the same grade. Standardized tests that measure your verbal skills are divided into two broad categories: vocabulary tests and tests of writing ability.

The best way to prepare for standardized tests is to work consistently at your subjects during the school year. Reading widely and learning the rules of test taking also help. The following hints will help you achieve success when you take a standardized test.

Hints for Taking Standardized Tests

1. Read the test directions carefully. Answer sample questions to be sure you are following the instructions correctly.
2. Try to relax. You can expect to be a little nervous, but concentrate on doing your best.
3. Skim the entire test to get an overview of the kinds of questions you will be asked.
4. Plan your time carefully. Be aware of how much time you are allotted for each part of the test.
5. Answer first those questions you find easiest. Skip questions you find too difficult, coming back to them later if you have time.
6. Read all the choices before selecting the best answer. If you are not sure of an answer, try to eliminate choices that are obviously incorrect. Educated guessing can often help.
7. Check your answers if you have time. Be sure you have correctly marked your answer sheet.

Vocabulary Tests

Two kinds of questions appear frequently on standardized vocabulary tests. One kind asks you to recognize an antonym—a word opposite to another in meaning. A second kind asks you to identify an analogy—a relationship between two sets of paired words.

Antonyms. Antonym questions test your ability to recognize words most nearly opposite in meaning. An antonym for *strength,* for example, is *weakness.* An antonym for *flatter* is *insult.* Your task on an antonym question is to locate, among a choice of four or five words, the opposite of a word in capital letters.

Try to find the antonym for *secretive* among the list of choices in the following question.

SECRETIVE   (A) silent (B) straightforward
(C) content (D) nominated (E) hostile

The answer is *straightforward.* A person who is secretive is not open or outgoing in speech. A person who is straightforward is direct and open. The words *secretive* and *straightforward* are antonyms.

The other choices are incorrect. *Silent* is a synonym, not an antonym, for *secretive.* Though someone who is secretive may be *content* or *hostile,* neither word is an opposite of *secretive. Nominated* has nothing to do with *secretive.*

Keep in mind that although you may not recognize every word on a test of this kind, there are ways you can figure out the meanings of unfamiliar words. For example, a prefix, root, or suffix can sometimes provide a clue to the meaning of an unfamiliar word.

Consider the word *immaturity.* You know that the prefix *im-* means "not" and that the root *mature* means "having completed natural growth." You also know that the suffix *-ity* means "state of." With this knowledge you would be able to choose *adulthood* as an antonym for *immaturity,* even if *immaturity* was not part of your vocabulary.

EXERCISE 4 Recognizing Antonyms
Write the letter of the word that is most nearly opposite in meaning to the word in capital letters.

  1. PASSIVE   (A) thoughtful (B) glum (C) sporty
     (D) active (E) cooperative

2. ALIEN   (A) similar (B) strange (C) foreign
   (D) agreeable (E) dull
3. COMPLEX   (A) mysterious (B) complicated
   (C) simple (D) fancy (E) harmless
4. MONOTONOUS   (A) double (B) noisy
   (C) boring (D) difficult (E) varying
5. ANIMATED   (A) inactive (B) bold (C) open
   (D) outstanding (E) irritable
6. INNOCENCE   (A) kindliness (B) guilt
   (C) victory (D) greed (E) sadness
7. LOITER   (A) delay (B) repair (C) shrink
   (D) hasten (E) increase
8. SOMBER   (A) mournful (B) simple (C) damp
   (D) cheerful (E) healthful
9. CAUTIOUS   (A) suspicious (B) superstitious
   (C) foolhardy (D) challenging (E) stern
10. INDIFFERENT   (A) alike (B) similar
    (C) unique (D) concerned (E) amused
11. DESCEND   (A) agree (B) climb (C) struggle
    (D) defend (E) shame
12. IMPRISON   (A) catch (B) arrange (C) free
    (D) enslave (E) punish
13. INDULGE   (A) reveal (B) annoy (C) keep
    (D) discipline (E) empty
14. UNKEMPT   (A) orderly (B) disorganized
    (C) polite (D) respectful (E) harmful
15. IMPULSIVE   (A) courageous (B) different
    (C) awkward (D) deliberate (E) bold
16. POTENT   (A) powerless (B) dangerous
    (C) logical (D) false (E) tiny
17. TRIVIAL   (A) daring (B) meaningless (C) evil
    (D) shared (E) important
18. EQUIVALENT   (A) certain (B) different
    (C) sturdy (D) cruel (E) noisy
19. MINUTE   (A) festive (B) late (C) gigantic
    (D) ordinary (E) active
20. INCREDIBLE   (A) sympathetic (B) normal
    (C) annoying (D) believable (E) motivated

Analogies. Analogy questions test your skill at figuring out relationships between words. Your first step on an analogy question is to determine how the two words in capital letters are related. Your second step is to find a pair of words among the choices that has the same relationship.

In the following example, find the lettered pair of words that has the same analogy as *handlebars* and *bicycle.*

> HANDLEBARS : BICYCLE :: (A) moose : antlers
> (B) tire : fender   (C) cabin : airplane
> (D) steering wheel : automobile   (E) golf : sport

The analogy is a part-to-whole relationship. Handlebars are part of a bicycle, specifically the part that steers it. The answer is *steering wheel : automobile* because the relationship between the two items is that of a part to the whole, and because the function of the part in both pairs of words is to steer.

The other choices are incorrect. *Moose : antlers* follows the word order whole-to-part, instead of part-to-whole. *Tire : fender* includes two parts of an automobile, but no whole. In *cabin : airplane* the function of the part, the cabin, is not that of steering. The relationship in *golf : sport* is item-to-category, rather than part-to-whole.

Writing a sentence that expresses the relationship between two pairs of words in an analogy question can help you figure out the answer. For example, the sentence for the analogy above should be worded, *"Handlebars* are the part that steers a *bicycle* in the same way that a *steering wheel* is the part that steers an *automobile."*

Remember that the word order in an analogy must be correct. If the main pair of words in the analogy is in cause-to-effect order, for example, the answer should not be in effect-to-cause order. Also remember to think of all the possible meanings of a word. If one meaning of a word does not fit the analogy, consider another meaning. For example, *shady* can mean either "shadowy" or "dishonest."

The following chart will help you figure out some of the common types of analogies.

Common Types of Analogies	
ANALOGY	**EXAMPLE**
word : synonym	plain : simple
word : antonym	hasten : delay
part : whole	lens : camera
cause : effect	burn : pain
worker : tool	secretary : typewriter
worker : product	cobbler : shoes
item : purpose	pencil : write
item : category	chipmunk : rodent

EXERCISE 5 Recognizing Analogies

Write the letter of the word pair that has the same relationship as the word pair in capital letters.

1. DENTIST : DRILL :: (A) calendar : date
   (B) sculptor : chisel   (C) lumberjack : forest
   (D) eyeglasses : sight   (E) hammer : carpenter
2. HORSE : MAMMAL :: (A) insect : beetle
   (B) beaver : fish   (C) snake : reptile
   (D) trout : halibut   (E) animal : tiger
3. HASTEN : HURRY :: (A) laugh : talk
   (B) trust : doubt   (C) stammer : whisper
   (D) attempt : try   (E) explain : understand
4. RANCH : CATTLE :: (A) people : city
   (B) chickens : coop   (C) garden : vegetables
   (D) automobiles : garage   (E) clowns : circus
5. CALM : RESTLESS :: (A) vague : indefinite
   (B) tiny : small   (C) colorless : transparent
   (D) loud : noisy   (E) gloomy : brilliant
6. DAISY : FLOWER :: (A) rye : grain   (B) fish : trout
   (C) violet : rose   (D) yellow : petal   (E) garden : soil
7. FOUNDATION : BASE :: (A) handle : door
   (B) shoes : belt   (C) ruler : inch
   (D) guest : visitor   (E) top : bottom
8. DIRECTOR : MOVIE :: (A) doctor : patient
   (B) cook : diet   (C) conductor : symphony
   (D) teacher : school   (E) building : architect

9. COWARD:BRAVERY :: (A) judge:law
   (B) criminal:honesty   (C) politician:power
   (D) samaritan:kindness   (E) hero:courage
10. ARCHERY:TARGET :: (A) bowling:pins
    (B) tennis:shoes   (C) basketball:swimming
    (D) golf:clubs   (E) horses:polo
11. ICE:FREEZE :: (A) mixture:stir   (B) study:book
    (C) debate:argument   (D) chill:frost
    (E) steam:boil
12. BRIGHTEN:LAMP :: (A) sit:chair
    (B) cool:refrigerator   (C) number:count
    (D) plan:calendar   (E) handle:open
13. CLIENT:CUSTOMER :: (A) dial:clock
    (B) salesperson:purchaser
    (C) computer:typewriter   (D) peak:summit
    (E) square:circle
14. BATON:CONDUCTOR :: (A) ship:captain
    (B) animal:zoologist   (C) banker:money
    (D) camera:photographer   (E) carpenter:saw
15. TAILOR:JACKET :: (A) designer:illustration
    (B) stone:mason   (C) case:lawyer
    (D) review:critic   (E) stitch:seamstress
16. GLUE:STICK :: (A) wheel:rotate
    (B) focus:binoculars   (C) staple:attach
    (D) knot:rope   (E) paper:recycle
17. QUESTION:RESPONSE :: (A) read:translation
    (B) give:gift   (C) ask:directions
    (D) offer:acceptance   (E) answer:request
18. FREQUENT:SELDOM :: (A) ornate:plain
    (B) numerous:plentiful   (C) decimal:point
    (D) mature:honest   (E) often:usual
19. SILK:MATERIAL :: (A) table:desk
    (B) pulp:paper   (C) granite:rock
    (D) lizard:snake   (E) bird:roadrunner
20. INFURIATE:ENRAGE :: (A) defend:offend
    (B) experiment:test   (C) laugh:cry
    (D) anger:forgive   (E) condemn:praise

Tests of Writing Ability

Two kinds of standardized tests measure writing ability: the objective test of standard written English and the writing sample. The objective test is a multiple-choice test that asks you to identify sentence errors. The writing sample is an essay test that requires you to write one or more original paragraphs on an assigned topic.

Tests of Standard Written English. Tests of standard written English contain sentences with three or more underlined words or phrases. The directions ask you to decide whether there is an error in grammar, usage, word choice, punctuation, or capitalization in any one of the underlined parts. Study the sentence below and identify the sentence error.

Some scientists <u>believe</u> that the first <u>dog's</u> <u>were</u>
           A   B   C
tamed over 10,000 years ago<u>.</u> <u>No error</u>
                        D   E

The answer is <u>B</u>. The word <u>dogs</u> should not have an apostrophe because it is a plural, not a possessive.

The following are a few of the common errors you should check for on the test of standard written English.

- lack of agreement between subject and verb
- lack of agreement between pronoun and verb or pronoun and antecedent
- incorrect spelling or use of a word
- missing, misplaced, or unnecessary punctuation
- missing or unnecessary capitalization

Some sentences on this kind of test contain no errors. Before you choose answer *E*, however, be sure that you have carefully examined every part of the sentence. Also keep in mind that the parts of the sentence that are not underlined are correct. Some of those parts may help you locate errors in the underlined parts.

EXERCISE 6 Recognizing Errors in Writing

Write the letter that is below the underlined word or punctuation mark that is incorrect. If the sentence contains no error, write *E*.

A
Matter
of
Degree

1. Temperatures on summer nights <u>are</u> often <u>cooler</u> in the
                                  A   **B**
   suburbs <u>then</u> <u>in</u> the city.   <u>No error</u>
        C   **D**   **E**

2. One reason for the difference <u>is</u> <u>that</u> suburbs have <u>less</u>
                                   A **B**   **C**
   buildings <u>than</u> the city has.   <u>No error</u>
           D   **E**

3. During the day city streets, sidewalks<u>,</u> and <u>buildings</u>
                                       A   **B**
   <u>absorb</u> the <u>Summer</u> heat.   <u>No error</u>
      C   **D**   **E**

4. At night the suburbs <u>cool</u> down<u>,</u> but<u>,</u> the city <u>does</u> not.
                        A   **B** **C**   **D**
   <u>No error</u>
    E

5. Buildings and streets <u>release</u> the heat absorbed during
                           A
   the day<u>,</u> this heat <u>keeps</u> the city warm<u>.</u>   <u>No error</u>
        B   **C**   **D**   **E**

6. The suburbs <u>have</u> more trees and grass that <u>hold</u>
              A   **B**   **C**
   rainwater near the surface<u>.</u>   <u>No error</u>
                   D   **E**

7. The water <u>evaporates</u> in the heat<u>,</u> and <u>cools</u> down the
              A   **B**   **C**
   temperature<u>.</u>   <u>No error</u>
         D   **E**

8. Furthermore, the trees<u>,</u> <u>like</u> a fan<u>,</u> <u>keeps</u> a breeze
                        A **B**   **C** **D**
   blowing.   <u>No error</u>
            E

9. Tall and unbending<u>,</u> the buildings in the city <u>retain</u> the
                  A   **B**
   warm air <u>as</u> an oven <u>does</u>.   <u>No error</u>
          C   **D**   **E**

10. <u>Its</u> easy to understand why <u>people</u> often <u>try</u> to leave the
     A   **B**   **C**
    city on a hot <u>July</u> weekend.   <u>No error</u>
                D   **E**

EXERCISE 7   Recognizing Errors in Writing

Write the letter that is below the underlined word or punctuation mark that is incorrect. If the sentence contains no error, write *E*.

1. Bottle-nosed dolphins <u>are</u> highly <u>intelligent</u> mam-
        A   **B**
mals with keen eyesight<u>_and hearing<u>.</u>   <u>No error</u>
                        C   **D**   **E**

2. If we <u>had</u> left home sooner<u>,</u> we could <u>of</u> climbed
        A   **B**   **C**
to the top of the <u>mountain</u>.   <u>No error</u>
                    D   **E**

3. Which <u>was</u> the <u>larger</u> dinosaur—the *Triceratops*<u>,</u>or
        A   **B**   **C**
the *Apatosaurus*<u>?</u>   <u>No error</u>
                D   **E**

4. Both my <u>brothers</u>-in-<u>law</u> <u>subscribe</u> to the magazine
            A   **B C**
"<u>Inventions</u>" each year.   <u>No error</u>
  D   **E**

5. The   techniques   in   <u>James</u>   <u>Whistler's</u>   paintings
                            A   **B**
<u>was</u> influenced by <u>Japanese</u> woodcuts. <u>No error</u>
C   **D**   **E**

6. Every <u>Fourth</u> of <u>July</u> our family celebrates by going
        A   **B**
to a <u>neighborhood</u> picnic<u>!</u>   <u>No error</u>
    C   **D**   **E**

7. Every member of the class <u>is</u> <u>reminded</u> to pay <u>their</u>
                            A   **B**   **C**
dues by <u>February</u> 9.   <u>No error</u>
        D   **E**

8. The four main parts of a ship <u>are</u> <u>:</u> the hull, the
                                A **B**
propellers, the rudder<u>,</u> and the engines<u>.</u>   <u>No error</u>
                    C   **D**   **E**

9. When Lewis and Clark traveled to the <u>Pacific</u><u>,</u>
                                        A   **B**
which states did <u>they</u> cross<u>?</u>   <u>No error</u>
                C   **D**   **E**

10. You <u>should'nt</u> <u>have</u> missed the bicycle race<u>;</u> <u>two</u>
        A   **B**   **C** **D**
contestants broke county records. <u>No error</u>
                                  E

The 20-Minute Essay. The essay part of a standardized test consists of an assigned topic and guidelines to aid you in writing an essay of approximately 175 to 200 words. You will be judged on your ability to express yourself.

When writing the 20-minute essay, you will use many of the techniques you use when taking a classroom essay test. *(See pages 594–595.)* However, a 20-minute essay may differ from those required on a classroom essay test in several ways. Keep the following guidelines in mind.

- You may be told not to erase mistakes, but to draw a neat line through any material you want to omit.
- Listen carefully to instructions to find out if you may write notes or an outline in the examination book. You will be graded on your essay only, not on your outline or notes.
- Keep your time limit in mind.

EXERCISE 8 Writing a 20-Minute Essay
Choose one of the following essay topics. Allow yourself exactly 20 minutes to outline and write your finished paper.

1. If you were to spend a year on a spaceship and could take along only two books, which ones would you take? Give reasons for your choices.
2. Choose a club or other activity you think should be added to the activities at your school. Persuade the other members of your student body to support your suggestion.

CHAPTER REVIEW

A. Write the letter of the word that is most nearly opposite in meaning to the word in capital letters.

1. FORBID   (A) trespass (B) inquire (C) allow
   (D) whisper   (E) prohibit
2. MOBILE   (A) stationary (B) movable
   (C) expensive   (D) crowded   (E) dangerous

3. MODERATE   (A) mysterious (B) windy
(C) short (D) forgiving (E) extreme
4. PROHIBIT   (A) ban (B) permit (C) warn
(D) display (E) sell
5. LOATHE   (A) threaten (B) hate (C) adore
(D) scold (E) advise
6. INSPIRE   (A) breathe (B) repeat (C) hope
(D) discourage (E) worry
7. SCARCE   (A) present (B) plentiful (C) heavy
(D) brave (E) fearful
8. CONDENSE   (A) cut (B) drop (C) expand
(D) strain (E) measure
9. JUVENILE   (A) plentiful (B) adult (C) large
(D) angry (E) pale
10. VAGUE   (A) stimulating (B) continuous
(C) valuable (D) specific (E) cloudy

B. Write the letter of the word pair that has the same relationship as the word pair in capital letters.

1. NICKEL:COIN :: (A) valuables:gold
(B) duck:goose (C) insect:bites
(D) table:chair (E) hammer:tool
2. CONTENT:DISSATISFIED :: (A) lazy:happy
(B) hungry:sleepy (C) grateful:thankful
(D) stable:dependable (E) friendly:hostile
3. RASH:MEASLES :: (A) sniffles:influenza
(B) doctor:illness (C) throat:tonsillitis
(D) bone:fracture (E) bronchitis:coughing
4. CARDIOLOGIST:HEARTS :: (A) police:patrol
(B) plants:biologist (C) doctors:patients
(D) computer:operator (E) dentist:teeth
5. STEREO:RECORD :: (A) grape:bunch
(B) size:color (C) automobile:parking lot
(D) recorder:cassette (E) rain:snow
6. STATE:GOVERNOR :: (A) legislator:people
(B) king:land (C) teacher:classroom
(D) tree:forest (E) city:mayor

7. FOUNDATION : HOUSE :: (A) base : statue
(B) valley : river (C) peak : mountain
(D) forest : tree (E) chair : legs

8. CAT : FELINE :: (A) carrot : orange (B) kitten : yarn
(C) rabbit : hop (D) dog : canine (E) equine : horse

9. PAINTINGS : MUSEUM :: (A) sea : ships
(B) play : actors (C) books : library
(D) combination : safe (E) typewriter : keys

10. ARGUE : DEBATE :: (A) think : speak
(B) interest : show (C) catch : trap
(D) hinder : help (E) free : enslave

C. Write the letter that is below the underlined word or punctuation mark that is incorrect. If the sentence contains no error, write *E*.

A Wise Choice

1. Hunting their <u>prey</u> at dusk or after dark<u>,</u> <u>owls</u> are <u>bird's</u>
$\quad$ **A** $\qquad\qquad$ **B** **C** $\qquad$ **D**
of the night. $\quad$ <u>No error</u>
$\qquad\qquad\qquad$ **E**

2. All members of the owl <u>family</u> <u>have</u> short necks, large
$\qquad\qquad\qquad\qquad$ **A** $\quad$ **B**
heads<u>,</u> and very<u>,</u> keen hearing. $\quad$ <u>No error</u>
$\quad$ **C** $\qquad$ **D** $\qquad\qquad\qquad$ **E**

3. Barn owls, more <u>than</u> any <u>others</u><u>,</u> are the subject of
$\qquad\qquad\qquad$ **A** $\qquad$ **B** **C**
<u>stories</u> about haunted houses. $\quad$ <u>No error</u>
D $\qquad\qquad\qquad\qquad$ **E**

4. <u>These</u> owls <u>sometimes</u> roost in barns<u>;</u> belfries<u>,</u> or
$\quad$ **A** $\qquad\quad$ **B** $\qquad\qquad\qquad$ **C** $\qquad$ **D**
abandoned houses. $\quad$ <u>No error</u>
$\qquad\qquad\qquad$ **E**

5. All owls, but <u>especially</u> barn owls, <u>can</u> <u>accurately</u> be
$\qquad\qquad$ **A** $\qquad\qquad\qquad$ **B** $\quad$ **C**
called <u>winged</u> mousetraps. $\quad$ <u>No error</u>
$\qquad$ **D** $\qquad\qquad\qquad$ **E**

Appendix

READING A TEXTBOOK

Understanding and remembering what you read is the key to successful studying. Use the following steps to help you get the most from the material you read in your textbooks.

1. Preview the chapter. Before reading a chapter, read its introduction and conclusion. Then skim the material on each page of the chapter to get an overview of the content. Pay particular attention to headings, terms in heavy type, pictures, captions, graphs, maps, and charts.

2. Read the chapter carefully. To ensure complete comprehension, read at a slower pace than you would use for reading a story or novel. Think about what you have read. Consider how the information relates to information in other sections of the text. If necessary, reread a particularly difficult section until you understand it completely.

3. Take notes. As you read the chapter, take notes in either outline or summary form. *(See pages 611–612.)* Note-taking is a valuable tool for analyzing and remembering what you read. Your notes will also provide you with a ready-made study guide at test time.

4. Reread the chapter. Read the chapter a second time, without pausing to take notes. Because you are already familiar with the material, you will retain much more of the information and gain a better understanding of any sections that seemed confusing to you.

5. Review. When you have completed the assignment, study your notes. Some books provide questions for you to answer. The questions are designed to highlight the major ideas in the chapter. Answer them to ensure that you have thoroughly understood the material. If parts of the chapter are still unclear to you, write a list of questions to ask during class discussion. It may also be helpful to discuss the chapter with a classmate.

TAKING NOTES

Note-taking is an important skill for helping you remember what you have read in a textbook or heard during a lecture. Notes are also a valuable study aid in preparing for a test.

Two methods for taking notes are the modified outline and the summary. In a *modified outline,* words and phrases are used to record main ideas and important details. A modified outline can be especially useful in studying for a multiple-choice test, because it allows you to see the most important details and facts.

In a *summary,* sentences are used to express important ideas in your own words. Summaries are especially useful in preparing for an essay test. Writing a summary requires you to think about the information, to see relationships between ideas, and to draw conclusions. It is also good practice in stating information briefly and clearly.

Whether taking notes in modified outline form or in summary form, you should include only main ideas and important details. In the following passage from a science textbook, the essential information is underlined. Following the passage are examples of notes in both modified outline form and summary form.

All fish . . . have certain characteristics in common. All fish have backbones and are cold-blooded. In addition, most fish breathe through gills. The gills are found on each side of a fish's head. Gills take up oxygen that is dissolved in water. As a fish opens its mouth, water passes into its mouth and over the gills. In the gills molecules of oxygen diffuse from the water into the blood. At the same time carbon dioxide passes out of the blood into the water.

Fish have other characteristics. For example, most fish have scales which cover and protect their bodies. Another characteristic common to many fish is fins. Fins aid fish in swimming. Certain fins act as steering guides. The fins also help keep fish balanced in water. Most fish also have streamlined bodies. The head and tail are smaller and more pointed than the middle part of the fish. Streamlined bodies help fish swim by making it easier to push water aside.

MODIFIED OUTLINE

Characteristics of Fish
1. Have backbones and are cold-blooded (all)
2. Breathe through gills (most)
3. Have scales, fins, and streamlined bodies (most)

SUMMARY

Characteristics of Fish
    There are two characteristics that all fish have in common — backbones and cold-bloodedness. Most fish breathe through gills and have scales for protection. Most fish also have fins and streamlined bodies for efficient swimming.

The following guidelines will help you take clear, well-organized notes.

Taking Notes

- Record only the main ideas and important details.
- Use the titles, subtitles, and words in special type or color to help you select the most important information.
- Use your own words; do not copy word for word.
- Use as few words as possible.

Modified Outline
- Use words and phrases.
- Use main ideas for headings.
- List any supporting details under each heading.

Summary
- Write complete sentences, using your own words.
- Show the relationship between ideas, being careful to use only the facts stated in the textbook or lecture.
- Include only essential information.
- Organize ideas logically.

STUDYING FOR A TEST

You should begin to study for a test long before test day. To do well on a test, you must keep up with your daily reading assignments, take clear and complete notes, and review the material in each subject regularly.

Developing Effective Study Habits. If you develop good study habits, you will find them useful for test taking as well as for daily classroom assignments. Use the procedures below to help you study more effectively.

How to Study Effectively

- Choose an area that is well lighted and free from noise.
- Equip your study area with everything you need for reading and writing, including a dictionary and a thesaurus.
- Keep an assignment book for recording assignments and due dates.
- Allow plenty of time for studying. Begin your reading and writing assignments early.

Preparing for Tests. If you keep up with your assignments and take good notes, you will have no difficulty preparing for tests. The guidelines below will help you do your best.

How to Prepare for a Test

1. Study the notes you took in class and those you took on assigned reading.
2. Focus on topics that were discussed in class or stressed by the teacher.
3. Review the questions at the end of main sections in your textbook. Write the answer to each question to help you organize your thoughts and recall important details.
4. Review any prior tests or quizzes you have taken that cover the material on which you will be tested.

USING STANDARD MANUSCRIPT FORM

The appearance of your composition can be almost as important as its content. A paper with jagged margins and words crossed out or crowded together is difficult to read. A neat, legible paper, however, makes a positive impression on your reader. Your teacher may provide you with a list of requirements for preparing the final copy of a composition, report, or other written work. Use that list or the following guidelines for standard manuscript form to help you prepare the final copy of your manuscript.

Standard Manuscript Form

1. Use standard-size 8½- by 11-inch white paper. Use one side of the paper only.
2. If handwriting, use black or blue ink. If typing, use a black typewriter ribbon and double-space the lines.
3. Leave a 1¼-inch margin at the left and a 1-inch margin at the right. The left margin must be even. The right margin should be as even as possible, without too many hyphenated words.
4. Put your name, the course title, the name of your teacher, and the date in the upper right-hand corner of the first page.
5. Center the title about 2 inches from the top of the first page. Do not underline or put quotation marks around your title.
6. If handwriting, skip 2 lines between the title and the first paragraph. If typing, skip 4 lines.
7. If handwriting, indent the first line of each paragraph 1 inch. If typing, indent 5 spaces.
8. Leave a 1-inch margin at the bottom of all pages.
9. Starting on page 2, number each page in the upper right-hand corner. Begin the first line 1 inch from the top of the page.

The following sample illustrates the first page of a type-written composition.

614

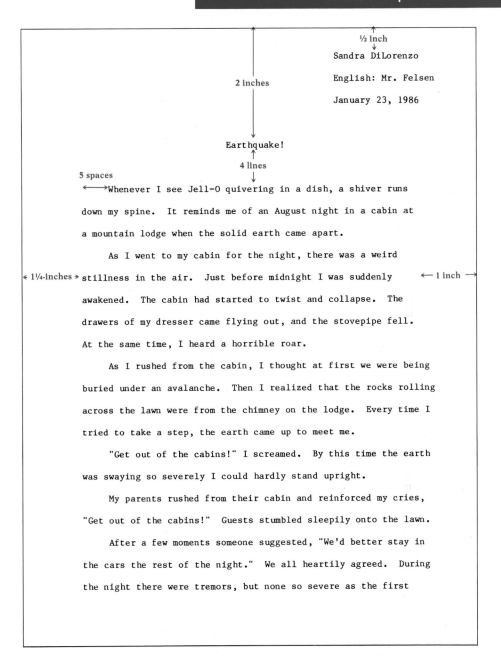

½ inch

2 inches

Sandra DiLorenzo

English: Mr. Felsen

January 23, 1986

Earthquake!

4 lines

5 spaces

Whenever I see Jell-O quivering in a dish, a shiver runs

down my spine. It reminds me of an August night in a cabin at

a mountain lodge when the solid earth came apart.

As I went to my cabin for the night, there was a weird

1¼-inches stillness in the air. Just before midnight I was suddenly   ← 1 inch →

awakened. The cabin had started to twist and collapse. The

drawers of my dresser came flying out, and the stovepipe fell.

At the same time, I heard a horrible roar.

As I rushed from the cabin, I thought at first we were being

buried under an avalanche. Then I realized that the rocks rolling

across the lawn were from the chimney on the lodge. Every time I

tried to take a step, the earth came up to meet me.

"Get out of the cabins!" I screamed. By this time the earth

was swaying so severely I could hardly stand upright.

My parents rushed from their cabin and reinforced my cries,

"Get out of the cabins!" Guests stumbled sleepily onto the lawn.

After a few moments someone suggested, "We'd better stay in

the cars the rest of the night." We all heartily agreed. During

the night there were tremors, but none so severe as the first

In addition to using standard form, you should always proofread your completed work carefully. Also, keep in mind the following guidelines and the rules taught in the usage, mechanics, and spelling chapters of this book.

Dividing Words. Although you should avoid dividing words whenever possible, sometimes doing so is necessary to keep the right-hand margin of your paper fairly even. Follow the rules on pages 360–361 for dividing words.

Writing Numbers. In general, spell out the numbers one through ten. Use numerals for numbers above ten.

> three   ten   11   34   105   3,487   425,297

To avoid six or more zeros, a combination of numerals and words may be used.

> one million   11 million   55 billion   2.5 billion

Always spell out a number at the beginning of a sentence, or revise the sentence.

> One hundred fifty-six scientists attended last year.
> Last year 156 scientists attended.

Use numerals for dates, street and room numbers, page numbers, percents, decimals, and times with A.M. or P.M.

> July 4, 1776   room 5   page 3   9 percent   8:30 A.M.

Using Abbreviations. Most abbreviations should be avoided in formal writing. Do not abbreviate names of states, countries, days of the week, months, weights, or measurements. See page 304 for examples of abbreviations that may be used in formal writing.

Quoting Long Passages. When you write a report, you might want to support a point by quoting a long passage from a book. When quoting a passage of more than one paragraph, place quotation marks at the beginning of each paragraph—but at the end of only the last paragraph. *(See pages 338–339.)* Remember to give credit to the author for the quoted material. *(See pages 569–573.)*

USING PROOFREADING SYMBOLS

Proofreading symbols make revising and editing easier. The most commonly used symbols are shown below. Use these symbols when you revise and edit your writing.

Proofreading Symbols

Symbol	Meaning	Example
∧	insert	Jupiter ∧has 13 moons.
ℓ	delete	Denmark has a ~~wet~~/damp climate.
....	let it stand	Socrates was a ~~Greek~~ philosopher.
#	add space	The bald#eagle is not really bald.
⌒	close up	The wheels smacked the run⌒way.
∼	transpose	Please only take one.
ɴo ¶	no paragraph	ɴo ¶Then we found the answer.
¶	new paragraph	¶The next day we met Zoron.
≡	capital letter	Severe storms hit the south.
/	lowercase letter	The bicyclists headed /South.

Sample Student Paper with Proofreading Symbols

¶ More than a century ago, the Cardiff giant was the talk

of New/York. The huge stone figure, over ten feet tall,

was un⌒earthed by workmen digging a well near the village

of Cardiff⊙∧

ɴo ¶ Archaeologists and ∲octors examined the figure/ and

decided it was a petrified human being. The figure ~~goes~~ went

on exhibit ∧and ~~it~~ was sold and resold until ~~it's~~ its∧ price reached

$200,000.ℓ The ∧n physicians discovered#that the figure had

no ~~petrified~~ heart or lungs. It was solid gypsum! Even

after the hoax was exposed, the Cardiff Giant remained

popular. Dozens of Cardiff Giants appeared in fairs and

exhibits throughout the United ≡states. ~~It~~ ∧The figure was one of the

(popular) great⌒ attractions of the time.

LISTENING TO DIRECTIONS

Both in school and at work, you receive many directions that require careful listening. While listening may seem easy, the fact is that many people do not know how to listen carefully. Like any other skill, good listening must be learned and practiced.

The most common listening fault that people make is to assume that they know what a person is going to say before he or she has finished speaking. The result is they stop listening. When a task is assigned to you, listen carefully to *all* instructions. Keep in mind that doing a good job requires two basic skills: (1) the ability *to understand* the assignment and (2) the ability *to do* the assignment. The first skill is often the key to success, since the quality of your work is meaningless if the task you complete is not the one you were asked to do. The following techniques will help you improve your ability to understand and follow directions.

Listening to Directions

1. Do not assume you already know what to do before the speaker is finished. Listen carefully to *all* instructions.

2. Write down the directions as soon as you receive them. The longer you wait, the greater the chance you will forget or misunderstand the assignment.

3. If any part of the directions is unclear, ask specific questions that will help you understand the assignment. Remember that the person giving the directions wants you to get them right.

4. Use common sense when carrying out the assignment. If part of what you are doing does not make sense to you, then either you have misunderstood the directions or the directions were faulty. Check with the person who gave you the assignment.

5. When you have completed a task, review the directions to make sure that you have followed all the instructions completely.

LISTENING FOR INFORMATION

Listening to a speech or a lecture requires that you pay close attention in order to gain information and to evaluate what you hear.

Concentrate on the speaker's words. Sit comfortably but stay alert. Focus on what the speaker is saying, without being distracted by noise or by the speaker's appearance or mannerisms.

Determine the speaker's purpose. As the speaker begins, determine the purpose of the speech—to inform, to explain, or to persuade.

Listen for verbal clues. Identify the speaker's main ideas. Often a speaker will use verbal signals such as the following to emphasize important points.

Let me begin	Also consider	Most important
Remember that	Finally	In summation

Notice nonverbal clues. A speaker may use gestures that will help you understand a key point. The movement of an arm or a change in the pace of speaking, for example, can signal that the speaker is saying something important.

Evaluate the information. Listen critically and evaluate what you hear. Try to separate fact from opinion. Watch out for propaganda devices that try to persuade you to believe as the speaker does. One such device is the slogan. A slogan is a simple word or phrase that oversimplifies a complex issue by reducing it to a word or a phrase.

Take notes. Writing notes can help you organize your thoughts and remember details. Use a modified outline when you take notes on a speech. You may also find it helpful to write a summary of the speech. *(See pages 611–612.)*

SPEAKING TO AN AUDIENCE

A speech may be formal or informal, long or short. Whatever its nature, you will find the following guidelines helpful.

Choosing and Limiting a Subject

The first step in preparing a speech is to choose the subject of your speech carefully.

How to Choose and Limit a Subject

1. Choose a subject that interests you and is likely to interest your audience.
2. Choose a subject that you know well or can research thoroughly.
3. Limit the subject to one that can be covered in the time allowed.
4. Determine the purpose of your speech—to explain or inform, to persuade, or to entertain.

Gathering Information

After you have chosen and limited your topic, begin to gather information. One source of information is your own experience. You may know more about your subject than you realize. Start by brainstorming. *(See pages 520–521.)* Jot down your ideas freely without stopping to evaluate each one.

You may want to interview people who are knowledgeable about your subject. Make a list of the questions you want to ask during the interview. The usefulness of the information you gather will depend in large part on how well you have prepared your questions.

Another excellent source of information is the library. Look for useful encyclopedia articles, books, and magazines. *(See pages 416–422.)*

Taking Notes

Take notes throughout your research. If you take notes based on personal experience, group your ideas into categories. *(See pages 521 – 522.)* If you interview someone, take notes in modified outline form or use a tape recorder. If you plan to use quotations, write down accurately the words you intend to quote and use quotation marks.

Note cards are the best way to record information from encyclopedias, magazines, and books. Note cards make it easy to organize the information later. The following sample note card was written by a student preparing for a speech on hot-air balloons.

Sample Note Card

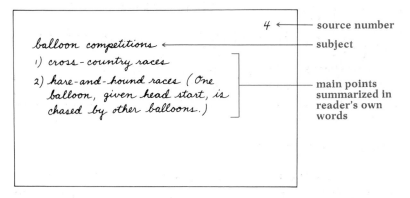

Organizing Information

When you have finished gathering information, group your notes into two or more main categories. Then use the categories to write an outline for the body of your speech. Begin by arranging the categories in a logical order. Then assign each category, or main topic, a Roman numeral. Look over your notes again and begin adding subtopics and supporting points under your main topics. *(See pages 521 – 524.)* Use the form that follows as a guide when you outline the body of your speech.

Form for Outlining a Speech

Limited Subject: _____

Body: I. (Main Topic)
      A. (Subtopic 1)
         1. (Supporting Detail)
         2. (Supporting Detail)
         3. (Supporting Detail)
      B. (Subtopic 2)
         1. (Supporting Detail)
         2. (Supporting Detail)
      C. (Subtopic 3)
   II. (Main Topic)
      A. (Subtopic 1)
      B. (Subtopic 2)

When you complete the outline, you will be ready to write your introduction and conclusion. To catch the interest of your audience, begin the introduction with an anecdote, an unusual fact, a question, or an attention-getting quotation. Include a thesis statement that indicates the main idea and the purpose of your speech. *(See pages 526–527.)*

The conclusion of the speech is your final opportunity to reinforce the ideas you want your listeners to remember. Restate your thesis statement in your conclusion. The last few sentences of your speech should signal the audience that you have finished.

Preparing to Deliver the Speech

Although you will rehearse your speech, you should not memorize it. Instead, use either your outline or cue cards to remind you of the important points of your speech. Cue cards contain key words and phrases or key topics listed in the order you want to follow in your speech. The kind of cue card you make will depend on the type of information in your speech and on your style of presentation. The following is an example of a cue card for a speech entitled "Computers in the Classroom."

Sample Cue Card

> 2
>
> _Advantages of computers in the classroom_
> - save time
> - allow for individual instruction
>
> _Disadvantages of computers in the classroom_
> - cost money
> - limit interaction between teacher and student

Number your cue cards to help keep them in order. Make sure that the wording of each card is easy to follow. A good set of cue cards will help you speak with confidence.

Rehearsing the Speech

Practice your speech until you know it well. If possible, record your speech on a tape recorder. Listen to your delivery and note where you should use more emphasis, show greater enthusiasm, or speak more distinctly.

Delivering the Speech

If you have researched your subject well, planned the content, and rehearsed, you will deliver a good speech. Be confident! You are now an expert on your subject.

Tips for Delivering a Speech

1. Relax and breathe deeply before you speak.
2. Glance at your outline or cue cards to refresh your memory. Avoid reading your speech.
3. Look at your audience. Either make eye contact or focus on points just behind the audience.
4. Speak slowly, clearly, and loudly enough to be heard.
5. Use gestures and facial expressions to help you emphasize your main points.

GLOSSARY OF COMPUTER TERMS

Computers, which have become an important part of our lives, have introduced a large number of new words into our language. The following glossary will help you become familiar with some common computer terms.

algorithm: a set of rules providing a step-by-step procedure for solving a problem

assembly language: a computer language that makes it possible to write machine language instructions in a simplified form, using specified abbreviations

backup: files and programs copied onto a second disk or tape; used to prevent loss of data

BASIC: *B*eginner's *A*ll-purpose *S*ymbolic *I*nstruction *C*ode, an easy-to-use language for computer programming

binary: a number system in which all digits are 0 or 1

bit: a binary digit, that is, a 0 or a 1

bug: an error in a computer program or system

byte: a group of adjacent binary digits that the computer processes as a unit

card: a printed electronic circuit board that is added to a microcomputer to extend its capabilities

cathode-ray tube (CRT): a vacuum tube that acts as a video screen for displaying letters, numbers, symbols, and graphics

central processing unit (CPU): the part of a computer system that interprets and executes instructions

character: a letter, number, punctuation mark, or other symbol

chip: a tiny integrated circuit, often made with silicon

COBOL: *c*ommon *b*usiness *o*riented *l*anguage, a computer language used mainly for business programs

code: a set of symbols and rules for writing programs

computer system: a computer with its hardware and software

cursor: a special symbol, often a flashing line or rectangle, showing where the next character will appear on a CRT screen

data: information that can be processed by a computer

debugging: correcting mistakes in a computer program

disk drive: a device for recording and retrieving information on floppy disks

624

documentation: written material that accompanies a computer program or system and explains its use

floppy disk: a magnetic storage disk, usually 5¼ or 8 inches in diameter, enclosed in a square protective envelope

flowchart: a diagram showing the logic and sequence between various parts of a program

FORTRAN: *for*mula *tran*slation, a computer language designed mainly for programming in the sciences

hardware: the physical equipment and components in a computer system: CRT's, keyboards, and printers, for example

input: introduce information into a computer

input/output (I/O): the process of entering and retrieving information with a computer system

K: the number 2 to the 10th power (1024), used to designate the size of a computer's memory; a computer memory of 64K would store 65,536 bytes

machine language: mathematical language a computer can deal with directly

magnetic disk: a flat circular plate with a magnetic surface, for storing data

microcomputer: a small, low-cost computer

microprocessor: typically, a chip containing the CPU for a microcomputer, and thus the "brains" of the system

modem: *mo*dulator + *dem*odulator, a device that allows computers and terminals to communicate over telephone lines

Pascal: a popular, structured programming language

program: (1) a set of instructions directing the computer to perform certain operations in a given sequence; (2) to design, write, and test a program

RAM (*random access memory*): temporary memory that the computer user can control through programming and erasing

read: the computer's method for sensing information in storage

ROM (*read only memory*): fixed, permanent memory built into the computer by the manufacturer

software: programs, usually on magnetic disks or tapes, created for use with hardware

system: a group of people, machines, materials, and techniques needed to accomplish a task

time-sharing: a means by which a CPU is shared by users on several terminals at the same time

WRITING A RÉSUMÉ

A résumé is a summary of your work experience, education, and interests. The purpose of a résumé is to give a potential employer a brief but positive overview of your qualifications for a job. The following guidelines and model will help you write your own résumé.

How to Write a Résumé

Form
1. Use one sheet of white 8½- by 11-inch paper.
2. Use even margins and leave space between sections.

Work Experience
1. List your most recent job first.
2. Include part-time, summer, and volunteer jobs.
3. For each job list the dates you worked, your employer's name, your title, and your primary responsibilities.

Education
1. List the name and address of each school and the years you attended.
2. List any special courses you have taken that would help make you a valuable employee.

Skills, Activities, Awards, Interests
1. List skills, such as typing, computer programming, or fluency in a foreign language, that relate to the position for which you are applying.
2. List school or community activities in which you have participated, such as music lessons or volunteer work.
3. List awards or certificates of merit you have earned.
4. Include your hobbies and special interests.

References
1. Give the names and addresses of people who have agreed to give you a recommendation, or state that references are available on request.
2. As references, list one previous employer, one teacher or school administrator, and one family friend.

Model of a Résumé

Organize a résumé so that the information is easy to read. Note that the use of capital letters, underlining, and spacing will help the reader find important information.

Thomas Williams
21 Stuart Street
Galesburg, Illinois 61401
Telephone: 427-9865

WORK EXPERIENCE

1985 - present	<u>Daily News</u>, 151 Oak Road, Galesburg, Illinois 61401 <u>Position</u>: Newspaper boy <u>Responsibilities</u>: Delivered newspaper to 60 homes
June 1984 - August 1984	Camp Windego, 9 Hill Road, Galesburg, Illinois 61401 <u>Position</u>: Kitchen staffer <u>Responsibilities</u>: Stocked shelves, cleaned kitchen

EDUCATION

1985 - present	John Adams High School, 82 Willow Street, Galesburg, Illinois 61401 <u>Special Courses</u>: computer programming, accounting
1983 - 1985	Eastview Middle School, 107 Curtis Road, Galesburg, Illinois 61401

SPECIAL SKILLS   Speak Spanish, program in BASIC, type 35 words per minute

ACTIVITIES   Ninth-grade class treasurer, YMCA volunteer

AWARDS   YMCA Citizenship Award for volunteer work, Young Musicians Award in eighth grade

SPECIAL INTERESTS   Computers, music, sports

REFERENCES   Available on request

627

COMPLETING A JOB APPLICATION

When you apply for a job, you may be asked to fill out an application form. Application forms vary, but most of them ask for similar kinds of information. It would be helpful to prepare your information ahead of time so that you will be ready to complete the form when you apply for a job. The following is a list of items that you will most likely need to know in order to complete a job-application form.

- The current date
- Your complete name, address, and telephone number
- Your date and place of birth
- Your Social Security number
- Names and addresses of schools you have attended, dates attended, and year of graduation
- Any special courses or advanced degrees
- Names and addresses of employers for whom you have worked and the dates you were employed
- Any part-time, summer, and volunteer jobs
- Names and addresses of references. (Obtain permission beforehand from each person you intend to list as a reference.)

When you fill out a job-application form, use the following general guidelines.

Completing a Job-Application Form

1. Print all information neatly and legibly.
2. Be sure your answers are accurate and complete.
3. Do not leave blanks. If a section does not apply to you, write *N/A (not applicable)*.
4. List schools attended and work experience in order, giving the most recent first.
5. If you mail the application form, include a brief cover letter stating the job you are applying for.

BARTOW'S DEPARTMENT STORE
EMPLOYMENT APPLICATION

Date __September 1, 1986__

Name __Paula__ __Jane__ __Samuels__
      FIRST   MIDDLE   LAST

Address __414 Broad Street,__ __Garfield,__ __Pennsylvania__ __19015__
        STREET   CITY   STATE   ZIP CODE

Phone __(215) 874-3198__   Social Security Number __181-98-0945__

Have you ever been employed here before? _____ Yes __✓__ No   If so, when? __N/A__

Date of Birth __November 15, 1973__ Place of Birth __Evanston, Illinois__
           MONTH DAY YEAR   CITY   STATE

Work Permit Number (if under 18) __8754__

Married? _____ Yes __✓__ No   Number of children __N/A__

EDUCATION

College or University __N/A__   From __N/A__ to __N/A__

Vocational Training __N/A__   From __N/A__ to __N/A__

Senior High School __N/A__   From __N/A__ to __N/A__

Junior High School __Wilson Junior High School__ From __1985__ to __Present__

Elementary School __Bradford School__   From __1979__ to __1985__

PREVIOUS WORK EXPERIENCE

Year	Employer	Address	Position
1985- present	Bart's Drug Store	211 Main Street, Garfield	Stock clerk
1984- 1985	PA Red Cross	22 Third Avenue, Garfield	Volunteer aid
1983- 1984	Reese Family	45 Durand Road, Garfield	Baby-sitter

REFERENCES

Name	Address	Occupation
1. Carl Smith, Wilson Junior High School, 14 Main Street, Garfield, Principal		
2. Jane Bart, Bart's Drug Store, 211 Main Street, Garfield, Manager		
3. Michael Reese, 45 Durand Road, Garfield, Accountant		

Applicant's Signature __Paula Jane Samuels__

INTERVIEWING FOR A JOB

When you apply for a job, the employer may ask you to come in for an interview. The way you present yourself during the interview may determine whether or not you get the job.

An excellent way to prepare for an interview is to learn as much as possible about the employer's business. The more you know about what the employer does and how the business operates, the better you will be able to discuss the job for which you are interviewing. The following suggestions will help you increase your chances of success at an interview for employment.

Interviewing for a Job

1. Present a neat, clean appearance.
2. Be on time for the interview.
3. Be polite to the interviewer.
4. Look at the interviewer when you speak.
5. Speak clearly and distinctly.
6. Answer all questions carefully and honestly.
7. Ask questions about the job that show your interest in the work and in the place of employment.
8. Thank the interviewer when the interview is over.
9. Follow up the interview with a letter thanking the interviewer and expressing your interest in the position. Give reasons why you think you are a good candidate for the job.

Index
Tab Index

Index

633

Tab Index

GRAMMAR

Chapter 9   Verbals and Verbal Phrases

Chapter 10   Clauses

Chapter 11   Sound Sentences

USAGE

Chapter 12   Using Verbs

Chapter 13   Using Pronouns

Chapter 14   Subject and Verb Agreement

Chapter 15   Using Adjectives and Adverbs

MECHANICS

Chapter 16   Capital Letters

Chapter 17   End Marks and Commas

Chapter 18   Underlining and Quotation Marks

Chapter 19   Other Punctuation

COMPOSITION

Acknowledgments

The authors and editors have made every effort to trace the ownership of all copyrighted selections found in this book and to make full acknowledgment of their use. Grateful acknowledgment is made to the following authors, publishers, agents, and individuals for their permission to reprint copyrighted materials.

Pages 172, 298, and 351. "Jesse Owens," "The Amazing Amazon," and "Moth or Butterfly?" from "Dash It All," "The Mouth of the Amazon River is 150 Miles Wide," and "Beauty and the Beast." Reprinted by permission of A & W Publishers, Inc., from *THE 2ND MAMMOTH BOOK OF TRIVIA* by Bruce D. Witherspoon. Copyright © 1982 by Hart Associates.

Pages 321 and 338. "Before Her Time" from "Any Requests?" Also "Speed Demon — 19th Century Style." Reprinted by permission of A & W Publishers, Inc., from *TRIVIATA: A Compendium of Useless Information.* Compiled by Timothy T. Fullerton. Copyright © 1975 by Hart Publishing Company, Inc.

Page 418. "SPIELBERG, STEVEN." Copyright © 1982, Marquis Who's Who, Inc. Reprinted by permission from *Who's Who in America*, 42nd Edition.

Page 421. "news," "nibble," and "niche." Copyright © 1961 by G. P. Putnam's Sons, *The Roget Dictionary*, Copyright 1931, 1936 by C. O. Sylvester Mawson. Printed in the United States of America.

Page 422. "Mathews, David," "Matioff, Gregory," "Matter, Interstellar," and "Milky Way." *Abridged Readers' Guide to Periodical Literature.* Copyright © 1983 by the H. W. Wilson Company. Material reproduced by permission of the publisher.

Page 441. "This Is Going to Hurt Just a Little Bit," from *I'm a Stranger Here Myself,* by Ogden Nash. Copyright © 1938 by Ogden Nash. Reprinted by permission of Little, Brown and Company.

Page 447. "The Red River," from "Return to Gods Country," by Eric Sevareid, from the September 1981 issue of *Audubon* magazine. Reprinted by permission of the publisher.

Pages 487–488. "Rescue!" Adapted from *RESCUE! TRUE STORIES OF HEROISM* by L. B. Taylor, Jr. Copyright © 1978 by L. B. Taylor, Jr. Used by permission of Franklin Watts, Inc.

Pages 511–512. "Cat Lovers, Dog Lovers," from *Country Chronicle*, by Gladys Taber. Reprinted by permission of J. B. Lippincott Company.

Pages 545–549. Ernest Hemingway, "A Day's Wait" from *Winner Take Nothing.* Copyright © 1933 by Charles Scribner's Sons; copyright renewed 1961 by Mary Hemingway. Reprinted with permission of Charles Scribner's Sons.